THE SOCIAL SCIENCE OF QANON

QAnon has emerged as the defining conspiracy group of our times, and its far-right conspiracies are extraordinary for their breadth and extremity. Bringing together scholars from psychology, sociology, communications, and political science, this cutting-edge volume uses social science theory to investigate aspects of QAnon. Following an introduction to the "who, what, and why" of QAnon in Part I, Part II focuses on the psychological characteristics of QAnon followers and the group's methods for recruiting and maintaining these followers. Part III includes chapters at the intersection of QAnon and society, arguing that society has constructed QAnon as a threat and that the social need to belong motivates its followers. Part IV discusses the role of communication in promoting and limiting QAnon support, while Part V concludes by considering the future of QAnon. *The Social Science of QAnon* is vital reading for scholars and students across the social sciences and for legal and policy professionals.

MONICA K. MILLER is a foundation professor with a split appointment between the Department of Criminal Justice and the interdisciplinary Social Psychology PhD program at the University of Nevada, Reno. She is also adjunct faculty at the Grant Sawyer Center for Justice Studies and an affiliate of the Department of Gender, Race, and Identity. She is coeditor of the NYU Press book series Psychology and Crime, the Springer series Advances in Psychology and Law, and the American Psychology and Law Society book series published by APA Books.

THE SOCIAL SCIENCE OF QANON

A New Social and Political Phenomenon

EDITED BY

MONICA K. MILLER

University of Nevada, Reno

Shaftesbury Road, Cambridge CB2 8EA, United Kingdom

One Liberty Plaza, 20th Floor, New York, NY 10006, USA

477 Williamstown Road, Port Melbourne, VIC 3207, Australia

314–321, 3rd Floor, Plot 3, Splendor Forum, Jasola District Centre, New Delhi – 110025, India

103 Penang Road, #05–06/07, Visioncrest Commercial, Singapore 238467

Cambridge University Press is part of Cambridge University Press & Assessment, a department of the University of Cambridge.

We share the University's mission to contribute to society through the pursuit of education, learning and research at the highest international levels of excellence.

www.cambridge.org
Information on this title: www.cambridge.org/9781316511534

DOI: 10.1017/9781009052061

First published 2023

A catalogue record for this publication is available from the British Library.

Library of Congress Cataloging-in-Publication Data
NAMES: Miller, Monica K., editor.
TITLE: The social science of QAnon : a new social and political phenomenon / edited by Monica K. Miller.
DESCRIPTION: Cambridge ; New York, NY : Cambridge University Press, 2023. | Includes bibliographical references.
IDENTIFIERS: LCCN 2023006546 (print) | LCCN 2023006547 (ebook) | ISBN 9781316511534 (hardback) | ISBN 9781009055024 (paperback) | ISBN 9781009052061 (epub)
SUBJECTS: LCSH: QAnon conspiracy theory. | Social movements. | Information society. | Social sciences–Network analysis.
CLASSIFICATION: LCC HV6275 .S549 2023 (print) | LCC HV6275 (ebook) | DDC 001.9/8–dc23/eng/20230417
LC record available at https://lccn.loc.gov/2023006546
LC ebook record available at https://lccn.loc.gov/2023006547

ISBN 978-1-316-51153-4 Hardback
ISBN 978-1-009-05502-4 Paperback

To Jim Richardson, who encouraged my interest in studying religion and social groups, in mentoring, and in publishing. You have inspired many. May this book be one small piece of your ever-expanding legacy.

Contents

PART III QANON AND SOCIETY

PART IV THE ROLE OF COMMUNICATION IN PROMOTING AND LIMITING QANON SUPPORT

PART V THE FUTURE OF QANON

Contributors

WASIM AHMED University of Stirling

KELLY-ANN ALLEN Monash University

AMARNATH AMARASINGAM Queens University

MARC-ANDRE ARGENTINO Concordia University

JOHN A. BANAS University of Oklahoma

ELENA BESSARABOVA University of Oklahoma

MIKEY BIDDLESTONE University of Kent

CHRISTOPHER BOYLE University of Adelaide

DAVID G. BROMLEY Virginia Commonwealth University

M. KATIE CUNIUS University of Nevada, Reno

KAREN M. DOUGLAS University of Kent

CHARLES P. EDWARDS University of Nevada, Reno

ADAM M. ENDERS University of Louisville

RICKY GREEN University of Kent

PAVAN HOLUR UCLA

DAKOTA JOHNSTON Queen's University

TATYANA KAPLAN University of Nevada, Reno

MARGARET L. KERN University of Melbourne

CAOMHAN MCGLINCHEY University of Exeter

ARIAL R. MEYER Washington State University

ZOE A. MORRIS Monash University

SHARDAY MOSURINJOHN Queens University

JOSEPH PIERRE University of California

JAMES T. RICHARDSON University of Nevada, Reno

VWANI ROYCHOWDHURY UCLA

SHADI SHAHSAVARI UCLA

MARC SMITH Social Media Research Foundation

ROBBIE M. SUTTON University of Kent

TIMOTHY R. TANGHERLINI University of California, Berkeley

CAROLINA TRELLA University of Kent

JOSEPH USCINSKI University of Miami

JARED M. WRIGHT TED, University in Ankara

STUART A. WRIGHT Lamar University

Preface

This book was inspired by lively conversations with Tatyana Kaplan during the COVID-19 pandemic. As two social psychologists, we were curious about this phenomenon of QAnon. I began the adventure of finding experts who could write chapters to explain various aspects of QAnon. Many weeks and conversations later, a book proposal was born.

Writing chapters and editing and publishing a book are no small feats in general. Doing so during a pandemic – while learning to juggle one's other duties (teaching, administration) online and at home and while personally experiencing COVID-19 and/or caring for those experiencing COVID-19 – is even more impressive. Our team tackled countless societal and personal challenges for two years to make this book a reality. There are many people I need to thank because, without them, this book would not exist. First, thanks to the chapter authors, who provided ideas that shaped the book, wrote these intriguing chapters, and made changes without complaint. Additionally, I'd like to thank Janka Romero at Cambridge University Press, who helped polish up the proposal and offered helpful advice at every stage. Thanks also to all of the reviewers, who made helpful suggestions that certainly improved the book. Finally, thanks to Rowan Groat and the publishing and production team at Cambridge University Press, who helped make the book a beautiful reality.

I'm proud of this team of hard-working professionals. We hope readers enjoy our perspectives on this group that has changed society since its emergence in 2017. May future researchers use this book as a starting point to challenge and expand the ideas it contains.

PART I

Introduction to QAnon

CHAPTER 1

The "Who, What, and Why" of QAnon

Monica K. Miller

"Shall we play the game again?"

This cryptic quote was posted on 8kun, an anonymous message board, on June 24, 2022 (Thompson, 2022). The poster is a person (or persons) known only as "Q," the leader of a group called QAnon (short for Q Anonymous). The group is largely online, gathering virtually on chat boards and social media. The group discusses the various clues (called "Q-drops") posted by Q and other leaders (see Chapter 3) and tries to decipher their meaning. Some followers are more invested, however, gathering at conventions and rallies in person. The group has prompted promotional products, including a video called "Great Awakening" and a book *Calm Before the Storm* (see Chapters 2 and 12). Although QAnon started in the USA, the group's influence is now international (see Chapters 8 and 17), and about 20 percent of Americans believe the core beliefs of QAnon (PRRI, 2021).

In order to understand this phenomenon, it is important to start at the beginning. In 2017, a message board poster calling themselves "Q Clearance Patriot" (later given the nickname "Q") posted on the website 4chan. The poster initially posted "Open your eyes . . . Many in our govt worship Satan" (Kirkpatrick, 2022), and they went on to predict that Hillary Clinton would be arrested on October 30, 2017. Although this prediction did not come true, the post garnered the attention of many people, and some key players actively promoted the messages (Beverley, 2020). While there is much speculation, no one knows for sure who Q is. Followers believe they are a high-ranking government official who is part of a plan to punish perceived wrongdoers. Another leading theory is that Q has been multiple people. Linguistic analysis suggests that Q's posts were originally written by Paul Ferber, one of the first of Q's followers, but then later were written by Ron Watkins, who operated one of the chat boards Q often used (Kirkpatrick, 2022). Both men have denied being Q, but linguistic experts say that their prose and language patterns suggest that they were the authors of Q's posts (Kirkpatrick, 2022).

QAnon leaders have used many recruitment tactics, including hashtag hijacking, in which QAnon talking points and/or disinformation are inserted into the conversation of a trending hashtag (e.g. #Election2020; see Chapters 8 and 12). QAnon nonbelievers unknowingly became exposed to QAnon messages and some eventually became believers. The movement grew rapidly, with a possible increase in growth occurring in 2020 (see Chapters 5 and 8, but see Chapter 9 for a counterpoint). However, Q fell silent after President Trump's 2020 election defeat. The mysterious message above, posted on June 24, 2022, could signal a renewed interest in the group that is the subject of this book.

As it grew and evolved to include broader conspiracies, QAnon attracted the attention of the public, social media, the FBI, and lawmakers (see Chapters 4 and 8). QAnon has some characteristics of conspiracy groups, quasi-religious groups, social movements, and organizations that are sometimes called "cults." While QAnon has some traits that are similar to aspects of all of these groups, it focuses on conspiracies; therefore, this book will label it as a conspiracy group. This introductory chapter begins by briefly discussing the beliefs, leadership, and history of the group. The chapter then discusses the quantity and diversity of QAnon followers, introducing some of the reasons people are attracted to QAnon. The chapter moves on to discuss similarities and differences among QAnon and other conspiracy groups. Finally, the chapter concludes with an overview of the themes in each part of this book.

The overall purpose of this book is to use social science theories to answer questions regarding QAnon and inspire a future generation of researchers to study this new and novel group that could have an influence on the USA's future. This book focuses specifically on the *social science* of QAnon. Psychosocial factors are those at the intersection of the individual person and the social environment. Together, psychology and society shape every aspect of life, from our day-to-day behavior to our life-altering choices. The social situation is an input into these choices and behaviors, and it is an output as a result. The QAnon phenomenon is no exception, as followers are influenced by society and their group to act and believe in certain ways – and society is changed as a result. This book will investigate the psychosocial factors at play in the phenomenon that is QAnon.

The scientific research *specifically* on QAnon is scarce. While there are books dedicated to conspiracy theories and new religious movements, this book is the first that I know of that applies social science theories to explain

QAnon specifically (for more on QAnon in general, see Beverley, 2020). As such, the book takes the approach of applying existing theories to QAnon-related phenomena rather than rehashing research that has already been published. Thus, every chapter presents a unique perspective on this novel topic that is emerging as yet another controversy of the 2020s.

What Is QAnon?

QAnon is, at the most basic level, a conspiracy theory. But it is also part religion, part political group, and part social movement. No matter how it is labeled, it is a moneymaker for many individual people and groups. Chapters 2, 16, and 17 discuss many of QAnon's differences from and similarities to other organizations such as the company NXIVM, social movements, various new religious movements, terrorist groups, and other conspiracy groups. Chapters 2 and 14 compare QAnon to alternate-reality or role-playing games.

QAnon shares many characteristics with religious groups, yet it lacks other characteristics, leading authors to call QAnon "quasi-religious" or a "hyper-real religion" (Franks et al., 2013; see also Chapters 16 and 17 of this volume). Q often quotes the Bible and infers that God supports their efforts (see Chapters 16 and 17 for more on the religious characteristics of QAnon). No one is born into QAnon, as are some members of religious minority groups.

QAnon also has similarities to and differences from *nonreligious* groups. QAnon does not typically keep incriminating information about its members (as did the company NXIVM) to prevent them from leaving the group. Indeed, there is not even a "membership roster." QAnon is not as violent as some terrorist groups, but it does have a general "mission." And QAnon is much more of a participatory group than most conspiracy groups in which followers are more consumers than producers or replicators of the conspiracy.

Finally, like many other groups, QAnon has globalized, becoming part of the cultures of many countries (especially in Europe), and it has the potential to spread worldwide. Internationally, the conspiracies vary somewhat, but they have similar themes (e.g. immigration, COVID-19-related economic downturn, or restrictions to "personal liberties"; see Chapter 8). Some QAnon conspiracies implicate international heads of state such as Angela Merkel and Boris Johnson; some support Trump, including calling on Trump to "Make Germany Great Again" (see also Chapters 8 and 17 for more on the spread of QAnon internationally). Thus, QAnon has many similarities to and differences from various types of groups. The section below called "What Is QAnon" details some of the unique characteristics of QAnon as a conspiracy group.

The difficulty of categorizing QAnon stems, in part, from the diversity of its beliefs. QAnon's basic beliefs are summarized throughout this book (in greatest detail in Chapters 8 and 9). In general, QAnon followers believe a host of conspiracies that generally propose that former President Trump is in the process of bringing down a cabal of satanic pedophiles and cannibals, who are part of the "Deep State" that runs a sex-trafficking ring and controls the government. The cabal allegedly consists mainly of Democrats, entertainers, and religious figures. These alleged wrongdoers are Satan-worshippers who harvest adrenochrome from children by sacrificing them. They predict that there will be a "Great Awakening," when their prophecies will come true and the evildoers will be exposed and punished.

The group has had a diverse range of alleged effects on individual people, families, and society (see Chapters 2, 5, and 17). For example, some followers have committed crimes in the name of QAnon; some have lost touch with family members by allowing QAnon to consume their lives; some have become consumed by fear, paranoia, and even violence. Yet many – likely most – will continue to function normally or even benefit from the social interactions and sense of belonging that they receive from following QAnon. One of QAnon's mottos, "Where We Go One, We Go All," signifies the importance of belonging and togetherness. Chapters 8 and 11 further discuss these effects related to the need to belong.

Whether QAnon is a conspiracy group, a religion, or something else, it is almost certainly a moneymaker for many people. For instance, there are numerous books on QAnon (e.g. how to interpret Q's messages and how to prepare for the "Great Awakening"). Some of these books have been very popular, with a book called *QAnon: An Invitation to the Great Awakening* once ranking at number 56 of all books, number 9 of all books about politics, and number 1 of all books about censorship on Amazon (Collins, 2019). QAnon supporters can buy shirts, hats, flags, car stickers, baby clothes, and any number of other goods. Conventions are also potential moneymakers, with attendees spending money to attend and buy merchandise. Additionally, YouTube "content creators" provide messages (e.g. tutorials regarding QAnon's beliefs and interpretations of Q's messages). Large numbers of viewers help these creators generate substantial amounts of money (see Chapter 12).

In sum, QAnon is a novel social entity that emerged in 2017 and – although primarily a US phenomenon – has spread internationally. The authors of this book all provide glimpses into the identity of QAnon as a whole and its individual followers.

Who Believes in QAnon?

QAnon has a broad following, with some who are *complete* believers, but many who believe only a subset of QAnon conspiracies (much like some religious followers do not believe all of their religion's teachings). Chapter 2 proposes a typological continuum that categorizes QAnon believers into "fence-sitters," "true believers," "activists," and "apostates."

It is difficult to calculate how many followers QAnon has, considering that there is no membership list. Even so, QAnon is remarkable because its size is likely unprecedented: Some estimates of its unofficial following range into the hundreds of thousands – perhaps even over a million, judging from social media group membership. But just because someone follows a QAnon social media page or believes some of the QAnon conspiracies does not mean that they are a "member." Chapter 9 notes that only 5–8 percent of Americans supported QAnon as of 2019–2020 (when that chapter was written). In a 2021 poll, 20 percent of Americans agreed with one of the major prophecies of QAnon: "There is a storm coming soon that will sweep away the elites in power and restore the rightful leaders." And 15 percent agreed with the major holding of QAnon that "the government, media, and financial worlds in the U.S. are controlled by a group of Satan-worshipping pedophiles who run a global child sex trafficking operation" (PRRI, 2021).

Support is not uniform across all Americans, however. A study found that 45 percent of self-identifying Republicans had favorable attitudes toward QAnon (The Economist/YouGov, 2021) and 27 percent of white evangelicals thought that the statement "Donald Trump has been secretly fighting a group of child sex traffickers that include prominent Democrats and Hollywood elites" was either "mostly" or "completely" accurate (Cox, 2021). These percentages are higher than those for all other political or religious groups. Chapter 8 further details evidence of the size of QAnon.

While not all of the people in the PRRI survey likely would identify as QAnon followers, this poll indicates that a nontrivial number of people agree with these QAnon-related statements. Thus, the beliefs of QAnon are fairly widespread. This begs the question answered in the next section: Why?

Why Do People Follow QAnon?

There are many reasons why people are attracted to QAnon. For instance, QAnon presents an exciting mystery, full of clues and puzzles (called Q-drops) left by other followers or an anonymous leader (named Q) believed to be a high-ranking political leader. As such, following QAnon is similar to playing an ever-changing, massive multiplayer video game (see Chapters 2 and 14). Further, followers participate in real time and can easily access other followers if they have access to the internet and the ability to read, post, and repost social media messages. These aspects might attract some followers to QAnon.

Although some people might jump to the conclusion that QAnon followers are somehow abnormal, there is no evidence that they, as a group, are delusional or have serious mental illness (see Chapter 2), nor are they "brainwashed" (see Chapter 7). Chapter 9, however, suggests that QAnon support is driven by antiestablishment sentiments and antisocial personality traits.

Additionally, there are numerous psychological and sociological explanations detailing the types of people might become QAnon followers. For instance, Chapter 2 suggests that a person's need for certainty, control, and closure – as well as symptoms associated with depression, anxiety, or substance abuse – could encourage someone to follow QAnon. Further, people who believe that society's values are being threatened (called "system identity threat") are more likely to believe in conspiracies (see Chapter 8), and these beliefs help meet the person's existential, epistemic, and social needs. The role of emotion in QAnon support is discussed in Chapter 6. Affect – and affective polarization – can prompt conspiratorial beliefs, spread of misinformation, and violent behavior.

Further, Chapter 4 discusses how membership could be related to cognitive *processes* (e.g. delusional ideation, teleological thinking, cognitive closure), *biases* (e.g. groupthink, confirmation bias, jumping to conclusions bias), and *traits* (e.g. narcissism, Machiavellianism, political affiliation). Similarly, Chapter 7 discusses how QAnon members use techniques such as "foot in the door" to recruit new members, and Chapter 2 provides anecdotal evidence for how members go "down the rabbit hole" and end up entrenched in QAnon.

Data suggest that QAnon has become normalized within society (Pierre, 2020). Indeed, research has indicated that labeling something a "conspiracy" does not reduce people's belief in the idea, indicating perhaps that the media's romanticized portrayal of conspiracies has led the term "conspiracy" to lose its stigma (Wood, 2016). With this negative connotation removed, people are free to believe in QAnon and reap the benefits of belonging to its community (see Chapter 11).

The events of 2020 could have contributed to the attractiveness of QAnon (see Chapters 2, 5, and 8, but see Chapter 9 for another perspective). These include Donald Trump's presidency, COVID-19, Black Lives Matter, and other social events. Chapter 5 posits that parasite stress theory, moral foundations theory, and terror management theory can partially explain the shift toward conservative values that contributed to QAnon's popularity. The events of 2020 could have increased support for conspiracy theories, and this increased support allowed QAnon followers to justify the group's harmful actions (e.g. spreading false COVID-19 information or committing violence; see also Chapter 15 for more on the harms of disinformation) as predicted by moral disengagement theory (see also Chapter 8).

With so many psychosocial influences encouraging support for QAnon, it is little surprise that the group has taken hold within a nontrivial proportion of the population. For the same reasons, it is also difficult to counter the group's messages or dissuade followers to abandon their beliefs in the conspiracy. Chapter 15 discusses the techniques of debunking and "prebunking" – both designed to prevent the spread of disinformation.

In sum, there are numerous reasons why people believe in QAnon. Many of these reasons are not unique to QAnon. So is it "just another conspiracy theory"? As discussed in the next section, the answer is both "yes" and "no."

Is QAnon "Just Another Conspiracy Theory"?

QAnon is the latest in a series of conspiracy narratives that have arisen throughout American history (see Chapter 10) and are grounded in folklore (see Chapter 14). Chapter 10 describes the witchcraft narrative in 1692 Salem and the 1980s satanic cult narrative. It is thus worth exploring whether QAnon is "just another conspiracy theory."

Many chapters in this book explore possible ways in which QAnon is similar to and different from other such groups that are primarily religious, political, or social. For example, QAnon has a clear leader and primary (virtual) meeting places, which are more common traits of quasi-religious groups than of most conspiracy groups. QAnon's conspiracies are many, unlike some singular-belief conspiracy groups (e.g. a group that believes that the Earth is flat). QAnon's conspiracies are extraordinary for their breadth and extremity, as described in Chapter 10. These conspiracies include those about the 2020 presidential election, the faked death (and predicted reappearance) of John F. Kennedy, Jr., sex trafficking, COVID-19, and climate change – just to name a few. Further, QAnon is unique because it is continually adapting and incorporating new conspiracies. It also aligns itself with other lifestyle and conspiracy groups in order to attract more members (see Chapter 17).

QAnon is also unique because of the attention it gets from the media, the marketplace, and political leaders. Social media took monumental steps to prevent QAnon groups from promoting false claims (see Chapters 12–14 for more on social media and QAnon). For instance, Facebook banned QAnon on October 6, 2020, because of its belief that QAnon was spreading disinformation (see also Chapters 12, 13, and 17). Although QAnon books were some of its top sellers (Collins, 2019), Amazon stopped selling any QAnon-related material (e.g. books, clothing) in early 2021 after the January 6 insurrection in Washington, DC (Pena, 2021).

Additionally, QAnon is not a typical conspiracy group because of the attention it is getting from high-level leaders. President Trump has called QAnon followers "people who love our country" and has supported congressional candidates who support QAnon. In all, over a dozen congressional candidates on the 2020 ticket were QAnon followers to varying degrees (see Chapter 5 for more on QAnon and political candidates and Chapter 9 for more on QAnon and politics).

Additionally, QAnon is a unique conspiracy group because of the concern it has raised about possible violence (see Chapters 5 and 9) and the harms associated with disinformation (see Chapter 15). A number of QAnon followers have committed crimes in the name of QAnon. Although QAnon itself does not directly call for violence, members sometimes take it upon themselves to act. Other people have spread harmful disinformation, including a conspiracy claiming that 5G communication towers were to blame for COVID-19 – or even that COVID-19 does not exist (see Chapters 13 and 15). A precursor event to QAnon, called Pizzagate, occurred during the 2016 election year. Presidential candidate Hillary Clinton's leaked emails allegedly contained coded messages about a pizza restaurant in Washington, DC that was allegedly operating a satanic child sex-trafficking ring in its basement. In December 2016, a North Carolina man traveled to the restaurant in Washington, DC to "self-investigate" the claims, bringing with him an assault rifle. He fired three shots in the restaurant, including into a door he believed to lead to the basement. The pizza restaurant did not, in fact, have a basement (see Chapter 12 for more). Nevertheless, this conspiracy regarding Hillary Clinton's involvement in a satanic child sex-trafficking ring grew and spread and was adopted as a core belief by QAnon. More recently, in August 2021, Matthew Coleman killed his children and later claimed to have been enlightened by QAnon (Meeks et al., 2021).

In part due to instances such as these, the FBI considers QAnon a threat, and on October 2, 2020, a bipartisan bill condemning QAnon was passed in the House of Representatives. Months later, the FBI's fears about the danger that QAnon posed proved correct: QAnon followers were active in the January 6, 2021, insurrection in Washington, DC (see Chapters 4 and 5).

In sum, QAnon is both similar to and different from other conspiracy groups. Little research has been conducted, however, that is directly about QAnon. This book offers a review of existing research on QAnon, includes some original research, and offers avenues for future research.

Overview of the Book

This book contains four parts. Each of the seventeen chapters relies on relevant social science theory and research, applying these to QAnon. This introductory chapter lays the foundation for the rest of the book. It presents a broad summary of information about the QAnon group, its followers, their beliefs, and their consequences.

Part II concerns how QAnon attracts and maintains followers. It contains six chapters that describe the psychological characteristics (e.g. cognition, traits, motivations, affect) that might be common among QAnon followers. QAnon might be particularly attractive to people with these characteristics. This part also describes the methods QAnon uses to recruit and maintain followers.

Part III focuses on the interaction between QAnon and society. Two chapters situate the QAnon phenomenon amid modern events (e.g. the COVID-19 pandemic) and the political world. Two other chapters assess how society has constructed QAnon as a threat, and how the need to affiliate with and belong to a social group can motivate followers.

Part IV examines the role of communication in promoting and limiting QAnon support. Its four chapters discuss how language and social networking can attract followers and spread messages. This is particularly true in the case of social media – which is a fundamental aspect of QAnon (see Chapters 12 and 14). Understanding QAnon's messages is one step toward debunking them – the topic of the final chapter in this part.

Part V discusses the future of QAnon. Chapter 16 presents one potential way to study QAnon in the future: investigating how QAnon might be similar to or different from other more well-studied groups (e.g. religious groups or organizations such as NXIVM). While this book largely focuses on QAnon as a conspiracy group, this chapter offers a different perspective and encourages researchers to take multiple approaches to studying QAnon in the future – for instance, by studying it as a religious group rather than only studying it as a conspiracy group. Chapter 17 builds on the themes presented in the previous chapters and notes how QAnon has shifted and adapted with changing events (e.g. Trump losing the 2020 election). It makes predictions about the condition in which QAnon might exist in the future and how it might continue to change, offering areas of study for future research.

Conclusion

There are many reasons why it is necessary to study QAnon: (1) one in five Americans polled believed at least one of the main theories posited by QAnon (PRRI, 2021); (2) the January 6 hearings held in July 12, 2022, attempted to establish some link between Donald Trump and QAnon followers; (3) numerous QAnon supporters have already become lawmakers in 2022; and (4) Ron Watkins – who might be Q himself – obtained enough signatures to be on the Arizona congressional ballot in August 2022 (Schwenk, 2022). Because these events all suggest that the influence of QAnon persists, all of the chapters in this book offer avenues for future scholarship. This is not an easy endeavor, however. QAnon lacks any kind of group structure and is largely a virtual movement. This fluidity makes it difficult for researchers to study it. QAnon is one example of how virtual social movements have shaped the ways in which researchers conduct investigations. Chapters 9, 13, and 14 suggest specific ways in which to conduct such research, while Chapter 15 offers methods for debunking misinformation such as that spread by QAnon. All of the chapters in this book offer ways to apply social science theories in order to further understand QAnon – and conspiracy groups more generally. Chapter 17 – the book's conclusion – offers predictions about the future of QAnon, noting that it has a unique ability to adapt and persist. As such, the authors of Chapter 17 predict that QAnon is likely to remain a significant force, both in the USA and globally. Therefore, QAnon is an important psychosocial phenomenon that deserves to be researched by trained scientists. The authors of the all of chapters in this book and I hope that this book is a first step in encouraging further study of QAnon.

REFERENCES

Beverley, J. A. (2020). *The QAnon Deception: Everything You Need to Know About the World's Most Dangerous Conspiracy Theory*. EqualTime Books.

Collins, B. (2019, March 4). On Amazon, a QAnon conspiracy book climbs the charts-with an algorithmic push. www.nbcnews.com/tech/tech-news/amazon-qanon-conspiracy-book-climbs-charts-algorithmic-push-n979181

Cox, D. A. (2021, March 4). Social isolation and community disconnection are not spurring conspiracy theories. www.americansurveycenter.org/research/social-isolation-and-community-disconnection-are-not-spurring-conspiracy-theories/#_edn11

Franks, B., Bangerter, A., & Bauer, M. W. (2013). Conspiracy theories as quasi-religious mentality: An integrated account from cognitive science, social representations theory, and frame theory. *Frontiers in Psychology*, *4*, 1–12.

Kirkpatrick, D. D. (2022). Who Is Behind QAnon? Linguistic Detectives Find Fingerprints. www.nytimes.com/2022/02/19/technology/qanon-messages-authors.html

Meeks, A., Campbell, J., & Caldwell, T. (2021, August 12). California man allegedly confesses to killing his children, refers to QAnon and Illuminati conspiracy theories. www.cnn.com/2021/08/12/us/father-kills-children-qanon-california-mexico/index.html

Pena, C. (2021, January 12). Amazon removes QAnon merchandise from its marketplace. www.nbcnews.com/business/business-news/amazon-removes-qanon-merchandise-its-marketplace-n1253937

Pierre, J. (2020). Mistrust and misinformation: A two-component, socio-epistemic model of belief in conspiracy theories. *PsyArXiv Preprints*, 1–29. https://doi.org/10.31234/osf.io/xhw52

PRRI. (2021, February 23). Understanding QAnon's Connection to American Politics, Religion, and Media Consumption. www.prri.org/research/qanon-conspiracy-american-politics-report

Schwenk, K. (2022, March 22). Ron Watkins, QAnon Figurehead, Will Be on the Ballot in Arizona. www.phoenixnewtimes.com/news/qanon-leader-ron-watkins-will-be-on-arizona-primary-ballot-13276203

Thompson, S. A. (2022, June 25). The Leader of the QAnon Conspiracy Theory Returns. www.nytimes.com/2022/06/25/technology/qanon-leader-returns.html

The Economist/YouGov. (2021). The Economist/YouGov Poll, January 10–12, 2021. https://docs.cdn.yougov.com/4yijjbkc2z/econTabReport.pdf

Wood, M. J. (2016). Some dare call it conspiracy: Labeling something a conspiracy theory does not reduce belief in it. *Political Psychology*, *37*, 695–705.

PART II

Recruiting and Maintaining Followers

CHAPTER 2

Down the Conspiracy Theory Rabbit Hole

How Does One Become a Follower of QAnon?

Joseph Pierre

Introduction

Because the shared beliefs that fall under the QAnon umbrella include outlandish narratives involving Satan-worshippers harvesting adrenochrome from children, it can be tempting to dismiss them as evidence of delusional thinking or mental illness. This chapter provides a more normative account of conspiracy beliefs, highlighting the social, epistemic, and political forces that can steer people to become adherents of QAnon as a mass movement. Although existing models of ideological group affiliation can inform a modern understanding of QAnon, it is ultimately argued that there are many potential paths to QAnon affiliation, as well as many variations and degrees of belief in QAnon ideology.

The Psychological Needs That QAnon Feeds

An empirical account of how one becomes an adherent of QAnon is complicated by several issues, not the least of which is that it is difficult to define what it means to be "an adherent of QAnon." Belief conviction exists on a continuum such that the threshold to define a QAnon believer, follower, or adherent is a matter of degree, and people might move back and forth across that threshold over time. In addition, the beliefs and ideologies that fall under the QAnon umbrella are diverse, such that followers might embrace one aspect but reject another. Finally, QAnon affiliation is primarily an online phenomenon that has spread internationally without any formal structure or leadership such that followers are not card-carrying members of any singular organizational entity. Methodological examination of adherents is therefore difficult, and, to date, there has been little to no published systematic research that addresses the phenomenon of how people have come to identify as "Anons."

In the absence of specific research data, understanding how one becomes an adherent of QAnon can be extrapolated from research on other similar phenomena, but as discussed in Chapter 16 of this volume, QAnon defies easy categorization. Certainly, the central dogma of QAnon – that America if not the world at large is imperiled by a liberal, pedophilic, Satan-worshipping "Deep State" – represents a conspiracy theory. But the alignment of QAnon ideology with American conservativism and with the election of Republican politicians at local and national levels who have identified with the cause suggests that QAnon can also be understood as a political movement and by-product of a global rise in populism (Stephansky, 2020). Several authors have alternatively claimed that QAnon is best understood as a cult or a new religious movement (Argentino, 2020a, 2020b; LaFrance, 2020; Lyttleton, 2020). Still others have highlighted that QAnon represents a kind of alternate-reality game (ARG) with potentially addictive qualities (Hawkins, 2020; Rosenberg, 2019). It is therefore unclear what kind of comparable research might be best applied to understand how people become QAnon adherents or whether any one model represents a best fit. Nonetheless, modeling QAnon based on different perspectives – as conspiracy theory, political movement, cult, and role-playing game – can at least provide speculative insight into how people might become followers and why it might be difficult to reverse that affiliation. As with the familiar "blind men and the elephant" metaphor, such perspectives are not mutually exclusive.

For an example of this nonmutual exclusivity, one aspect of participation in QAnon for some involves assuming the role of "bakers" who decipher cryptic messages posted online in the form of "Q-drops," "breadcrumbs," and "stringers" that purportedly convey meaningful political insights and predict future events. Given that Q's predictions have invariably failed to occur, some have suggested that "the best way to think of QAnon may be not as a conspiracy theory, but as an unusually absorbing alternate-reality game . . ." (Rosenberg, 2019), while others have acknowledged that it is a "dangerous conspiracy theory," but it also "pushes the same buttons that [ARGs] do, whether by intention or coincidence" (Hon, 2020). Modeling QAnon as an ARG with an active role-playing component highlights the potentially absorbing and compulsive aspects of participation, similar to that of other forms of "behavioral addition" involving video games and the Internet. Proposed diagnostic criteria for "internet gaming disorder" as a psychiatric disorder include preoccupation and inability to control time spent involved online, use of internet gaming to escape or relieve negative mood states, loss of interest in previous forms of entertainment, and loss of significant relationships and educational/job opportunities as a result (Sussman et al., 2018). Along with symptoms of anxiety, impulsivity, depression, and substance use disorder, social deficits and social isolation are thought to be risk factors for the syndrome (Sussman et al., 2018). Such findings offer likely parallels to account for the rise in popularity of QAnon during the COVID-19 pandemic, when many people were spending more time at home online.

Similar psychological needs predicting affiliation emerge when conceptualizing QAnon as a cult or a new religious movement. As discussed in Chapter 16, the extent to which QAnon, which lacks a traditional charismatic leader and whose coercive group dynamics are mostly confined to online spaces, qualifies as a cult remains debatable. However, some of its theological and apocalyptic elements are unquestionably "cultic" (Lyttleton, 2020), with significant ideological overlap with evangelical Christianity (Argentino, 2020b). Previous research on cult membership has revealed that affiliation is often driven by life dissatisfaction, "ideological hunger," and social vulnerability, leading to a search for emotional affiliation and group cohesion (Galanter, 1990; Rousselet et al., 2017; Ungerleider & Wellisch, 1979). As with internet gaming disorder, cult participation is also often preceded by psychiatric symptoms suggestive of depressive, anxiety, and substance use disorders (Rousselet et al., 2017). Modeling QAnon as a kind of internet cult therefore reinforces the likelihood that affiliation in recent years has been fueled by disenchantment with the state of the world, a sense of anomie and disconnection from society at large, the appeal of attaining novel group affiliation as a "Q Patriot," and faith in President Trump as a kind of messianic savior.

A converging profile of attraction to QAnon is further suggested by modeling it as an amalgam of conspiracy theories. As will be discussed more thoroughly in Chapters 3 and 4 of this volume, psychological research has found that the tendency to believe in conspiracy theories is associated with a veritable laundry list of personality traits, psychological needs, and cognitive quirks, although it is likely that some are more relevant to specific conspiracy theories than others (Pierre, 2020b). Both public awareness of and social media posts about QAnon exploded in 2020, coincident with the COVID-19 pandemic, Black Lives Matter protests, and the reelection campaign of President Trump (Gallagher et al., 2020; Pew Research Center, 2020). The concomitant rise in popularity of QAnon suggests that psychological needs for certainty, control, and closure that have been associated with conspiracist ideation and are often heightened during times of societal crisis and upheaval might have been particularly salient drivers of attraction to QAnon as a conspiracy theory narrative during that time.

"Hooks" and Online Recruitment

Contrary to stereotypes, social isolation might not be a significant determinant of vulnerability to belief in QAnon conspiracy theories (Cox, 2021). A more normalizing "socio-epistemic" framework to understand belief in conspiracy theories proposes that mistrust and misinformation are central interactive components (Pierre, 2020b). As both a conspiracy theory and populist political movement, QAnon is rooted in mistrust of elites, liberals, Democrats, and the so-called Deep State, as well as the allegedly "fake news"–peddling mainstream media. It has therefore been referred to as a "right-wing," "pro-Trump" conspiracy theory, with polls from late 2020 and early 2021 demonstrating that 45 percent of self-identifying Republicans had favorable opinions of QAnon (The Economist/YouGov, 2021), 23 percent believed that Satan-worshipping elites were running a child sex ring trying to control politics and media, and 72 percent believed that the "Deep State" was working to undermine President Trump (Ipsos, 2020).

According to the socio-epistemic model of belief in conspiracy theories, mistrust in authoritative sources of information leads to a search for counter-narratives and a biased vulnerability to misinformation and disinformation, which are ubiquitous online. In the case of QAnon, conspiratorial counter-narratives have been widely promoted by influential commentators from conservative outlets such as Fox News and One America News Network (OANN), conspiracy theory entrepreneurs like Alex Jones and Lin Wood, political candidates elected to office like Marjorie Taylor Greene, and President Trump himself. Social media has likewise served as a "petri dish," allowing conspiracy theories to proliferate and reach a wide audience, with both conservative and liberal media coverage contributing to nearly 60 percent of Americans having at least some familiarity with QAnon as of early 2021 (The Economist/YouGov, 2021).

Whether intentionally or not, QAnon has gained followers through social media outreach using various "hooks" to attract followers from groups with ideological overlap. Anecdotal accounts detail such "recruitment" among Christian evangelicals attracted to Q's use of Bible quotations, apocalyptic predictions about the "Great Awakening" and the coming "Storm," as well as recycled "Satanic Panic" narratives from the 1980s about pedophilia and eating babies (Ohlheiser, 2020; Rogers,

2021). Polls from early 2021 found that 33 percent of evangelicals believed that "QAnon claims" were either somewhat or very accurate (Morning Consult, 2021) and that 27 percent of white evangelicals (the highest rate for any category of religious group) rated the claim that "Donald Trump has been secretly fighting a group of child sex traffickers that include prominent Democrats and Hollywood elites" as either "mostly" or "completely" accurate (Cox, 2021).

QAnon's "hijacking" of the #SaveTheChildren "hashtag" (a legitimate fundraising campaign run by the Save The Children Fund) and its subsequent adoption of #SaveOurChildren allowed conspiracy theories about child trafficking (e.g. that the online furniture company Wayfair was trafficking children within shipping boxes) to find a receptive audience (Roose, 2020; Spring, 2020). In 2020, QAnon also managed to attract untold numbers to in-person rallies to protest child trafficking; many soon unwittingly came to realize that the events had been organized to promote the much broader QAnon agenda (Zadrozny & Collins, 2020).

In a similar fashion, QAnon followers were recruited through outreach to "wellness" groups and "lifestyle influencers" based on less obvious connections between conspiracy theories and health, spirituality, yoga, and alternative medicine, a union that has been labeled "conspirituality" (Love, 2020; Ward & Voas, 2011). Based on the appeal of "soft-core" narratives described as "pastel QAnon" (Aubrey, 2020), hard-core QAnon conspiracy theories such as those related to 5G networks causing COVID-19 were able to gain traction among those within wellness groups whose mistrust of science, technology, and Western medicine manifests as "bullshit receptivity" and a tendency to believe in pseudoscience and health misinformation (Hart & Graether, 2018; Scherer et al., 2021). Likewise, QAnon conspiracy theories about Bill Gates intending to use COVID-19 vaccinations to implant microchips into people for tracking purposes fostered the convergence of QAnon with conspiracy theory believers from the antivaccination movement (Cook, 2020; Dickinson, 2021).

The Plural of Anecdote Is Data

To summarize thus far, while there is no evidence that belief in QAnon conspiracy theories represents delusional thinking or is reflective of mental illness per se (Pierre, 2019, 2020a; Pies & Pierre, 2021), the process of becoming a QAnon follower can be understood as an expression of individual psychological vulnerability to conspiracy theory belief, cult affiliation, and ARG engagement. In addition, QAnon can be viewed through a larger "socio-epistemic" lens of hyperpolarized politics and populism, mistrust in authoritative sources of information, the ubiquity of misinformation, and online recruitment through like-minded ideological groups. Based on this pluralistic perspective, the process of becoming a QAnon follower appears to involve initial resonance with conservative politics, populist ideals such as mistrust of government and the need to "drain the swamp," or one of several "hooks" that overlap with QAnon ideology. Deeper affiliation with QAnon then emerges from immersion in online spaces where exposure to QAnon rhetoric is pervasive.

In the absence of systematized research on the process of becoming a QAnon follower, anecdotal accounts can be useful to validate or refute this portrayal. Several such accounts have been published over recent years. One of the first, from 2018, described a woman whose boyfriend, who had previously been a "staunch conservative," became concerned about online information claiming Hillary Clinton was a pedophile, was impressed by a QAnon video on YouTube called "Great Awakening," and over the next several months started "constantly reading QAnon posts on Twitter, checking threads while eating breakfast, and spending hours researching new Q 'drops' or theories to determine whether they're true" (Minutalglio, 2018). A subsequent portrait of several loved ones who became QAnon followers described parents who became QAnon followers "when they decided to get rid of cable TV and start watching YouTube" and a husband who got into trouble at work due to his immersion in QAnon online and insisted that his wife watch and be quizzed about QAnon-related videos in order to win her to the cause (Lamoureux, 2019). Another told of a father with a long-standing interest in aliens who found QAnon while looking into conspiracy theories about the moon landing, 9/11 being an inside job, and the US government being controlled by shape-shifters and then became more heavily invested after he gave up watching the major networks for news (Grable, 2020). By the fall of 2020, as COVID-19 continued and after Black Lives Matters protests had spread worldwide, such narratives – told by family members and other loved ones – started appearing in increasing numbers, echoing an uptick in postings on online support forums like Reddit's r/QAnonCasualities and r/ReQovery (Carrier, 2021; Dickson, 2020; Grametz, 2020; Jaffe & Del Real, 2021; Lytvynenko, 2020; Watt, 2020).

After Marjorie Taylor Greene won a seat in the US Congress, *The Washington Post* published an article detailing her path to QAnon and public office (Kranish et al., 2021). After starting as a gym owner, she became "entranced by QAnon" during the Trump presidency, achieved notoriety as a social media influencer promoting QAnon dogma, and ran a successful political campaign supported by "key Republicans" based on her "ability to tap into the far-right online world."

Following the "storming of the US Capitol" in January 2021, additional portraits of QAnon followers were published in the mainstream media, including that of Melissa Rein Lively, a thirty-five-year-old public relations professional who went into a "tailspin, searching for answers" during the economic crisis of the COVID-19 pandemic (Andrews, 2020b). Through "natural wellness and spirituality spaces she inhabited online," she ultimately became consumed with "doom-scrolling on the internet" and "found answers in QAnon" that were "horrifying," yet "oddly comforting." Valerie Gilbert, a fifty-seven-year-old "Harvard-educated writer and actress" who was previously part of the "anti-establishment left," described that her "world opened up in Technicolor for me … like the Matrix" during Pizzagate (Roose, 2021). QAnon subsequently "took over her life and yanked her politics sharply to the right" as she took on the role of a self-described "digital soldier" and "meme queen," posting online throughout the day and cutting ties with friends in the process. Larry Cook, a "one-time healthy-lifestyle guru" turned prominent antivaccine activist, "opened his mind to the Q worldview" after reading *Calm Before the Storm* in 2020 (Dickinson, 2021). He described how "discovering QAnon suddenly gave him a context for his distrust of mainstream medicine and his sense of being persecuted and silenced by social media." Ashli Babbit, a thirty-five-year-old Air Force veteran and one-time supporter of Barack Obama, adopted QAnon as a cause after leaving military service and became an active viewer of conservative media, supporter of President Trump, and promoter of QAnon conspiracy theories on social media (Jamison et al., 2021). After breaching barricaded doors during the Capitol insurrection, she was shot and killed by police.

The story of Jitarth Jadeja, a man who became a QAnon follower in 2017 but later came to believe it was all a hoax, was carried in several major news outlets starting in the fall of 2020 (Andrews, 2020a; Dickson, 2020; Lord & Naik, 2020), culminating in a CNN interview in which he apologized to Anderson Cooper for "thinking you ate babies" (Anderson Cooper 360, 2021). During a time when he was struggling in school, feeling overwhelmed, and socially isolated, Jadeja heard about QAnon through Alex Jones and InfoWars, found solace in it, and felt "energized" by deciphering Q-drops (Andrews, 2020a; Lord & Naik, 2020). Soon, he found himself so immersed that he became disconnected from both friends and reality (Lord & Naik, 2020). After two years, he became increasingly bothered by logical inconsistencies within QAnon claims. He finally came to see QAnon as a "slick con" (Dickson, 2020), and he found support and a way out within Reddit subforums such as r/Qult_Headquarters (Lord & Naik, 2020).

Down the Rabbit Hole: A Typology of Believing

Anecdotal portrayals, especially those exclusively published within the so-called liberal mainstream media, hardly constitute objective data. But they do provide validation of the previously detailed potential entry points into QAnon and reinforce the centrality of online immersion in the process of becoming a QAnon believer.

Indeed, research investigating online users who participate in conspiracy theory forums has determined that falling down the proverbial rabbit hole of conspiracy theory belief is not a passive process, but an active one in which users seek out others with like-minded beliefs (Klein et al., 2019). However, such research has also emphasized the importance of distinguishing those who passively endorse conspiracy theories in private and those who actively engage with them in social spaces, whether online or in person. Other research has likewise challenged the idea of what it means to be a QAnon follower. For example, an analysis of Reddit users from 2018 reported a meaningful distinction between "casual" and "hard-core" QAnon followers, with the vast majority belonging to the former group and only a small minority producing most of the QAnon content online (Chang, 2018). A similar survey from 2020 found significant heterogeneity among QAnon supporters, many of whom endorsed support for the larger movement but were often unaware of its more outrageous claims or endorsed specific QAnon-related ideologies as "true" despite encountering them for only the first time during the survey (Edelman, 2020; Schaffner, 2020).

Other studies have found evidence for considerable variation within the details of conspiracy theory beliefs, leading to the conclusion that they represent "stories of individuation" reflecting "thirty shades of truth" (Raab et al., 2013). Franks et al. (2017) performed semi-structured, in-person interviews of conspiracy theory supporters and found support for a spectrum model consisting of five "ascending typologies" of conspiracy theory worldview endorsement that varies according to belief conviction, self-view, attitudes toward in-group and out-group members, and action. According to their model, Type 1 includes those who feel "something isn't right" but keep an open mind as they seek answers to questions, whereas

Type 2 describes those who feel as if "there's more to reality than meets the eye," are skeptical of official narratives, and have begun to explore alternative sources of information. Type 3 includes those who have become committed to a specific conspiracy theory and feel a sense of community based on questioning and rejecting official narratives, while Type 4 has given up questioning in favor of "truth-seeking conversion," membership within an "enlightened" conspiracy theory community, and dismissal of nonbelievers as "sheep" or "asleep." Finally, Type 5 describes those who come to regard all reality as an illusion, view explanations for world events in supernatural terms, and feel a "mystical sense of connectedness" among fellow conspiracy theory believers. Along this continuum, engagement with conspiracy theory communities and commitment to political action become increasingly strong. Franks et al. (2017) hypothesize that their "ascending typologies" represent a "personal journey" and "trajectory" of conspiracy theory belief "conversion."

A spectrum model – that is, a continuum with discrete points along the way – of conspiracy belief aligns with other continuous models of delusions and delusion-like beliefs, which have been quantified along cognitive dimensions of belief conviction, preoccupation, and extension (Pierre, 2001, 2019). Just how deep one goes down the QAnon rabbit hole can therefore be measured in terms of both belief and behavior. As with any kind of scale, however, it is important to consider how many points are included in a measurement device's range and the practical relevance of distinguishing between any two points. Because the five typologies offered by Franks et al. (2017) seem to have blurry borders and unclear pragmatic distinctions between types, a simpler model encompassing a more complete range of belief and ideological affiliation is proposed here.

Nonbelievers

Nonbelievers do not endorse belief in conspiracy theories and, broadly speaking, trust in institutions of authority and epistemic sources of information.

Fence-Sitters

Fence-sitters are those who are skeptical and mistrustful of authoritative sources of information, are "looking for answers," and are considering the validity of conspiracy theory counternarratives. The term "fence-sitter" is borrowed from research on vaccine hesitancy that has demonstrated that interventions to counter belief in misinformation and conspiracy theories are most effective among those with intact cognitive flexibility, whose belief conviction remains malleable (Betsch et al., 2015). As with the distinction between those who believe in metaphorical versus literal interpretations of the Bible, fence-sitters might look favorably on QAnon as a movement but stop short of actually endorsing specific QAnon conspiracy theories. It is likely that the large majority of "QAnon followers" are fence-sitters, with significant heterogeneity among them (Chang, 2018; Edelman, 2020; Schaffner, 2020).

True Believers

Adopting a term from Hoffer's (1951) treatise on mass movements, "true believers" endorse belief in conspiracy theories, whether individually or more broadly, with strong conviction. Such conviction is possible because institutions of authority and "facts" are dismissed as untrustworthy as well as through support from social networks where conspiracy theories are embraced to the exclusion of previous relationships and social responsibilities.

True believers often view their endorsed ideology as a component of their identity, with QAnon supporters proudly identifying as "Anons" and "Q Patriots." When belief and identity become fused, a perceived attack on one's beliefs can be regarded as a personal assault and existential threat. The degree to which cherished beliefs are protected through cognitive dissonance is often directly proportional to one's commitment to the belief and time invested in the cause. In the case of QAnon, such cognitive dissonance is typically resolved by "doubling down" on belief conviction and "moving the goalposts" of predictions about future events.

Activists

Activists have decided that they must act on beliefs in order to defend them or to fight for the cause. This category decouples action from the continuum of belief, in recognition of the myriad factors beyond belief itself or its cognitive dimensions that motivate behavior, including affect and emotion (see Chapter 6 of this volume for more on the link between QAnon and emotion) as well as financial gain. QAnon activism might take the form of creating or recirculating online content, solving Q-drops as a "baker," selling QAnon merchandise as a "conspiracy theory entrepreneur" (Sunstein & Vermeule, 2009), attending in-person rallies, or more drastic acts of criminal behavior or violence.

Note, however, that the line between productive and "healthy" political activism or religious evangelism on the one hand and "extremism" or "radicalization" on the other is often blurred and interpreted subjectively (as they say, "one man's terrorist is another man's freedom fighter"; Borum, 2011). In addition, while some research has suggested that radicalization and political violence are driven by ideological passion, a quest for significance, group identity and dynamics, grievance, and perceived threat (Kruglanski et al., 2017; McCauley & Moskalenko, 2008; Rip et al., 2012), few if any contributory factors are reliable predictors possessing high sensitivity (Piccinni et al., 2018; Sawyer & Hienz, 2017).

Apostates

Apostates have renounced belief in conspiracy theories along with membership in the social networks that support them. Research on cult membership indicates that becoming an apostate is typically caused by loss of faith due to social and family interventions, being unable to resolve ideological contradictions, experiences of abuse, and conflicts within one's social network (Rousselet et al., 2017). Anecdotal accounts of apostates such as Jitarth Jadeja and others support the conclusion that, for some QAnon followers, repeated predictions by Q that did not come to pass have stretched cognitive dissonance to its breaking point.

This categorical model of ideological affiliation is proposed as a framework to test several potential hypotheses about the continuum of conspiracy theory belief conviction and identification with ideological groups. For example, to what extent is there a dose-related effect whereby the amount of time spent within social networks that support conspiracy theory beliefs is proportional to conviction and therefore predictive of transitioning from nonbeliever, to fence-sitter, to true believer? What other factors drive transitions from one category to the next, not only in terms of belief, but also regarding activism or apostasy? Does a "clinical staging" model predict the efficacy of specific interventions within different categories?

How Does One Become a Follower of QAnon

While we can look to previous research on similar phenomena to speculate on how one becomes a follower, QAnon remains a relatively novel form of political, religious, and conspiratorial ideology that has been largely propagated through the internet in just the past few years. It will no doubt continue to evolve over time such that a more thorough characterization will require dedicated research efforts in the years to come.

In the meantime, if we are to attempt to characterize how one becomes a follower of QAnon, we must first recognize the myriad subcategories of that identity and pathways of individuation. It has been said that "radicalization" – the extreme end of activism – "constitutes a multifinite and equifinite process" with "multiple potential outcomes as well as multiple pathways to any given outcome" involving "an individual-level process embedded in [a] social and temporal context level" and "a range of experiences across [an] individual's lifetime" (Sawyer & Hienz, 2017: 47, 50). Such a statement applies even more so to the analysis of how one moves along the much broader spectrum of ideological nonbeliever, fence-sitter, true believer, activist, and apostate.

Asking how one becomes a follower of QAnon is akin to asking how one comes to identify with other ideologies such as being a Catholic, a Democrat, or a Freudian psychoanalyst. While identifying macroscopic stereotypes associated with QAnon affiliation can be instructive, there will always be exceptions to such stereotypes across people. A more granular understanding of the process therefore requires a much closer examination of personal narrative accounts, where no two stories of individuation are ever quite the same.

REFERENCES

Anderson Cooper 360. (2021, January 30). Former QAnon supporter to Cooper: I apologize for thinking you ate babies. *CNN.com*. www.cnn.com/videos/us/2021/01/30/anderson-cooper-former-qanon-supporter-special-report-sot-ac360-vpx.cnn

Andrews, T. M. (2020a, October 24). He's a former QAnon believer. He doesn't want to tell his story, but thinks it might help. *The Washington Post*. www.washingtonpost.com/technology/2020/10/24/qanon-believer-conspiracy-theory/

(2020b, November 11). She fell into QAnon and went viral for destroying a Target mask display. Now she's rebuilding her life. *The Washington Post*. www.washingtonpost.com/technology/2020/11/11/masks-qanon-target-melissa-rein-lively/

Argentino, M.-A. (2020a, May 18). The church of QAnon: Will conspiracy theories form the basis of a new religious movement? *The Conversation*. https://theconversation.com/the-church-of-qanon-will-conspiracy-theories-form-the-basis-of-a-new-religious-movement-137859

(2020b, May 28). In the name of the father, son, and Q: Why it's important to see QAnon as a "hyper-real" religion. *Religion Dispatches*. https://religiondispatches

.org/in-the-name-of-the-father-son-and-q-why-its-important-to-see-qanon-as-a-hyper-real-religion/

Aubrey, S. (2020, September 27). "Playing with fire": The curious marriage of QAnon and wellness. *The Sydney Morning Herald*. www.smh.com.au/lifestyle/health-and-wellness/playing-with-fire-the-curious-marriage-of-qanon-and-wellness-20200924-p55yu7.html

Betsch, C., Korn, L., & Holtmann, C. (2015). Don't try to convert the anti-vaccinators, instead target the fence-sitters. *Proceedings of the National Academy of Sciences of the United States of America*, *112*, E6725–E6726.

Borum, R. (2011). Radicalization into violent extremism I: A review of social science theories. *Journal of Strategic Security*, *4*, 7–36.

Carrier, A. (2021, February 19). "This crap means more to him than my life": When QAnon invades American homes. *Politico*. www.politico.com/news/magazine/2021/02/19/qanon-conspiracy-theory-family-members-reddit-forum-469485

Chang, A. (2018, August 8). We analyzed every QAnon post on Reddit. Here's who QAnon supporters actually are. *Vox*. www.vox.com/2018/8/8/17657800/qanon-reddit-conspiracy-data

Cook, J. (2020, November 28). Online anti-vax communities have become a pipeline for QAnon radicalization. *Huffington Post*. www.huffpost.com/entry/qanon-anti-vax-coronavirus_n_5fbeb0c0c5b61d04bfa6921a

Cox, D. A. (2021, March 4). Social isolation and community disconnection are not spurring conspiracy theories. www.americansurveycenter.org/research/social-isolation-and-community-disconnection-are-not-spurring-conspiracy-theories/#_edn11

Dickinson, T. (2021, February 10). How the anti-vaxxers got red-pilled. *Rolling Stone*. www.rollingstone.com/culture/culture-features/qanon-anti-vax-covid-vaccine-conspiracy-theory-1125197/

Dickson, E. (2020). Former QAnon followers explain what drew them in – and got them out. *Rolling Stone*. www.rollingstone.com/culture/culture-features/ex-qanon-followers-cult-conspiracy-theory-pizzagate-1064076/

Edelman, G. (2020, October 6). QAnon supports aren't quite who you think they are. *Wired*. www.wired.com/story/qanon-supporters-arent-quite-who-you-think-they-are/

Franks, B., Bangerter, A., Bauer, M. W., Hall, M., & Noort, M. C. (2017). Beyond "monologicality"? Exploring conspiracist worldviews. *Frontiers in Psychology*, *8*, 861.

Galanter, M. (1990). Cults and zealous self-help movements: A psychiatric perspective. *American Journal of Psychiatry*, *147*, 543–551.

Gallagher, A., Davey, J., & Hart, M. (2020). The genesis of a conspiracy theory. Institute for Strategic Dialogue. www.isdglobal.org/wp-content/uploads/2020/07/The-Genesis-of-a-Conspiracy-Theory.pdf

Grable, R. R. (2020, May 21). My father, the QAnon conspiracy theorist. *Narratively*. https://narratively.com/my-father-the-qanon-conspiracy-theorist/

Grametz, J. (2020, August 11). Reddit community QAnon Casualties share stories of conspiracy cult. *News.com.au*. www.news.com.au/technology/online/social/reddit-community-qanon-casualties-share-stories-of-conspiracy-cult/news-story/8a48754da503954647a61f91d22b304b

Hart, J., & Graether, M. (2018). Something's going on here: Psychological predictors of belief in conspiracy theories. *Journal of Individual Differences, 39*, 229–237.

Hawkins, E. (2020, September 9). Dr. Joseph Pierre: UCLA psychiatrist takes on QAnon and "rescuing" loved ones. *Heavy*. https://heavy.com/news/2020/09/joseph-pierre-qanon/

Hoffer, E. (1951). *The true believer: Thoughts on the nature of mass movements*. Harper & Row.

Hon, A. (2020, August 5). What alternate reality games teach us about the dangerous appeal of QAnon. *Vice*. www.vice.com/en/article/qj4xbm/what-alternate-reality-games-teach-us-about-the-dangerous-appeal-of-qanon

Ipsos. (2020, December 30). More than 1 in 3 Americans believe a "deep state" is working to undermine Trump. www.ipsos.com/en-us/news-polls/npr-misinformation-123020

Jaffe, G., & Del Real, J. A. (2021, February 23). Life amid the ruins of QAnon: "I wanted my family back." *The Washington Post*. www.washingtonpost.com/nation/interactive/2021/conspiracy-theories-qanon-family-members/

Jamison, P., Natanson, H., Cox, J. W., & Horton, A. (2021, January 10). "The storm is here": Ashli Babbitt's journey from Capital "guardian" to invader. The Washington Post. www.washingtonpost.com/dc-md-va/2021/01/09/ashli-babbitt-capitol-shooting-trump-qanon/

Klein, C., Clutton, P., & Dunn, A. G. (2019). Pathways to conspiracy: The social and linguistic precursors of involvement in Reddit's conspiracy theory forum. *PLoS ONE, 14*(11), e0225098.

Kranish, M., Thebault, R., & McCrummen, S. (2021, January 30). How Rep. Marjorie Taylor Greene, promoter of QAnon's baseless theories, rose with support from key Republicans. *The Washington Post*. www.washingtonpost.com/politics/greene-qanon-house-trump-republicans/2021/01/30/321b4258-623c-11eb-ac8f-4ae05557196e_story.html

Kruglanski, A. W., Jasko, K., Chernikova, M., Dugas, M., & Webber, D. (2017). To the fringe and back: Violent extremism and the psychology of deviance. *American Psychologist, 72*, 217–230.

LaFrance, A. (2020, June). The prophesies of Q. *The Atlantic*. www.theatlantic.com/magazine/archive/2020/06/qanon-nothing-can-stop-what-is-coming/610567/

Lamoureux, M. (2019, July 11). People tell us how QAnon destroyed their relationships. *Vice*. www.vice.com/en/article/xwnjx4/people-tell-us-how-qanon-destroyed-their-relationships

Lord, B., & Naik, R. (2020, October 18). He went down the QAnon rabbit hole for almost two years. Here's how he got out. *CNN*. www.cnn.com/2020/10/16/tech/qanon-believer-how-he-got-out/index.html

Love, S. (2020, December 16). "Conspirituality" explains why the wellness world fell for QAnon. *Vice*. www.vice.com/en/article/93wq73/conspirituality-explains-why-the-wellness-world-fell-for-qanon

Lyttleton, J. (2020, July 5). Is QAnon a cult? *The Millennial Source*. https://themilsource.com/2020/07/05/is-qanon-a-cult/

Lytvynenko, J. (2020, September 18). Friends and family members of QAnon believers are going through a "surreal goddamn nightmare." www.buzzfeednews.com/article/janelytvynenko/qanon-families-friends

McCauley, C., & Moskalenko, S. (2008). Mechanisms of political radicalization: Pathways towards terrorism. *Terrorism and Political Violence*, *20*, 415–433.

Minutaglio, R. (2018, August 24). My boyfriend reads QAnon theories. I still love him – but I'm worried. *Esquire*. www.esquire.com/news-politics/a22664244/qanon-boyfriend-conspiracy-theorist-my-partner-deep-state/

Morning Consult. (2021). National tracking poll #2101102. *Morning Consult*. https://assets.morningconsult.com/wp-uploads/2021/02/01222231/2101102_crosstabs_MC_TECH_QANON_Adults_v1.pdf

Ohlheiser, A. (2020, August 26). Evangelicals are looking for answers online. They're finding QAnon instead. *MIT Technology Review*. www.technologyreview.com/2020/08/26/1007611/how-qanon-is-targeting-evangelicals/

Pew Research Center. (2020, November 16). 5 facts about the QAnon conspiracy theories. www.pewresearch.org/fact-tank/2020/11/16/5-facts-about-the-qanon-conspiracy-theories/

Piccinni, P., Marazziti, D., & Veltri, A. (2018). Psychopathology of terrorists. *CNS Spectrums*, *23*, 141–144.

Pierre, J. M. (2001). Faith or delusion: At the crossroads of religion and psychosis. *Journal of Psychiatric Practice*, *7*(3), 163–172.

(2019). Integrating non-psychiatric models of delusion-like beliefs into forensic psychiatric assessment. *American Academy of Psychiatry and the Law*, *47*, 171–179.

(2020a). Forensic psychiatry versus the variety of delusion-like beliefs. *American Academy of Psychiatry and the Law*, *48*, 327–334.

(2020b). Mistrust and misinformation: A two-component, socio-epistemic model of belief in conspiracy theories. *Journal of Social and Political Psychology*, *8*, 617–641.

Pies, R. W., & Pierre, J. M. (2021, February 4). Believing in conspiracy theories in not delusional. *Medscape Psychiatry*. www.medscape.com/viewarticle/945290

Raab, M. H., Ortlieb, S. A., Auer, N., Guthmann, K., & Carbon, C.-C. (2013). Thirty shades of truth: Conspiracy theories as stories of individuation, not of pathological delusion. *Frontiers in Psychology*, *4*, 406.

Rip, B., Vallerand, R. J., & Lafreniere, M. K. (2012). Passion for a cause, passion for a creed: On ideological passion, identity threat, and extremism. *Journal of Personality*, *80*, 573–602.

Rogers, K. (2021, March 4). Why QAnon has attracted so many white evangelicals. *FiveThirtyEight*. https://fivethirtyeight.com/features/why-qanon-has-attracted-so-many-white-evangelicals/

Roose, K. (2020, August 12). QAnon followers are hijacking the #SaveTheChildren movement. *New York Times*. www.nytimes.com/2020/08/12/technology/qanon-save-the-children-trafficking.html

(2021, January 17). A QAnon "digital soldier" marches on, undeterred by theory's unraveling. *New York Times*. www.nytimes.com/2021/01/17/technology/qanon-meme-queen.html

Rosenberg, A. (2019, August 7). I understand the temptation to dismiss QAnon. Here's why we can't. *The Washington Post*. www.washingtonpost.com/opinions/2019/08/07/qanon-isnt-just-conspiracy-theory-its-highly-effective-game/

Rousselet, M., Duretete, O., Hardoun, J. B., & Grall-Bronec, M. (2017). Cult membership: What factors contribute to joining of leaving? *Psychiatry Research*, *257*, 27–33.

Sawyer, J. P., & Heinz, J. (2017). What makes them do it? Individual-level indicators of extremist outcomes. In G. LaFree & J. D. Freilich (Eds.), *The handbook of criminology and terrorism* (1st ed. pp. 47–61). Wiley.

Schaffner, B. (2020). QAnon and conspiracy beliefs. *Institute for Strategic Dialogue*. www.isdglobal.org/wp-content/uploads/2020/10/qanon-and-conspiracy-beliefs.pdf

Scherer, L. D., McPhetres, J., Pennycook, G., Kempe, A., Allen, L. A., Knoepke, C. E., Tate, C. E., & Matlock, D. D. (2021). Who is susceptible to online health misinformation? A test of four psychosocial hypotheses. *Health Psychology*, *40*(4), 274–284.

Spring, M. (2020, July 15). Wayfair: The false conspiracy about a furniture firm and child trafficking. *BBC News*. www.bbc.com/news/world-53416247

Stephansky, J. (2020, October 16). In QAnon-linked US candidates, populism meets conspiracy. *Al Jazeera*. www.aljazeera.com/news/2020/10/16/in-qanon-linked-us-candidates-populism-meets-conspiracy

Sunstein, C. R., & Vermeule, A. (2009). Conspiracy theories: Causes and cures. *Journal of Political Philosophy*, *17*, 202–227.

Sussman, C. J., Harper, J. M., Stahl, J. L., & Weigle, P. (2018). Internet and video game addictions: Diagnosis, epidemiology, and neurobiology. *Child and Adolescent Psychiatry Clinics of North America*, *27*, 307–326.

The Economist/YouGov. (2021). The Economist/YouGov Poll, January 10–12, 2021. https://docs.cdn.yougov.com/4yijjbkc2z/econTabReport.pdf

Ungerleider, J. T., & Wellisch, D. K. (1979). Coercive persuasion (brainwashing), religious cults, and deprogramming. *American Journal of Psychiatry*, *136*, 279–282.

Ward, C., & Voas, D. (2011). The emergence of conspirituality. *Journal of Contemporary Religion*, *26*, 103–121.

Watt, C. S. (2020, September 23). The QAnon orphans: People who have lost their loved ones to conspiracy theories. *The Guardian*. www.theguardian.com/us-news/2020/sep/23/qanon-conspiracy-theories-loved-ones

Zadrozny, B., & Collins, B. (2020, August 21). QAnon looms behind national rallies and viral #SaveTheChildren hashtags. *NBC News*. www.nbcnews.com/tech/tech-news/qanon-looms-behind-nationwide-rallies-viral-hashtags-n1237722

CHAPTER 3

Psychological Motives of QAnon Followers

Ricky Green, Carolina Trella, Mikey Biddlestone, Karen M. Douglas, and Robbie M. Sutton

In this chapter, we consider whether recent theoretical developments in the psychological conspiracy theory literature can also be extended to belief in QAnon conspiracy theories. Although there is little empirical research on QAnon, research demonstrating the psychological factors that render belief in conspiracy theories more likely has grown significantly over the past two decades. This growing body of research has led scholars to conclude that people are motivated (often unconsciously) to believe in conspiracy theories in an attempt to satisfy important psychological needs (Douglas et al., 2017; see also Biddlestone et al., 2021; Douglas et al., 2019; van Prooijen, 2020 for further elaborations). Specifically – drawing on past theorizing on ideological beliefs (see Jost et al., 2008) – Douglas and colleagues (2017) argued that people are motivated to endorse conspiracy theories in an attempt to satisfy the following needs: (1) existential – the need to feel secure and in control of one's life; (2) epistemic – the need for a consistent and accurate understanding of the world; and (3) social – the need to feel positive about one's self and one's social groups.

We aim to revisit this framework with QAnon followers and the conspiracy theories they tend to endorse in mind. At the time of writing this chapter, however, there is no published empirical research examining the psychological factors associated with belief in QAnon conspiracy theories. Nevertheless, there is good reason to believe that – like belief in other conspiracy theories – belief in QAnon conspiracy theories can also be explained by the motives regarding these psychological needs. In the following sections, therefore, we draw on what is known so far about QAnon followers – through media, anecdotal portrayals, and academic literature – to argue that the three needs (existential, epistemic, and social) that motivate conspiracy beliefs in general might also motivate belief in QAnon conspiracy theories.

Existential Motives

People experience an important existential need to feel secure and in control of their lives (Douglas et al., 2017). Unfortunately, however, people often experience barriers to satisfying this need, and for some people this appears to attract them to conspiracy theories. In this section, we describe research suggesting that endorsement of conspiracy theories is a motivated response to compensate for thwarted existential needs before discussing how this research can explain belief in QAnon conspiracy theories.

How Existential Motives Relate to Belief in Conspiracy Theories

Early research revealed that people scoring high in general anxiety are more prone to believing in conspiracy theories (Grzesiak-Feldman, 2007). Grzesiak-Feldman (2013) replicated and extended this effect experimentally: Students in an anxiety-inducing situation (i.e. waiting for a school exam to begin) scored higher on conspiracy beliefs compared to students in a neutral situation. In a similar vein, Green and Douglas (2018) found that attachment anxiety – feelings of anxiety toward personal relationships (Mikulincer & Shaver, 2017) – predicted belief in conspiracy stereotypes (e.g. of Jews, bankers[1]), general notions of conspiracy (e.g. the government permits or perpetrates acts of terrorism on its own soil, disguising its involvement), and specific conspiracy theories (e.g. the attack on the Twin Towers was not a terrorist action but a governmental plot). Green and Douglas (2018) argued that these relationships might exist due to the tendency for people with high attachment anxiety to catastrophize – that is, to view or present situations as considerably worse than they actually are. Further research supported this hypothesis, showing that attachment anxiety predicted catastrophizing in a number of domains (e.g. pain, stress, social situations), each of which, in turn, predicted greater belief in general notions of conspiracy (Green & Douglas, 2020). These findings suggest that endorsement of conspiracy theories could be another means to catastrophize life's problems for people with attachment anxiety as an attempt to garner attention and support from friends, family, and partners.

Some people hold worldviews that purport their environment to be inherently disorderly, highly threatening, and occupied by malevolent

[1] Some people believe that Jewish people are secretly in control of the global financial system (Kofta et al., 2020).

people (Federico et al., 2013). This is referred to as a "dangerous worldview," and research has demonstrated it to be a robust predictor of belief in conspiracy theories (e.g. Hart & Graether, 2018; Leiser et al., 2017). In fact, Hart and Graether (2018) showed that a dangerous worldview stood out as a central predictor of belief in conspiracy theories when controlling for the effects of other known predictors of these beliefs in multiple regression models. These studies suggest that some people are simply motivated to believe in conspiracy theories due to alignment with their threatening view of the world, wherein conspiring groups with nefarious intentions are plotting to control and do harm to the masses.

Are Existential Motives Associated with Belief in QAnon Conspiracy Theories?

There is much to suggest that QAnon conspiracy beliefs might take root from some of these existential threat motives. For instance, many of the propositions of the theories associated with QAnon are alarmingly threatening. For example, some QAnon followers believe that young children are being trafficked and harvested for their blood in order to extract a fictional chemical called "adrenochrome," to be consumed by the Satan-worshipping global elite as a means to stay young and invigorated (Friedberg, 2020). If believed, this is a terrifying reality to exist in; if not believed, it sounds more like the plot of a satanic horror movie. For people who have high anxiety or who tend to catastrophize, this potential threat might be too large to ignore. Indeed, research shows that anxiety and catastrophizing are associated with a heightened sensitivity toward threats (Petrini & Arendt-Nielsen, 2020; Richards et al., 2014). The child-trafficking threat might therefore play on people's preexisting anxieties about the world and draw them toward this particular QAnon conspiracy theory.

There are other indications that people are attracted to QAnon when they are experiencing threats to existential needs. For example, some ex-QAnon followers have reported having anxiety issues to journalists when they were initially being drawn into QAnon (Moskalenko, 2021). Further, when Twitter banned #WWG1WGA from trending on its platform, QAnon followers circumvented this and instead began using #SaveTheChildren. It was reported that this workaround could have increased the reach of the QAnon child-trafficking conspiracy theory as it was shared by some celebrity influencers and attracted the attention of "suburban moms," who began increasingly showing their support for QAnon (North, 2020; Peterson, 2020). Bracewell (2021) compared this

QAnon conspiracy theory to past right-wing populist women's movements, noting that they targeted women's anxieties regarding real, ongoing problems of sexual violence toward children and women perpetrated by men. This suggests that perceived existential threats regarding child welfare or sexual violence from men might motivate some people to believe in the child-trafficking QAnon conspiracy theory. Endorsement and dissemination of this conspiracy theory could therefore appear to provide a sense of security for some people (Douglas et al., 2017), such as through them helping to end child trafficking by shining a light on the supposed Satan-worshipping elite and their wrongdoings.

It is also likely that some people who believe in this conspiracy theory are probable candidates for holding a dangerous worldview, which seems to fit perfectly with the QAnon child-trafficking narrative, but also with the QAnon worldview in general. For example, QAnon followers also view the world in somewhat biblical terms, in that they see themselves as fighting against a dark, evil force that wants to destroy the soul of their nation and ultimately the world (Pettipiece, 2021), reflecting characteristics of a dangerous worldview. This suggests that some people will be motivated to believe in QAnon conspiracy theories as they fit their view of the world as being inherently dangerous and occupied by malevolent people.

These existential motivations are not the only motives at play, however. Indeed, scholars have argued that existential threat motives trigger epistemic sensemaking processes (van Prooijen, 2020), which we now discuss.

Epistemic Motives

People have an epistemic need to understand the world they live in. However, people also have different thinking styles and perceive the world in different ways from one another (Douglas et al., 2017). Some of these thinking styles are associated with a greater tendency to hold conspiracy beliefs. In this section, we describe research that suggests that belief in conspiracy theories is motivated by epistemic needs – underpinned by gut feelings and biased thinking styles – before discussing whether this research can help to explain belief in QAnon conspiracy theories.

How Epistemic Motives Relate to Belief in Conspiracy Theories

Thinking styles vary from more analytical (or "rational"; i.e. evaluating the information a person has gathered and organized) to more intuitive (or "experiential"; i.e. understanding reality in the moment, omitting logic or analysis; e.g. Norris & Epstein, 2011). Research has shown that belief in conspiracy theories is associated with belief in simple solutions to complex problems (van Prooijen, 2017) and less analytical thinking (e.g. Barron et al., 2018; Wagner-Egger et al., 2018). Further, Swami and colleagues (2014) found that improving people's analytical thinking (i.e. by improving verbal and cognitive fluency) reduced their endorsement of conspiracy theories compared to a control group who did not receive analytical thinking training. Moreover, research has shown that belief in conspiracy theories is instead associated with an intuitive thinking style (see Chapter 4 of this volume for more on the traits of QAnon believers). For example, intuitive thinkers are more receptive to "bullshit" (statements that appear impressive but are actually nonsensical), which has been associated with belief in conspiracy theories (Hart & Graether, 2018). Finally, Pytlik and colleagues (2020) found conspiracy beliefs to be more strongly associated with more intuitive thinking than less analytical thinking. In fact, in this study, the relationship between the "jumping to conclusions" bias (i.e. making hasty decisions based on little evidence) and conspiracy beliefs was explained by intuitive thinking.

Belief in conspiracy theories has been associated with a number of other cognitive biases. For example, research has shown that people who tend to perceive patterns where they do not exist (illusory pattern perception) are more likely to believe in conspiracy theories (van Prooijen et al., 2018). Specifically, participants who thought a series of random coin toss results (presented in written format) were predetermined scored more highly on conspiracy beliefs. Further, this effect was more pronounced when participants were instructed to find patterns in the coin toss results. Similarly, people who commit the conjunction fallacy – the tendency to overestimate the likelihood of co-occurring events – have also been found to have stronger conspiracy beliefs (Brotherton & French, 2014; Dagnall et al., 2017). In other research, people who had a tendency to attribute agency and intentionality where they do not exist also found conspiracy theories appealing (Douglas et al., 2016). For example, participants who agreed with statements such as "the average mountain [has] free will" and "the environment experiences emotions" were more likely to believe in a number of different conspiracy theories.

These cognitive processes demonstrate some of the different ways in which people perceive the world, showing that conspiracy beliefs tend to be motivated by biased and less cognitively taxing thinking patterns. This makes sense when considering some central features of many conspiracy theories, such as their resistance to falsifiability and lack of direct evidence

(Douglas et al., 2017). Taken together, these studies demonstrate that, as opposed to rational, analytically driven thinking, belief in conspiracy theories appears to be motivated by intuitive thinking (or "gut feelings"), which are exemplified by cognitive styles attuned to pattern-seeking and over-ascriptions of agency.

Are Epistemic Needs Associated with Belief in QAnon Conspiracy Theories?

QAnon followers appear to follow a pattern of intuitive thinking. For instance, the particular conspiracy theories of QAnon have been thoroughly debunked, showing that the evidence is heavily piled against QAnon's claims (Hennessy, 2020). Notwithstanding the lack of evidence, some QAnon followers continue to believe that "the storm" is coming, which is a conspiracy theory claiming that President Donald Trump thwarted the so-called Deep State and that multiple arrests of prominent Democrats (including Barack Obama) were imminent (Martineau, 2017). However, no such arrests have ever come to fruition. In spite of this, QAnon followers continue to "trust the plan" even in the face of this irrefutable evidence (Sommer, 2021). This suggests that QAnon followers perhaps have a tendency to follow their intuition – or their "gut feelings" – rather than think analytically or rationally about the claims proposed by QAnon conspiracy theories.

Considering the cognitive biases that were discussed above with the QAnon phenomenon in mind, the popularity of "Q" and their cryptic "Q-drops" (see Chapter 4 of this volume for more on biases related to QAnon) could hinge on some of these cognitive biases being evident in QAnon followers. For example, Q regularly prompts their followers to scour previous Q-drops for clues by telling them "you have more than you know" and guiding them to "refer to past crumbs" (see IAmBecauseWeAre, 2018 for transcripts of Q-drops). Essentially, Q is exploiting people's cognitive biases to make their followers more prone to finding connections that support their conspiracy theories. This could be compared to the effect we described above in which people demonstrated increased conspiracy beliefs after being instructed to find patterns in their environment (see van Prooijen et al., 2018). Further, another aspect of the Q-drops is that they are invariably nonsensical; however, QAnon followers appear to make sense of them.[2] Indeed, some ardent followers

[2] This also suggests that QAnon followers might be receptive to statements that appear impressive but are actually nonsensical (i.e. "bullshit" receptivity; Hart & Graether, 2018).

are called "bakers," whose role is to decipher these cryptic Q-drops (Schwartz, 2018). These "bakers" tend to make spurious connections between the Q-drops and events that happen in the real world. This is also similar to the conjunction fallacy (e.g. Brotherton & French, 2014), in which people have a bias to perceive events as co-occurring. Taken together, this suggests that QAnon followers, and especially those who consider themselves "bakers," exhibit cognitive biases that motivate them to find patterns and connections that support QAnon conspiracy theories. Next, we describe research that suggests that conspiracy beliefs are also motivated by an attempt to satisfy social needs.

Social Motives

People might also be motivated to endorse conspiracy theories in order to meet social needs to defend and maintain the self- and group image (Douglas et al., 2017). In particular, conspiracy theories appeal to people who are attempting to meet needs at three levels of self-definition: their *individual*, *relational*, and *collective* selves (Biddlestone et al., 2021). In this section, we summarize research showing that belief in conspiracy theories is motivated by each of these social needs before discussing whether this research can help to explain belief in QAnon conspiracy theories.

How Individual Self Motives Relate to Belief in Conspiracy Theories

People seek to protect and maintain their self-image (Sedikides & Gaertner, 2011). Early research suggested that belief in conspiracy theories might be used to shift the blame of personal inadequacy onto others (Abalakina-Paap et al., 1999). While updated findings have provided nuance to this claim – namely that it could be other motives that seek to protect and enhance the self that drive conspiracy beliefs rather than low self-esteem itself (e.g. Cichocka et al., 2016b; see also Biddlestone et al., 2022) – they have also shown that a need for uniqueness is commonly implicated in the formation of conspiracy beliefs (e.g. Imhoff & Lamberty, 2017; Lantian et al., 2017). All conspiracy theories provide believers with a sense of possessing special coveted knowledge (see Sternisko et al., 2020), which some people might identify as an opportunity to gain ego boosts by demonstrating their worth, proving that they are not expendable (Leary, 2005; see also Biddlestone et al., 2021).

How Relational Self Motives Relate to Belief in Conspiracy Theories

Relational needs seek to establish, maintain, and enhance interpersonal relationships (Sedikides & Gaertner, 2011). Experiencing a loss of social ties is linked to increased psychological vulnerability (e.g. Poon et al., 2020). In response, people might attempt to reestablish interpersonal bonds to curtail these existential concerns by gaining social support (Leary, 2005). Biddlestone and colleagues (2021) argue that, in this case, conspiracy theories could be used to form relationships by providing a topic for people to share their interests and epistemic concerns with one another (see Klein et al., 2018, 2019). However, publicly supporting conspiracy beliefs can lead to expectations of further social exclusion (Lantian et al., 2018), thus potentially creating a loop of social exclusion that might only be remedied by seeking social support through other means. One way by which this could occur is through identification with established communities.

How Collective Self Motives Relate to Belief in Conspiracy Theories

Collective needs refer to identification with valued social groups (Sedikides & Gaertner, 2011). Conspiracy theories accuse malevolent out-groups of secretly plotting against the in-group with nefarious intentions (Zonis & Joseph, 1994). These out-groups can be a collaboration of powerful people or relatively powerless minority groups (see Nera et al., 2021). Regardless, much like the self-protective use of conspiracy theories by narcissists, conspiracy theories can be used to blame out-groups for in-group shortcomings. For example, narcissistic in-group identification – an insecure form of group identification capturing the defensive belief that one's in-group does not receive the recognition it deserves (see Golec de Zavala et al., 2009) – is robustly shown to predict belief in conspiracy theories about supposedly threatening out-groups (e.g. Cichocka et al., 2016a) as well as a more general conspiracist mindset (Golec de Zavala & Federico, 2018; see also Bertin et al., 2021; Sternisko et al., 2020).

Are Social Needs Associated with Belief in QAnon Conspiracy Theories?

Regarding the individual self, all conspiracy theories are argued to provide the promise of holding special coveted knowledge (Sternisko et al., 2023). Indeed, followers of QAnon are often documented as claiming to carry out their own research online (Mamic, 2020) by deciphering and piecing together Q's cryptic Q-drops (IAmBecauseWeAre, 2018). This illustrates the conviction that people must engage in their own investigations rather than believe in official narratives, and that this will ultimately lead to uncovering secret knowledge. Therefore, it appears likely that a need for uniqueness would also drive these processes associated with QAnon conspiracy beliefs through attempts to enhance one's self-image.

With regard to the relational self, many reports of the breaking of interpersonal relationships between family members and friends have been attributed to QAnon beliefs (e.g. Watt, 2020), with online forums (e.g. "r/QAnonCasualties"; Reddit, 2019) popping up as support groups for those losing their loved ones to QAnon. The contentious worldview associated with "going down the rabbit hole" has been likened to an addiction (Coda Story, 2021; for a psychological review on the "rabbit hole" phenomenon, see Sutton & Douglas, 2022), and thus seems to represent a frequently observed strain on relationships that can result in various forms of social exclusion. Coda Story's mini-documentary also contains repeated references to spouses witnessing noticeable changes in their partners' personalities, causing stressful interpersonal circumstances that give the impression that they have lost their loved ones forever (see also Chapter 11 of this volume for more on QAnon and the need to belong).

Finally, QAnon beliefs clearly appeal to needs regarding the collective self. QAnon is well-known as an online phenomenon, with most of its ideas spreading online through self-affirming online communities, often with established identity markers (Kochi, 2021; see also Klein et al., 2018, 2019). Furthermore, QAnon is often cited as "taking off" during the Trump presidency (e.g. Tollefson, 2021). Crucially, QAnon beliefs encompass pro-Trump rhetoric, often echoing talking points touted by him during his election campaign and presidency, such as references to the "Deep State" (Abramson, 2017). This partisan component implies a favored in-group and nefarious out-group. Therefore, supporters of Trump have been able to use QAnon beliefs to blame any shortcomings of the administration and Republican party – or in-group – on secret plots carried out by out-groups, such as the "Deep State" or members of the Democratic Party. This side to QAnon might have already proved itself to be the most dangerous to society, culminating in a form of collective action in the attempted insurrection of the US Capitol on January 6, 2021 (Spocchia, 2021).

Summary, Caveats, and Future Research

Research on the psychology of conspiracy theories suggests that people are motivated to believe in conspiracy theories in a misguided attempt to satisfy important psychological needs (e.g. Biddlestone et al., 2021; Douglas et al., 2017, 2019; Jutzi et al., 2020; van Prooijen, 2020). As we noted previously, however, there is a dearth of empirical literature on the psychological factors associated with belief in QAnon conspiracy theories specifically. Nevertheless, in the process of highlighting the extant literature, we argue that these needs might also motivate belief in the QAnon conspiracy theory.

In this chapter, we aimed to provide a psychological structure to QAnon conspiracy beliefs through the use of a well-established framework (Douglas et al., 2017, 2019), arguing that QAnon followers might also be motivated to believe in QAnon conspiracy theories to satisfy existential, epistemic, and social needs. However, although belief in one conspiracy theory strongly predicts belief in another conspiracy theory (see Wood et al., 2012), the psychological motives framework has not been tested on QAnon directly. In fact, scholars have yet to even psychometrically validate a QAnon conspiracy beliefs scale. Considering that QAnon has been active for four years, this gap in the literature leaves ample opportunity to understand *if* and *how* QAnon followers are different from or similar to believers in other conspiracy theories. For example, one way to test the motives framework against QAnon conspiracy belief would be to present online questionnaires with measures of the relevant motives, such as a dangerous worldview scale (e.g. Duckitt et al., 2002) or a measure of illusory pattern seeking with the use of "Q-drops" (see van Prooijen et al., 2018) and observing their relationships with belief in QAnon conspiracy theories. Experimentally manipulating the salience of motives such as the need for uniqueness would allow researchers to confirm whether QAnon conspiracy theories are also appealing to those seeking to enhance their self-image (e.g. Lantian et al., 2017). The relationships between these motives and QAnon conspiracy beliefs could also be compared with belief in other conspiracy theories to test their psychological overlap. While a full overview of all of the motives that might drive QAnon conspiracy beliefs is beyond the scope of the current chapter, a wider array of motives that are additionally included in established frameworks should also be considered in similar designs (see Douglas et al., 2017, 2019).

The QAnon conspiracy theory has been described as a "grand narrative" (Vesoulis, 2018), vaguely tying together stories of ritualistic pedophilia, child trafficking, and pseudo-cannibalism (drinking blood) with elements of cultish religious fanaticism (e.g. Pettipiece, 2021). This eclectic mix of threats might provide a useful context in which to investigate how people cope with these overwhelming concerns. Similarly, the myriad of peripheral theories that make up the QAnon grand narrative could be used to study potential typologies of conspiracy believers (see Franks et al., 2017), detailing the psychological profiles of people at different stages of going down the QAnon "rabbit hole." While we would expect notable overlap between the motives that drive conspiracy beliefs in the literature and belief in QAnon conspiracy theories, this characteristic of an all-encompassing grand narrative likely makes QAnon a unique context that can be used to extend researchers' understanding of these psychological processes.

Conclusion

Research investigating the psychological motivations of QAnon followers and the conspiracy theories they tend to endorse is (surprisingly) nonexistent. Nevertheless, drawing on recent theorizing on why people are drawn to conspiracy theories in general (Douglas et al., 2017), we have concluded that QAnon followers might also be motivated to believe in QAnon conspiracy theories as means to satisfy existential, epistemic, and social needs. Indeed, QAnon followers might be motivated to endorse QAnon conspiracy theories since they align with their threatening view of the world. They might also be motivated to believe in "Q" and their "Q-drops" as they appeal to people's cognitive biases, especially intuitive, pattern-seeking tendencies. Finally, QAnon followers might also be motivated to endorse QAnon theories to feel unique (bolstering the individual self), as a basis for forming interpersonal bonds (maintaining the relational self), and to defend the group image (defending the collective self). A future challenge for researchers will be to test this framework empirically.

REFERENCES

Abalakina-Paap, M., Stephan, W. G., Craig, T., & Gregory, W. L. (1999). Beliefs in conspiracies. *Political Psychology*, *20*(3), 637–647.

Abramson, A. (2017, March 8). President Trump's allies keep talking about the "Deep State". What's that? *Time*. https://time.com/4692178/donald-trump-deep-state-breitbart-barack-obama/

Barron, D., Furnham, A., Weis, L., Morgan, K. D., Towell, T., & Swami, V. (2018). The relationship between schizotypal facets and conspiracist beliefs via cognitive processes. *Psychiatry Research*, *259*, 15–20.

Bertin, P., Nera, K., Hamer, K., Uhl-Haedicke, I., & Delouvée, S. (2021). Stand out of my sunlight: The mediating role of climate change conspiracy beliefs in the relationship between national collective narcissism and acceptance of climate science. *Group Processes and Intergroup Relations.* https://doi.org/10.31234/osf.io/cnmfa

Biddlestone, M., Green, R., Cichocka, A., Douglas, K. M., & Sutton, R. M. (2022). A systematic review and meta-analytic synthesis of the motives associated with conspiracy beliefs. *PsyArXiv.*

Biddlestone, M., Green, R., Cichocka, A., Sutton, R. M., & Douglas, K. M. (2021). Conspiracy beliefs and the individual, relational, and collective selves. *Social and Personality Psychology Compass, 15*(10), e12639.

Bracewell, L. (2021). Gender, populism, and the QAnon conspiracy movement. *Frontiers in Sociology, 5*, 615727.

Brotherton, R., & French, C. C. (2014). Belief in conspiracy theories and susceptibility to the conjunction fallacy. *Applied Cognitive Psychology, 28* (2), 238–248.

Cichocka, A., Marchlewska, M., & De Zavala, A. G. (2016a). Does self-love or self-hate predict conspiracy beliefs? Narcissism, self-esteem, and the endorsement of conspiracy theories. *Social Psychological and Personality Science, 7*(2), 157–166.

Cichocka, A., Marchlewska, M., Golec de Zavala, A., & Olechowski, M. (2016b). "They will not control us": Ingroup positivity and belief in intergroup conspiracies. *British Journal of Psychology, 107*(3), 556–576.

Coda Story. (2021, June 9). Living with Q: How QAnon is Destroying the Private Lives of Americans [Video]. www.youtube.com/watch?v=eTNkFfkxGjM

Dagnall, N., Denovan, A., Drinkwater, K., Parker, A., & Clough, P. (2017). Statistical bias and endorsement of conspiracy theories. *Applied Cognitive Psychology, 31*(4), 368–378.

Douglas, K. M., Sutton, R. M., Callan, M. J., Dawtry, R. J., & Harvey, A. J. (2016). Someone is pulling the strings: Hypersensitive agency detection and belief in conspiracy theories. *Thinking & Reasoning, 22*(1), 57–77.

Douglas, K. M., Sutton, R. M., & Cichocka, A. (2017). The psychology of conspiracy theories. *Current Directions in Psychological Science, 26*(6), 538–542.

Douglas, K. M., Uscinski, J. E., Sutton, R. M., Cichocka, A., Nefes, T., Ang, C. S., & Devari, F. (2019). Understanding conspiracy theories. *Political Psychology, 40*, 3–35.

Duckitt, J., Wagner, C., Du Plessis, I., & Birum, I. (2002). The psychological bases of ideology and prejudice: Testing a dual process model. *Journal of Personality and Social Psychology, 83*(1), 75–93.

Federico, C. M., Weber, C. R., Ergun, D., & Hunt, C. (2013). Mapping the connections between politics and morality: The multiple sociopolitical orientations involved in moral intuition. *Political Psychology, 34*(4), 589–610.

Franks, B., Bangerter, A., Bauer, M. W., Hall, M., & Noort, M. C. (2017). Beyond "monologicality"? Exploring conspiracist worldviews. *Frontiers in Psychology, 8*, 861.

Friedberg, B. (2020, July 31). The dark virality of a Hollywood blood-harvesting conspiracy. *Wired*. www.wired.com/story/opinion-the-dark-virality-of-a-hollywood-blood-harvesting-conspiracy/

Golec de Zavala, A., & Federico, C. M. (2018). Collective narcissism and the growth of conspiracy thinking over the course of the 2016 United States presidential election: A longitudinal analysis. *European Journal of Social Psychology*, *48*(7), 1011–1018.

Golec de Zavala, A. G., Cichocka, A., Eidelson, R., & Jayawickreme, N. (2009). Collective narcissism and its social consequences. *Journal of Personality and Social Psychology*, *97*(6), 1074–1096.

Green, R., & Douglas, K. M. (2018). Anxious attachment and belief in conspiracy theories. *Personality and Individual Differences*, *125*, 30–37.

(2020, July). Making mountains out of molehills: Anxious attachment, belief in conspiracy theories, and the tendency to exaggerate life's problems [Conference Session]. International Society of Political Psychology, Virtual Event.

Grzesiak-Feldman, M. (2007). Conspiracy thinking and state–trait anxiety in young Polish adults. *Psychological Reports*, *100*(1), 199–202.

(2013). The effect of high-anxiety situations on conspiracy thinking. *Current Psychology*, *32*(1), 100–118.

Hart, J., & Graether, M. (2018). Something's going on here: Psychological predictors of belief in conspiracy theories. *Journal of Individual Differences*, *39*(4), 229–237.

Hennessy, M. (2020, July 29). Debunked: The conspiracy theories around the so-called Hollywood drug adrenochrome. *TheJournal.ie*. www.thejournal.ie/adrenochrome-mark-zuckerberg-5160653-Jul2020/

IAmBecauseWeAre. (2018). *QAnon – The storm*. Word Press. Retrieved June 1, 2021, from https://krypt3ia.files.wordpress.com/2018/08/q_s_posts_-_cbts_-_7–2-0.pdf

Imhoff, R., & Lamberty, P. K. (2017). Too special to be duped: Need for uniqueness motivates conspiracy beliefs. *European Journal of Social Psychology*, *47*(6), 724–734.

Jost, J. T., Ledgerwood, A., & Hardin, C. D. (2008). Shared reality, system justification, and the relational basis of ideological beliefs. *Social and Personality Psychology Compass*, *2*(1), 171–186.

Jutzi, C. A., Willardt, R., Schmid, P. C., & Jonas, E. (2020). Between conspiracy beliefs, ingroup bias, and system justification: How people use defense strategies to cope with the threat of COVID-19. *Frontiers in Psychology*, *11*, 578586.

Klein, C., Clutton, P., & Dunn, A. G. (2019). Pathways to conspiracy: The social and linguistic precursors of involvement in Reddit's conspiracy theory forum. *PLoS ONE*, *14*(11), e0225098.

Klein, C., Clutton, P., & Polito, V. (2018). Topic modeling reveals distinct interests within an online conspiracy forum. *Frontiers in Psychology*, *9*, 189.

Kochi, S. (2021, February 2). How does the QAnon conspiracy theory spread online? *Media Diversity Institute*. www.media-diversity.org/how-does-qanon-spread-online/

Kofta, M., Soral, W., & Bilewicz, M. (2020). What breeds conspiracy antisemitism? The role of political uncontrollability and uncertainty in the belief in Jewish conspiracy. *Journal of Personality and Social Psychology*, *118*(5), 900–918.

Lantian, A., Muller, D., Nurra, C., & Douglas, K. M. (2017). "I know things they don't know!" *Social Psychology*, *48*(3), 160–173.

Lantian, A., Muller, D., Nurra, C., Klein, O., Berjot, S., & Pantazi, M. (2018). Stigmatized beliefs: Conspiracy theories, anticipated negative evaluation of the self, and fear of social exclusion. *European Journal of Social Psychology*, *48* (7), 939–954.

Leary, M. R. (2005). Sociometer theory and the pursuit of relational value: Getting to the root of self-esteem. *European Review of Social Psychology*, *16* (1), 75–111.

Leiser, D., Duani, N., & Wagner-Egger, P. (2017). The conspiratorial style in lay economic thinking. *PLoS ONE*, *12*(3), e0171238.

Mamic, A. (2020, December 15). What it means to "do your own research." *Medium*. https://medium.com/illumination-curated/what-it-means-to-do-your-own-research-c00cf5c25056

Martineau, P. (2017, December 19). The storm is the new Pizzagate – Only worse. *Intelligencer*. https://nymag.com/intelligencer/2017/12/qanon-4chan-the-storm-conspiracy-explained.html

Mikulincer, M., & Shaver, P. R. (2017). *Attachment in adulthood: Structure, dynamics, and change* (2nd ed.). Guilford Publications.

Moskalenko, S. (2021, March 25). Many QAnon followers report having mental health diagnoses. *The Conversation*. https://theconversation.com/many-qanon-followers-report-having-mental-health-diagnoses-157299

Nera, K., Wagner-Egger, P., Bertin, P., Douglas, K., & Klein, O. (2021). A power-challenging theory of society, or a conservative mindset? Upward and downward conspiracy theories as ideologically distinct beliefs. *European Journal of Social Psychology*, *51*(4–5), 740–757.

Norris, P., & Epstein, S. (2011). An experiential thinking style: Its facets and relations with objective and subjective criterion measures. *Journal of Personality*, *79*(5), 1043–1080.

North, A. (2020, September 18). How #SaveTheChildren is pulling American moms into QAnon. *Vox*. www.vox.com/21436671/save-our-children-hashtag-qanon-pizzagate

Peterson, A. H. (2020, October 29). The real housewives of QAnon: How conspiracy theorists co-opted #SavetheChildren to lure suburban moms into Q's labyrinth. *ELLE*. www.elle.com/culture/a34485099/qanon-conspiracy-suburban-women/

Petrini, L., & Arendt-Nielsen, L. (2020). Understanding pain catastrophizing: Putting pieces together. *Frontiers in Psychology*, *11*, 603420.

Pettipiece, T. (2021, March 21). History repeats itself: From the New Testament to QAnon. *The Conversation*. https://theconversation.com/history-repeats-itself-from-the-new-testament-to-qanon-156915

Poon, K.-T., Chen, Z., & Wong, W.-Y. (2020). Beliefs in conspiracy theories following ostracism. *Personality and Social Psychology Bulletin*, *46*(8), 1234–1246.

Pytlik, N., Soll, D., & Mehl, S. (2020). Thinking preferences and conspiracy belief: Intuitive thinking and the jumping to conclusions-bias as a basis for the belief in conspiracy theories. *Frontiers in Psychiatry*, *11*, 568942.

Reddit. (2019). [r/QAnonCasualties]. Have a friend or loved one taken in by QAnon? Look here for support, resources and a place to vent [Subreddit]. *Reddit*. www.reddit.com/r/QAnonCasualties/

Richards, H. J., Benson, V., Donnelly, N., & Hadwin, J. A. (2014). Exploring the function of selective attention and hypervigilance for threat in anxiety. *Clinical Psychology Review*, *34*(1), 1–13.

Schwartz, M. (2018, September 11). A trail of "bread crumbs," leading conspiracy theorists into the wilderness. *The New York Times*. www.nytimes.com/2018/09/11/magazine/a-trail-of-bread-crumbs-leading-conspiracy-theorists-into-the-wilderness.html

Sedikides, C., Gaertner, L., & O'Mara, E. M. (2011). Individual self, relational self, collective self: Hierarchical ordering of the tripartite self. *Psychological Studies*, *56*(1), 98–107.

Sommer, W. (2021). *Trust the plan: The rise of QAnon and the conspiracy that reshaped America*. HarperCollins.

Spocchia, G. (2021, January 9). What role did QAnon play in the capitol riot? *The Independent*. www.independent.co.uk/news/world/americas/us-election-2020/qanon-capitol-congress-riot-trump-b1784460.html

Sternisko, A., Cichocka, A., Cislak, A., & Van Bavel, J. J. (2023). National narcissism predicts the belief in and the dissemination of conspiracy theories during the COVID-19 pandemic: Evidence from 56 countries. *Personality and Social Psychology Bulletin*, *49*(1), 48–65.

Sternisko, A., Cichocka, A., & Van Bavel, J. J. (2020). The dark side of social movements: Social identity, non-conformity, and the lure of conspiracy theories. *Current Opinion in Psychology*, *35*, 1–6.

Sutton, R. M., & Douglas, K. M. (2022). Rabbit hole syndrome: Inadvertent, accelerating, and entrenched commitment to conspiracy beliefs. *Current Opinion in Psychology*, *48*, 101462.

Swami, V., Voracek, M., Stieger, S., Tran, U. S., & Furnham, A. (2014). Analytic thinking reduces belief in conspiracy theories. *Cognition*, *133*(3), 572–585.

Tollefson, J. (2021). Tracking QAnon: How Trump turned conspiracy-theory research upside down. *Nature*, *590*(7845), 192–193.

van Prooijen, J. (2017). Why education predicts decreased belief in conspiracy theories. *Applied Cognitive Psychology*, *31*(1), 50–58.

(2020). An existential threat model of conspiracy theories. *European Psychologist*, *25*(1), 16–25.

van Prooijen, J., Douglas, K. M., & De Inocencio, C. (2018). Connecting the dots: Illusory pattern perception predicts belief in conspiracies and the supernatural. *European Journal of Social Psychology*, *48*(3), 320–335.

Vesoulis, A. (2018, August 3). Here's why experts worry about the popularity of QAnon's conspiracy theory. *Time*. https://time.com/5356851/what-is-qanon

Wagner-Egger, P., Delouvée, S., Gauvrit, N., & Dieguez, S. (2018). Creationism and conspiracism share a common teleological bias. *Current Biology*, *28*(16), R867–R868.

Watt, C. S. (2020, September 23). The QAnon orphans: People who have lost loved ones to conspiracy theories. *The Guardian*. www.theguardian.com/us-news/2020/sep/23/qanon-conspiracy-theories-loved-ones

Wood, M. J., Douglas, K. M., & Sutton, R. M. (2012). Dead and alive. *Social Psychological and Personality Science*, *3*(6), 767–773.

Zonis, M., & Joseph, C. M. (1994). Conspiracy thinking in the Middle East. *Political Psychology*, *15*(3), 443–459.

CHAPTER 4

Cognitive Processes, Biases, and Traits That Fuel QAnon

Arial R. Meyer and Monica K. Miller

Introduction

QAnon is a conspiracy group that has adopted a mixture of novel and well-established theories, most with undertones of xenophobia and anti-Semitism (Anti-Defamation League, n.d.c). QAnon's presence is prevalent throughout social media platforms, far-right and other extremist protests, and many news outlets (Ingram, 2020; Sen & Zadrozny, 2020; Tolan et al., 2021). One major concern about this prevalence is that QAnon spreads disinformation as a "construction of alternative facts" (Marwick & Partin, 2020; see Chapter 12 of this volume for more on QAnon and social media and disinformation). The spreading of this disinformation is dangerous because, on a macro-level, it can lead to riots, violence, and other crimes. For example, the insurrection at the US Capitol on January 6, 2021, was associated with belief in disinformation about the 2020 presidential election (Anti-Defamation League, n.d.b; Moskalenko & McCauley, 2021). On a micro-level, belief in disinformation can also lead to self-harm (e.g. ingesting disinfectants as a COVID-19 prevention or cure; Nelson et al., 2020) or other harmful behaviors (e.g. spitting on others during a global pandemic, undermining social distancing guidelines; Greene & Murphy, 2021).

On a national scale, QAnon poses a security threat (Amarasingam & Argentino, 2020), which is why the FBI has labeled QAnon a potential domestic terrorist threat (Winter, 2019). The dangers are compounded when leaders express opinions that are inconsistent with those of experts and empirical evidence (Garry et al., 2021; Nelson et al., 2020). For example, Donald Trump, while still in the midst of his presidency, claimed that the 2020 election was a fraud (West, 2021), despite many election security experts stating otherwise (Cybersecurity and Infrastructure

Security Agency, 2020). Trump's claim of a fraudulent election was a major contributing factor to the insurrection at the Capitol, in which many QAnon followers were involved (Moskalenko & McCauley, 2021). This is cause for concern, especially when considered with the findings of a 2018 study showing that misinformation and disinformation online often spread quicker and achieve greater reach than does verified information (Vosoughi et al., 2018).

The QAnon movement quickly gained momentum in 2020 (see Chapter 8 of this volume for more on QAnon in the year 2020), though support has since been described as "meager and stable" in 2021 (Enders et al., 2022). Despite this support, little is known about the cognitive processes, biases, and traits of QAnon followers. This chapter discusses the cognitive processes, biases, and traits (e.g. beliefs and individual characteristics) possibly associated with QAnon followers. The ability to distinguish *how* and *why* people are susceptible to following such a conspiracy movement is crucial to helping people leave the movement before their support becomes too extreme and affects their social and professional lives. For example, many families in America are negatively affected when a family member supports QAnon (Goldenberg et al., 2020). As such, conspiracy theories are harmful at the individual level, the family level, and the societal level.

Cognitive processes (e.g. delusional ideation), cognitive biases (e.g. jumping to conclusions [JTC] bias), and personal traits (e.g. narcissism) could all relate to the tendency to believe conspiracy theories like QAnon. The effects of QAnon are not only apparent in online spaces, but the effects have also spread to the real world, which makes understanding the cognitive processes, biases, and traits of followers even more important. For example, QAnon followers are running for political office (Zitser & Ankel, 2021), and many related political protests and rallies have turned violent (Amarasingam & Argentino, 2020).

This chapter has four sections; each relies on research related to conspiracy theories in general and on anecdotes about QAnon followers. This allows for speculation about how QAnon followers might be similar to or different from followers of other groups. The first section discusses possible cognitive processes of QAnon followers, offering specific examples. The second section includes a discussion of cognitive biases, and the third section offers a discussion of individual traits that are possibly common among QAnon followers. The concluding section of this chapter offers some general observations and future directions for research.

Possible Cognitive Processes of QAnon Followers

It is likely that QAnon followers have some common cognitive processes, yet little research has been conducted in this area. In this chapter, we identify a few cognitive processes that might be common among QAnon followers, based largely on the body of research on believers of conspiracy theories in general. Cognitive processing refers to the way in which information is received, processed, reduced, stored, and utilized (Krch, 2011). Examples of cognitive processes include attention, higher reasoning, memory, and many others. Cognitive processing is important because it allows humans to interact intelligibly with each other and the broader world. Delusional ideation, teleological thinking, cognitive closure, and the process laid out by Pierre's (2020) socio-epistemic model are just some possible cognitive processes common to QAnon followers.

Delusional Ideation

Delusional ideation – a misleading or mistaken belief or idea – is commonly associated with conspiricism (Dagnall et al., 2015). People experiencing delusional ideation, from an attribution psychology perspective, tend to attribute negative events to other people or external circumstances rather than to themselves (Kiran & Chaudhury, 2009). For example, paranoia is a type of delusional ideation in which the afflicted person believes that others are threatening or conspiring against them. These characteristics of paranoid delusional ideation combined with conspiracist thinking might surface due to distorted perceptions (Meller, 2002).

Indeed, QAnon followers have displayed a pattern of believing unsubstantiated ideas and predictions; such beliefs are the main tenet of delusional ideation. QAnon originated when "Q," an anonymous 4chan user, began to post claims of being a US government official with top-secret clearance (Papasavva et al., 2020). For example, Q told followers to prepare for March 4, 2021, when the "Storm" would happen; this is the belief that Donald Trump would be reinstated as President on that date (Brockell, 2021). As the date passed and President Biden remained the President of the USA, Q dropped another supposed date of August 13, 2021, as the date Trump would be reinstated, which has since passed without coming to fruition (Reimann, 2021). This pattern of unwavering belief in ideas and predictions made by leaders in the QAnon movement, despite constantly being disproven, is a clear indication of delusional ideation. From the perspective of QAnon followers, Donald Trump losing the election is a negative occurrence that they attribute to being the fault of others (e.g. claiming the election was stolen by Democrats). This tends to be the response of QAnon followers, as it is much easier to blame another party than it is not only to admit defeat, but also to admit that Trump might be falling out of favor and thus lost the election due to his own actions.

Another example of delusional ideation among QAnon followers is the unsubstantiated claim that Bill Gates created the COVID-19 vaccine in order to microchip the general population. Despite the inadequate evidence to support such claims, many QAnon followers still believe this to be true (Goldenberg et al., 2020). This contributed to the already prevalent antivaccination propaganda. As supported by a Facebook study, there appears to be an overlap between vaccine hesitancy and support of QAnon (Klar, 2021). This is likely due to QAnon's "abundance of pseudoscience and COVID-19 vaccine conspiracy theories" (Garry et al., 2021, p. 166). Though any person can experience delusional ideation, this could be a common cognitive process among QAnon followers.

Teleological Thinking and Creationism

Teleological thinking is the attribution of a purpose and cause to natural events and entities; this type of thinking is a predictor of conspiracism (Wagner-Egger et al., 2018). Teleological thinking is correlated with creationism (Novella, 2018) – the belief that the universe is a product of divine creation as outlined in the Bible (Ruse, 2003). Creationism is often seen as the antithesis of evolution (Metz et al., 2020). Friedman (2021) adds that having a strong inclination to find structure and purpose in this world leads people who believe in the Bible (i.e. Christians) to be more susceptible to belief in conspiracy theories as a way to explain events.

Journalists have compared QAnon followers to followers of the "Christian Right" and "Tea Party" (Enders et al., 2022). Given that creationism often results from teleological thinking and a large number of QAnon followers are Christian (Miller, 2021), it is likely that many QAnon followers will exhibit patterns of teleological thinking. Moreover, Q is known to quote scriptures from the Bible, lending further credence to the idea that there is a relationship between teleological thinking and QAnon followers (see Chapter 16 of this volume for a more detailed comparison of QAnon and religious groups).

Cognitive Closure

When human needs of certainty are not met, conspiracy theories become attractive because they offer certainty and security (Abrams, 2020). Cognitive closure is the psychological need to reduce ambiguity and attain certainty. Conspiracy theories are alluring because they satiate important social psychological motives (Douglas et al., 2017; see also Chapter 3 of this volume).

The year 2020 is an example of an unprecedented, ambiguous, and stressful period for humans worldwide (see Chapter 8 for more on why the events of 2020 might have contributed to the spread of QAnon). The global COVID-19 pandemic caused heightened perceptions of uncertainty, danger, and urgency, likely encouraging people to seek cognitive closure. Although QAnon existed prior to the pandemic, QAnon blossomed at its start. QAnon offers clear enemies, a narrative of triumphing over evil, and a way to participate in this worthy cause (Bratich, 2020). In this sense, conspiracy theories can be psychologically reassuring (Romer & Jamieson, 2020), especially for those experiencing lack of control and security. Indeed, a former QAnon follower explained that the allure of QAnon was based on his own skepticism of explanations he received from mainstream media, which led him to seek alternative answers to explain what he perceived as governmental corruption (Dickson, 2020). The need for cognitive closure is a possible explanation for both *why* people turn to the QAnon movement and *how* they find it.

Socio-epistemic Model

Pierre's (2020) two-component socio-epistemic model explains the pervasiveness of conspiracy theories as well their variation. The first component of this model is that belief in conspiracy theories is rooted in epistemic mistrust. Mistrust in government is associated with general conspiracist ideation and conspiracies related to government (Imhoff & Lamberty, 2018; Richey, 2017). This mistrust in government becomes further justified by each known occurrence of corruption (Pierre, 2020). The second component of this model is misinformation processing. This is described as an active process that occurs after a loss of trust in orthodox institutions, which results in a spiraling search for alternative answers to those available from authority accounts (Pierre, 2020). This is a possible explanation for why people turn to conspiracy theories; these theories typically "represent the antithesis of authoritative accounts" (Pierre, 2020, p. 10). The person does not necessarily conjure up a conspiracy theory when searching for an alternative explanation; the conspiracy theories are convenient and readily accessible when someone searches for them.

Furthermore, QAnon followers display a deep distrust of the government. The dominating theory of this movement revolves around this distrust; for instance, a major belief of QAnon is that the government is run by satanic pedophiles (Goldenberg et al., 2020). Government officials such as former President Barack Obama, former Senator Hillary Clinton, and current President Joe Biden have all been identified by QAnon followers as enemies of the QAnon movement. As discussed above, many people have faced uncertainty since the start of the COVID-19 pandemic, and this caused tension between governments and their citizens. In fact, 78 percent of Americans believe that the COVID-19 crisis was the fault of the US government (Lee, 2020). It stands to reason that, when faced with the stress and uncertainty of a global pandemic, people would seek out explanations for the existence of the COVID-19 virus, even when they are provided with such explanations by the (untrusted) government. Whether it is labeling the pandemic a hoax or believing it to be a governmental scheme to plant microchips in citizens, QAnon offers alternative explanations, even if they are baseless. QAnon followers, in general, fit both components of the socio-epistemic model.

Possible Cognitive Biases of QAnon Followers

People create their subjective reality based on their own perceptions (Meterko, 2021). This happens through cognitive biases, which influence a person's thinking patterns, judgments, and perceptions, often leading to erroneous conclusions. Not only are conspiracy theories reinforced by how humans are cognitively hardwired, but they also appear to reinforce existing biases (Friedman, 2021). Some cognitive biases are more common than others, but a few that are particularly suited to QAnon followers include groupthink and group polarization, confirmation bias and motivated reasoning, and the JTC bias, as discussed in the following subsections.

Groupthink and Group Polarization

First coined by psychologist Irving Janis in 1972, groupthink is a cognitive bias that occurs when members of a group prioritize harmony and conformity over reality (Lee, 2019). Individual group members conform to their group for the sake of peace and harmony, often reaching a consensus without critical evaluation of alternatives (Murata et al., 2015). These group members might normally be considered intelligent, competent human beings, but, nonetheless, they can still find themselves susceptible to such biased, faulty decision-making (Janis, 2007). Groupthink is commonly used to explain large-scale political movement trends (Walker, 2002) through people conforming to the beliefs of other members in their group (e.g. a political party).

Conformity is prioritized over reality in the QAnon movement. Even if a follower wants to speak up and express doubt, they often go along with the majority for fear of social isolation and punishment (Chandler, 2020; Crews, 2021). This can become harmful, as QAnon does have a punitive component, which makes leaving the movement even harder for followers (Klepper, 2021; see Chapter 11 of this volume for more on QAnon and the need to belong). Also, QAnon followers are generally intelligent people who like to seek out knowledge, but they also tend to overlook and discount experts, researchers, and scientists (Marwick & Partin, 2020). Groupthink and group polarization are cognitive biases that are potentially common among QAnon followers.

Confirmation Bias and Motivated Reasoning

Humans have a tendency to discount information that contradicts their position in favor of information that confirms their position, which is referred to as confirmation bias. Confirmation bias occurs through selective exposure, biased interpretation, and biased memory. Selective exposure refers to the human tendency to seek out information that supports one's own beliefs to avoid cognitive dissonance (Lazer et al., 2018). Biased interpretation refers to the tendency of humans to interpret information in a way that supports one's existing beliefs (McKee & Stuckler, 2010). Finally, biased memory is the phenomenon of having a better memory for information that supports (rather than opposes) one's existing beliefs (Frost et al., 2015).

Similarly to confirmation bias, motivated reasoning is a cognitive bias that refers to the cognitive processing of only partial information, meaning that only such information that further supports the belief is processed (e.g. see Douglas et al., 2019). Essentially, motivated reasoning occurs when a person is faced with facts that are contradictory to their strong personal beliefs (Douglas et al., 2019). Fischele (2000, p. 154) suggests that motivated reasoning explains why there is such variance in public reactions to various political scandals: It is "often the nature of the scandal itself that provides justifications needed to maintain prior beliefs." However, other research suggests that motivated reasoning might not play as big of a role in belief in conspiracy theories as was previously thought (Pennycook & Rand, 2020).

Likewise, QAnon followers frequently dismiss the knowledge of and research conducted by experts in the field if their conclusions differ from QAnon followers' beliefs. Faced with such contradictions, followers are motivated to process information in a way that will conform to their preexisting beliefs and thoughts. They seek confirmation of their beliefs through communication with their group of like-minded people, strengthening their belief that their own beliefs are indeed accurate. As a result, QAnon followers commonly become estranged from friends and family who do not hold the same beliefs (Goldenberg et al., 2020), choosing to expose themselves only to like-minded QAnon followers.

Further, QAnon followers also interpret certain information differently from nonfollowers. The number seventeen is significant to QAnon because Q is the seventeenth letter of the alphabet, and QAnon followers often interpret information including the number seventeen in a way that supports their existing beliefs (Moore, 2018). In short, QAnon followers display many of the main characteristics and processes of confirmation bias, though empirical evidence on this matter is still needed.

Jumping to Conclusions Bias

The JTC bias is a cognitive bias that influences people – often those with high levels of paranoia and delusions – toward hasty decision-making (Johnstone et al., 2017). People who display the JTC bias require less information to make a decision and become more confident about the decisions they made compared to people without this bias. Additionally, those who display the JTC bias are more likely to believe conspiracy theories than those without who do not display this bias (Pytlik et al., 2020). The JTC bias is a relatively normal phenomenon, and QAnon followers are not immune to it. Thus, QAnon followers who experience the JTC bias might be more likely than those without the bias to endorse conspiracy theories, such as the theory that China created the COVID-19 virus in a lab. The JTC bias could have led someone to believe this theory immediately, even though there was insufficient evidence to support the theory at the time – and they might retain that belief even after studies concluded that the virus was not created in a lab (Centers for Disease Control and Prevention, 2020). Though more research is needed, it is possible that this bias is prevalent among QAnon followers.

Possible Traits of QAnon Followers

There are traits (e.g. beliefs and individual characteristics) that might be shared among QAnon followers that could relate to the tendency to believe conspiracies. This section will suggest that QAnon followers might have traits such as holding anti-Black and anti-Semitic attitudes, narcissism, Machiavellianism, and their particular political affiliation.

Anti-Black and Anti-Semitic Attitudes

Negative attitudes toward Black peoples can promote a willingness to believe in conspiracy theories (Pasek et al., 2015; see generally Fischele, 2000; Nyhan, 2010). Friedman (2021) discusses the enabling relationship between belief in conspiracy theories and prejudices toward racial-ethnic and religious minorities. For example, a popular racist conspiracy called "white replacement theory" is the belief that white Europeans are being replaced by nonwhite immigrants from Africa and the Middle East; supporters of this theory believe this will cause the extinction of the white race (Anti-Defamation League, 2021).

There are numerous examples of QAnon followers exhibiting these attitudes. Online QAnon spaces are rife with anti-Semitic propaganda (Goldenberg et al., 2020). For example, QAnon perpetuates the blood libel conspiracy theories, which claim Jews kidnapped Christian children to use their blood for religious, ritualistic purposes (Anti-Defamation League, n.d.a). It is apparent that these anti-Semitic attitudes are not kept secret from the public; anti-Semitist symbols were used by QAnon followers during the insurrection at the Capitol in early 2021 (Schor, 2021). Additionally, in their online efforts to push the #SaveTheChildren agenda, QAnon posted almost exclusively about Caucasian children (Bloom, 2021), despite the fact that African American children are overrepresented in child sex trafficking and are more likely to be victimized (Human Trafficking Search, 2014). In short, anti-Black and anti-Semitic attitudes might be common among QAnon followers, though more research on this is needed.

Narcissism

Past research has identified a link between narcissism and belief in conspiracy theories (Cichocka et al., 2015); thus, QAnon followers might also have this trait. Narcissism is characterized by an inability to take criticism, low self-esteem, and a disregard for others' feelings. Narcissists tend to be hard patients to treat in a clinical setting because they often resent the perceived power of the clinician and reject their treatment/advice (Yakeley, 2018), which is similar to the way in which many QAnon followers reject the advice and treatment of medical experts regarding COVID-19. Indeed, collective narcissism is associated with the belief and dissemination of COVID-19 conspiracy theories (Sternisko et al., 2023). Moreover, people with low self-esteem appear to be more likely to accept conspiracy theories (Bowes et al., 2020) because such people generally have negative perceptions of humanity (Cichocka et al., 2015).

QAnon followers possess many of the key characteristics of narcissism. First, QAnon followers tend to discount the knowledge of experts, scientists, and institutions in favor of "populous expertise." Second, although it is not currently known whether QAnon followers have low levels of self-esteem, a crucial aspect of self-esteem involves connecting with others, which can often be achieved through social media networking websites (Jhangiani & Tarry, 2014). QAnon followers predominantly communicate through social media websites such as 4chan, 8chan, and even Facebook (Zuckerman & McQuade, 2019) and Parler (Mak, 2021). People with low self-esteem can visit social media websites in an effort to connect with others, often finding like-minded people who will help boost their personal self-esteem. It is plausible that following QAnon helps narcissistic followers to reinforce their sense of grandiosity.

Machiavellianism

Machiavellianism is a personality trait characterized by interpersonal manipulation (Aïn et al., 2013, p. 1) and low levels of empathy (Aïn et al., 2013). Because it is also associated with increased susceptibility to belief in conspiracy theories (Hughes & Machan, 2021), many QAnon followers might have this trait. For instance, the end goal of QAnon is to violently eliminate political opponents of the movement (Goldenberg et al., 2020), which is one of many examples of QAnon's support for radical action against perceived enemies. This hyper-fixation has caused numerous acts of violence and terrorism in the USA, such as the January 6,

2021 Capitol insurrection (Moskalenko & McCauley, 2021), violence at Black Lives Matter rallies (Bloom, 2020), countless murders, including of one QAnon follower's own children (Amarasingam & Argentino, 2020; Sommer, 2020), as well as kidnappings (Sommer, 2020).

Political Affiliation

Halpern et al. (2019) suggest that it is more likely for someone politically affiliated with the right (i.e. conservative) to believe in conspiracy theories than it is for someone politically affiliated with the left (i.e. liberal). Generally, conservatives tend to claim political falsehoods as truth more often than liberals (Garrett & Bond, 2021). For example, conservatives are more likely to endorse conspiracy theories about climate change (van der Linden et al., 2020). Broadly speaking, QAnon is a right-wing conspiracy group (Marwick & Partin, 2020). Accordingly, about a third of Republicans who report that they have a large friendship group of Trump supporters also say that the beliefs of QAnon are mostly or completely true (Cox, 2021). However, it is not necessarily affiliation with the right or left that encourages QAnon support but rather the extremity of this affiliation (see Chapter 9 of this volume for more on QAnon and the politics of 2020; Enders et al., 2022), as conspiracy theories are more likely to be believed at political extremes (van Prooijen et al., 2015).

Republicans continue to become more deeply embedded with the QAnon movement as time passes; some QAnon followers have even been elected to various political positions, and others plan to run for office in the coming years (Crews, 2021; Zitser & Ankel, 2021). For example, Republican J. R. Majewski has openly admitted to supporting QAnon and breaching police barricades at a "Stop the Steal" rally, and he ran for Congress in Ohio (Zitser & Ankel, 2021). Rep. Marjorie Taylor Greene, a once-proud supporter of QAnon (Domonoske, 2020), became a US Representative in 2021 (Mosley & Raphelson, 2021); she claimed in 2023 that she got "sucked in" to believing in QAnon because of the internet (Wade, 2023).

Conclusion and Future Directions

Conspiracy theories are relatively common occurrences, as evidenced throughout history (e.g. those surrounding the Kennedy assassination and 9/11, as well as the beliefs held by flat-earthers). Indeed, approximately half of Americans believe in at least one disproven conspiracy theory (Oliver & Wood, 2014). News outlets have suggested that, as of the late 2010s, society has entered an "age of conspiricism" (Stanton, 2020; Willingham, 2020). Largely due to the internet and social media websites, conspiracy theories are more readily accessible now than they once were (Wood & Douglas, 2015). Although research suggests that belief in conspiracy theories has not grown more prevalent (van Prooijen & Douglas, 2017), updated research is needed to account for QAnon, as well as recent events such as the COVID-19 pandemic. Because there is a link between belief in conspiracy theories and experiencing crisis situations (Uscinski & Parent, 2014), it is likely that people of all eras will experience conspiracy beliefs while in the midst of societal crisis (van Prooijen & Douglas, 2017). Therefore, this is an area in need of more research.

A second avenue for future research concerns the similarities and differences between QAnon and other groups – and their believers. In some ways, QAnon is not particularly unique among conspiracy groups. For example, in comparing QAnon followers to those of other conspiracy/extremist groups, both are motivated by a "sense of existential threat" (Goldenberg et al., 2020, p. 7). And like those of other populist groups, QAnon followers pit themselves against powerful elites (Bracewell, 2021), as evidenced through a public discourse analysis of QAnon posts (Chandler, 2020). At the micro-level, future research could test whether different types of conspiracy theories attract different types of people. For instance, research has indicated that people who follow some conspiracy theories in general are high in narcissism (e.g. Cichocka et al., 2015), but it is unclear whether this is true of QAnon followers as well. While there is a sizable body of research into other conspiracy groups, much less research has been conducted that is specific to QAnon. Thus, much more research is needed to fully understand the people who follow QAnon.

Future studies could also use varying methodologies to gain a fuller understanding of QAnon and its followers. Most studies conducted on QAnon are one-shot surveys. Future studies should implement different strategies (e.g. longitudinal studies) to better understand the types of people who believe in the QAnon conspiracy movement and how their characteristics and beliefs might change over time. For instance, future studies could better test for the JTC bias among QAnon followers by determining how much information a potential follower needs before believing in QAnon. Similarly, how much counterevidence is enough to make followers question QAnon and eventually quit believing – or do QAnon followers engage in behaviors (e.g. biased information searching) that allow them to continue believing in the face of contrary evidence?

While still exploratory, this application of the possible cognitive processes and traits of QAnon followers helps us to understand who is more susceptible to believing in conspiracy movements like QAnon. This understanding is crucial if society is to combat the danger and violence that arise within extremist groups like QAnon. If it is found that QAnon followers display many of the same cognitive processes and traits of other conspiracy theorists, then this movement is not as unique as it might seem. Even so, understanding all conspiracy theories – and those who support them – is critical to combating misinformation and protecting the well-being of society.

REFERENCES

Abrams, Z. (2020, November 18). What do we know about conspiracy theories? *American Psychological Association*. www.apa.org/news/apa/2020/11/conspiracy-theories

Aïn, S. E., Carré, A., Fantini-Hauwel, C., Baudouin, J. Y., & Besche-Richard, C. (2013). What is the emotional core of the multidimensional Machiavellian personality trait? *Frontiers in Psychology*, *4*(1), 454.

Amarasingam, A., & Argentino, M.-A. (2020). The QAnon conspiracy theory: A security threat in the making? *Combating Terrorism Center*, *13*(7). https://ctc.usma.edu/the-qanon-conspiracy-theory-a-security-threat-in-the-making/

Anti-Defamation League. (n.d.a). Blood Libel: A False, Incendiary Claim Against Jews. www.adl.org/education/resources/glossary-terms/blood-libel

(n.d.b). The dangers of disinformation. www.adl.org/education/resources/tools-and-strategies/the-dangers-of-disinformation

(n.d.c). QAnon. www.adl.org/qanon

(2021, April 19). "The Great Replacement": An explainer. www.adl.org/resources/backgrounders/the-great-replacement-an-explainer

Bloom, M. (2020, May 30). Far-right infiltrators and agitators in George Floyd protests: Indicators of white supremacists. *Just Security*. www.justsecurity.org/70497/far-right-infiltrators-and-agitators-in-george-floyd-protests-indicators-of-white-supremacists/

(2021, July 5). We knew QAnon is anti-Semitic. Now, we know it's racist, too. *Bulletin for Atomic Scientists*. www.google.com/amp/s/thebulletin.org/2021/07/we-knew-qanon-is-anti-semitic-now-we-know-its-racist-too/amp/

Bowes, S. M., Costello, T. H., Ma, W., & Lilenfield, S. O. (2020). Looking under the tinfoil hat: Clarifying the personological and psychopathological correlates of conspiracy theories. *Journal of Personality*, *89*(3), 422–436.

Bracewell, L. (2021). Gender, populism, and the QAnon conspiracy movement. *Frontiers in Sociology*, *5*, 615727.

Bratich, J. (2020, October 23). Rutgers expert explains QAnon. *Rutgers Today: Research & Innovation*. www.rutgers.edu/news/rutgers-expert-explains-qanon

Brockell, G. (2021, March 4). Why March 4 matters to QAnon extremists, leading to fears of another Capitol attack. *The Washington Post*. www.washingtonpost.com/history/2021/03/03/march-4-qanon-trump-inauguration/

Centers for Disease Control and Prevention. (2020, July 1). Identifying the source of the outbreak. www.cdc.gov/coronavirus/2019-ncov/science/about-epidemiology/identifying-source-outbreak.html

Chandler, K. J. (2020). Where we go 1 we go all: A public discourse analysis of QAnon. *McNair Scholars Research*, *13*(1). https://commons.emich.edu/mcnair/vol13/iss1/4

Cichocka, A., Marchlewska, M., & Golec de Zavala, A. (2015). Does self-love or self-hate predict conspiracy theories? Narcissism, self-esteem, and endorsement of conspiracy theory. *Social Psychology and Personality Science*, *7*(2), 157–166.

Cox, D. A. (2021, March 4). Social isolation and community disconnection are not spurring conspiracy theories. *Survey Center on American Life*. www.americansurveycenter.org/research/social-isolation-and-community-disconnection-are-not-spurring-conspiracy-theories/

Crews, G. (2021). Folie à Deux in the 21st century: QAnon and the American dream delusion. In C. S. Bentch & G. A. Crews (Eds.), *Mitigating mass violence and managing threats in contemporary society* (pp. 75–84). IGI Global.

Cybersecurity and Infrastructure Security Agency. (2020, November 12). Joint statement from Elections Infrastructure Government Coordinating Council & the Election Infrastructure Sector Coordinating Executive Committees. www.cisa.gov/news/2020/11/12/joint-statement-elections-infrastructure-government-coordinating-council-election

Dagnall, N., Drinkwater, K., Parker, A., Denovan, D., & Parton, M. (2015). Conspiracy theory and cognitive style: A worldview. *Frontiers in Psychology*, *6*, 206.

Dickson, E. J. (2020, September 23). Former QAnon followers explain what drew them in – And got them out. *Rolling Stone*. www.rollingstone.com/culture/culture-features/ex-qanon-followers-cult-conspiracy-theory-pizzagate-1064076/amp/

Domonoske, C. (2020, August 12). QAnon supporter who made bigoted videos win GA. primary, likely heading to Congress. *NPR*. www.npr.org/2020/08/12/901628541/qanon-supporter-who-made-bigoted-videos-wins-ga-primary-likely-heading-to-congre

Douglas, K. M., Sutton, R. M., & Cichocka, A. (2017). The psychology of conspiracy theories. *Current Directions in Psychological Science*, *26*(6), 538–542.

Douglas, K. M., Uscinski, J. E., Sutton, R. M., Cichocka, A., Nefes, T., Ang, C. S., & Deravi, F. (2019). Understanding conspiracy theories. *Political Psychology*, *40*(1), 3–35.

Enders, A. M., Uscinski, J. E., Klofstad, C. A., Wuchty, S., Seelig, M. I., Funchion, J. R., Murthi, M. N., Premaratne, K., & Stoler, J. (2022). Who supports QAnon? A case study in political extremism. *Journal of Politics*, 84(3), https://doi.org/10.1086/717850

Fischele, M. (2000). Mass response to the Lewinski Scandal: Motivated reasoning or Bayesian updating? *International Society of Political Psychology*, *21*(1) 135–156.

Friedman, R. A. (2021). Why humans are vulnerable to conspiracy theories. *Psychiatric Services*, *72*(1), 3–4.

Frost, P., Casey, B., Griffin, K., Raymundo, L., Farrell, C., & Carrigan, R. (2015). The influence of confirmation bias on memory and source monitoring. *Journal of General Psychology*, *142*(4), 238–252.

Garrett, R., & Bond, R. M. (2021). Conservatives' susceptibility to political misperceptions. *Science Advances*, *7*(23), eabf1234.

Garry, A., Walther, S., Mohamed, R., & Mohammed, A. (2021). QAnon conspiracy theory: Examining its evolution and mechanisms of radicalization. *Journal for Deradicalization*, *26*, 152–216.

Goldenberg, A., Riggleman, D., Baumgartner, J., March, L., Reid-Ross, A., & Finkelstein, J. (2020). The QAnon conspiracy: Destroying families, dividing communities, undermining democracy. *Network Contagion Research Institute*. https://networkcontagion.us/wp-content/uploads/NCRI-%E2%80%93-The-QAnon-Conspiracy-FINAL.pdf

Greene, C. M., & Murphy, G. (2021). Quantifying the effects of fake news on behavior: Evidence from a study of COVID-19 misinformation. *Journal of Experimental Psychology*, *27*(4), 773–784.

Halpern, D., Valenzuela, S., Katz, J., & Miranda, J. P. (2019). From belief in conspiracy theories to trust in others: Which factors influence exposure, believing, and sharing of fake news. In G. Meiselwitz (Ed.), *Social computing and social media. Design, human behavior and analytics* (pp. 217–232). HCII 2019. Lecture Notes in Computer Science, vol 11578. Springer.

Hughes, S., & Machan, L. (2021). It's a conspiracy: COVID-19 conspiracies link to psychopathy, Machiavellianism, and collective narcissism. *Personality and Individual Differences*, *171*, 110559.

Human Trafficking Search. (2014). Human trafficking: Not all black or white. https://humantraffickingsearch.org/human-trafficking-not-all-black-or-white/

Imhoff, R., & Lamberty, P. K. (2018). How paranoid are conspiracy believers? Toward a more fine-grained understanding of the connect and disconnect between paranoia and belief in conspiracy theories. *European Journal of Social Psychology*, *48*, 909–926.

Ingram, M. (2020, August 13). The QAnon cult is growing and the media is helping. *Columbia Journalism Review*. www.cjr.org/the_media_today/the-qanon-conspiracy-cult-is-growing-and-the-media-is-helping.php

Janis, I. L. (2007). Groupthink. In R. P. Vecchio (Ed.), *Leadership: Understanding the dynamics of power and influence in organizations* (2nd ed., pp. 157–169). University of Notre Dame Press.

Jhangiani, R., & Tarry, H. (2014). *Principles of social psychology.* BC Campus.

Johnstone, K. M., Chen, J., & Balzan, R. P. (2017). An investigation into the jumping-to-conclusions bias in social anxiety. *Consciousness and Cognition, 48*, 55–65.

Kiran, C., & Chaudhury, S. (2009). Understanding delusions. *Industrial Psychiatry Journal, 18*(1), 3–18.

Klar, R. (2021, March 15). Facebook study finds overlap between vaccine hesitancy and QAnon. *The Hill.* https://thehill.com/policy/technology/543273-facebook-study-finds-overlap-between-vaccine-hesitancy-and-qanon

Klepper, D. (2021, January 29). Checked by reality, some QAnon supporters seek a way out. *Associated Press: PBS News.* www.pbs.org/newshour/nation/checked-by-reality-some-qanon-supporters-seek-a-way-out

Krch, D. (2011). Cognitive processing. In J. S. Kreutzer, J. DeLuca, & B. Caplan (Eds.), *Encyclopedia of clinical neuropsychology* (p. 627). Springer.

Lazer, D., Baum, M., Benkler, Y., Berinsky, A., Greenhill, K., Menczer, F., Metzger, M. J., Nyhan, B., Pennycook, G., Rothschild, D., Schudson, M., Sloman, S. A., Sunstein, C. R., Thorson, E. A., Watts, D. J., & Zittrain, J. (2018). The science of fake news. *Science, 359*(6380), 2–4.

Lee, M. (2020, October 5). Poll: Many Americans blame virus crises on U.S. government. *The Associated Press.* https://apnorc.org/poll-many-americans-blame-virus-crisis-on-us-government/

Lee, Y. (2019). Groupthink as a system of the decision making process. *Applied Psychology Opus.* https://wp.nyu.edu/steinhardt-appsych_opus/groupthink/

Mak, A. (2021, January 13). Where MAGA insurrectionists and QAnon followers will post now. *Slate.* https://slate.com/technology/2021/01/twitter-facebook-parler-gab-telegram-maga-qanon.html

Marwick, A., & Partin, W. C. (2020). The construction of alternative facts: "QAnon" researchers as scientistic selves. *Paper presented at AoIR 2020: The 21st Annual Conference of the Association of Internet Researchers.* Virtual event: AoIR. http://spir.aior.org

McKee, M., & Stuckler, D. (2010). How cognitive biases affect our interpretation of political messages. *British Medical Journal, 340*(7753), 936–937.

Meller, T. (2002). Agency panic and the culture of conspiracy. In P. Knight (Ed.), *Conspiracy nation: The politics of paranoia in post-war America* (pp. 57–81). NYU Press.

Meterko, V. (2021, August 19). What is cognitive bias and how does it contribute to wrongful conviction. *Innocence Project.* https://innocenceproject.org/what-is-cognitive-bias-how-it-contributes-to-wrongful-conviction/

Metz, S. E., Weisberg, D. S., & Weisberg, M. (2020). A case of sustained internal contradiction: Unresolved ambivalence between evolution and creationism. *Journal of Cognition and Culture, 20*(3–4), 338–354.

Miller, D. T. (2021). Characterizing QAnon: Analysis of YouTube comments presents new conclusions about a popular conservative conspiracy. *First Monday*, *26*(2). https://doi.org/10.5210/fm.v26i2.10168

Moore, R. (2018, November 22). Lucky 17, Q, and the "tippy top" White House: How conspiracy theories are being turbo-charged in Trump's America. ITV News. www.itv.com/news/2018-11-22/lucky-17-q-and-the-tippy-top-president-how-conspiracy-theories-are-being-turbo-charged-into-donald-trumps-america

Moskalenko, S., & McCauley, C. (2021). QAnon: Radical opinion versus radical action. *Perspectives on Terrorism*, *15*(2), 142–146.

Mosley, T., & Raphelson, S. (2021, January 29). Who is Marjorie Taylor Green? What the Congresswoman's rise means for the future of the GOP. *Wbur*. www.wbur.org/hereandnow/2021/01/29/marjorie-taylor-greene-gop

Murata, A., Nakamura, T., & Karwoski, W. (2015). Influences of cognitive biases in distorted decision making and leading to critical unfavorable incidents. *Safety*, *1*, 44–58.

Nelson, T., Kagan, N., Critchlow, C., Hillard, A., & Hsu, A. (2020). The danger of misinformation in the COVID-19 crisis. *Missouri Medicine*, *117*(6), 510–512.

Novella, S. (2018). Teleology and conspiracy thinking. *Neurologica*. https://theness.com/neurologicablog/index.php/teleology-and-conspiracy-thinking/

Nyhan, B. (2010). Why the "death panel" myth wouldn't die: Misinformation in the health care Reform Debate. *The Forum 8*. https://journalistsresource.org/wp-content/uploads/2012/07/Why-Death-Panel-Myth-Wont-Die.pdf

Oliver, J. E., & Wood, T. J. (2014). Conspiracy theories and the paranoid style(s) of mass opinion. *American Journal of Political Science*, *58*(4), 952–966.

Papasavva, A., Blackburn, J., Stringhini, G., Zannettou, S., & De Cristofaro, E. (2020). "Is it a Qoincidence?": A first step towards understanding and characterizing the QAnon movement on Voat.co. *Computers and Society*. https://doi.org/10.48550/arXiv.2009.04885

Pasek, J., Stark, T. H., Krosnick, J. A., & Tompson, T. (2015). What motivates a conspiracy theory? Birther beliefs, partisanship, liberal–conservative ideology, and anti-Black attitudes. *Electoral Studies*, *40*, 482–489.

Pennycook, G., & Rand, D. G. (2020). Who falls for fake news? The roles of bullshit receptivity, overclaiming, familiarity, and analytic thinking. *Journal of Personality*, *88*(2), 185–200.

Pierre, J. (2020). Mistrust and misinformation: A two-component, socio-epistemic model of belief in conspiracy theories. *Journal of Social and Political Psychology*, *8*(2), 617–641.

Pytlik, N., Soll, D., & Mehl, S. (2020). Thinking preferences and conspiracy belief: Intuitive thinking and the jumping to conclusions-bias as a basis for the belief in conspiracy theories. *Frontiers in Psychiatry*, *11*, 568942.

Reimann, N. (2021, August 13). QAnon marked Friday as Trump "reinstatement" day – here are other flop predictions of Trump's return. *Forbes*. www.forbes.com/sites/nicholasreimann/2021/08/13/qanon-marked-friday-as-tru

mp-reinstatement-day-here-are-other-flop-predictions-of-trumps-return/?sh=7e0e14982a77

Richey, S. (2017). A birther and a truther: The influence of the authoritarian personality on conspiracy beliefs. *Politics & Policy, 45*, 465–485.

Romer, D., & Jamieson, K. H. (2020). Conspiracy theories as a barrier to controlling the spread of COVID-19 in the U.S. *Social Science & Medicine, 263*, 113356.

Ruse, M. (2003, August 30). Creationism. *Stanford Encyclopedia of Philosophy*. https://plato.stanford.edu/entries/creationism/

Schor, E. (2021, January 13). Anti-Semitism seen in Capitol insurrection raises alarms. *Associated Press: US News*. www.usnews.com/news/politics/articles/2021-01-13/anti-semitism-seen-in-capitol-insurrection-raises-alarms

Sen, A., & Zadrozny, B. (2020, August 10). QAnon groups have millions of members on Facebook, documents show. *NBC News*. www.nbcnews.com/tech/tech-news/qanon-groups-have-millions-members-facebook-documents-show-n1236317

Sommer, W. (2020, August 15). QAnon promotes pedo-ring conspiracy theories. Now they're stealing kids. *The Daily Beast*. www.thedailybeast.com/qanon-promotes-pedo-ring-conspiracy-theories-now-theyre-stealing-kids

Stanton, Z. (2020). You're living in the golden age of conspiracy theories. *Politico*. www.politico.com/news/magazine/2020/06/17/conspiracy-theories-pandemic-trump-2020-election-coronavirus-326530

Sternisko, A., Cichocka, A., Cislak, A., & Van Bavel, J. J. (2023). National narcissism and the belief and dissemination of conspiracy theories during the COVID-19 pandemic: Evidence from 56 countries. *Personality and Social Psychology Bulletin*, 49(1), 48–65.

Tolan, C., Kuznia, R., & Ortega, B. (2021, January 7). Insurrection fueled by conspiracy groups, extremists, and fringe movements. CNN. www.cnn.com/2021/01/07/us/insurrection-capitol-extremist-groups-invs/index.html

Uscinski, J. E., & Parent, J. M. (2014). *The ages of conspiracies*. Oxford University Press.

van der Linden, S., Panagopoulos, C., Azevedo, F., & Jost, J. (2020). The paranoid style in American politics revisited: An ideological asymmetry in conspiratorial thinking. *Political Psychology, 42*(1), 23–51.

van Prooijen, J. W., & Douglas, K. M. (2017). Conspiracy theories as a part of history: The role of societal crisis situations. *Memory Studies, 10*(3), 323–333.

van Prooijen, J. W., Krouwel, A. P. M., & Pollet, T. (2015). Political extremism predicts belief in conspiracy theories. *Social Psychological and Personality Science, 6*(5), 570–578.

Vosoughi, S., Roy, D., & Aral, S. (2018). The spread of true and false news online. *Science, 359*, 1146–1151.

Wade, P. (2023, January 8). MTG, a Member of Congress, blames "the Internet" for her past QAnon beliefs. *Rolling Stone*. www.rollingstone.com/politics/politics-news/marjorie-taylor-greene-blames-internet-qanon-beliefs-1234657579/

Wagner-Egger, P., Delouvée, S., Gauvrit, N., & Dieguez, S. (2018). Creationism and conspiracism share a common teleological basis. *Current Biology*, *28*, R847–R870.

Walker, L. E. A. (2002). Politics, psychology, and the Battered Women's Movement. *Journal of Trauma Practice*, *1*(1), 81–102.

West, D. M. (2021, January 11). The role of misinformation in Trump's insurrection. *Brookings*. www.brookings.edu/blog/techtank/2021/01/11/the-role-of-misinformation-in-trumps-insurrection/

Willingham, A. J. (2020, October 3). How the pandemic and politics gave us a golden age of conspiracy theories. *CNN*. www.cnn.com/2020/10/03/us/conspiracy-theories-why-origins-pandemic-politics-trnd/index.html

Winter, J. (2019, August 1). Exclusive: FBI document warns conspiracy theories are a new domestic terrorism threat. *Yahoo News*. www.yahoo.com/now/fbi-documents-conspiracy-theories-terrorism-160000507.html

Wood, M. J., & Douglas, K. M. (2015). Online communication as a window to conspiracist worldviews. *Frontiers in Psychology*, *6*, 836.

Yakeley, J. (2018). Current understanding of narcissism and narcissistic personality disorder. *BJPsych Advances*, *24*(5), 305–315.

Zitser, J., & Ankle, S. (2021, June 27). A Trump loving insurrectionist and a convicted stalker are among 36 QAnon supporters running for Congress in 2022. *Insider*. www.businessinsider.com/the-36-qanon-supporters-running-congress-in-the-2022-midterms-2021-6

Zuckerman, E., & McQuade, M. (2019). QAnon and the emergence of the unreal. *Journal of Design and Science*. https://doi.org/10.21428/7808da6b.6b8a82b9

CHAPTER 5

The Role of Moral Cognitions in the Growth of QAnon

M. Katie Cunius and Monica K. Miller

The COVID-19 pandemic altered people's lifestyles and limited their ability to socialize. This caused people to have ample time to watch the news and scroll through social media, allowing the popularization of conspiracy groups such as QAnon. QAnon's popularization is further supported by the conservative shift that occurred during the pandemic (Kawrowski et al., 2020; O'Shea et al., 2022; Rosenfeld & Tomiyama, 2021) and throughout former President Trump's term in office. QAnon has been associated with violent acts, such as the January 6 insurrection (Legare & Rosen, 2022). These violent acts, which generally go against society's moral standards, could be justified by QAnon supporters through the use of moral cognitions. These moral cognitions can be explained by parasite stress theory (PST), moral foundations theory (MFT), terror management theory (TMT), and moral disengagement theory (MDT).

This chapter will discuss the relationship between the COVID-19 pandemic and President Trump's term in office, and it will associate these events with the emergence of QAnon. It will then explain the justification of QAnon's actions using moral cognitions. Uncertain times encourage a conservative shift in beliefs, which allows for conspiracy groups such as QAnon to emerge and affect their supporters' moral cognitions to further encourage these beliefs (see Chapters 3, 4, and 16 of this volume for more on the characteristics of QAnon followers).

Parasite Stress Theory

The COVID-19 pandemic created an environment of uncertainty of a type that had not previously been experienced. This uncertainty forced people to seek stability and comfort in known places, which created a reliance on traditional values and conservatism (Karwowski et al., 2020; see also Chapter 8 of this volume). This means people with strong conservative values likely grew stronger in their beliefs, and those who were uncertain in their beliefs might have shifted toward conservativism. This section will apply PST to the COVID-19 pandemic and explain how this might have caused a shift in some people's values.

Assumptions of Theory

PST predicts that, when a person feels threated by an infection, they will alter their beliefs and responses to cope with the infection's perceived risk (Schaller, 2011; Thornhill & Fincher, 2014). This theory originates from evolutionary psychology to explain humans' "behavioral immune system" (Schaller, 2011) that encapsules humans' emotional, cognitive, or impulsive responses to a perceived risk of infection to both minimize and avoid the infection (Schaller, 2011; Thornhill & Fincher, 2014). These psychological and behavioral responses are a person's defense mechanisms that protect them from the infection's risk (Thornhill & Fincher, 2014). Such responses are influenced by a person's own ideas and by the perceived characteristics that they assign to the disease, which impact their subsequent reactions (Tybur et al., 2013). Due to this novel threat and a desire for stability, a person could revert to conservative values to help calm their anxiety about the infection's risk.

Conservative Shift in Relation to Parasite Stress Theory

The perceived risk of COVID-19 likely has caused many people to shift toward more conservative and traditional values. This shift is evident in multiple areas of a person's life, including in terms of gender roles (Rosenfeld & Tomiyama, 2021) and political views (e.g. right-wing authoritarianism; Kawrowski et al., 2020). These conservative values, such as strong family ties and right-wing authoritarianism, create a social in-group that is positively associated with PST (Fincher & Thornhill, 2012). Therefore, this in-group, created based on conservative values, is more likely to align with the behaviors associated with PST. This in-group, consisting of people with shared characteristics and beliefs, reduces the infection's perceived risk because the group can be a support system and a mechanism for coping with the disease. This is partly because, when people feel threatened, they shift toward structure, which in politics can be associated with conservatism and the perceived stability found in conservative candidates (Karwowski et al., 2020).

Further, people could perceive out-groups as infectious threats (Pazhoohi & Kingstone, 2021). This occurred throughout the COVID-19 pandemic with the rise in Asian hate crimes throughout the world because of the pandemic's origination in Wuhan, China (Human Rights Watch, 2020). Although people of Asian ethnicity were not the cause of the pandemic, some people perceived them as a representation of the infection and so as a threat similar to the infection itself. This hate is increased when people have higher confidence in the government, which in the USA was led by Republican President Trump. This confidence in government increases feelings of conservatism, xenophobia, and authoritarianism (Pazhoohi & Kingstone, 2021; see Chapter 9 of this volume for more on the politics of QAnon).

In sum, the perceived threat of COVID-19 encourages a dependence on traditional (Rosenfeld & Tomiyama, 2021) and conservative values (Kawrowski et al., 2020). This conservative shift can help a person manage their fear of infection by relying on in-group members, causing subsequent suspicion of out-group members. This increases trust in and reliance on members within one's own group. Thus, the perceived threat of COVID-19, as described by PST, explains how the threat and uncertainty of a disease shift people's beliefs toward conservatism.

Moral Foundations Theory

Along with PST, MFT can explain the relationship between the pandemic and people's shift toward conservative beliefs. However, this theory can also explain how prominent political figures affect a person's shift in beliefs, such as former President Trump. This section will discuss how MFT would predict a conservative shift in beliefs.

Assumptions of Theory

MFT can be used to predict a person's conservative shift in beliefs because of the COVID-19 pandemic and Trump's presidency. This theory describes how people's innate moral intuitions (i.e. foundations) develop in response to adaptive challenges, which then form a person's moral judgments (Haidt & Joseph, 2004). This theory consists of five main foundations: purity/derogation, authority/subversion, loyalty/betrayal, fairness/cheating, and care/harm (Graham et al., 2018). The *purity/derogation* foundation describes humans' need to make accurate judgments about an infection's perceived risk, which can include fear of dissimilar others (Graham et al., 2018). The *authority/subversion* foundation describes a person's preference for a hierarchical system and a distinct authority figure (Graham et al., 2018), such as conservatives' preferences for former President Trump and a strong government. The *loyalty/betrayal* foundation portrays loyal people as patriots and disloyal people as traitors (Graham et al., 2018). The foundation of *fairness/cheating* describes how people monitor others' behaviors to judge a person's fairness (Graham et al., 2018). The *care/harm* foundation describes the sensitivity a person feels toward another person or a person's desire to harm when another person is victimized (Graham et al., 2018), which can relate to the out-groups formed because of COVID-19's perceived threat, as previously discussed.

Moral foundations are taught throughout cultures and generations to establish the virtues and values that people are expected to follow (Graham et al., 2013; Haidt & Graham, 2007). Therefore, these foundations have been best understood by comparing the emphases that each culture puts on the foundations (e.g. Graham et al., 2011), and this approach has been applied to other areas such as politics (e.g. Graham et al., 2009; Malka et al., 2016). Although research has been conducted comparing these foundations between groups to better understand who uses which foundation, comparisons of groups are not critical to understanding the main components of the theory. For the current purposes, it is important to know how foundations are used when making a decision or judgment. These moral judgments are often thought to be associative, effortless, and automatic (Graham et al., 2013). Thus, a person determines the risk of COVID-19 by considering their perceived risk of the disease and the risk suggested by government officials. This perception helps them justify and form their beliefs, actions, and judgments.

Conservative Shift in Relation to Moral Foundations Theory

Conservative beliefs have been affiliated with predicting a person's moral foundations (Hatemi et al., 2019), with conservatives placing equal weight across the five foundations of morality (Graham et al., 2013, including binding foundations (loyalty, authority, purity; Graham et al., 2013; Malka et al., 2016). Contrasting with conservatives, liberals tend to focus on individualizing foundations (harm/care, fairness/reciprocity). This partially is a result of how conservatives and liberals differentially decide what is valuable and moral (Kawrowski et al., 2020). For instance, conservatives would rely on an authority figure (i.e. Trump), but liberals likely would not because of the different foundations that the groups rely on when making their decisions. This is exemplified by ideals such as conservatives placing value in domains like traditional gender roles (i.e. purity foundation; Kawrowski et al., 2020) and liberals believing a person's gender does not determine their role within society. Within these moral foundations, conservatives strongly emphasize moral issues relating to loyalty (e.g. patriotism), authority (e.g. law and order), and purity (e.g. religious and traditional restrictions; Graham et al., 2018). For example, conservatives might emphasize pride in their country and faith in government. These foundations increase values attributed to in-group (conservative) membership. The moral foundations that are associated with conservative beliefs can be attributed to people's trust in and reliance on President Trump's perception of the pandemic. For example, if President Trump questioned the health advice from Dr. Anthony S. Fauci[1] in relation to COVID-19, then Trump's supporters would question Fauci's advice too because of their faith in Trump. This loyalty further distances the in-group (conservatives) from the out-group (liberals), establishing trust within group members and reinforcing their beliefs.

To many conservatives, Trump was also perceived as a strong authority figure, making conservatives more likely to respect any rules and opinions handed down from Trump (Graham et al., 2018). In times of uncertainty, this strong authority figure would attract people seeking stability and confidence. Further, conservative attitudes would be strengthened through entrenchment and persuasion (Day et al., 2014). This strengthening of beliefs could also apply to moderates who have faith in the government and perceive Trump as an authority figure, which could result in shifting their beliefs toward conservatism. However, if these people do not perceive Trump as a legitimate authority figure, then they would not be persuaded toward conservatism based on these values.

This perception of Trump as a legitimate authority figure could impact perceptions regarding COVID-19 guidelines, which further solidifies the shift in conservative values, as stated in above. When conservatives assess the risk posed by the pandemic, they likely compare their perceived risk of infection to the risk described by President Trump (Pazhoohi & Kingstone, 2021). This has been referred to as the "Faith in Trump" effect, in which confidence in Trump and his handling of the pandemic are positively associated with defying COVID-19 protocols (Cullen et al., 2022; Graham et al., 2020). This effect is associated with conservatives

[1] Dr. Fauci is the Director of the National Institute of Allergy and Infectious Diseases and has provided information and guidance on the COVID-19 pandemic (National Institute of Allergy and Infection Diseases, n.d.).

perceiving COVID-19 as lower in risk as compared to people with other political ideologies (Shao & Hoa, 2020). This faith in authority also relates to high binding moral foundations (e.g. authority, group cohesion, obedience, and self-sacrifice), which are all associated with conservative beliefs.

The COVID-19 pandemic and former President Trump strengthened people's binding foundations, authority foundation, loyalty foundation, and purity foundations, which strengthened their conservative beliefs and allowed people with moderate beliefs to shift toward conservatism. Although people's morals are formed from the same five foundations, people's beliefs and judgments differ depending on the importance placed within each foundation. This explains the differing opinions between groups, such as conservatives and liberals.

Terror Management Theory

As previously discussed, people's perception of an infectious risk can cause a conservative shift in their beliefs. Additionally, a person's realization of *mortality*, such as that stemming from an infectious disease, can also cause a conservative shift, as explained by TMT (see Chapter 8 for more on TMT). COVID-19 might have heightened awareness of a person's mortality, causing a psychological response that affected their worldview (Solomon et al., 2015). For many, this heightened awareness resulted in a conservative shift, leading people to rely on traditional beliefs and their in-groups to find stability. The perception of threat and desire for group membership are associated with both the pandemic, as previously discussed, and with former President Trump (e.g. Cohen et al., 2017; Greenberg & Kosloff, 2008; Pyszcynski, 2004).

Assumptions of Theory

TMT does not directly relate to a person's perceived risk of infection but instead describes the effect of a person's awareness that death is inevitable and the subsequent psychological response that arises from this awareness (Greenberg et al., 1986). When a person is aware of their mortality, they strive for a meaningful and significant life to manage this fear (Solomon et al., 2015). This significant life is dependent on the person's cultural worldview, which relates to their beliefs and increases their self-esteem. This worldview then decreases their anxiety and death-related thoughts (Solomon et al., 2015).

A person's perceived threat of mortality and strong cultural worldview reinforce their personal viewpoints and diminish threats to their beliefs (Solomon et al., 2015). This perceived mortality can also cause a strengthening in conservative values as an attempt to seek stability (e.g. Pyszcynski, 2004; Weise et al., 2008). Thus, when a conservative or moderate person is aware of their mortality, they will strengthen their personal beliefs and increase their trust in leaders who share similar beliefs. During the specific time of COVID-19, liberals would likely not strengthen their trust in authority because they did not perceive Trump as a strong authority figure. However, if a liberal authority figure was in office, then this strengthening of values could be replicated among liberals.

Conservative Shift in Relation to Terror Management Theory

TMT can be applied to the COVID-19 pandemic and Trump's presidency to explain how a person's mortality awareness can cause a shift toward conservative beliefs. TMT would predict that the heightened awareness of mortality caused by COVID-19 (Horner et al., 2023) would increase reliance on traditional values, causing a conservative shift. This acknowledgment of mortality can cause people to reevaluate their existing beliefs and strengthen their conservative views and allegiances to those in conservative parties. This is because, when mortality salience is increased, the reliance on charismatic leaders increases to mitigate this terror threat (Cohen et al., 2017; Greenberg & Kosloff, 2008; Pyszcynski, 2004). Conservatives also increase their aggression toward out-group members (e.g. liberals) by being prejudicing toward and stereotyping out-group members (Greenberg & Kosloff, 2008). This mortality threat and strengthened in-group identification can then increase support for nationalism (Pyszcynski, 2004). This increases intolerance of out-group members who dissent from their personal views, which results in an increase in hostility. It also can increase desire for vengeance, such as participating in violent behaviors toward dissenting others (e.g. liberals).

Tension is increased between in-group and out-group members when mortality is salient because people strengthen their relationships with others who maintain a similar worldview to them (high mortality threat) to validate their beliefs and create an anxiety buffer (Ahmed et al., 2021). However, this anxiety buffer and worldview could be threatened by the implemented COVID-19 protocols, which required precautionary measures such as social distancing. These protocols threaten the values of close relationships and subsequently hinder a person's anxiety buffer. Although frustrations surrounding these protocols were present among all people regardless of their political affiliation, people with conservative beliefs were strongly against these measures, and some actively protested these protocols (e.g. Bergengruen, 2022).

In sum, when a person's mortality is threatened, those with both strong and weak conservative beliefs will seek a strong leader and in-group members (Weise et al., 2008). This support then increases a person's self-perception (e.g. self-esteem), perceived security, and the strength of their beliefs. Thus, TMT can explain the effect of the pandemic and President Trump's role in the conservative shift that could occur when a person realizes their impermanence.

Integrating the Theories in Relation to QAnon

The theories above all describe how the COVID-19 pandemic and simultaneous Trump presidency could predict why some people became more conservative during this time. Conservative beliefs and moral cognitions allow the emergence of extremist conspiracy groups such as QAnon. Further, this conservative shift also encourages belief in QAnon and support for the group's actions.

Moral Foundations Theory and Parasite Stress Theory

MFT and PST are related because both theories can explain an infection's perceived threat (i.e. COVID-19) and the influence of Trump as an authority figure on the formation of a person's subsequent moral judgments. Specifically, the moral foundation of care/harm relates to PST because people avoid infection by making judgments about the infection's perceived risk. Further, the foundation of caring and fairness can predict a person's behavioral compliance with COVID-19 protocol measures (Chan, 2021). If a person perceives COVID-19 as low in risk, they are more likely to oppose health restrictions because the person has a low care and fairness foundation. This perception of risk is reinforced through the government's portrayal of the risk (authority foundation), such as Trump's portrayal of COVID-19, which reinforced conservative values. This value placed in the government's perception of the pandemic can also relate to the binding foundation of loyalty, which is associated with an increase in conservatism, along with the foundation of authority (Karwowski et al., 2020).

Moral Foundations Theory, Parasite Stress Theory, and Terror Management Theory

The realization of mortality associated with the perceived threat of COVID-19 increases nationalism and group identification (Pyszczynski, 2004). This is associated with an intolerance for dissent, hostility toward those who are different, and a desire for vengeance (Pyszczynski, 2004). When a person's perception of their mortality is heightened, they increase their use of prejudice toward out-group members, increase their likelihood to stereotype out-group members, and increase their reliance on charismatic leaders (authority foundation; Greenberg & Kosloff, 2008). This process increases aggression toward out-group members. One reason for this is because in-group members can find support among people with similar beliefs in times of uncertainty. These three theories can help explain the role of a person's moral cognitions in their conservative shift toward belief in QAnon. Further, the combination of these theories allows us to understand the role that the COVID-19 pandemic and former President Trump played in strengthening these beliefs and in the growth of QAnon.

Conservative Shift in Relation to QAnon

A conservative shift and increased reliance on conservative leaders create an acceptance of dissent, hostility, and vengeance toward people who oppose a group's beliefs (Pyszczynski, 2004). This allows QAnon members to act in a deviant and at times harmful way with perceived support from these leaders. For example, former President Trump has referred to QAnon members as "patriots" who are fighting for their country (Rubin et al., 2021).

This conservative shift also allowed people to accept and support the actions of QAnon because of their shared potential out-groups (e.g. liberals). QAnon members believe high-power elites, including liberals, run a satanic pedophilia ring. Thus, groups who also dislike liberals might relate to QAnon because of this belief, allowing QAnon members to publicly announce their beliefs without facing repercussions from their in-group members.

The beliefs that create a conservative shift can allow for conspiracy beliefs to grow. As previously discussed, a perceived threat (e.g. COVID-19) can contribute to a conservative shift, as described by PST and TMT. Conservatives are associated with a lower perceived risk of COVID-19 and thus a lower rate of safety compliance (Timberg & Dwoskin, 2021), which also are associated with conspiracy beliefs (Maftei & Holman, 2022). Therefore, these shared beliefs can foster support for QAnon and increase the prevalence of the group through the spread of their information. PST describes how COVID-19 can cause people to rely on their in-group because of the perceived threat of COVID-19, which is further explained by TMT (Pyszczynski, 2004). This in-group was strengthened because of former President Trump, specifically in relation to his perceptions of the pandemic according to the foundations of authority, patriotism, and loyalty according to MFT (Graham et al., 2018). The actions of QAnon members resulting from the conservative shift that occurred during the pandemic and in association with former President Trump can be justified by moral disengagement mechanisms.

Moral Disengagement and Harm Caused by QAnon

Along with the theories offered above, MDT can explain the cognitive processing a person uses to justify their decisions (Bandura et al., 1996). Although harmful acts (e.g. violence) do not represent an innate characteristic of QAnon, such acts are often linked to QAnon (e.g. Keith, 2022; Legare & Rosen, 2022). QAnon members can use mechanisms of moral disengagement to justify these harms and rationalize their sense of morality.

Assumptions of Theory

Morals are the set of values and norms specific to a person's culture that dictate their expected social behaviors (Moll et al., 2005). Moral disengagement can be used by QAnon members to justify the group's harm caused to others. This justification can be accomplished through one of eight cognitive mechanisms: moral justification, euphemistic language, advantageous comparison, displacement of responsibility, diffusion of responsibility, distortion of consequences, attribution of blame, and dehumanization (Bandura et al., 1996). Moral justification is the process of making a harmful act socially acceptable or at least less harmful to society (Bandura et al., 1996). Euphemistic language is the choosing of words to portray the action as a valued service. Advantageous comparison is the process of contrasting the act in question with a more reprehensible act. Displacement of responsibility is the shifting of responsibility away from the offender onto another person. Diffusion of responsibility is reducing an individual person's responsibility by applying responsibility to the whole group or shifting it onto other events. Distortion of consequences occurs when the perceived harm is minimized because the act benefits another person. Attribution of blame is the process of assigning cause to the victim to justify the harm caused. Dehumanization is the process of diminishing the human qualities attributed to the victim. These mechanisms are used by QAnon supporters to justify the group's violent acts and the misinformation spread by QAnon members.

Harm Caused by QAnon Members

QAnon's beliefs have caused harmful acts that are both physically violent (e.g. Bleakley, 2021; Keith, 2022; Legare & Rosen, 2022) and harmful to society's understanding of COVID-19 (e.g. Timberg & Dwoskin, 2021; Wendling, 2020). These harms deviate from society's moral standards, and thus the acts need to be justified by QAnon supporters. To justify these acts, QAnon supporters can use moral disengagement mechanisms.

Violent Actions

QAnon's beliefs have contributed to violent acts that have harmed others and are perceived as justified by its supporters. For example, many QAnon supporters believe Hollywood elites and Democratic leaders are running a pedophilia ring and that it is the duty of QAnon members to save these children (Beckett, 2020). Thus, there have been reports of members kidnapping their own children for fear of them being trafficked (Beckett, 2020). This belief is also associated with events such as Pizzagate, in which QAnon supporters believed a sex-trafficking ring was located under a pizza shop in Washington, DC. To protest this, QAnon supporters attempted to blow up a "satanic temple monument" to make people aware of Democratic pedophiles and the event of Pizzagate itself (Bleakley, 2021).

One of the most prominent events QAnon was involved in was the January 6 insurrection – the storming of the Capitol because of the belief that the 2020 election was fraudulent. QAnon supporters at this rally were in support of engaging in violent acts, such as stating President Biden, former Vice President Mike Pence, and Dr. Fauci should be hung and Nancy Pelosi[2] should be killed (Keith, 2022). Although these are examples of verbal violence, the January 6 insurrection is also associated with physical violence, such as the assaulting of Capitol police officers. These

[2] Speaker of the House from 2019 to the present (2022).

supporters demonstrated little remorse and instead wished more violence had occurred (Legare & Rosen, 2022).

Spread of Public Health Misinformation

A second harm QAnon encourages is the spread of COVID-19 misinformation. Conservatism is associated with the belief that the media exaggerate information related to the COVID-19 pandemic (Calvillo et al., 2020). Further, conspiracy ideations are associated with lower perceived risk and compliance with safety measures (Maftei & Holman, 2022). An example of QAnon followers' skepticism surrounding the pandemic is their belief that COVID-19 is a cover-up for Democrat's satanic sex-trafficking ring (Wendling, 2020). This belief has caused supporters to encourage the burning of masks and refusing COVID-19 testing and vaccinations. QAnon members believe the COVID-19 vaccines cause death and that those who are vaccinated are COVID-19 super-spreaders (Timberg & Dwoskin, 2021). Further, they believe that the vaccines are aiding a corrupt government and drug companies who intend to depopulate the Earth and gain social control (Timberg & Dwoskin, 2021).

Moral Disengagement Mechanisms Justify QAnon's Actions

There are several moral disengagement mechanisms that can justify QAnon's harm and rationalize its actions that go against society's moral standard. Moral disengagement not only rationalizes the offender's actions, but also allows people with similar beliefs to identify with the group and rationalize supporting such harmful acts.

The first moral disengagement mechanism is moral justification. Moral justification is a common mechanism that can be used by QAnon members to justify violent acts toward people (e.g. political leaders) who QAnon supporters believe are involved in child-kidnapping schemes. This group believes that any action that removes a child from harm's way is morally just because this saves the child from satanic worshippers (Beckett, 2020). Thus, any acts that cause harm to Democrats or downplay the severity of COVID-19 are justified because they expose the more severe crime of pedophilia – the epitome of moral depravity (Garry et al., 2021; Spring & Wendling, 2020). Moral justification has further been used to justify violence associated with the pandemic in other ways. For example, QAnon supporters have said "give me the vaccine and I'll give them bullets" (Timberg & Dwoskin, 2021). By suggesting President Joe Biden and Dr. Fauci deserve to be hung and Nancy Pelosi should be shot in the head (Keith, 2022), these supporters are justifying such violent actions and portraying them as punishments for the government's evil acts.

Another justification of violence toward government officials occurs when QAnon supporters blame the victims of the harm for bring about that harm. QAnon blames the COVID-19 virus on prominent Democratic leaders and other countries (i.e. China). This blame then justifies violence toward these Democratic leaders (e.g. Biden, Dr. Fauci) and justifies hate toward Asian people (e.g. referring to the virus as the "Chinese virus"; Moyniham & Porembescu, 2022). Simply put, harm is justified because these groups are seen as having brought the harm on themselves by causing COVID-19.

Similarly, displacement of responsibility – the third moral disengagement mechanism – shifts the responsibility related to the harm away from the offender and onto an unaffiliated third party. Thus, the third party is used as a scapegoat, and QAnon supporters encourage violent behavior against this third party as a punishment for causing the pandemic. Further, turning these people into perpetrators justifies the harm done to them because they are no longer perceived as victims.

The combination of moral justification, attribution of blame, and dehumanization can be used to justify the assault of police officers during the January 6 insurrection (Legare & Rosen, 2022). The officers at the Capitol were perceived as part of the "problem" – an obstacle protecting the results of a fraudulent election. Thus, the violence against them was perceived as deserved because they acted as a roadblock to destroying a corrupt government; the protesters demonstrated little remorse for their actions, and some wished more violence had occurred (Legare & Rosen, 2022). QAnon supporters blamed the police officers for protecting a tyrannical government and justified their violence because "in the face of tyranny, violence is the answer" (Legare & Rosen, 2022). Through this dehumanization, moral justification, and shifting of blame toward the police officers and others supporting the government's actions, the harm that QAnon supporters caused (e.g. police officers being attacked) was minimized (Castano, 2008; Leidner et al., 2010).

Distortion of consequences is the fourth moral disengagement mechanism, and this can be used by QAnon supporters to justify their morally questionable acts. QAnon supporters spread vaccine misinformation by stating that these vaccines are depopulating the country and those who are vaccinated are COVID-19 super-spreaders (Timberg & Dwoskin, 2021). Thus, the consequences of spreading harmful misinformation are distorted so that it is seen as positive instead of negative.

Euphemistic language – the fifth moral disengagement mechanism – is evident in the support shown between QAnon and conservative leaders. Trump has called QAnon supporters "patriots" who "love our country," and he has said that their actions are evidence of fighting against pedophilia (Rubin et al., 2021). Trump's support of QAnon allowed for the spread of misinformation through the portrayal of QAnon's actions as just and patriotic. This government support could change the perception that outsiders have of QAnon, increasing the group's following.

In sum, what many people would perceive as immoral and rarely justified is perceived as warranted and patriotic by QAnon members and their supporters. Moral cognition theories (i.e. PST, MFT and TMT) explain the growth of QAnon, and moral disengagement mechanisms allow QAnon to do harm. These theories that explain the support for and growth of QAnon can also be applied to other conspiracy groups, as discussed next.

Similarities in the Use of Moral Cognitions in Other Conspiracy Groups

Moral cognitions can be useful for understanding the cognitive processes of radical information (e.g. understanding the conservative shift, applying moral disengagement mechanisms to QAnon's actions). Conspiracy groups form because of the need to understand one's own environment, the need to feel safe and in control of one's environment, and the need to maintain one's self-image (Douglas et al., 2017). Regardless of the group's beliefs, people must morally justify their decisions, which can be accomplished through moral cognitive processes. This chapter specifically discusses the extremist conspiracy group QAnon; however, there are groups that exist with similar beliefs to QAnon and counterconspiracy groups (e.g. antifa) that could use the same logics to justify their perspectives (e.g. increased reliance on in-group members).

Further, these conspiracy groups all attract people with low self-efficacy, low self-control, and weak law-relevant morality (Rottweiler & Gill, 2022). This creates an increased desire to engage in everyday crimes (Jolley et al., 2019; Rottweiler & Gill, 2022). The dangerousness of this has been discussed above in terms of how these situations and a person's cognitions can be used to justify these crimes and other violent intentions. Thus, the factors discussed above do not specifically explain the increase in support for QAnon – QAnon is simply the chosen conspiracy group that has been used as an example. These factors could be used to justify supporting any conspiracy group in general, allowing a person to support whichever group is most relevant to them.

Conclusion

QAnon's increase in popularity can be partially attributed to the COVID-19 pandemic and former President Trump shifting people toward conservative values. This shift in values can be explained through PST, MFT, TMT, and MDT. These theories help explain the factors that encourage people to search for a group to identify with, leading them to form strong beliefs that align themselves with that group. These beliefs spread easily due to the increase in free time and access to social media caused by the pandemic. These values can encourage the actions of QAnon, whether these are violent actions or the spread of misinformation. The justification of these actions is rationalized through moral cognitions. Despite this chapter focusing on QAnon, the use of theories to explain and justify support for QAnon can be applied to other conspiracy groups as well.

Researchers could investigate the implications of these theories for other similar groups and experimentally manipulate variables related to conspiracy followers' cognitive processes to better understand people's support of conspiracy groups. Although QAnon is prevalent because of the current social climate, understanding the cognitive processes that motivate people to support these conspiracy groups could help researchers to understand these groups' beliefs and actions (see Chapter 3 for more on the motives of QAnon followers). The manipulation of these cognitive processes could affirm the previously found conservative shift associated with PST, MFT, TMT, and MDT. Applying such findings to other conspiracy groups could also explain how these beliefs strengthen a person's membership within such groups. Future studies must take these theories and directly apply their concepts to QAnon and other conspiracy groups to better understand the factors associated with a conspiracy group's moral cognitions.

REFERENCES

Ahmed, R., Ahmed, A., & Barkat, W. (2021). Behavioral limitations of individuals for coping with COVID-19: A terror management perspective. *Journal of Human Behavior in the Social Environment*, *31*(1–4), 97–118.

Bandura, A., Barbaranelli, C., Caprara, G. V., & Pastorelli, C. (1996). Mechanisms of moral disengagement in the exercise of moral agency. *Journal of Personality and Social Psychology*, *71*(2), 364–374.

Beckett, L. (2020, October 16). QAnon: A timeline of violence linked to the conspiracy theory. *The Guardian*. www.theguardian.com/us-news/2020/oct/15/qanon-violence-crimes-timeline

Bergengruen, V. (2022, January 26). How the anti-vax movement is taking over the right. *Time*. https://time.com/6141699/anti-vaccine-mandate-movement-rally/

Bleakley, P. (2021). Panic, pizza and mainstreaming the alt-right: A social media analysis of Pizzagate and the rise of the QAnon conspiracy. *Current Sociology*. https://doi.org/10.1177/00113921211034896

Calvillo, D. P., Ross, B. J., Garcia, R. J., Smelter, T. J., & Rutchick, A. M. (2020). Political ideology predicts perceptions of the threat of COVID-19 (and susceptibility to fake news about it). *Social Psychological and Personality Science*, *11*(8), 1119–1128.

Castano, E. (2008). On the perils of glorifying the in-group: Intergroup violence, in-group glorification, and moral disengagement. *Social and Personality Psychology Compass*, *2*(1), 154–170.

Chan, E. Y. (2021). Moral foundations underlying behavioral compliance during the COVID-19 pandemic. *Personality and Individual Differences*, *171*, 110463.

Cohen, F., Solomon, S., & Kaplin, D. (2017). You're hired! Mortality salience increases Americans' support for Donald Trump. *Analyses of Social Issues and Public Policy*, *17*(1), 339–357.

Cullen, F. T., Graham, A., Jonson, C. L., Pickett, J. T., Sloan, M. M., & Haner, M. (2022). The denier in chief: Faith in Trump and techniques of neutralization in a pandemic. *Deviant Behavior*, *43*, 829–851.

Day, M. V., Fiske, S. T., Downing, E. L., & Trail, T. E. (2014). Shifting liberal and conservative attitudes using moral foundations theory. *Personality and Social Psychology Bulletin*, *40*(12), 1559–1573.

Douglas, K. M., Sutton, R. M., & Cichocka, A. (2017). The psychology of conspiracy theories. *Current Directions in Psychological Science*, *26*(6), 538–542.

Fincher, C. L., & Thornhill, R. (2012). Parasite-stress promotes in-group assortative sociality: The cases of strong family ties and heightened religiosity. *Behavioral and Brain Sciences*, *35*(2), 61–79.

Garry, A., Walther, S., Rukaya, R., & Mohammed, A. (2021). QAnon conspiracy theory: Examining its evolution and mechanisms of radicalization. *Journal for Deradicalization*, *26*(3), 152–216.

Graham, A., Cullen, F. T., Pickett, J. T., Jonson, C. L., Haner, M., & Sloan, M. M. (2020). Faith in Trump, moral foundations, and social distancing defiance during the coronavirus pandemic. *Socius*, *6*, 1–23.

Graham, J., Haidt, J., Koleva, S., Motyl, M., Iyer, R., Wojcik, S. P., & Ditto, P. H. (2013). Moral foundations theory: The pragmatic validity of moral pluralism. *Advances in Experimental Social Psychology*, *47*, 55–130.

Graham, J., Haidt, J., Motyl, M., Meindl, P., Iskiwitch, C., & Mooijman, M. (2018). Moral foundations theory: On the advantages of moral pluralism over moral monism. In K. Gray & J. Graham (Eds.), *Atlas of moral psychology* (pp. 211–222). The Guilford Press.

Graham, J., Haidt, J., & Nosek, B. A. (2009). Liberals and conservatives rely on different sets of moral foundations. *Journal of Personality and Social Psychology, 96*(5), 1029–1046.

Graham, J., Nosek, B. A., Haidt, J., Iyer, R., Koleva, S., & Ditto, P. H. (2011). Mapping the moral domain. *Journal of Personality and Social Psychology, 101* (2), 366–385.

Greenberg, J., & Kosloff, S. (2008). Terror management theory: Implications for understanding prejudice, stereotyping, intergroup conflict, and political attitudes. *Social and Personality Psychology Compass, 2*(5), 1881–1894.

Greenberg, J., Pyszczynski, T., & Solomon, S. (1986). The causes and consequences of a need for self-esteem: A terror management theory. In R. F. Baumeister (Ed.), *Public self and private self* (pp. 189–212). Springer.

Haidt, J., & Graham, J. (2007). When morality opposes justice: Conservatives have moral intuitions that liberals may not recognize. *Social Justice Research, 20*(1), 98–116.

Haidt, J., & Joseph, C. (2004). Intuitive ethics: How innately prepared intuitions generate culturally variable virtues. *Daedalus, 133*(4), 55–66.

Hatemi, P. K., Crabtree, C., & Smith, K. B. (2019). Ideology justifies morality: Political beliefs predict moral foundations. *American Journal of Political Science, 63*(4), 788–806.

Horner, D. E., Sielaff, A., Pyszczyznski, T., & Greenberg, J. (2023). Terror management and the COVID-19 pandemic. In M. K. Miller (Ed.), *The social science of the COVID-19 pandemic: A call to action for researchers.* Oxford University Press. Manuscript in progress.

Human Rights Watch. (2020, October 28). Covid-19 fueling Anti-Asian racism and xenophobia worldwide. www.hrw.org/news/2020/05/12/covid-19-fueling-anti-asian-racism-and-xenophobia-worldwide

Jolley, D., Douglas, K. M., Leite, A. C., & Schrader, T. (2019). Belief in conspiracy theories and intentions to engage in everyday crime. *British Journal of Social Psychology, 58*(3), 534–549.

Karwowski, M., Kowal, M., Groyecka-Bernard, A., Białek, M., Lebuda, I., Sorokowska, A., & Sorokowski, P. (2020). When in danger, turn right: Does COVID-19 threat promote social conservatism and right-wing presidential candidates? *Human Ethology, 35*, 37–48.

Keith, M. (2022, January 8). QAnon influencer who spread conspiracy theories and misinformation about COVID-19 dies after contracting the virus. *Business Insider*. www.businessinsider.com/anti-vaxx-qanon-influencer-dies-after-contracting-covid-2022-1

Legare, R., & Rosen, J. (2022, January 27). QAnon follower from South Carolina who admitted he assaulted officers on January 6 sentenced to 44 months in prison. *CBS News*. www.cbsnews.com/news/january-6-nicolas-languerand-qanon-assault-sentence-44-months/

Leidner, B., Castano, E., Zaiser, E., & Giner-Sorolla, R. (2010). Ingroup glorification, moral disengagement, and justice in the context of collective violence. *Personality and Social Psychology Bulletin*, *36*(8), 1115–1129.

Maftei, A., & Holman, A. C. (2022). Beliefs in conspiracy theories, intolerance of uncertainty, and moral disengagement during the coronavirus crisis. *Ethics & Behavior*, *32*, 1–11.

Malka, A., Osborne, D., Soto, C. J., Greaves, L. M., Sibley, C. G., & Lelkes, Y. (2016). Binding moral foundations and the narrowing of ideological conflict to the traditional morality domain. *Personality and Social Psychology Bulletin*, *42*(9), 1243–1257.

Moll, J., Zahn, R., de Oliveira-Souza, R., Krueger, F., & Grafman, J. (2005). The neural basis of human moral cognition. *Nature Reviews Neuroscience*, *6*(10), 799–809.

Moynihan, D., & Porumbescu, G. (2020, September 16). Analysis | Trump's "Chinese virus" slur makes some people blame Chinese Americans. But others blame Trump. *The Washington Post*. www.washingtonpost.com/politics/2020/09/16/trumps-chinese-virus-slur-makes-some-people-blame-chinese-americans-others-blame-trump/

National Institute of Allergy and Infectious Diseases. (n.d.). Anthony S. Fauci, M.D., former NIAID director. www.niaid.nih.gov/about/director

O'Shea, B. A., Vitriol, J. A., Federico, C. M., Appleby, J., & Williams, A. L. (2022). Exposure and aversion to human transmissible diseases predict conservative ideological and partisan preferences. *Political Psychology*, *43*(1), 65–88.

Pazhoohi, F., & Kingstone, A. (2021). Associations of political orientation, xenophobia, right-wing authoritarianism, and concern of COVID-19: Cognitive responses to an actual pathogen threat. *Personality and Individual Differences*, *182*, 111081.

Porumbescu, G., Moynihan, D., Anastasopoulos, J., & Olsen, A. L. (2022). When blame avoidance backfires: Responses to performance framing and outgroup scapegoating during the COVID-19 pandemic. *Governance*. https://doi.org/10.1111/gove.12701

Pyszczynski, T. (2004). What are we so afraid of? A terror management theory perspective on the politics of fear. *Social Research: An International Quarterly*, *71*(4), 827–848.

Rosenfeld, D. L., & Tomiyama, A. J. (2021). Can a pandemic make people more socially conservative? Political ideology, gender roles, and the case of COVID-19. *Journal of Applied Social Psychology*, *51*(4), 425–433.

Rottweiler, B., & Gill, P. (2022). Conspiracy beliefs and violent extremist intentions: The contingent effects of self-efficacy, self-control and law-related morality. *Terrorism and Political Violence*, *34*, 1485–1504.

Rubin, O., Bruggeman, L., & Steakin, W. (2021). QAnon emerges as recurring theme of criminal cases tied to US capitol siege. *ABC News*. https://abcnews.go.com/US/qanon-emerges-recurring-theme-criminal-cases-tied-us/story?id=75347445

Schaller, M. (2011). The behavioral immune system and the psychology of human sociality. *Philosophical Transactions of the Royal Society*, *366*, 3418–3426.

Shao, W., & Hao, F. (2020). Confidence in political leaders can slant risk perceptions of COVID–19 in a highly polarized environment. *Social Science & Medicine*, *261*, 1–6.

Solomon, S., Greenberg, J., & Pyszczynski, T. (2015). *The worm at the core: On the role of death in life*. Random House.

Spring, M., & Wendling, M. (2020, September 2). How Covid-19 myths are merging with the QAnon conspiracy theory. *BBC News*. www.bbc.com/news/blogs-trending-53997203

Thornhill, R., & Fincher, C. L. (2014). The parasite-stress theory of sociality, the behavioral immune system, and human social and cognitive uniqueness. *Evolutionary Behavioral Sciences*, *8*(4), 257–264.

Timberg, C., & Dwoskin, E. (2021, March 11). With Trump gone, QAnon groups focus fury on attacking coronavirus vaccines. *The Washington Post*. www.washingtonpost.com/technology/2021/03/11/with-trump-gone-qanon-groups-focus-fury-attacking-covid-vaccines/

Tybur, J. M., Lieberman, D., Kurzban, R., & DeScioli, P. (2013). Disgust: Evolved function and structure. *Psychological Review*, 120(1), 65–84.

Weise, D. R., Pyszczynski, T., Cox, C. R., Arndt, J., Greenberg, J., Solomon, S., & Kosloff, S. (2008). Interpersonal politics: The role of terror management and attachment processes in shaping political preferences. *Psychological Science*, *19*(5), 448–455.

Wendling, M. S. (2020, September 2). How COVID-19 myths are merging with the QAnon conspiracy theory. *BBC News*. www.bbc.com/news/blogs-trending-53997203

CHAPTER 6

Emotions and the QAnon Conspiracy Theory

Elena Bessarabova and John A. Banas

Emotions and the QAnon Conspiracy Theory

Emotions permeate every aspect of human social functioning and have profound consequences for behaviors and decision-making (Frijda, 1987; Lazarus, 1991; Lerner & Keltner, 2000). Each discrete emotion is associated with a specific cognitive activity, physiological response, and action tendency (Lerner & Keltner, 2001). Emotions elicit distinct cognitive appraisals tied to the core meaning of the event that produced a particular emotion (Lazarus, 1991; Smith & Ellsworth, 1985), and those appraisals subsequently determine a variety of outcomes consistent with a specific emotion (Lerner & Keltner, 2001). The role of affect is complex, as it can have adaptive consequences determining successful human interaction and societal functioning, but it can be also a source of irrationality and bias (Bessarabova et al., 2020).

In what follows, we discuss the role of emotions in conspiratorial beliefs, focusing specifically on the QAnon conspiracy theory. In the chapter, we detail how emotions affect susceptibility to and dissemination of conspiratorial beliefs along with information processing and action tendencies associated with different types of emotions. The chapter concludes with a discussion of potential variables and mitigation strategies that might curb the proliferation of conspiratorial beliefs and a few suggestions for future research directions.

Emotions and Susceptibility to Conspiratorial Beliefs

Both positive and negative affective states influence how people become receptive to conspiratorial beliefs. Fearful/anxious psychological states along with stress are among the factors determining the endorsement of conspiratorial ideas (e.g. Grzesiak-Feldman, 2013; Swami et al., 2016). The appeal of conspiracies for people in the state of fear makes sense:

Conspiracy theories offer straightforward causal explanations for uncontrollable and upsetting events, providing seemingly rational accounts of social reality (Swami et al., 2016). Conspiracies can aid emotional regulation by providing fearful people with a sense of order and control (Douglas et al., 2019). Empirical evidence indicates that state and trait anxiety are positively related to conspiratorial thinking: For instance, state and trait anxiety were positively associated with conspiratorial beliefs about Jewish, German, and Arabic cultural out-groups (Grzesiak-Feldman, 2013), and trait anxiety was positively correlated with the endorsement of anti-Semitic conspiracies among high-school males (Grzesiak-Feldman, 2007). Similarly, by priming anxiety about the US economic crisis, Radnitz and Underwood (2017) found increased acceptance of a nonexistent conspiracy theory created for the purpose of the experimental induction (see Chapter 4 of this volume for more on the traits associated with QAnon support).

Fear and anxiety, along with stress and lost control, all seem to factor into the proliferation of QAnon. The rise of QAnon happened against the backdrop of one of the deadliest pandemics in recent history, which, when paired with trying economic times (e.g. the widening of the gap between the rich and poor, stagnating wages, a reduction in employment opportunities), does make the world seem unpredictable, chaotic, scary, stressful, and difficult to navigate (see Chapter 8 of this volume for more on the role of the events of 2020 in QAnon support). QAnon tells its supporters that even though forces of evil are conspiring against them, these forces have been identified and will be dealt with harshly. These main tenets of QAnon might help restore a sense of order, alleviate anxiety, and provide an illusion of control.

However, managing anxiety and negative affect is not the only reason why people are captivated by QAnon. Following QAnon is filled with positive affective experiences. As Roose (2021) notes, for QAnon believers the movement provides a sense of community and also functions as a significant source of entertainment. Daly (2020) compared QAnon to a massively multiplayer online video game, which gamifies solving mysteries and being in the know about secret knowledge. Like video games, QAnon invites its followers to participate in a shared social reality that has familiar characters and captivating plots (Roose, 2021). By offering supporters opportunities to participate in group missions – coordinated attacks on the enemy, similar to raids in some video games – it fosters a sense of camaraderie that promotes belonging (Daly, 2020). Overall, QAnon provides an immersive, wildly entertaining, and exciting experience, which likely contributes to why so many people became susceptible to its appeal (see Chapter 11 of this volume for more on QAnon and the need to belong).

Emotions and the Spread of Misinformation

Emotions have been shown to determine the transmission of information, with content containing intense (high-arousal) emotions being disseminated the most (Berger, 2011; Lewandowsky et al., 2012). Relative to emotionally neutral content, information intended to evoke anger, fear, disgust, or happiness is more likely to be shared through viral networks as well as interpersonal interactions (Berger & Milkman, 2012; Cotter, 2008; Heath et al., 2001; Peters et al., 2009). Similar effects were demonstrated with high-arousal, activating emotions of positive (awe) or negative (anger or anxiety) valence compared to deactivating emotions of low arousal (sadness), indicating that sad content was less likely to be shared, and high-arousal content (regardless of valence) was transmitted the most (Berger & Milkman, 2012).

These kinds of patterns of results were also found in research examining the relationships between emotions and the spread of misinformation. For instance, Vosoughi et al. (2018) analyzed a large corpus of fact-checked and widely spread Twitter news stories across a span of ten years and found that, relative to factual information that was shared, false news that went viral contained more novel information (i.e. likely producing awe and surprise). Furthermore, in replies to false news, Twitter users were more likely to reveal feelings of fear, disgust, and surprise relative to true stories that produced feelings of sadness and joy (Vosoughi et al., 2018). Given that information is more likely to be spread if it has strong emotional undertones (Berger & Milkman, 2012), people responding to fake information with surprise and strong negative emotional reactions can create a vicious cycle, contributing to the further spread of conspiratorial and unsubstantiated beliefs.

Because fearmongering and outrage seem to be such prevalent tactics in enticing readers to interact with news content (Reis et al., 2015), the fact that negative emotions contribute to the spread of misinformation is not surprising, but the role of positive, high-intensity affect in the dissemination of misinformation might seem counterintuitive. The reason why positive content, in general, is more likely to be shared could be due to self-presentation concerns: People like interacting with others who communicate in a positive and upbeat fashion and avoid people who bring them down (Berger & Milkman, 2012). Thus, sharing positive content, regardless of its accuracy, is one way to be seen in a positive light and be liked by others.

QAnon capitalizes on the motivational power of both positive and negative emotions and the intensity of emotional experience. QAnon information is rarely presented in emotionally neutral tones, and instead strong emotional language is used to agitate supporters, which likely contributes to how widespread it has become (see Chapter 8 of this volume for a discussion of QAnon's popularity). Q's posts, however, do not only promote fear and outrage: Although claiming that a pedophile ring is running the country is likely to induce anger and fear, suggesting that there is a plan and that help is on the way can make people feel hopeful, reassuring supporters that they should "trust the plan" and that "there's more good than bad" (Hoback, 2021).

Emotions and Information Processing

Recent research demonstrates that the endorsement of conspiratorial beliefs and misinformation might be an emotional affair rather than a cognitive one, with people who are emotionally invested being most susceptible to the appeal of conspiratorial and unsubstantiated beliefs (Sanchez & Dunning, 2021). Emotional investment wherein one's own political worldview is infused with positive affect and opposing worldviews are seen through a negative emotional lens is known as *affective polarization* (Iyengar et al., 2019). Affective polarization is prevalent among QAnon supporters, who tend to describe the movement and their leader in positive affective terms, using rhetoric filled with anticipation, excitement, and hope; in contrast, the language used in reference to the opposition tends to rely predominantly on negative affect and is fraught with expressions of anger, fear, and disgust (Hoback, 2021).

Affective polarization influences how people process information (see Chapter 4 of this volume for more on cognitive processing). Given that group affiliation and core beliefs are central to how people define themselves (Tajfel, 1981; Verplanken & Holland, 2002), unfavorable information that challenges those beliefs or threatens self-identity is dissonant (Aronson, 1992) and thus likely to be discounted. Conversely, favorable information about groups that are important to the self and unfavorable information about groups people oppose can help affirm the individual self-concept and reinforce one's worldview, and thus such information is more likely to be endorsed and trusted, especially by those who are emotionally involved (Sanchez & Dunning, 2021). Since QAnon supporters appear to be emotionally intertwined with the movement, they are more likely to endorse politically friendly misbeliefs, even the most egregious ones (e.g. that the Democrats in charge not only molest children but also consume their victims to prolong their lives; Roose, 2021) because endorsing such beliefs is affectively rewarding. As Sanchez and Dunning (2021) explain:

> [P]eople endorse misbeliefs ... to satisfy epistemic aims, that is, to render their environment understandable and predictable, to feel safe and in control, and to maintain positive self-image and status for the self and their social group (Douglas & Sutton, 2018; Douglas et al., 2017). Such belief allows them to feel affirmed and "in the know" rather than anxious (Morgan et al., 2013). In contrast, endorsing unfriendly political beliefs offers no such gain in validation ... Endorsing such information contradicts one's worldview, questions one's knowledge and objectivity, and brings preferred outcomes into greater doubt. As such, partisans should be motivated to deny rather than endorse such misbeliefs. (p. 2)

QAnon exists in a particular informational space where affective polarization thrives. Q-drops appear first in the dark corners of the internet (different message boards over time, some of which – ironically for a movement dedicated to fighting high-power pedophiles – do contain videos of actual child pornography) and then are aggregated on more user-friendly and less disturbing websites like QMaps (Turton & Brustein, 2020). The "analysis" of Q-drops is done by various people and YouTube personalities – fans of the movement and true believers – who use emotionally laden language to engage with their followers. In this *new paradigm of truth*, the opinions of those with legitimate authority and expertise are questioned and discounted, and anybody can proclaim themselves to be an expert (Weeks & Garrett, 2019; see Chapter 13 of this volume for an analysis of such messages). Compared to other social media platforms (like Facebook or Twitter) where QAnon supporters might encounter attitudinally heterogeneous beliefs and might have to engage in uncivil, anger-fueled discussions, retreating to attitudinally consistent venues is one approach to regulate anger.

Although QAnon supporters might flock to friendly sources to avoid anger, being angry is unavoidable in QAnon. Embracing QAnon's worldview necessitates believing that the world is fundamentally unjust and run by people praying on innocents by committing unspeakable acts. Because perceptions of injustice represent one of the core appraisals igniting anger (van Zomeren et al., 2018), thinking about the central tenets of QAnon should activate affective and cognitive processes consistent with the profile of people in angry states. Specifically, anger can result in confirmation bias and unwillingness to consider new ideas and motivate exposure to and endorsement of attitudinally friendly information, regardless of its accuracy (Huddy et al., 2007; MacKuen et al., 2010; Valentino et al., 2008; Weeks, 2015). Consumption of partisan content has been shown to promote misinformation (e.g. Meirick & Bessarabova, 2016; see Weeks & Garett, 2019 for a discussion), including unsubstantiated and conspiratorial beliefs.

Angry people, however, do sometimes abandon the comforts of attitudinally friendly sources to venture into hostile venues seeking out identity-threatening information (Arpan & Nabi, 2011; Han & Arpan, 2017). Because anger is an approach emotion (motivating action to restore a desired state/interrupted goal; Carver & Harmon-Jones, 2009), attempts to engage with the opposing side make sense. However, it appears to be a motivated engagement: Seeking out such identity-threatening information does not seem to be driven by accuracy concerns because the information from the opposing side is sought "for the purpose of future debate, assessing the nature and extent of negative information about the group, defending existing views (e.g. Arpan & Nabi, 2011; Hwang et al., 2008; Matthes, 2011), and/or ... to be ready to discuss issues with non-likeminded others (Mutz, 2006)" (Han & Arpan, 2017, pp. 260–261).

Anger also seems to result in the preference for subsequent information that is matched in emotional tone (i.e. angry people want more information that makes them angry), and if the emotional tone is matched, angry people are more likely to find the information convincing (Weeks & Garrett, 2019). For example, DeSteno et al. (2004) found that feeling angry about anti-American demonstrations in the Middle East made participants endorse an anger-framed appeal about local taxes more than when the appeal was framed to evoke sadness. Studying unsubstantiated beliefs, Na et al. (2018) likewise reported that, relative to a low-anger condition, when people were made angry after reading about the mismanagement of a health crisis, they were also more likely to accept a rumor – unsubstantiated information – that matched the emotion in the original article (i.e. also contained anger-inducing themes). These effects of preference for affectively congruent information are troubling, as they suggest that people are more likely to accept misinformation because it matches how they feel. Given that anger is often used to signal-boost misinformation (Reis et al., 2015), false claims that evoke anger are likely to be accepted as true, especially if they promote attitudinally consistent falsehoods (Weeks & Garett, 2019). It is not surprising then that when QAnon followers helped spread and promote misinformation about COVID-19, social justice protests, and the 2020 election (Roose, 2021), many of these stories appealed to anger. Perhaps when anger is stirred by one conspiracy theory, being exposed to the angering information about other conspiratorial beliefs makes people more likely to endorse and spread other conspiracies and misinformation (see Chapters 12 and 13 of this volume for more on misinformation).

Emotions and Actions

QAnon supporters have gone beyond chatrooms and online conversations, moving from a fringe group clad in "Q" T-shirts of die-hard Trump supporters into the mainstream (Tornoe, 2021), and they quickly progressed from violent rhetoric to action. From murdering a crime boss in New York believed by the assailant to be a member of the Deep State, multiple kidnappings and assassination plots (Beckett, 2020) to the alleged participation in the deadly insurrection at the Capitol (Tornoe, 2021), violence or attempts at violence committed by QAnon believers have been on the rise, prompting the Department of Homeland Security to list QAnon as a domestic terror group at an increased risk of violence (Levy & Kesling, 2021). Emotions, particularly anger, are likely to play a role in the increase in violent actions. As one QAnon supporter (now convicted on terrorism charges for bridge obstruction with a heavily armed vehicle; AP News, 2020) explains, his decision to resort to violence was motivated by frustration that the highly anticipated mass arrests have not been happening, and he consequently acted upon "a series of poorly constructed decisions that were based on emotional pain" (Brean & Hawkins, 2018, para. 11).

Resorting to extreme action because of anger is consistent with how angry people act. Anger results from perceptions of goal interruption (Lazarus, 1991), hardship, or injustice (van Zomeren et al., 2018). Based on the appraisal tendency framework, anger makes people feel certain and in control (Lerner & Keltner, 2000). As an approach emotion, anger motivates attempts to confront injustice (Carver & Harmon-Jones, 2009) and has been shown to predict a wide range of collective action (see van Zomeren et al., 2018 for a review). One theory – the anger activism model – predicts that anger's action potential is at its highest when anger is intense and efficacy beliefs (i.e. a perception of a route to remedy the problem or correct the injustice) are strong (Turner, 2007).

The model predicts that, under these conditions, people are likely to go to great lengths to fix the problem and to be willing to engage in behaviors that require effort. Although empirical support for the anger activism model's predictions has been mixed, the connection between anger and activism attitudes and intentions is well demonstrated, as anger has been shown to increase intentions to engage in action to end smoking (Ilakkuvan et al., 2017), to participate in activism against unfair university policies (Turner et al., 2020), to increase support for various causes (mediated through increased efficacy beliefs; Austin et al., 2020), as well as to fight against companies marketing unhealthy, excessively sweet beverages to children (Skurka, 2019).

In addition to activism, anger motivates people to take punitive action against anger-inducing entities. Anger stems from the appraisals of offense and perceptions of accountability (Lerner et al., 1998), motivating attributions of blame (Lerner & Keltner, 2000, 2001; Smith & Ellsworth, 1985) and attempts at retribution (Nabi, 2003). Nabi (2003), for instance, experimentally manipulated anger and fear in messages targeting drunk driving and tested the effect of each emotion on decision-making. She found that fear prompted participants to list societal causes for drunk driving along with protective solutions, whereas anger made participants write down personal attributions (e.g. the offender's carelessness or stupidity) and suggest punitive solutions (e.g. harsher sentences for offenders). Because angry people are more likely to see other people or entities as being responsible for their anger (Lerner & Keltner, 2000), action fueled by anger is often directed at some out-group that can be held responsible for the injustice (van Zomeren et al., 2018). There are many examples of retributive action targeting out-groups perpetrated by QAnon supporters, with the January 6, 2021, insurrection in Washington, DC being the most notable one.

Mitigation Approaches to Stopping the Proliferation of QAnon

In addition to examining the role of emotions in the spread of QAnon, we explore potential variables and mitigation approaches that could be helpful in curbing the proliferation of QAnon propaganda as well as other conspiracy theories. Recently, there has been an increase in research testing a variety of mitigation techniques attempting to find effective solutions. Below, we detail several of those variables and mitigation approaches, focusing specifically on the methods that could help address the affective influences underlying the susceptibility to and propagation of conspiratorial beliefs.

In considering why people endorse outrageous conspiracy theories, a lack of intelligence seems like an easy and obvious answer. If that is the case, then educational and informational techniques should be effective at reducing misinformation. Consistent with this idea, some research indicates that education (e.g. Cox, 2021) and intelligence (e.g. Pennycook & Rand, 2019) do seem to make people less susceptible to conspiracies and misinformation. However, research focusing on how emotionally invested people process information suggests that although intelligence might reduce the endorsement of misinformation in general, when beliefs are tied to a person's identify or are central to their worldview, emotional investment hijacks the ability to rationally process information, resulting instead in affective polarization.

Sanchez and Dunning's (2021) study demonstrates the role of emotional investments in information processing. Their participants were given either attitudinally consistent or discrepant political misinformation and were asked to imagine that most people believed in the statements they read. Finding out that many people endorsed the opposite-party misinformation made participants dissonant, and seeing consensus regarding misinformation that favored their political beliefs made them feel validated. Then, participants were given the opportunity to rate the extent to which they believed the information they read earlier was true and to indicate how the process of rating made them feel. Emotionally invested participants were eager to denounce political misinformation that favored the opposite side and, as a result, felt more validated because it helped "repair" the emotional distress from previous exposure to dissonant information (see Chapter 4 of this volume for more on cognitive biases).

Given how emotionally invested QAnon supporters are, attempting to debias people through media literacy or debunking efforts is likely to be futile. Attitudinally discrepant information highlighting inconsistencies and falsehoods within the conspiracy theory would only make staunch QAnon supporters feel inadequate and in need of validation to help reaffirm their worldview. Because (as discussed earlier) emotionally invested people are highly attuned to the affective consequences of the information they receive, they would likely approach new information with an eye toward identity affirmation and consistency instead of accuracy. As a result, attitudinally inconsistent information will be rejected, possibly motivating even greater support for the movement.

A more effective strategy is to make people resilient to misinformation before they become emotionally invested. Several approaches might be useful in this respect. First, to help people resist the affective techniques used to spread misinformation, some research indicates that developing *emotional intelligence* – a skill associated with "being able to accurately perceive and reflect on emotional content, to make correct links between emotion and context, and the ability to regulate one's own emotional reactivity" – can be beneficial in making people less prone to falling for the emotionally manipulative tactics used to disseminate fake news (Preston et al., 2021, p. 2). Consistent with this idea, a study with participants from the UK found that more emotionally intelligent participants, who were better able to disregard the emotionally charged content presented in misinformation, were also better equipped to assess the veracity of information (Preston et al., 2021). Thus, developing and practicing one's emotional intelligence skills might help people to be more savvy information consumers, making them less likely to become susceptible to fake news and conspiracy propaganda. Future research should explore how emotional intelligence relates to affective polarization, examining directly the appeal of QAnon propaganda.

Second, encouraging analytic processing of information could also help make affective manipulation (e.g. clickbait, fearmongering) less effective. Given that conspiratorial ideas become more attractive in times of stress, uncertainty, and lost control, attempts at promoting deliberative thinking might be challenging because stress impairs analytic thinking and undermines people's ability to critically evaluate information (Starcke & Brand, 2012). Furthermore, relying on intuitive instead of analytic approaches to information processing has been shown to promote endorsement of a wide range of conspiracy theories (e.g. New World Order; Swami et al., 2014). To promote critical thinking, training people to ask themselves "Is the source being manipulative?" or "Is the use of emotion genuine or is it done to trick me into doing something?" might be sufficient to make people critically evaluate information and check the intention behind an emotional appeal. Research indicates that when people are aware that a message or a source used emotion to induce persuasion, and the intent is seen as manipulative, they become reactant and less likely to be persuaded or to comply with what the message is advocating (e.g. Bessarabova et al., 2015).

Third, as discussed above, many QAnon beliefs are fueled by anger, and when anger is associated with core identity beliefs (political/worldview beliefs being some of them), this could result in biased information processing, confirmation bias, motivated information-seeking (e.g. Han & Arpan, 2017; MacKuen et al., 2010), and the endorsement of partisan misinformation (Weeks, 2015). Given these approaches to information processing, committed QAnon supporters will be unlikely to consider and be swayed by new information critical of QAnon. Thus, as noted, debunking QAnon to its angry followers is likely to be ineffective. A better approach is a "prebunking" technique grounded in decades of inoculation theory research (e.g. McGuire, 1961, see also the meta-analysis of inoculation effects in Banas & Rains, 2010). This mitigation approach entails making people motivated to defend themselves against conspiratorial beliefs and then providing them with information on, for example, how emotionally laden conspiracy propaganda can be identified, along with the counterarguments that are useful in defending oneself against future persuasion attempts from sources spreading conspiracies and other misinformation. Several studies have confirmed the efficacy of the inoculation approach against conspiracy theories (e.g. Banas & Miller, 2013; Banas et al., 2022; see Chapter 15 of this volume for more information on how inoculation theory works in preventing conspiratorial ideation). Future research should specifically test the effectiveness of inoculation strategies against the affective manipulation used in conspiracy theories.

Finally, another effective approach might be countering the QAnon movement using some of its own techniques. Given that QAnon relies heavily on gamification (Roose, 2021), serious video games can be used to educate people about conspiratorial influences and to help them spot affective misinformation (see Chapter 15 of this volume). Serious video games have been successful at mitigating a wide range of biases, including conformation bias, fundamental attribution error, and the bias blind spot (e.g. Bessarabova et al., 2016; Lee et al., 2021). Recently, there have been attempts at using online games to teach people how to identify misinformation that have revealed some promising findings (e.g. Roozenbeek & van der Linden, 2019). Given the popularity of video games among younger people, future research could be particularly fruitful in this direction.

Comparing QAnon to Other Groups

QAnon is an umbrella conspiracy that has borrowed its content heavily from other conspiracy theories (e.g. the Kennedy assassination, the 9/11 Truth movement), and even its main premise that the world is run by some shadowy cabal is rooted in centuries-old anti-Semitic tropes (Roose, 2021). Thus, in terms of the belief system, QAnon, at its core, is not new. What is new is how the movement has been able to capitalize on new technologies and go beyond fearmongering and scare tactics to create a fun, interactive experience wherein people from different walks of life can congregate. Followers have positive affective experiences with QAnon because decoding the latest Q-drops is exciting, and so is discussing theories with fellow believers. In a world where people feel disconnected, QAnon offers a sense of community and bonding with like-minded people. Thus, it is not surprising how widespread this conspiracy theory has become.

In terms of other affective processes described in the chapter, the effects of emotions, contributing to the proliferation of conspiratorial beliefs and biased information processing, are not specific to QAnon. Affective polarization, for instance, is a trend that tracks well with the mainstream politics in the USA: As a 2016 Pew poll indicates, about half of Democrats and Republicans described the opposite party with fear and anger, and over 40 percent of respondents viewed the other side as a threat to America (Pew Research Center, 2016).

Conclusions

QAnon poses a significant threat to democracy and the well-being of American society. It capitalizes on positive and negative emotions to create a captivating experience for its followers while simultaneously promoting fear and energizing its supporters through appeals to anger. In some respects, QAnon functions similarly to video games, creating interactive and immersive experiences that have attracted many people. Because QAnon uses the motivational power of anger, the increased engagement and the rise of violence perpetrated by QAnon supporters are likely to continue. Therefore, it becomes particularly important to prevent the conspiratorial ideas of QAnon from spreading further. To combat the affective strategies underlying QAnon, potential approaches (as outlined in this chapter) might involve developing and practicing emotional intelligence skills to help recognize the manipulative affective strategies used by the outlets promoting misinformation and conspiratorial beliefs, emphasizing critical and analytic thinking, and using preemptive strategies to inoculate those who have not yet succumbed to QAnon propaganda. To match the gamification strategies employed by QAnon, researchers should continue looking into gaming and video game strategies to make preventative communication tactics more palatable to users. Overall, the processes and mitigation techniques described in this chapter have implications beyond the QAnon conspiracy theory and could be applied to address other types of conspiratorial beliefs and the spread of misinformation in general.

REFERENCES

AP News. (2020, December 22). Man gets prison for 2018 armed Hoover Dam bridge barricade. *AP News*. https://apnews.com/article/kingman-las-vegas-arizona-colorado-river-nevada-f1ab90c182bbd94a1511a3cdb8f6786a

Aronson, E. (1992). The return of the repressed: Dissonance theory makes a comeback. *Psychological Inquiry*, *3*, 303–311.

Arpan, L. M., & Nabi, R. L. (2011). Exploring anger in the hostile media process: Effects on news preferences and source evaluation. *Journalism and Mass Communication Quarterly*, *88*, 5–22.

Austin, L., Overton, H., McKeever, B. W., & Bortree, D. (2020). Examining the rage donation trend: Applying the anger activism model to explore communication and donation behaviors. *Public Relations Review*, *46*, 1–8.

Banas, J. A., & Miller, G. (2013). Inducing resistance to conspiracy theory propaganda: Testing inoculation and meta-inoculation strategies. *Human Communication Research*, *40*, 1–24.

Banas, J. A., & Rains, S. A. (2010). A meta-analysis of research on inoculation theory. *Communication Monographs*, *77*, 281–311.

Banas, J. A., Bessarabova, E., Talbert, N., & Penkauskas, M. (2022). Inoculating against anti-vax conspiracies. Paper presented at the *National Communication Association*, New Orleans, LA.

Beckett, L. (2020, October 16) QAnon: A timeline of violence linked to the conspiracy theory. *The Guardian*. www.theguardian.com/us-news/2020/oct/15/qanon-violence-crimes-timeline

Berger, J. (2011). Arousal increases social transmission of information. *Psychological Science*, *22*, 891–893.

Berger J., & Milkman K. L. (2012). What makes online content viral? *Journal of Marketing Research*, *49*, 192–205.

Bessarabova, E., Banas, J. A., & Bernard, D. R. (2020). Emotional appeals in message design. In D. O'Hair & M. J. O'Hair (Eds.), *Handbook of applied communication research* (pp. 103–122). Sage.

Bessarabova, E., Piercy, C., King, S., Vincent, C., Dunbar, N. E., Burgoon, J. K., Miller, C. H., Jensen, M., Elkins, A., Wilson, D., Wilson, S. N., & Lee, Y.-H. (2016). Mitigating bias blind spot via a serious video game. *Computers in Human Behavior*, *62*, 452–466.

Bessarabova, E., Turner, M. M., Fink, E. L., & Blustein, N. B. (2015). Extending the theory of reactance to guilt appeals: "You ain't guiltin' me into nothin'." *Zeitschrift für Psychologie*, *223*, 215–224.

Brean, H., & Hawkins, D. (2018, July 13). Suspect in Hoover Dam standoff writes Trump, cites conspiracy in letters. *Las Vegas Review Journal*. www.reviewjournal.com/crime/courts/suspect-in-hoover-dam-standoff-writes-trump-cites-conspiracy-in-letters/

Carver, C. S., & Harmon-Jones, E. (2009). Anger is an approach-related affect: Evidence and implications. *Psychological Bulletin*, *135*(2), 183–204.

Cotter, E. M. (2008). Influence of emotional content and perceived relevance on spread of urban legends: A pilot study. *Psychological Reports*, *102*, 623–629.

Cox, D. A. (2021, February 11). After the ballots are counted: Conspiracies, political violence, and American exceptionalism. *The American Survey Center*. www.americansurveycenter.org/research/after-the-ballots-are-counted-conspiracies-political-violence-and-american-exceptionalism/

Daly, K. (2020, August 18). How QAnon works like a video game to hook people? *Axios*. www.axios.com/qanon-video-game-cbbacb1e-969c-4f07-93cd-69e41bc6feeb.html

DeSteno, D., Petty, R. E., Rucker, D. D., Wegener, D. T., & Braverman, J. (2004). Discrete emotions and persuasion: The role of emotion-induced expectancies. *Journal of Personality and Social Psychology*, *86*, 43–56.

Douglas, K. M., & Sutton, R. M. (2018). Why conspiracy theories matter: A social psychological analysis. *European Review of Social Psychology*, *29*(1), 256–298.

Douglas, K. M., Sutton, R. M., & Cichocka, A. (2017). The psychology of conspiracy theories. *Current Directions in Psychological Science*, *26*(6), 538–542.

Douglas, K. M., Uscinski, J. E., Sutton, R. M., Cichocka, A., Nefes, T., Ang, C. S., & Deravi, F. (2019). Understanding conspiracy theories. *Political Psychology*, *40*, 3–35.

Frijda, N. H. (1987). Emotion, cognitive structure, and action tendency. *Cognition and Emotion*, *1*, 115–143.

Grzesiak-Feldman, M. (2007). Conspiracy thinking and state–trait anxiety in young Polish adults. *Psychological Reports*, *100*, 199–202.

(2013). The effect of high-anxiety situations on conspiracy thinking. *Current Psychology*, *32*, 100–118.

Han, Y.-H., & Arpan, L. (2017). The effects of news bias-induced anger, anxiety, and issue novelty on subsequent news preferences. *Advances in Journalism and Communication*, *5*, 256–277.

Heath, C., Bell, C., & Sternberg, E. (2001). Emotional selection in memes: The case of urban legends. *Journal of Personality and Social Psychology*, *81*, 1028–1041.

Hoback, C. (2021). Q: Into the storm [Documentary]. HBO.

Huddy, L., Feldman, S., & Cassese, E. (2007). On the distinct political effects of anxiety and anger. In W. R. Neuman, G. E. Marcus, A. Criegler, & M. MacKuen (Eds.), *The affect effect: Dynamics of emotion in political thinking and behavior* (pp. 202–230). University of Chicago Press.

Hwang, H., Pan, Z., & Sun, Y. (2008). Influence of hostile media perception on willingness to engage in discursive activities: An examination of mediating role of media indignation. *Media Psychology*, *11*, 76–97.

Ilakkuvan, V., Turner, M. M., Cantrell, J., Hair, E., & Vallone, D. (2017). The relationship between advertising-induced anger and self-efficacy on persuasive outcomes. *Family & Community Health*, *40*(1), 72–80.

Iyengar, S., Lelkes, Y., Levendusky, M., Malhotra, N., & Westwood, S. J. (2019). The origins and consequences of affective polarization in the United States. *Annual Review of Political Science*, *22*, 129–146.

Lazarus, R. S. (1991). *Emotion and adaptation*. Oxford University Press.

Lee, Y., Dunbar, N., Miller, C. H., Bessarabova, E., Jensen, M., Wilson, S. N., Elizondo, J., Burgoon, J., & Valacich, J. (2021). Mitigating bias and improving professional decision making through digital game play. In J. Raessens, B. Schouten, J. Jansz, T. d. l. H. Conde-Pumpido, M. Kors, & R. Jacobs (Eds.), *Persuasive gaming in context* (pp. 239–258). Amsterdam University Press.

Lerner, J. S., & Keltner, D. (2000). Beyond valence: Toward a model of emotion specific influences on judgment and choice. *Cognition and Emotion, 14*(4), 473–493.

(2001). Fear, anger, and risk. *Journal of Personality and Social Psychology, 81*(1), 146–159.

Lerner, J. S., Goldberg, J. H., & Tetlock, P. E. (1998). Sober second thought: The effects of accountability, anger and authoritarianism on attributions of responsibility. *Personality and Social Psychology Bulletin, 24*, 563–574.

Levy, R., & Kesling, B. (2021, January 27). DHS issues its first national terrorism bulletin for domestic extremists. *Wall Street Journal*. www.wsj.com/articles/dhs-issues-national-terrorism-alert-for-domestic-extremists-11611770893

Lewandowsky, S., Ecker, U. K. H., Seifert, C. M., Schwarz, N., & Cook, J. (2012). Misinformation and its correction: Continued influence and successful debiasing. *Psychological Science in the Public Interest, 13*(3), 106–131.

MacKuen, M., Wolak, J., Keele, L., & Marcus, G. E. (2010). Civic engagements: Resolute partisanship or reflective deliberation. *American Journal of Political Science, 54*, 440–458.

Matthes, J. (2011). Exposure to counterattitudinal news coverage and the timing of voting decisions. *Communication Research, 39*, 147–169.

McGuire, W. J. (1961). The effectiveness of supportive and refutational defenses in immunizing and restoring beliefs against persuasion. *Sociometry*, 24, 184–197.

Meirick, P. C., & Bessarabova, E. (2016). Epistemic factors in selective exposure and political misperceptions on the right and left. *Analyses of Social Issues and Public Policy, 16*(1), 36–68.

Morgan, C. A., III, Southwick, S., Steffian, G., Hazlett, G. A., & Loftus, E. F. (2013). Misinformation can influence memory for recently experienced, highly stressful events. *International Journal of Law and Psychiatry, 36*(1), 11–17.

Mutz, D. C. (2006). *Hearing the other side: Deliberative versus participatory democracy*. Cambridge University Press.

Na, K., Garrett, R. K., & Slater, M. D. (2018). Rumor acceptance during public health crises: Testing the emotional congruence hypothesis, *Journal of Health Communication, 23*(8), 791–799.

Nabi, R. L. (2003). Exploring the framing effects of emotion: Do discrete emotions differentially influence information accessibility, information seeking, and policy preference? *Communication Research, 30*, 224–247.

Pennycook, G., & Rand, D. G. (2019). Lazy, not biased: Susceptibility to partisan fake news is better explained by lack of reasoning than by motivated reasoning. *Cognition*, *188*, 39–50.

Peters, K., Kashima, Y., & Clark, A. (2009). Talking about others: Emotionality and the dissemination of social information. *European Journal of Social Psychology*, *39*, 207–222.

Pew Research Center. (2016). Partisanship and political animosity in 2016. www.pewresearch.org/politics/2016/06/22/partisanship-and-political-animosity-in-2016/

Preston, S., Anderson, A., Robertson, D. J., Shephard, M. P., & Huhe, N. (2021). Detecting fake news on Facebook: The role of emotional intelligence. *PLoS ONE*, *16*(3), e0246757.

Radnitz, S., & Underwood, P. (2017). Is belief in conspiracy theories pathological? A survey on the cognitive roots of extreme suspicion. *British Journal of Political Science*, *47*, 113–129.

Reis, J., Benevenuto, F., Olmo, P., Prates, R., Kwak, H., & An, J. (2015). Breaking the news: First impressions matter on online news. *Proceedings of the 9th International Conference on Web and Social Media, ICWSM 2015*, Oxford, UK, May 26–29 (pp. 357–366). https://ink.library.smu.edu.sg/sis_research/5339

Roose, K. (2021, June 15). What is QAnon, the viral pro-Trump conspiracy theory? *New York Times*. www.nytimes.com/article/what-is-qanon.html

Roozenbeek, J., & van der Linden, S. (2019). The fake news game: Actively inoculating against the risk of misinformation. *Journal of Risk Research*, *22*, 570–580.

Sanchez, C., & Dunning, D. (2021). Cognitive and emotional correlates of belief in political misinformation: Who endorses partisan misbeliefs? *Emotion*, *21* (5), 1091–1102.

Skurka, C. (2019). You mad? Using anger appeals to promote activism intentions and policy support in the context of sugary drink marketing to kids. *Health Communication*, *34*(14), 1775–1787.

Smith, C. A., & Ellsworth, P. C. (1985). Patterns of cognitive appraisal in emotion. *Journal of Personality and Social Psychology*, *48*, 813–838.

Starcke, K., & Brand, M. (2012). Decision making under stress: A selective review. *Neuroscience and Biobehavioral Reviews*, *36*, 1228–1248.

Swami, V., Furnham, A., Smyth, N., Weis, L., Lay, A., & Clow, A. (2016). Putting the stress on conspiracy theories: Examining associations between psychological stress, anxiety, and belief in conspiracy theories, *Personality and Individual Differences*, *99*, 72–76.

Swami, V., Voracek, M., Stieger, S., Tran, U. S., & Furnham, A. (2014). Analytic thinking reduces belief in conspiracy theories. *Cognition*, *133*(3), 572–585.

Tajfel, H. (1981). *Human groups and social categories: Studies in social psychology*. Cambridge University Press.

Tornoe, R. (2021, March 1). Journalists battle the misinformation pandemic *Editor & Publisher*. www.editorandpublisher.com/stories/journalists-battle-the-misinformation-pandemic,187699

Turner, M. M. (2007). Using emotion in risk communication: The anger activism model. *Public Relations Review*, *33*, 114–119.

Turner, M. M., Richards, A. S., Bessarabova, E., & Magid, Y. (2020). The effects of anger appeals on systematic processing and intentions: The moderating role of efficacy. *Communication Reports*, 33, 14–26.

Turton, W., & Brustein, J. (2020, October 7). QAnon high priest was just trolling away as a Citigroup tech executive. *Bloomberg*. www.bloomberg.com/news/features/2020-10-07/who-is-qanon-evangelist-qmap-creator-and-former-citigroup-exec-jason-gelinas

Valentino, N. A., Hutchings, V. H., Banks, A. J., & Davis, A. K. (2008). Is a worried citizen a good citizen? Emotions, political information seeking, and learning via the Internet. *Political Psychology*, *29*, 247–273.

van Zomeren, M., Saguy, T., Mazzoni, D., & Cicognani, E. (2018). The curious, context-dependent case of anger: Explaining voting intentions in three different national elections. *Journal of Applied Social Psychology*, *48*(6), 329–338.

Verplanken, B., & Holland, R. W. (2002). Motivated decision making: Effects of activation and self-centrality of values on choices and behavior. *Journal of Personality and Social Psychology*, *82*(3), 434–447.

Vosoughi, S., Roy, D., & Aral, S. (2018). The spread of true and false news online. *Science*, *359*(6380), 1146–1151.

Weeks, B. E. (2015). Emotions, partisanship, and misperceptions: How anger and anxiety moderate the effect of partisan bias on susceptibility to political misinformation. *Journal of Communication*, *65*, 699–719.

Weeks, B. E., & Garrett, R. K. (2019). Emotional characteristics of social media and political misperceptions. In J. E. Katz & K. K. Mays (Eds.), *Journalism and truth in an age of social media* (pp. 236–250). Oxford University Press.

CHAPTER 7

Recruitment to QAnon

Ordinary Persuasion and Human Agency or "Brainwashing"?

James T. Richardson

This chapter discusses recruitment techniques used by QAnon, which is viewed by some as a new quasi-religious movement or a movement that has infiltrated some churches (Argentino, 2020; Beaty, 2020; LaFrance, 2020; also see Chapter 16 of this volume). I compare and contrast QAnon recruitment techniques to those of new religious movements (NRMs) and political movements from the 1960s, 1970s, and 1980s in America. As with earlier movements, QAnon uses existing networks among family, friends, and colleagues for recruitment, but QAnon also has used internet sites that allow its postings. QAnon then builds on those initial contacts with social psychological techniques such as "foot-in-the-door" by starting with small activities meant to hook potential converts to the QAnon cause. Other social psychological processes for developing commitment are also relevant, as will be discussed. First, an examination of research findings on recruitment to NRMs and political movements of the 1960s and onward will be offered as background to QAnon and to demonstrate important differences as well.

Recruitment to Political and Religious Movements of Past Decades

The 1960s were times of great turmoil in America brought on by the Vietnam War and overt racism and sexism in American society, among other pressures. Many young people rebelled against the institutional structures and values of society and sought other avenues of activity that would make their lives more meaningful. The rejection was most obvious with the many and large anti-Vietnam War demonstrations that occurred, in which many thousands of America's most educated and affluent youth protested American involvement in Southeast Asia.

Appreciation is expressed for helpful comments from David Bromley, Lorne Dawson, and Stuart Wright on an earlier version of this chapter.

These protests reached a crescendo after the invasion of Cambodia, and violence was often associated with such activities around the country. However, other forms of protest also developed, perhaps in part because of the apparent lack of effectiveness of antiwar protests. Thousands of America's youth became involved in the drug subculture, perhaps choosing to just "drop out" of American society completely. Many others began to participate in alternative religions of various kinds, including both indigenous ones based on variants of Christianity (i.e. Jesus Movement groups) and foreign religious movements derived from the cultures of the Far East and India.

The mass exodus of many of America's young people from their usual social locations and career trajectories caused considerable disquiet among societal leaders and especially the parents of those who were choosing rebellion, either political, religious, or through drugs. Explanations or "accounts" (Scott & Lyman, 1968) were sought to explain what was happening. "Outside agitators," liberal college professors, and other ideas were tried out as explanations of the disquiet among America's youth. However, solid research on these political movements by a few young (at the time) researchers, some of whom were themselves involved in these forms of rebellion, led to different conclusions (Flacks, 1967, 1973; Levine, 1986; Skolnick, 1969). What they found was that young people were not being duped by anyone but were acting out their values and exercising their human agency to show their unhappiness with what was happening in America. The Vietnam War and the racism and sexism that was rampant were not accepted by many members of the largest generation of college-educated young people in America's history. These young people sought major changes in American society, even though their efforts led to many clashes with authorities in society.

Even as these political movements were developing (and perhaps because of their perceived ineffectiveness) many young people sought other ways to live and other values to espouse. Alternative religions, often referred to by the pejorative term "cults" (Richardson, 1993a) or as NRMs by most scholars, developed and spread in America, attracting thousands of young people. Many of the most well-known and controversial were communal, including the Unification Church, Hare Krishna, Jesus Movement groups such as the Children of God, or the Bhagwan Rajneesh, which settled for years in eastern Oregon. These movement groups caused much consternation, and again explanations were sought as to why thousands of young people would leave their families, friends, schools, and career paths to join such groups, even if for only a short time period (which was the usual pattern). A very popular and self-serving "account" that developed and was promoted by those opposing such groups was that of "brainwashing."

Supposedly, the leaders of these new movements, some of whom were foreign, had developed a powerful psychotechnology that could overcome the will of the brightest and best in America, forcing them to succumb to the entreaties of those malevolent leaders. This explanation had a dubious intellectual heritage to be sure, deriving from efforts to propagandize about resocialization efforts after the communist takeover in China and to "explain" why a small number of American GIs refused repatriation after hostilities ceased in Korea (Lifton, 1961; Schein, 1961).

This odd intellectual heritage notwithstanding, "brainwashing" (and companion terms "mind control" and "psychological coercion") became a handy device or account to explain the development of interest in NRMs by many of America's youth. This pseudoscientific explanation (Anthony, 1990; Anthony & Robbins, 2004; Ginsburg & Richardson, 1998) was widely promoted by some parents of young NRM members, by mass media, and by other institutions in America, and was for a time even accepted in courts, leading to several large judgments against some NRMs by former members (most were overturned on appeal).

But sound research similar to that on the protest movements eventually overcame the simplistic brainwashing thesis, at least in some quarters, as researchers discovered that participants in NRMs were not tricked or duped but had come into those groups as "seekers" (Balch & Taylor, 1978; Levine, 1986; Richardson, 1985; Straus, 1976, 1979) trying to find a better way of life and a different ethic to guide behavior. They had rejected society's institutional structures, including regular churches, to look for a better way to live in an American society that seemed at the time very chaotic. As these dislocated young people were "floating" around American society, they encountered various groups of others like themselves who were seeking a better life. And sometimes they encountered an NRM willing to welcome them and offer shelter, food, and friendship, a package that was attractive to at least some of those young people. Sometimes recruitment was as simple as "coming to agree with your new best friend," who just happened to be part of a newer religious group (Stark & Bainbridge, 1980). And often participating in one of the NRMs had positive and ameliorative effects on the young people doing so, even if those positive effects were ignored by those opposing the rise of NRMs in American society (Galanter, 1978; Kilbourne & Richardson, 1984; 1988; Richardson, 1995).

As already noted, most who joined an NRM stayed only for a while in these groups; they "passed through" (Beckford, 1978; Richardson, 1978) them on the way to somewhere else – another NRM or to establish a family – only to "return home," thus reaffirming their previously rejected social location and career plans. Very high attrition rates were some of the best-kept secrets of most NRMs (see Barker, 1984; Bird & Reimer, 1982; Galanter, 1980; Richardson et al., 1986; Wright, 1987, among others). Because so many people were exercising their agency and leaving NRMs, the "brainwashing" thesis lacked explanatory power about why people joined NRMs. If, as claimed by some (Singer, 1979), "brainwashing" was a useful explanation, then why were the groups so small and why were so many leaving?

Eventually, the courts also rejected "brainwashing"-based explanations as inadmissible under usual standards of evidence acceptability in some cases in the early 1990s (Anthony, 1990; Anthony & Robbins, 2004; Ginsburg & Richardson, 1998; Richardson, 1991, 1993b, 2014a). But by that time so-called cult brainwashing had become hegemonic within American society, and many if not most ordinary Americans thought "brainwashing" was a full and adequate explanation of why young people were joining NRMs (Bromley & Breschel, 1992).

Differences, Similarities, and Overlap in Recruitment to NRMs and QAnon

There seem to be clear differences between recruitment targets of QAnon and those of most NRMs and political movements of earlier decades – that being the age and social location of most recruits. NRMs and political movements of a few decades ago focused on young people from relatively affluent backgrounds (Barker, 1984; Flacks, 1967, 1973; Richardson, 1985). Interest in QAnon has been most prevalent among older generations. Apparently QAnon has a huge and somewhat amorphous following in America and elsewhere, if news reports and polling results are to be believed. Devotees seem centered in older age and other demographic groups, although sound research on this hypothesis is lacking. QAnon may include many followers with considerable experience with alternate-reality games (ARGs; Berkowitz, 2021). This makeup of QAnon participants contrasts sharply with most NRMs, which were much smaller, with reasonably well-defined boundaries of belief and behavior, and usually offering some degree of a clear organizational structure. Political movements of earlier decades, while often transitory, also usually had more structure and boundaries than does the contemporary QAnon movement. And, of course, ARGs were not available back in the 1970s and 1980s for participants in religious and political movements.

While there are major differences between the recruitment efforts used by NRMs and political movements and by QAnon, there also was an important underlying set of assumptions about recruitment to QAnon and to political and religious movements, at least until the development of a "new paradigm" in recruitment and conversion research on NRMs and political movements described above (Kilbourne & Richardson, 1989). There was an early assumption of research on political and religious movements of the 1960s and 1970s that some sort of psychopathology explained involvement in such phenomena (Richardson, 1985; Stark, 1971). Those who participated were considered by many to be suffering a social deficiency or mental illness that, almost by definition, required intervention and treatment (Kilbourne & Richardson, 1984 Richardson, 1992, 1993b, 2014b). Contemporary mass media coverage of QAnon seems to assume aspects of the deterministic "old paradigm." There is some discussion about the need to intervene with QAnon devotees and perhaps even to consider "deprogramming" them (see also Chapter 16 of this volume), a term that arose because of efforts to forcibly extract participants from NRMs (Richardson, 2011; Thomas, 2021).

Another important similarity with recruitment to QAnon through the use of the internet was also evidenced to some degree by some of the NRMs that operated for a few decades in American society. As Dawson and Cowan (2004) have noted, some NRMs and other religious groups, especially pagan ones (Cowan, 2005), developed fairly sophisticated uses within recent decades of the new technologies that were evolving using the internet. Their edited volume was one of the first to focus attention on this important development and how it was being experienced by those involved in religious groups (also see Hadden & Cowan, 2000). Their substantive introduction to the volume starts with an assertion: "The Internet is changing the face of religion worldwide" (p. 1). They then offer considerable support for this thesis, as do the many chapters that follow. They make an important distinction between *religion online* and *online religion*, with the former referring to "... the provision of information about and/or services related to various religious groups and traditions," while the latter "... invites Internet visitors to participate in religious practices" (p. 7). However, they note that the distinction is an analytical one, and that there was considerable evidence of a growing tendency to encourage participation via the internet, something that has certainly been demonstrated by QAnon.

Dawson and Cowan (2004) discuss important differences in how religious groups recruit by using the internet versus other technologies, particularly radio and television, which are controlled by media elites who determine what content is broadcast. These differences are worth examining in light of QAnon's almost total focus on the internet to spread its message:

> (1) [T]he internet is an interactive and not simply a broadcast medium; (2) the internet is truly multimedial; (3) the internet employs hypertextuality[1]; (4) anyone can launch himself onto the World Wide Web with relative ease and little expense; (5) the internet is global in its reach. With comparatively small investment time, money, and knowledge, internet users can make their religious views known, at least potentially, to millions of others throughout the world ... [T]he World Wide Web is open in principle and in practice to almost anyone, no matter how unconventional his opinions. (Dawson & Cowan, 2004, p. 10)

Dawson and Cowan also offer prescient words of caution about the long-term effects of the integration of religion and the internet. Although some scholars were claiming that the internet was a "new dawn" and that its effects on religion would be dramatic and positive overall (see Brasher, 2001), Dawson and Cowan, while agreeing that there are positive aspects to what is happening, also discuss the "dark side" of the internet (p. 8). They cite a number of scholars who warn of dystopian tendencies occurring as use of the internet by religious groups was rapidly increasing. It was as if they anticipated what has developed with QAnon's nearly total dependence on the internet to convey its negative messaging and conspiracy theories (Beverly, 2020).

QAnon Recruitment: How Does It Occur?

Although there are many examples of QAnon involvement disrupting families (Jaffe & Del Real, 2021), a conclusion of most popular coverage into QAnon recruitment is that one's social groups affect one's beliefs and actions. People are more likely to affiliate if other members in their social network are already participating, a finding consistent with social movement and NRM recruitment research of decades ago. More broadly, the controversial and pseudoscientific term "brainwashing," which was often used to describe recruiting methods to NRMs, has been rejected as an explanation of QAnon followers (Schulson, 2021). QAnon participation

[1] Hypertext is text that contains hot links to other texts.

can more easily be explained by social psychological theories on persuasion and attitude change that assume active agency on the part of participants.

Richardson (1993c) offers a systematic critique of "brainwashing" theories (and of naive efforts by some social psychologists) to explain why young people were participating in NRMs. He also focuses on more useful subject-centered, agency-oriented theories of recruitment such as those presented by Moreland and Levine (1985) and Levine and Russo (1988). These researchers propose three psychological and social psychological processes that are involved in any recruitment: *evaluation*, *commitment*, and *role transition*. The first involves a mutual evaluation by the subject of recruitment and the group considering the new potential recruit to find out whether there are mutual benefits to recruitment. If so, then a multifaceted process of commitment is entered into by the individual person and the group (see Richardson, 1993c). If successful, commitment is achieved, then this process morphs into a role transition for the individual person, during which they learn about what is expected of them as a participant and begin acting the part of a full-fledged group member, with attendant ramifications.

The Levine/Moreland/Russo model, although developed before widespread development of the internet as a recruitment tool for groups and movements, nevertheless offers insights into QAnon recruitment. First, and importantly, the model is agency-oriented and assumes that people make decisions for themselves based on some sort of calculus depending on their circumstances, motivations, and knowledge. In short, the model assumes that *people decide on their own to participate in QAnon* (Thomas, 2021).[2] They might be enticed and intrigued by what they read online from QAnon enablers, but they are not being subjected to some sort of internet-based "brainwashing." There is no "omniscient leader" with magical powers that are effective over long distances via the internet (Richardson, 2021). For whatever reasons (and, granted, some of the reasoning offered seems quite far-fetched) recruits choose to continue accessing QAnon messages and, at the same time, shut out opposing views that might be accessed via the internet or from other sources such as

[2] The model also offers theorizing about the process of how an individual may leave a group or movement. Thus, it is useful to help us understand how and why some devotees are leaving QAnon and the processes through which this might be accomplished. There is at least one website devoted to QAnon defectors on Reddit (R/QAnonCasualties) demonstrating a growing interest in this (see Thomas, 2021), which is somewhat analogous to the focus on "deprogramming" and "exit counseling" that occurred with the spread of unpopular NRMs (Bromley & Richardson, 1983; Shupe & Bromley, 1980).

mainstream media (see also Chapter 12 of this volume for more on social media and QAnon). How long they remain devoted to QAnon ideas and conspiracy theories is, however, an open and empirical question that needs to be addressed.

Other social psychological theorizing might help with understanding how an initial relatively small involvement or exposure to QAnon messaging might be effective. So-called foot-in-the-door research, first presented in the 1960s (Freedman & Fraser, 1966) and developed more fully by others later (Pliner et al., 1974), offers ideas relevant to how so many people have gotten involved in QAnon. The underlying idea of this research is that, if one can get another person to make a small commitment to a cause, then that person will be much more susceptible to making a larger commitment later. This theory might have had some application to some recruitment to NRMs decades ago, but it certainly seems a fruitful way to approach an understanding of QAnon recruitment.

For instance, QAnon usurpation of the moniker "Save The Children" has drawn in many people for at least an initial contact with QAnon messaging. QAnon has taken over the "Save The Children" campaign by posting exaggerated claims about child kidnapping and sex trafficking to attract a sympathetic audience. Rahn and Patterson (2021) note that, according to the Associated Press, #SaveTheChildren was mentioned more than 800,000 times on Twitter in August 2020. Many people are interested in "saving children" and thus might click on QAnon-controlled internet sites seemingly dedicated to that cause. Once on such a site, they are steered via hyperlinks to sites informing them about the cabal of politicians and entertainers supposedly behind these alleged evils. QAnon also attempts to attract believers of other conspiracies (e.g. anti-vaccine, COVID-19 being caused by 5G towers, and, more recently, "stolen elections") and draw them into the world of QAnon. Those visiting QAnon-controlled sites are always encouraged to click on hyperlinks to many other strange ideas, and some end up "going down the rabbit hole" of QAnon conspiracy theories (see Chapter 2 of this volume).

One notable difference between recruitment to QAnon and recruitment to other more ordinary groups (including NRMs) is that the negotiation process engaged in between the group and the potential recruit is considerably attenuated. QAnon is open to anyone. There are no membership requirements, and no one who chooses to partake of the QAnon messages is refused. Indeed, given the easy access to the internet enjoyed by most citizens of the Western world, everyone is a potential recruit. Of course, given recent developments that have seen Facebook, Twitter, and

YouTube delete thousands of QAnon sites and posts, access to QAnon messaging has become somewhat more limited. But alternative sites are being developed to host QAnon messages, so the long-term effect of the decisions by major media organizations remains to be seen (and is yet another important research topic).

However, even if only a small minority of those who venture close to the QAnon "rabbit hole" actually accept the full QAnon message, this nevertheless represents a large number of people. And there are many different publics from which to draw participants into QAnon's world. The partisan divide in American politics has produced many more individuals who are susceptible to QAnon than would usually be the case. When the President of the USA (Donald Trump) is perceived by many as a QAnon sympathizer, this greatly increases the number of potential recruits who will "check it out" by doing an internet search, and as claimed by some (Berkowitz, 2021), those with experience with ARGs may be especially susceptible to QAnon entreaties. Some notable media figures such as Roseanne Barr are promoters of QAnon ideas, as are some well-known sports figures such as former Boston Red Socks pitcher Curt Shilling. Quite importantly, the Republican Party harbors a number of open devotees of QAnon, and the Party seems content to maintain a "big enough tent" to include them (Rosenberg, 2020). A significant proportion of evangelical Christians are believers in at least some QAnon ideas, and Christians generally might find themselves quite susceptible to QAnon messaging (Beverly, 2020; Jenkins, 2021; Rogers, 2021). There also is overlap of QAnon devotees with other groups such as those who view COVID-19 as a hoax and are antivaccination, those who oppose the Black Lives Matter movement, those sympathetic to white nationalist ideas, those who believe in satanic plots concerning children and childcare in America (Beverly, 2020; Richardson et al., 1991), and many other movements and groups disenchanted with ordinary life and politics.

Future Research Needs Regarding QAnon

There is very little systematic research on QAnon followers and QAnon itself available at present (see Garry et al., 2021 for an exception). Clearly, this oversight must be rectified if we are to come to grips with a phenomenon that could be a threat to the very existence of our democratic society. Some opinion polling is available that shows certain categories of people are more or less prone to accepting some of the predominant ideas promoted by QAnon, with expected breakdowns by political party, religious affiliation, gender, and a few other variables (Beverly, 2020). Beverly (2020) also offers some preliminary thoughts about why people are attracted to QAnon, including: (1) loss of institutional trust; (2) feeling a lack of purpose; (3) seeking clarity in unsettled times; (4) no restrictions on membership; (5) not everyone has to be a "true believer" and accept all QAnon teachings; (6) loneliness and seeking a sense of community; and (7) QAnon gives a feeling of being on the "inside track" concerning current events. Garry et al. (2021) summarizes a few reports that emphasize that QAnon participants with low self-control, low regard for the law, and high self-efficacy are more prone toward violence. Berkowitz (2021) hypothesizes that experience with ARGs also makes individuals more open to QAnon messaging.

However, the speculative efforts just mentioned represent a thin database on which to make well-founded assertions about QAnon. Thus, researchers do not really know who is susceptible to QAnon messaging, who joins, through what kinds of social processes, why some join and others do not, how long they remain as participants, what might cause them to leave, what happens to them if they leave, and who are "long-termers" who stay in the QAnon fold and become major interpreters of QAnon messages.[3]

Comparative research also is needed on the rapid spread of QAnon around the world into many other countries, a development showing that recruitment has been successful beyond the USA. How has such recruitment to QAnon occurred, and how has the QAnon message been able to appeal to citizens in so many different cultural settings? Utilizing a sophisticated digital disinformation platform, Storyzy,[4] developed in France, Garry et al. (2021) hypothesize that disinformation campaigns, coupled with the internet and social media, have greatly enabled the unprecedented global effect of QAnon. The authors explored the potential of several survey methods to obtain insights from QAnon followers

[3] We also need research on the organizational impacts of the defection of QAnon followers on activities promoted by QAnon messaging. The "distillation effect" (Milgram & Toch, 1969) that can contribute to extreme, even violent tendencies in some groups might be worth considering, especially in light of the propensity for violence that has been shown by some QAnon followers (Amarasingam & Argentino, 2020b).

[4] Storyzy is a French-based company that uses a Software as a Service (SaaS) tool to allow ". . . source analysis, topic analysis, chronology, country analysis, and social media analysis tools of disinformation sites, blogs, article, and topics" (Garry et al., 2021, p. 164).

on some social media platforms. More such careful research is needed around the globe.[5]

As researchers approach the study of QAnon, care must be taken to seek verifiable information and to avoid one's biases interfering with what is studied and the interpretation of research findings. Beverley (2020) offers sixteen helpful pieces of advice for those involved in research on QAnon, and reviewing those would be a useful exercise for any researchers approaching this challenging area of study regarding recruitment to QAnon or research more broadly.

A large body of research on such questions is available on NRMs, much of which was referred to above, and this research could provide models for what needs to happen concerning QAnon research. However, even the large body of research on NRMs had some lacunae, as indicated in one report (Richardson et al., 1993). This useful summary of research needs and suggestions for NRM research is worth reviewing as scholars plan future research on QAnon and its followers. The authors surveyed the available research, citing a number of additional kinds of research that were needed:

> Major problems with current research include (1) too many one-shot study designs; (2) problems with "compounded accounts" deriving from the interaction of subject accounts with researcher perspective; (3) need for more longitudinal research with "triangulation" of methods and sources, and better approximations of control group studies; (4) more replication and use of standardized instrumentation in research; (5) difficulties using therapy settings as data gathering situations; and (6) limitations on "happy member" research. (Richardson et al., 1993, p. 293)

These critiques all are applicable to QAnon research, as well – whether it is research about recruiting or other topics. Conducting such research will present many challenges given the very nature of the QAnon movement with its penchant for secrecy and even violence. The almost total dependency so far on polling data of nonparticipants and on anecdotal accounts by distraught family members of QAnon participants or former QAnon devotees must be overcome if our society is ever going to understand and counter the threats posed by QAnon.

Richardson et al. (1993) also offer suggestions for specific types of research that needed to be done in the context of NRMs, much of which also is

[5] Research on QAnon will have to grapple with the issue of how to research digital material, as QAnon is nearly totally dependent on the internet to communicate with its devotees. With this in mind, the following two sources are recommended for those seeking ways to proceed with research on QAnon's communications and other attributes that might be accessed using digital methodologies: Cheruvallil-Contractor and Shakkour (2016) and Possami-Inesedy and Nixon (2019).

applicable to QAnon recruitment. Included is organizational research – a challenging area, to be sure, given the amorphous structures of QAnon. However, a hierarchy of people in certain roles involved in interpreting Q's obtuse messages has evolved within QAnon (Beverly, 2020), and instead of continuing to ask "Who is Q?" researchers should focus on the developing authority structure within QAnon that includes a growing cadre of interpreters of QAnon messaging (e.g. "Who are these interpreters and how are they recruited?"). And, given the reticence of whoever Q is to identify themself and their recent lack of messaging, a focus on the "successor problem" that has faced some NRMs could be a fruitful line of research. Does the seeming disappearance of Q and efforts by others to assume their mantle of leadership have implications for recruitment to QAnon?

Research on the implications for QAnon recruitment of contacts between QAnon and other organizations such as political parties, hate groups, "sovereign citizen" groups, and other conspiracy theory promoters would be useful, as would information about QAnon participants' involvement with ARGs. The role of mass media of various types, including social media, in promulgating the views of QAnon would be informative, as would discourse analysis on the ambiguous messages themselves. And the effect of the deletion of thousands of QAnon postings and sites from social media (e.g. Facebook, Twitter, YouTube) raises a very important question about future recruitment to QAnon, given that ready access to social media has been significantly curtailed (see Chapter 12 of this volume for more on QAnon and social media).

In the aftermath of Trump's failure to overturn the election of Joe Biden as president and the importance of QAnon predictions that Trump would eventually prevail, research from NRM studies on "when prophecy fails" (Dawson, 1999; Festinger et al., 1956; Tumminia, 2005) is relevant. As this area of research has shown, when prophecies fail, this does not automatically mean that the group will disappear. Indeed, such groups might overcome their "cognitive dissonance" and simply reinterpret what happened, and even begin to promote their message more fervently; these findings have clear implications for QAnon recruitment. While it is clear that many QAnon devotees have become disillusioned with the failure of prophecies about Trump prevailing and becoming president again (Amarasingam & Argentino, 2020a; Dawson, 2021; Jaffe & Del Real, 2021), there are no data yet available showing this to be a major portion of QAnon adherents. (Indeed, there is even a suspicion that such reports are more wishful thinking on the part of major media outlets.) It is also unclear what effect this has had on recruitment. So, it seems that new "when prophecy fails" research on QAnon would be useful and would add to the growing literature in this area (see Chapters 3 and 4 of this volume for more on psychological processes in QAnon).

Some specific questions of considerable import bear special attention at this time. For instance, Elizabeth Neumann (2021), a former Department of Homeland Security administrator in the Trump administration, reported in a 60 Minutes interview that right-wing groups were taking advantage of the disillusionment of many QAnon adherents over the failed prophecies about Trump becoming president again by making efforts to recruit them to various radical movements. If this claim is accurate (see Amarasingam & Argentino, 2020b), finding out about these efforts to take advantage of possible QAnon "derecruitment" seems important. As noted above, research on attrition from NRMs contributed to gaining a fuller understanding of how recruitment operated and its limitations. Perhaps the same might be achievable regarding QAnon recruitment.

Thus, much more research on QAnon phenomena is needed. Hopefully, this can be done by a new generation of scholars, allowing much more to be learned about this very concerning – even threatening – development that has swept rapidly across America and into dozens of other nations.

Conclusion

This examination of QAnon recruitment reveals that most participants in this conspiratorial movement do so of their own volition, as also was found with research on participants in political and religious movements from decades earlier in America. However, there are major differences in the age of most participants and in the methods of contact and participation with the movement, which for QAnon is usually through use of the internet and social media. This examination also reveals that traditional social psychological theories are useful for understanding how QAnon recruitment operates. There is no need for magical pseudoscientific ideas such as "brainwashing" and "mind control" to explain recruitment to this important conspiracy-oriented movement.

REFERENCES

Amarasingam, A., & Argentino, M. A. (2020a, October 28). QAnon's predictions haven't come true; so how does the movement survive the failure of prophecy? *Religion Dispatches*. https://religiondispatches.org/qanons-predictions-havent-come-true-so-how-does-the-movement-survive-the-failure-of-prophecy/

(2020b). The QAnon conspiracy theory: A security threat in the making? *CTC Sentinel*, *13*(7). www.ctc.usma.edu/the-qanon-conspiracy-theory-a-security-threat-in-the-making/

Anthony, D. (1990). Religious movements and brainwashing litigation: Evaluating key testimony. In T. Robbins & D. Anthony (Eds.), *In gods we trust* (pp. 295–344). Transaction Publishers.

Anthony, D., & Robbins, T. (2004). Pseudoscience and minority religions: In J. T. Richardson (Ed.), *Regulating religion: Case studies from around the globe* (pp. 127–149). Kluwer.

Argentino, M. A. (2020, May 18). The church of QAnon: Will conspiracy theories form the basis of a new religious movement? *The Conversation*. https://theconversation.com/the-church-of-qanon-will-conspiracy-theories-form-the-basis-of-a-new-religious-movement-137859

Balch, R., & Taylor, D. (1978). Seekers and saucers: The role of the cultic milieu in joining an UFO cult. In J. T. Richardson (Ed.), *Conversion careers: In and out of the new religions* (pp. 95–116). Sage.

Barker, E. (1984). *The making of a Moonie: Brainwashing or choice?* Basil Blackwell.

Beaty, K. (2020, August 17). QAnon: The alternative religion that's coming to your church. *Religion News Service*. https://religionnews.com/2020/08/17/qanon-the-alternative-religion-thats-coming-to-your-church/

Beckford, J. (1978). Through the looking glass and out the other side: Withdrawal from Rev. Moon's Unification Church. *Archives des Science Sociales des Religious*, *45*, 95–116.

Berkowitz, R. (2021, May 11). QAnon resembles the games I design. But for believers, there is no winning. *Washington Post*. www.washingtonpost.com/outlook/qanon-game-plays-believers/2021/05/10/31d8ea46-928b-11eb-a74e-1f4cf89fd948_story.html

Beverly, J. (2020). *The QAnon deception: Everything you need to know about the world's most dangerous conspiracy theory*. EqualTime Books.

Bird, F., & Reimer, B. (1982). Participation rates in new religious movements and para-religious movements. *Journal for the Scientific Study of Religion*, *21*, 1–14.

Brasher, B. (2001). *Give me that online religion*. Jossey-Bass.

Bromley, D., & Breschel, E. (1992). General population and institutional elite support for control of new religious movements: Evidence from national survey data. *Behavioral Science and the Law*, *10*, 39–52.

Bromley, D., & Richardson, J. T. (1983). *The brainwashing/deprogramming controversy*. Edwin Mellen Press.

Cheruvallil-Contractor, S., & Shakkour, S. (2016). *Digital methodologies in the sociology of religion*. Bloomsbury.

Cowan, D. (2005). *Cyberhenge: Modern pagans on the internet*. Routledge.

Dawson, L. (1999). When prophecy fails and faith persists: A theoretical overview. *Nova Religio*, *3*(1), 60–82.

(2021, January 21). Keeping faith with Trump: The dangerous causes and consequences. *International Centre for Counter-Terrorism*. https://icct.nl/publication/keeping-faith-with-trump-the-dangerous-causes-and-the-consequences/

Dawson, L., & Cowan, D. (2004). *Religion online: Finding faith on the internet.* Routledge.

Festinger, L., Riecken, H., & Schachter, S. (1956). *When prophecy fails: A social and psychological study of a group that predicted the destruction of the world.* University of Minnesota Press.

Flacks, R. (1967). The liberated generation: An exploration of the roots of student protest. *Journal of Social Issues, 23*, 52–75.

(1973). *Youth and social change*. Markham.

Freedman, J., & Fraser, S. (1966). Compliance without pressure: The foot-in-the-door technique. *Journal of Personality and Social Psychology, 4*(2), 195–202.

Galanter, M. (1978). The "relief effect": A sociobiological model of neurotic stress and large group therapy. *American Journal of Psychiatry, 135*, 588–591.

(1980). Psychological induction into the lager group: Findings from a modern religious sect. *American Journal of Psychiatry, 137*, 1574–1578.

Garry, A., Walther, S., Rukaya, R., & Mohammed, A. (2021). QAnon conspiracy theory: Examining its evolution and mechanisms of radicalization. *Journal of Deradicalization, 26*, 152–216.

Ginsburg, G., & Richardson, J. T. (1998). "Brainwashing" evidence in light of *Daubert*. In H. Reece (Ed.), *Law and science* (pp. 265–288). Oxford University Press.

Hadden, J., & Cowan, D. (2000). *Religion on the internet: Research prospects and promises.* JAI Press.

Jaffe, G., & Del Real, J. (2021, February 23). Life among the ruins: "I want my family back." *Seattle Times*. www.seattletimes.com/nation-world/life-amid-the-ruins-of-qanon-i-wanted-my-family-back/

Jenkins, J. (2021, May 27). Survey: White evangelicals, Hispanic Protestants, Mormons most likely to believe in QAnon. *Religious News Service*. https://religionnews.com/2021/05/27/survey-white-evangelicals-hispanic-protestants-and-mormons-most-likely-believe-in-qanon/

Kilbourne, B., & Richardson, J. T. (1984). Psychotherapy and the new religions in a pluralistic society. *American Psychologist, 39*, 237–251.

(1988). A social psychological analysis of healing. *Journal of Integrative and Eclectic Psychotherapy, 7*(1), 20–34.

(1989). Paradigm conflict, types of conversion, and conversion theories. *Sociological Analysis, 50*(1), 1–21.

LaFrance, A. (2020, May 13). The prophecies of Q: American conspiracy theories are entering a dangerous new phase. *The Atlantic*. www.theatlantic.com/magazine/archive/2020/06/qanon-nothing-can-stop-what-is-coming/610567/g

Levine, S. (1986). *Radical departures: Desperate detours to growing up*. Harvest Books.

Levine, J., & Russo, E. (1988). Majority and minority influence. In C. Hedrick (Ed.), *Group processes* (pp. 13–54). Sage.

Lifton, R. (1961). *Thought reform and the psychology of totalism*. Victor Gollancz.

Milgram, S., & Toch, H. (1969). Collective behavior: Crowds and social movements. In G. Lindzey & E. Aronson (Eds.), *The handbook of social psychology.*

Vol. 4: Group psychology and phenomena of interaction (pp. 507–610). Addison-Wesley.

Moreland, R., & Levine, J. (1985). Socialization in small groups: Temporal change in individual–group relations. In L. Berkowitz (Ed.), *Advances in experimental social psychology* (pp. 143–169). Academic Press.

Neumann, E. (2021, February 19). Former DHS official: Right-wing extremists and white supremacists targeting QAnon followers for recruitment [Interview]. *60 Minutes*. www.cbsnews.com/news/qanon-conspiracy-capitol-riots-60-minutes-2021-02-19/

Pliner, P., Hart, H., Kohl, J., & Saari, D. (1974). Compliance without pressure: Some further data on the foot-in-the-door technique. *Journal of Experimental Social Psychology*, *10*, 17–24.

Possami-Inesedy, A., & Nixon, A. (2019). *The digital social: Religion and belief.* De Gruyter.

Rahn, W., & Patterson, D. (2021, March 29). What is the QAnon conspiracy theory? *CBS News*. www.cbsnews.com/news/what-is-the-qanon-conspiracy-theory/

Richardson, J. T. (1978). *Conversion careers: In and out of the new religions*. Sage.

(1985). The active versus passive convert: Paradigm conflict in conversion/recruitment research. *Journal for the Scientific Study of Religion*, *24*, 163–179.

(1991). Cult/brainwashing cases and the freedom of religion. *Journal of Church and State*, *33*, 55–74.

(1992). Mental health of cult consumers. In J. Schumacher (Ed.), *Religion and mental health* (pp. 233–244). Oxford University Press.

(1993a). Definitions of cult: From sociological-technical to popular-negative. *Review of Religious Research*, *34*(4), 348–356.

(1993b). Religiosity as deviance: Use and misuse of the DMS with participations new religions. *Deviant Behavior*, *14*, 1–21.

(1993c). A social psychological critique of "brainwashing" claims about recruitment to new religions. In J. Hadden & D. Bromley (Eds.), *The handbook of sects and cults in America* (pp. 75–97). JAI Books.

(1995). Clinical and personality assessment of participants in new religions. *International Journal of Psychology of Religion*, *5*(3), 145–170.

(2011). Deprogramming: From private self-help to governmental organized repression. *Crime, Law, and Social Change*, *55*, 321–336.

(2014a). Brainwashing and forensic evidence. In S. Morewitz & M. Goldstein (Eds.), *Handbook of forensic sociology* (pp. 77–85). Springer.

(2014b). "Brainwashing" and mental health. In H. Friedman (Ed.), *Encyclopedia of mental health* (2nd ed., pp. 210–215). Academic Press.

(2021). The myth of the omnipotent leader: Social construction of a misleading account of leadership in new religious movements. *Nova Religio*, *24*, 11–25.

Richardson, J. T., Balch, R., & Melton, G. (1993). Problems of research and data in the study of new religions. In J. Hadden & D. Bromley (Eds.), *The handbook of sects and cults in America* (pp. 213–229). JAI Books.

Richardson, J. T., Bromley, D., & Best, J. (1991). *The satanism scare*. Aldine de Gruyter.

Richardson, J. T., van der Lans, J., & Derks, F. (1986). Leaving and labeling: Voluntary and coerced disaffiliation from religious social movements. In F. Lang, G. Lang, & L. Kriesberg (Eds.), *Research in social movements, conflicts and change* (pp. 97–126). JAI Books.

Rogers, K. (2020, October 29). QAnon isn't going to take over Congress in 2020. But it's found a home in the GOP. *FiveThirtyEight*. https://fivethirtyeight.com/features/qanon-isnt-going-to-take-over-congress-in-2020-but-its-found-a-home-in-the-gop/

(2021, March 4). Why QAnon has attracted so many white evangelicals. *FiveThirtyEight*. https://fivethirtyeight.com/features/why-qanon-has-attracted-so-many-white-evangelicals/

Rosenberg, M. (2020, November 10). Republican voters take a radical conspiracy theory mainstream. *New York Times*. www.nytimes.com/2020/10/19/us/politics/qanon-trump-republicans.html

Schein, E. (1961). *Coercion persuasion*. W.W. Norton.

Schulson, M. (2021, February 24). Can cult studies offer help with QAnon? The science is thin. *Undark*. https://undark.org/2021/02/24/cult-studies-qanon/

Scott, M., & Lyman, S. (1968). Accounts. *American Sociological Review*, *33*(1), 46–62.

Shupe, A., & Bromley, D. (1980). *The new vigilantes: Anti-cultists and the new religions*. Sage.

Singer, M. (1979). Coming out of the cults. *Psychology Today*, *12*, 72–82.

Skolnick, J. (1969). *The politics of protest*. Ballentine Books.

Stark, R. (1971). Psychopathology and religious commitment. *Review of Religious Research*, *12*, 165–176.

Stark, R., & Bainbridge, W. (1980). Networks of faith: Interpersonal bonds and recruitment to cults and sects. *American Journal of Sociology*, *85*, 376–395.

Straus, R. (1976). Changing oneself: Seekers and the creative transformation of life experience. In J. Lofland (Ed.), *Doing social life* (pp. 252–273). John Wiley and Sons.

(1979). Religious conversion as a personal and collective accomplishment. *Sociological Analysis*, *40*, 158–165.

Thomas, P. (2021, April 15). "Deprogramming" QAnon followers ignores free will and why they adopted the beliefs in the first place." *The Conversation*. https://theconversation.com/deprogramming-qanon-followers-ignores-free-will-and-why-they-adopted-the-beliefs-in-the-first-place-158372

Tumminia, D. (2005). *When prophecy never fails: Myth and reality in a flying-saucer group*. Oxford University Press.

Wright, S. (1987). *Leaving cults: The dynamics of defection*. The Society for the Scientific Study of Religion.

PART III

QAnon and Society

CHAPTER 8

QAnon in the Year 2020
The Bigger Social Picture

Charles P. Edwards

The QAnon conspiracy theory emerged in late 2017 and initially posited that a group of "elites" or "Deep State" actors were Satan-worshipping pedophiles who sacrificed children and used their status in society or as high-ranking government officials to gain control (Garry et al., 2021). To combat these "Deep State" actors, an anonymous group provided veiled messages and information on the website 4chan and signed these messages as "Q Clearance Patriot." QAnon believers refer to this group simply as "Q" (Polarization & Extremism Research & Innovation Lab [hereafter PERI Lab], 2020). Despite existing for nearly three years, QAnon rose to prominence and gained international recognition in 2020. This exponential rise of QAnon begs the question: What about the social climate of 2020 allowed QAnon to flourish? This chapter will briefly review the social climate and events of 2020, examine how QAnon was able to spread and increase its membership, and discuss how various psychological theories could help to explain this growth.

The Social Climate of 2020

The year 2020 was marked by health crises, civil unrest, and political and social animosity. Although there were many events that exemplified these issues, this chapter will focus on three primary issues that shaped the social climate of 2020: the COVID-19 pandemic, the Black Lives Matter (BLM) movement, and the contentious 2020 US presidential election.

The COVID-19 pandemic will potentially be the most remembered aspect of 2020. The SARS-CoV-2 virus, which causes COVID-19, was discovered in late 2019 and rapidly spread across the globe. In the USA, COVID-19 was the underlying or contributing cause of death in 11.3 percent of all deaths in 2020 (377,883 deaths), making COVID-19 the third leading cause of death behind heart disease and cancer (Ahmad et al., 2021). To slow the spread of the virus, local and national mandates for social distancing, mask wearing, and quarantining were enacted until a vaccine could be created (AJMC Staff, 2021). Some research suggests that these mandates were effective at preventing hundreds of thousands of additional COVID-19 cases (Lyu & Wehby, 2020), though there was resistance against following the mandates in certain groups and parts of the country (Forsyth, 2020).

Amidst the COVID-19 lockdowns, BLM gained national attention and became a pivotal movement that shaped the second half of 2020. Having begun in 2013, BLM rose to prominence with calls for racial justice and the organization of marches against police brutality following the death of George Floyd at the hands of a police officer in May 2020 (Corley, 2021). These demonstrations sparked an international wave of protests and calls for racial justice and equality (Westerman, 2020). Along with this national attention came conspiracy theories and attempts to undermine the BLM organization through accusations and disinformation campaigns (Corley, 2021).

In the political sphere, 2020 started with the impeachment of President Donald Trump, although the Senate did not vote to remove President Trump from office (Zurcher, 2020; see Chapter 9 of this volume for more on the politics associated with QAnon). This set the tone for the upcoming election cycle, as 2020 was marked by political derision and divisiveness, which led to civil unrest (Solace Global, 2020). This carried throughout the primaries, the campaign trail, the presidential debates (Itzkowitz et al., 2020; Solace Global, 2020), and even after the election, with claims of fraud and attacks on the democratic process carrying through to 2021. These voter fraud claims were perpetuated by President Trump and led to an attack on the US Capital on January 6, 2021 (Mascaro, 2021).

Rise and Spread of QAnon in 2020

QAnon capitalized on the social turmoil and uncertainty of 2020, as seen by the group's increase in notoriety. One analysis suggests there was an over 800-percent increase in the number of articles published globally that mentioned QAnon from March 1, 2020, to November 1, 2020 (39,692 articles) compared to the prior eight months of July 1, 2019, to February 29, 2020 (4,207 articles; Garry et al., 2021). Many factors could account for this drastic increase, including a combination of social climate events and characteristics inherent to QAnon, such as QAnon believers' use of social media and online communication as well as the evolution of QAnon's messaging and ability to adapt to international issues (PERI Lab, 2020).

QAnon, Social Media, and Online Communication

Increased reliance on social media for information as well as the ease and anonymity of online communication played key roles in the spread of QAnon in 2020 (see Chapter 12 of this volume for more on social media and QAnon). Social media websites (e.g. Twitter, Facebook) lacked the ability to systematically fact-check information and claims on their platforms, which allowed disinformation to spread. Networks of QAnon believers capitalized on this by coordinating disinformation campaigns across multiple social media platforms (PERI Lab, 2020). Disinformation can act as propaganda akin to that used by terrorist or extremist groups and was used to delegitimize the US government (e.g. the election of Joe Biden; Garry et al., 2021). The anonymity provided by online communication allows people to read this disinformation and join these movements without personal repercussions. With young people having access to social media and with the COVID-19 pandemic leading to lockdowns and quarantines, more people than ever could be exposed to the disinformation spread on social media (Pantucci & Ong, 2021; PERI Lab, 2020).

QAnon used multiple tactics to increase their audience and the effectiveness of its disinformation. QAnon was known for partaking in hashtag hijacking, in which QAnon talking points and disinformation are inserted into the conversation of a trending hashtag (e.g. #Election2020; PERI Lab, 2020). This caused non-QAnon believers to be exposed to QAnon messaging if they were to search for that specific hashtag. Additionally, using online platforms allowed arguments presented by QAnon believers to appear more valid than if they were presented in a different medium. Illogical arguments might stand out in an article, and tone or physical demeanor can be used to establish the validity of a spoken argument (PERI Lab, 2020). These aspects are entirely lacking from online debate. QAnon believers typically attach links to other arguments as support for an argument rather than providing evidence for claims (PERI Lab, 2020). Lastly, QAnon would use multimodal forms of disinformation, such as adding images and videos to text, to appear more credible and convincing. One example is the "Plandemic" video that suggested COVID-19 was a government weapon (Hameleers et al., 2020; PERI Lab, 2020).

Social media platforms, such as Twitter and YouTube, did eventually attempt to quell this spread of disinformation. YouTube began banning and removing QAnon content in October 2020. Twitter started slightly earlier, removing QAnon-related accounts beginning July 21, 2020 (Garry et al., 2021). In fact, the first spike in publication of QAnon articles occurred the day after Twitter began banning QAnon accounts (Garry et al., 2021). Unfortunately, social media platforms faced a catch-22 – if QAnon believers could spread disinformation and messaging, then others might become radicalized despite the claims and messaging being dishonest or not factual. If, however, QAnon was deplatformed or banned by the social media platforms (e.g. removing QAnon users, banning links that mention QAnon-related disinformation), then QAnon believers would move to other platforms that were less strict (e.g. Gab, Parler). This could lead to deplatformed users becoming enmeshed in echo chambers and being exposed to increasingly radical beliefs (PERI Lab, 2020).

Evolution of QAnon Messaging

In addition to social media, QAnon has spread by adapting and modifying its core tenets and messages (see Chapters 10 and 13 of this volume for more about QAnon narratives). The QAnon conspiracy theory originally posited that a group of pedophilic, Satan-worshiping "elites" or "Deep State" actors sacrificed children and were usurping power and control (Garry et al., 2021; PERI Lab, 2020). These actors include Democratic politicians, celebrities, philanthropists, and billionaires (PERI Lab, 2020). Additionally, QAnon was not a single person but, rather, a group of anonymous, high-ranking military officers with Q-level clearance (hence, "QAnon") who were fighting against these Deep State elites from within the government (Garry et al., 2021).

QAnon believers' assertions regarding the core tenets that drew them to QAnon suggest that, over time, the core tenets that comprise QAnon have widened and shifted. QAnon believers who used Telegram – a messaging platform – were asked in late 2020 about what drew them to the conspiracy theory. Responses suggested that a significant portion were drawn to QAnon because of the classic, foundational tenets – 47 percent stated *Save The Children* was a primary factor, whereas 30 percent stated *Expose the Cabal of Democrats* as an important factor (Garry et al., 2021). Such a high percentage of respondents citing the foundational tenets as important drawing factors is not surprising. What is somewhat surprising, however, is the percentage of participants who were drawn to QAnon because of messaging surrounding more modern events – of additional response options, 39 percent cited *Keep President Trump in Power*, 37 percent cited *COVID-19 as a Control Tactic*, and 18 percent cited *Election Fraud Beliefs* (responses were not mutually exclusive; Garry et al., 2021). The fact that over a third of respondents (37 percent) were drawn to QAnon because of QAnon's messaging regarding COVID-19 – a virus that appeared approximately two years after QAnon – shows the ability of QAnon to evolve and adapt its messaging to current events.

This messaging adaptability partly explains the rise of QAnon in that the conspiracy theory can draw people in based on their personal beliefs and predispositions. Conservatives might be drawn to the conspiracies regarding the criminal activity by the leftist elites. Conspiracies about COVID-19 might draw in vaccine skeptics and science deniers. Voter fraud conspiracies might draw in supporters of President Trump. And the morally just *Save The Children* messaging could draw those who do not fit any of the previous categories.

Global Spread of QAnon

QAnon has spread internationally by adapting and modifying its messaging to relate to the major events, narratives, and conspiracies of other nations or even smaller localities (AFP, 2020). Website traffic to qanon.pub (a website for QAnon believers to find information) suggests that approximately three-quarters (76.6 percent) of this website's traffic is from the USA, meaning that nearly a quarter of this traffic is international (Garry et al., 2021). Countries such as Australia, Canada, Greece, South Africa, and Portugal represented the most international traffic that could be followed to qanon.pub. Regarding sources of "inbound links" (articles, websites, or ways that people were brought to qanon.pub), approximately two-thirds (65.8 percent) of them originate from US-based sources, meaning that over a third of these links originate internationally. These estimates could be skewed, though, because of virtual private networks (VPNs) or internet protocol (IP) address modifiers hiding the correct, original locations of such sources (Garry et al., 2021).

There is some debate regarding which country comprises the largest number of non-American QAnon believers. Certain analyses suggest that Germans comprise the largest non-US QAnon membership, whereas other analyses suggest that the French comprise the largest total of non-US QAnon believers (Garry et al., 2021). However, the analysis suggesting that France comprises the largest QAnon following outside the USA was conducted using Storyzy – a French software company that provides information about disinformation sites – and might have been biased due to the program's familiarity with French disinformation sources (Garry et al., 2021). Regardless of which country comprises the largest non-US QAnon following, the research suggests that there is a large European faction of QAnon believers.

The messaging for international sects of QAnon focuses on issues such as immigration, the COVID-19-related economic downturn, or restrictions to "personal liberties" (e.g. social distancing, mask mandates). More specifically, some QAnon conspiracies have focused on international heads of state, such as claims that Angela Merkel (the former Chancellor of Germany) and Emmanuel Macron (the French President) were "pawns" or part of the Deep State, or that Boris Johnson (the former British Prime Minister) was "installed" by Q to help then-President Trump fight against the Deep State (AFP, 2020). Germany in particular appears to be a hot spot for more than just QAnon internet activity; other, older conspiracy theories have intertwined their rhetoric with that of QAnon (e.g. the neo-Nazi Reichsbürger movement, which believes that the current country of Germany is not a legitimate state; BBC News – Europe, 2020) to form "Corona Rebels," an antimask group that organizes demonstrations against COVID-19 mask mandates (PERI Lab, 2020).

This global spread has also reached parts of Asia, as QAnon narratives have been adapted by the Japanese to fit their local context while also referencing the core, Americanized tenets of QAnon (Pantucci & Ong, 2021). One of the largest Japanese sects of QAnon believers, QArmyJapanFlynn, asserts that former President Trump is fighting against the Deep State and Satan-worshippers; they also show a specific reverence of General Michael Flynn, who served in President Trump's administration for only twenty-four days (The Straits Times, 2020). However, this same group propagates Japanese-specific messages, including the conspiracy that the Japanese government intentionally does not allow young women to focus on child-rearing and that the approval ratings for Yoshihide Suga (former Japanese Prime Minister) were fabricated (The Straits Times, 2020).

Psychological Explanation for QAnon Trends

The societal circumstances that encompassed 2020 allowed for QAnon to flourish. Global events, increased traffic and reliance on social media for information, and a conspiracy theory with adaptable messaging all contributed to the rise of QAnon. This, however, only answers *what* happened to allow QAnon to flourish and expand; it still leaves questions as to *why* people were drawn to and believed in QAnon. Psychology provides some explanations regarding the expansion of QAnon, including findings from research involving conspiracy theories, group membership, system identity threat (SIT), and terror management theory (TMT; see Chapters 3 and 4 of this volume for more on the psychology of QAnon)

Conspiracy Theories

It is important to define what constitutes a conspiracy theory. A *conspiracy* is the belief that two or more actors are secretly engaged in a plot that is typically considered unlawful or wicked (Douglas et al., 2019; van Prooijen & Douglas, 2017). These plots might center around a variety of goals, such as gaining wealth, increasing power, or violating agreements (Douglas et al., 2019). *Conspiracy theories* are attempts to explain significant events, such as political, economic, or societal changes, by claiming that there is a secret plot between two or more actors (Douglas et al., 2019; van Prooijen & Douglas, 2017).

By nature, people are motivated to reduce feelings of uncertainty or increase their sense of control, especially when their environment is highly uncertain or removes personal control (Van den Bos, 2009). This is, in part, because feelings of certainty and control allow people to lead effective lives – they can avoid environmental and societal threats while also make choices that improve their social acceptance and personal well-being. However, this is also because feelings of uncertainty relate to increases in anxiety (van Prooijen & Douglas, 2017). When an unexpected event occurs (e.g. an environmental and societal crisis), people might engage in anxiety and uncertainty reduction or control promotion by creating narratives to make sense of the new environment. These narratives provide reassurance that there is order in the world and that crises do not occur randomly (i.e. reducing uncertainty surrounding societal changes; van Prooijen & Douglas, 2017). When these new sense-making narratives are unfounded, though, the narratives might be viewed as conspiracy theories (Douglas et al., 2019). Indeed, increases in anxiety, powerlessness, and lack of control (i.e. feelings that would lead to sense-making narratives) are all related to increases in conspiracy theory beliefs (Constantinou et al., 2021; van Prooijen & Douglas, 2017).

Increases in conspiracy theory belief in times of uncertainty and societal crisis occurs because people feel they have less control over their environment (van Prooijen & Douglas, 2017). In fact, belief in conspiracy theories increases as the outcome of an event becomes increasingly negative, an idea referred to as "consequence–cause matching." For example, people are more likely to believe in a conspiracy theory if the president was assassinated than if the president was *almost* assassinated (McCauley & Jacques,

1979) or if a presidential assassination led to war than if the assassination did not lead to war (LeBoeuf & Norton, 2012). Looking at the events of 2020 (e.g. coverage of the COVID-19 death count, police brutality followed by nationwide BLM protests), the spread of QAnon is in line with this notion of societal crisis increasing conspiracy theory belief.

Despite conspiracy theories typically arising to increase certainty and control, conspiracy theory belief can relate to *more* powerlessness rather than less (van Prooijen & Douglas, 2017). Research suggests that conspiracy theory belief relates to increased feelings of powerlessness and anxiety, which can lead to maladaptive behaviors associated with the conspiracy theory. For instance, conspiracy theory belief regarding political figures relates to increased withdrawal from politics (Douglas & Sutton, 2008). Similarly, belief in climate change conspiracy theories relates to refusals to reduce carbon footprints (Jolley & Douglas, 2014b), and vaccine conspiracy theory belief relates to higher rates of refusal to vaccinate children (Jolley & Douglas, 2014a). This last finding is especially troubling, as one of the primary tenets of QAnon that evolved over the course of 2020 is that COVID-19 vaccines are a means of social control, with claims that the vaccines are a means to insert a tracker, to alter human DNA, or are meant to kill people for population control (Timberg & Dwoskin, 2021). This could lead QAnon believers to refrain from vaccinating themselves or their children from COVID-19, which might lead to variants of the virus emerging.

Another QAnon-specific element that could also explain the group's rise in 2020 is the number of high-profile people who pushed QAnon beliefs. This notion of "advertising towers" suggests that fringe belief groups elevate the messages of high-profile believers to market their ideas (PERI Lab, 2020). High-profile QAnon believers came from various backgrounds (e.g. athletes, movie stars, internet celebrities), although much of the focus was on politicians, such as Representatives Marjorie Taylor Greene and Lauren Boebert (Levin, 2021; Massie, 2021). None were more famous or integral in the QAnon conspiracy theory, though, than former President Donald Trump, who was cast as the primary force of "good" fighting against the Deep State (PERI Lab, 2020). Using such prominent political figures who were engaged in a contentious election in 2020 helped propagate QAnon beliefs and conspiracies.

Group Membership and Belonging

One major fallout from the COVID-19 pandemic was the legislation and advocation for people to socially distance, quarantine, or remain in their homes as much as possible. These practices created both *physical* and *social* isolation, in that people could not be physically near each other, which reduced physical contact and opportunities to socialize (Constaninou et al., 2021). Research suggests that social isolation relates to increases in loneliness, and both social isolation and loneliness relate to poorer physical and mental health for elderly adults and, sometimes, poorer mental health for young adults (e.g. increased levels of depression; Brady et al., 2020; Matthews et al., 2016).

A primary way to combat loneliness and isolation is through a sense of belonging (Allen, 2020; see also Chapter 11 of this volume for more on QAnon and the need to belong). This comes, in part, from group membership; group members can feel a sense of belonging that relates to feeling accepted, understood, liked, and appreciated. Therefore, because physical isolation during the COVID-19 pandemic was necessitated or recommended by government organizations (e.g. the Centers for Disease Control and Prevention; CDC), some people might have sought to alleviate their social isolation through an increased sense of belonging by means of group membership, which was readily provided online via conspiracy theory groups.

As previously discussed, social media and modern forms of online communication make it easier than ever to connect with others – reducing feelings of social isolation – and online groups can provide a sense of belonging (Allen, 2020; PERI Lab, 2020). Additionally, one of the tactics that QAnon believers implement to keep existing members engaged and draw in new members is a practice called "love bombing," in which QAnon believers are extremely warm, welcoming, supportive, and encouraging to other QAnon believers as they "follow breadcrumbs" to discover the "truth" (PERI Lab, 2020). QAnon believers share in the ideal that they are all together in a fight against evildoers and, therefore, will focus on emotionally supporting other believers through positive reinforcement (PERI Lab, 2020). This strong sense of support and community can alleviate the anxieties and negative effects of social isolation and loneliness.

Social Identity Threat

Like group membership, SIT focuses on a broader group membership – being a member of society – and examines the relationship between endorsement of conspiracy theory beliefs and perceptions of threats to society or social systems (Federico et al., 2018). SIT is predicated on the ideas that people desire to keep the existing social arrangements or systems in place (Jost et al., 2004) and will defend these systems (Jost & Hunyady, 2002) because challenges or threats to these social systems might threaten people's social identity that is tied to these systems (Federico et al., 2018). For example, if a person identifies with the country they live in, they might derive self-esteem, purpose, and meaning from that identity. However, threats of change to the nation might cause that person to undertake social identity defense tactics, such as defending the status quo and existing systems, to prevent reductions in self-esteem, purpose, or meaning. Research on SIT suggests that increases in perceptions of societal threats relate to increases in conspiracy theory endorsement (Federico et al., 2018).

Throughout 2020, myriad events could have been construed as threats to existing systems. Natural disasters and the pandemic were constant presences (e.g. wildfires in California, evidence supporting global warming, the COVID-19 pandemic) and threatened existing social systems (Kashima, 2021). However, there is little action to be taken to defend against these threats specifically; instead, defense actions could be taken against the measures that arose in the aftermath of these disasters. One such area related to the COVID-19 protocols, such as social distancing, quarantining, self-isolation, and wearing masks. SIT suggests that these changes pose a threat to social systems and, consequently, some people's social identity. Therefore, those who feel threatened by these changes would defend themselves against these threats by rallying against these changes. Constantinou and colleagues (2021) found support for this proposition in that, as conspiracy theory belief increases, adherence to COVID-19 protocols decreases.

Similar events in 2020 could also have created threats to existing systems. For example, BLM protests organized in response to the deaths of multiple Black men in police custody (e.g. George Floyd, Daniel Prude) were also tied to calls for cities and government entities to "defund the police" (BLM Global Network, 2020). This attempted change to the system and practices of policing could be viewed as a threat. Additionally, those who associate their social identity with conservatism and being Republican might have perceived the political events of 2020 – the impeachment proceedings of President Trump (Zurcher, 2020), the continual attacks on him based on his handling of the COVID-19 pandemic (Paz, 2020), and the general election cycle conflict (e.g. presidential debates; Cillizza, 2020) – as threats to the existing system of government, and so have instigated their defensive responses. The continual nature of this series of events means that some people might have perceived these events as a near-constant stream of threats to established social systems, which, as suggested by previous research (e.g. Federico et al., 2018), would increase their endorsement of conspiracy theories such as QAnon.

Terror Management Theory

Another psychological explanation that relates to the rise of QAnon during 2020 is TMT (see Chapter 5 of this volume for more on TMT and QAnon). TMT posits that a person's thoughts and awareness of their inevitable death can create a debilitating anxiety or existential threat. To combat this existential threat, people will adopt worldviews that outline a path to immortality, either literally (e.g. reincarnation, the afterlife) or figuratively (e.g. personal legacy, stories), and engaging in activities and thoughts that align with the adopted worldviews will increase personal self-esteem (Horner et al., in press), which can be bolstered by close and fulfilling relationships (Vail et al., 2019).

TMT offers three primary hypotheses: (1) Reminding someone of their eventual death will increase the desire to bolster their worldview, self-esteem, and close friendships (mortality salience hypothesis); (2) the bolstering of someone's worldview and self-esteem should reduce the anxiety associated with existential threat (anxiety-buffer hypothesis); and (3) threats to someone's worldview, self-esteem, and close friendships should make thoughts of death and existential threat more easily accessible (death-thought accessibility hypothesis; Greenberg & Arndt, 2011; Vail et al., 2019). Research on TMT supports these three hypotheses and can be applied to various worldviews (Greenberg & Arndt, 2011); however, many researchers focus on religious worldviews and beliefs. For example, when mortality salience is increased, religious people might attempt to improve their self-esteem and strengthen their close friendships by engaging in actions such as *bolstering* fellow believers, *derogating* nonbelievers, or *annihilating* those who pose the existential threat (if applicable; Vail et al., 2019). These actions would cause the person to become more entrenched in their religious beliefs, as the bolstering, derogating, and/or annihilation would need to be strictly related to the threatened worldview, and the actions serve as a buffer against anxiety induced by the existential threat and will, ideally, reduce death-thought accessibility (Greenberg & Arndt, 2011; Horner et al., in press; Vail et al., 2019).

These actions are all accentuated when the person is a *religious fundamentalist* (RF) or is intensely invested in their religious worldview and beliefs (Vail et al., 2019). This accentuation is because RFs believe that their religion is the only "correct" way to live and have a closed-minded orientation, meaning that there is no room for interpretation or flexibility regarding religious worldviews (e.g. the literal truth of the Bible). If a RF was confronted with an existential threat, that person might more strictly follow the worldview and behaviors ascribed by their religion (Vail et al., 2019), become aggressive in their derogation of nonbelievers (Altemeyer & Hunsberger, 1992), and have higher death-thought accessibility (Friedman & Rholes, 2007).

Some view QAnon as a quasi-religious organization (e.g. Kenes, 2021), meaning the TMT principles and logic applied to religious beliefs could be adapted to explain how TMT might relate to QAnon beliefs, especially in 2020. The constant media coverage of COVID-19 infection rates and death tolls combined with coverage of the deaths of Black men at the hands of the police (e.g. George Floyd, Daniel Prude) could be seen as constant existential threats that would increase mortality salience. QAnon believers might buffer against these existential threats by bolstering fellow believers and derogating nonbelievers. In fact, those reactions are in line with typical behaviors of QAnon believers; QAnon believers are known to be hostile toward nonbelievers but, simultaneously, to partake in the previously discussed "love bombing" (PERI Lab, 2020). This stark contrast in behaviors directed toward in-group versus out-group members could be seen as buffering existential threat-induced anxiety by improving self-esteem and promoting close relationships.

Also, because the acceptance of QAnon requires that believers have a close-minded orientation (e.g. black-and-white thinking about who is "good" and "evil"; PERI Lab, 2020), QAnon believers might react to mortality salience messages similarly to RFs. This would include more strictly following the tenets and principles of QAnon, becoming hostile toward nonbelievers, and attempting to annihilate those who pose an existential threat to QAnon beliefs (e.g. voting out politicians who do not align with QAnon, attacking lawmakers who would pass legislation against QAnon principles). This final component could also account for the mindset of some of the people who attacked the Capital building in Washington, DC, on January 6, 2021.

Future Directions

Moving forward, studying QAnon or, at the very least, a proxy for QAnon (e.g. former QAnon believers) is critical to better understand how QAnon adapts and spreads and how psychological theories might apply to the group. Researchers could interview current and former QAnon believers to establish what initially drew them to QAnon, what kept them involved, and how current believers might be persuaded to leave QAnon. These interviews could assess the effects of group membership, belonging, self-esteem, and threats to social systems as they relate to QAnon membership. Studies with QAnon believers could test TMT and SIT propositions by assessing whether there are significant differences in QAnon believers' likelihood to believe *other* conspiracy theories or to be affected by existential and system threats compared to nonbelievers.

Researchers could additionally examine how QAnon might expand in the future. TMT posits that existential threats will increase the desire to bolster worldviews, self-esteem, and relationships. Once the pandemic ends (i.e. the existential threat removed), how will that affect QAnon membership and expansion? QAnon has successfully pivoted and modified its messaging to increase membership and involvement, so it is plausible that the group could find new, innovative ways to attract and retain members. Researchers should monitor QAnon activity to assess membership levels, involvement, and recruitment tactics.

Lastly, the ease and effectiveness with which QAnon believers were able to disseminate disinformation have created a predicament for social media platforms regarding how they are to deal with conspiracy theories moving forward. Researchers should examine platforms' decisions regarding banning or removing conspiracy theory content and the consequences of those decisions. This could include monitoring the expansion of conspiracy theories that are not banned or removed from platforms, examining the effectiveness of measures taken to quell the spread of disinformation, and assessing traffic on social media platforms to determine whether users are migrating to or preferring certain platforms for conspiratorial discussions.

Conclusion

The social climate of 2020 provided, in a sense, a "perfect storm" in which QAnon could spread. The COVID-19 lockdowns drove more people online, and QAnon's ability to adapt its messaging and disseminate disinformation created a rise in QAnon believers. However, the constant shifting and adaptation of QAnon's core tenets to current events has created a conspiracy theory that is diffuse and ever-expanding. This constant shifting can make it difficult for researchers to study how psychological theories might apply to QAnon, as people might have been radicalized to join the group for a wide variety of reasons. Continued research on QAnon is critical, though, to better understand how belonging, SIT, and TMT might apply to QAnon.

REFERENCES

AFP. (2020, September 15). COVID as a "catalyst" for QAnon's rise in Europe. *France24*. www.france24.com/en/20200915-covid-a-catalyst-for-qanon-s-rise-in-europe

Ahmad, F. B., Cisewski, J. A., Miniño, A., & Anderson, R. N. (2021). Provisional mortality data – United States, 2020. *CDC Morbidity and Mortality Weekly Report*, *70*(14), 519–522.

AJMC Staff. (2021, January 1). A timeline of COVID-19 developments in 2020. *The American Journal of Managed Care*. www.ajmc.com/view/a-timeline-of-covid19-developments-in-2020

Allen, K. A. (2020). *The psychology of belonging*. Routledge.

Altemeyer, B., & Hunsberger, B. (1992). Authoritarianism, religious fundamentalism, quest, and prejudice. *International Journal for the Psychology of Religion*, *2*, 113–133.

BBC News – Europe. (2020, March 19). German police raid neo-Nazi Reichsbürger movement nationwide. *BBC News*. www.bbc.com/news/world-europe-51961069

BLM Global Network. (2020, July 6). What defund the police really means. *Black Lives Matter*. https://blacklivesmatter.com/what-defunding-the-police-really-means/?__cf_chl_jschl_tk__=pmd_52abba25e7f25e4b9e34a9b515c0d30615 14a6b7-1627912133-0-gqNtZGzNAjijcnBszQiO

Brady, S., D'Ambrosio, L. A., Felts, A., Rula, E. Y., Kell, K. P., & Coughlin, J. F. (2020). Reducing isolation and loneliness through membership in a fitness program for older adults: Implications for health. *Journal of Applied Gerontology*, *39*(3), 301–310.

Cillizza, C. (2020, October 23). Trump just handed Biden a devastating debate attack. *CNN*. www.cnn.com/2020/10/22/politics/trump-biden-final-debate-2020/index.html

Constantinou, M., Gloster, A. T., & Karekla, M. (2021). I won't comply because it is a hoax: Conspiracy beliefs, lockdown compliance, and the importance of psychological flexibility. *Journal of Contextual Behavioral Science*, *20*, 46–51.

Corley, C. (2021, May 25). Black Lives Matter fights disinformation to keep the movement strong. *NPR*. www.npr.org/2021/05/25/999841030/black-lives-matter-fights-disinformation-to-keep-the-movement-strong

Douglas, K. M., & Sutton, R. M. (2008). The hidden impact of conspiracy theories: Perceived and actual influence of theories surrounding the death of Princess Diana. *Journal of Social Psychology*, *148*(2), 210–222.

Douglas, K. M., Uscinski, J. E., Sutton, R. M., Cichocka, A., Nefes, T., Ang, C. S., & Deravi, F. (2019). Understanding conspiracy theories. *Political Psychology*, *40*, 3–35.

Federico, C. M., Williams, A. L., & Vitriol, J. A. (2018). The role of system identity threat in conspiracy theory endorsement. *European Journal of Social Psychology*, *48*(7), 927–938.

Forsyth, D. R. (2020). Group-level resistance to health mandates during the COVID-19 pandemic: A groupthink approach. *Group Dynamics: Theory, Research, and Practice*, *24*(3), 139–152.

Friedman, M., & Rholes, W. S. (2007). Successfully challenging fundamentalists beliefs results in increased death awareness. *Journal of Experimental Social Psychology*, *43*, 794–801.

Garry, A., Walther, S., Mohamed, R., & Mohamed, A. (2021). QAnon conspiracy theory: Examining its evolution and mechanisms of radicalization. *Journal for Deradicalization*, *26*, 152–216.

Greenberg, J., & Arndt, J. (2011). Terror management theory. In P. A. M. Van Lange, A. W. Kruglanski, & E. T. Higgins (Eds.), *Handbook of theories of social psychology* (pp. 398–415). Sage.

Hameleers, M., Powell, T. E., Van Der Meer, T. G., & Bos, L. (2020). A picture paints a thousand lies? The effects and mechanisms of multimodal disinformation and rebuttals disseminated via social media. *Political Communication*, *37*(2), 281–301.

Horner, D. E., Sielaff, A., Pyszczynski, T., & Greenberg, J. (in press). Terror management during and after the COVID-19 pandemic. In M. K. Miller (Ed.), *The social science of the COVID-19 pandemic: A call to action for researchers*. Oxford University Press.

Itzkowitz, C., Sonmez, F., Wagner, J., & Wang, A. B. (2020, September 30). Debate commission says it will change structure to ensure a "more orderly discussion." *The Washington Post*. www.washingtonpost.com/elections/2020/09/30/trump-biden-live-updates/

Jolley, D., & Douglas, K. M. (2014a). The effects of anti-vaccine conspiracy theories on vaccination intentions. *PLoS ONE*, *9*(2), e89177.

Jolley, D., & Douglas, K. M. (2014b). The social consequences of conspiracism: Exposure to conspiracy theories decreases intentions to engage in politics and to reduce one's carbon footprint. *British Journal of Psychology*, *105*(1), 35–56.

Jost, J. T., & Hunyady, O. (2002). The psychology of system justification and the palliative function of ideology. *European Review of Social Psychology*, *13*, 111–153.

Jost, J. T., Banaji, M. R., & Nosek, B. A. (2004). A decade of system justification theory: Accumulated evidence of conscious and unconscious bolstering of the status quo. *Political Psychology*, *25*, 881–919.

Kashima, Y. (2021). COVID-19, societal threats, and social psychology's self-imposed constraint. *Asian Journal of Social Psychology*, *24*(1), 30–33.

Kenes, B. (2021). QAnon: A conspiracy cult or quasi-religion of modern times? *European Center for Populism Studies*. www.populismstudies.org/wp-content/uploads/2021/03/ECPS-Organisation-Profile-Series-3.pdf

LeBoeuf, R. A., & Norton, M. I. (2012). Consequence–cause matching: Looking to the consequences of events to infer their causes. *Journal of Consumer Research*, *39*(1), 128–141.

Levin, B. (2021, February 4). Marjorie Taylor Greene: I only believe some of what QAnon says about Dems being satanic pedophile cannibals, okay? *Vanity Fair*. www.vanityfair.com/news/2021/02/marjorie-taylor-greene-fake-mea-culpa

Lyu, W., & Wehby, G. L. (2020). Community use of face masks and COVID-19: Evidence from a natural experiment of state mandates in the US. *Health Affairs*, *39*(8), 1419–1425.

Mascaro, L., Tucker, E., Jalonick, M. C., & Taylor, A. (2021, January 6). Pro-Trump mob storms US Capitol in bid to overturn election. *AP*. https://apnews.com/article/congress-confirm-joe-biden-78104aea082995bbd7412a6e6cd13818

Massie, G. (2021, March 19). Lauren Boebert shares QAnon conspiracy claiming Democratic arrests and resignations. *The Independent*. www.independent.co.uk/news/world/americas/us-politics/boebert-gop-qanon-congress-democrats-b1819868.html

Matthews, T., Danese, A., Wertz, J., Odgers, C. L., Ambler, A., Moffitt, T. E., & Arsenault, L. (2016). Social isolation, loneliness and depression in young adulthood: A behavioural genetic analysis. *Social Psychiatry & Psychiatric Epidemiology*, *5*, 339–348.

McCauley, C., & Jacques, S. (1979). The popularity of conspiracy theories of presidential assassination: A Bayesian analysis. *Journal of Personality and Social Psychology*, *37*(5), 637–644.

Pantucci, R., & Ong, K. (2021). Persistence of right-wing extremism and terrorism in the West. *Counter Terrorist Trends and Analyses*, *13*(1), 118–126.

Paz, C. (2020, November 2). All the President's lies about the coronavirus. *The Atlantic*. www.theatlantic.com/politics/archive/2020/11/trumps-lies-about-coronavirus/608647/

Polarization & Extremism Research & Innovation Lab. (2020, December 15). The QAnon conspiracy: Destroying families, dividing communities, undermining democracy. *Network Contagion Research Institute*. https://networkcontagion.us/wp-content/uploads/NCRI-%E2%80%93-The-QAnon-Conspiracy-FINAL.pdf

Solace Global. (2020, October 20). United States election 2020: A contentious election in an unusual year. *Solace Global*. www.solaceglobal.com/wp-content/uploads/2020/10/Solace-Advisory-US-Elections-2020-October-2020.pdf

The Straits Times. (2020, November 30). QAnon's rise in Japan shows conspiracy theory's global spread. *The Straits Times – International*. www.straitstimes.com/asia/east-asia/qanons-rise-in-japan-shows-conspiracy-theorys-global-spread

Timberg, C., & Dwoskin, E. (2021, March 11). With Trump gone, QAnon groups focus fury on attacking coronavirus vaccines. *The Washington Post*. www.washingtonpost.com/technology/2021/03/11/with-trump-gone-qanon-groups-focus-fury-attacking-covid-vaccines/

Vail, K. E., III, Soenke, M., & Waggoner, B. (2019). Terror management theory and religious belief. In C. Routledge & M. Vess (Eds.), *Handbook of terror management theory* (pp. 259–285). Academic Press.

Van den Bos, K. (2009). Making sense of life: The existential self trying to deal with personal uncertainty. *Psychological Inquiry*, *20*(4), 197–217.

van Prooijen, J. W., & Douglas, K. M. (2017). Conspiracy theories as part of history: The role of societal crisis situations. *Memory Studies*, *10*(3), 323–333.

Westerman, A. (2020, December 30). In 2020, protests spread across the globe with a similar message: Black Lives Matter. *NPR*. www.npr.org/2020/12/30/950053607/in-2020-protests-spread-across-the-globe-with-a-similar-message-black-lives-matt

Zurcher, A. (2020, February 5). Trump impeachment trial: What acquittal means for 2020 election. *BBC News*. www.bbc.com/news/world-us-canada-51331363

CHAPTER 9

QAnon and the Politics of 2020

Joseph Uscinski and Adam M. Enders

Introduction

The QAnon movement began in late 2017 when a person(s) claiming to be a government insider anonymously posted cryptic details on the 4chan imageboard about a supposed battle between Donald Trump and the "Deep State." Initially, QAnon attracted a small following and meager media attention. Despite billing themselves as an "online research community," followers of "Q" began participating in offline activities in 2018: They wore Q regalia to rallies for then-President Trump, and they even orchestrated kidnappings and acts of violence (Musgrave, 2018; Shammas, 2020). One supporter was convicted of domestic terrorism and another killed a mafia crime boss after a failed attempt to arrest New York Mayor Bill DeBlasio (Bump, 2019).

QAnon has been described as a cult, a "collective delusion," and a sign of mental illness (Ingram, 2020; Moorhouse & Malone, 2020). While the group shares some characteristics of cults and some followers show signs of psychopathology (Collins, 2020), QAnon's objectives (as far as one can discern them) are expressly political. Even though they do not espouse clear or consistent liberal or conservative policy goals (Enders et al., 2022), at the center of QAnon lore is the belief that the entire political establishment is profoundly corrupt, if not downright evil. Moreover, only a complete dismantling of the establishment (e.g. executing most politicians) can bring the change Q followers seek (Steck & Andrew, 2021). Such views naturally lend themselves to support for Donald Trump, who ran and governed as a political outsider bent on "draining the swamp" (Uscinski et al., 2021)

QAnon became intimately tied to the election of 2020, as Trump and his allies retweeted or spoke fondly of the group to motivate supporters (Samuels & Rodrigo, 2020), while Trump's opponents frequently pointed to the group's bizarre beliefs and actions (see Chapter 8 of this volume for more on how the events of 2020 affected QAnon). As the 2020 election neared, journalists increasingly pressed Trump on his support for the group and devoted considerable coverage to the numerous congressional candidates with ties to QAnon (Gabbatt, 2020). Although Trump lost the 2020 presidential election, two congressional seats went to candidates who had praised the group during their campaigns (Uscinski & Enders, 2021). Following the election, QAnon supporters were among the most visible at the January 6 Capitol riot.

Disconcerting as QAnon-related activity might seem, the movement has received only scant systematic attention from scholars, due both to the relative novelty of the movement and to the slow pace of academic publishing. Hence, much of the conventional wisdom about the basic characteristics of QAnon has been the product of journalistic inquiries. Having paid close attention to the news coverage garnered by the QAnon movement since 2018, we can identify four central claims about the group that frequently appear in the reporting:

(1) The QAnon movement is widely supported, perhaps as much as other political coalitions such as the Tea Party or the Christian Right.
(2) Support for the QAnon movement is growing and becoming "mainstream."
(3) The QAnon movement is born of "extreme" right-wing ideology.
(4) Support for QAnon is bred by social media activity and online information exposure.

While each of these inferences might at first seem reasonable, empirical support for each of them typically falls well below acceptable evidentiary standards employed in the social sciences. In this chapter, we put the conventional wisdom about the basic characteristics of the QAnon movement to the test. We utilize unique polling data from seven surveys of the American mass public spanning 2018–2021. These data allow us to track both the level of support for the QAnon movement and fluctuations in the scope of the movement over time. We fail to find evidence for the claims that QAnon has grown or become "mainstream." We also investigate the individual-level political, social, and psychological characteristics of QAnon supporters. Our findings are, again, sharply at odds with the conventional wisdom: Support for the movement appears to be less the product of left–right political orientations, such as partisanship and liberal–conservative ideology, and more the product of antiestablishment worldviews and antisocial personality traits. We conclude by discussing the political mechanisms that might have brought QAnon into the spotlight, as well at the potentially dangerous political consequences of the movement, despite its limited size and growth.

The Size and Growth of QAnon

News coverage of QAnon spiked during the summer of 2020, likely in response to: (1) the group frequently sharing conspiracy theories and misinformation about the pandemic; and (2) the use of QAnon-themed appeals coming from numerous candidates. Journalists tracking QAnon activity online frequently asserted that the movement was gaining support. For example, *CNN* argued QAnon was "dangerous and growing," *The Wall Street Journal* claimed it had "mainstream traction," *and VICE* lamented its "explosive growth" (Lamoureux, 2020; Seetharaman, 2020; Stelter, 2020). *The New York Times* even compared QAnon to the once-influential "Tea Party" (Roose, 2020), and *Salon* likened its scope to that of the "Christian Right" (Marcotte, 2020).

The inferences made by journalists regarding QAnon's size and growth were often supported by coarse examinations of social media activity, the presence of QAnon signs and T-shirts at Trump events, and the group's involvement in "Save The Children" rallies (Collins, 2020; Zadrozny & Collins, 2020). An obvious problem with this evidence is that it is largely anecdotal – it simply cannot be used to make valid inferences about the American population. Even sophisticated examinations of social media activity are beset by analytical hurdles (see Chapter 12 of this volume for more on QAnon and social media). For example, it can be difficult to tell which users – across groups and platforms – are unique, which users are sincere (rather than trolls), and how QAnon support stacks up against that for other fringe groups. This problem is compounded by the lack of definitional standards of what being a "QAnon believer" entails. Indeed, even though the results of public opinion polls were occasionally used to buttress claims about the size and scope of QAnon, many of the survey questions used to make such inferences either did not ask respondents about QAnon directly or asked respondents about conspiracy theories that both predate and exist outside the confines of QAnon.

Scope of the QAnon Movement

We investigate the size and growth of QAnon using seven repeated state-level and national polls from August 2018 to February 2021; two of these polls were administered in Florida (2018 and 2020) and five were

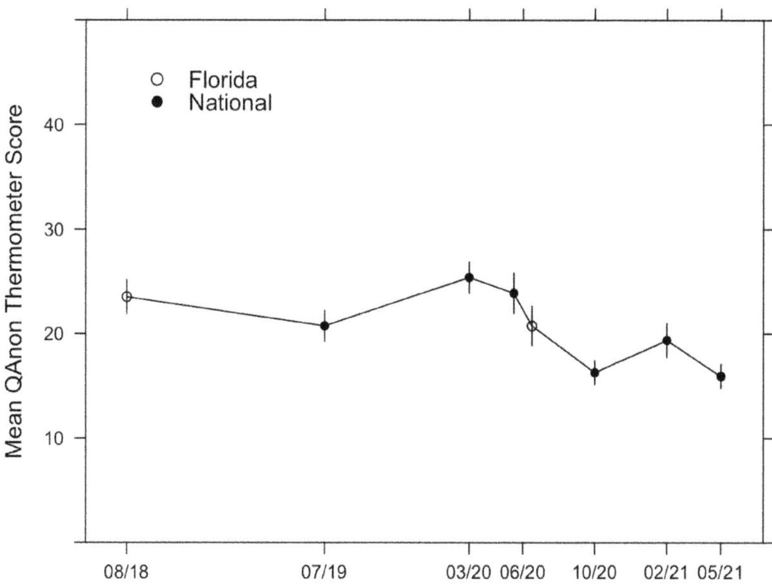

Figure 9.1 The average feeling thermometer scores (0–100) for the "QAnon movement" over time, with 95 percent confidence bands.

administered nationally from 2019 through 2021.[1] In these surveys, we asked respondents to rate their feelings toward the "QAnon movement" and other stimuli (e.g. political groups and leaders) using a "feeling thermometer." Feeling thermometers offer a rating scale that ranges from 0, denoting very "cold"/negative feelings, to 100, denoting very "warm"/ positive feelings. We asked respondents to rate their feelings toward the "QAnon *movement*" specifically, because QAnon followers frequently refer to themselves as a "research *movement*" and both the FBI and Congress consider QAnon a "movement." This definitional issue will be probed more carefully below.

The average thermometer score for each poll is plotted in Figure 9.1. In our first poll, of Floridians in August of 2018, the average thermometer score among respondents was 24. For context, respondents were also asked

[1] Sample sizes are as follows: August 2018 (n = 2,085), July 2019 (n = 2,000), March 2020 (n = 2,023), June 2020 (national, n = 1,040), June 2020 (Florida, n = 1,039), October 2020 (n = 2,015), February 2021 (n = 1,100), and May 2021 (n = 2,021). All polls, except the February 2021 poll, were administered by Qualtrics and designed to be representative of either the US adult population or Florida residents based on age, race, sex, and education. The February 2021 poll, which was also designed to be representative of the US adult population, was fielded by Lucid.

to rate Fidel Castro; QAnon was rated higher than the dictator by only 5 points on average. Given the palpable dislike of the Castro regime amongst Floridians, this is no endorsement of QAnon. Two years later, a June 2020 sample of Floridians rated the QAnon movement 21, indicating no growth in support over the course of two years. In our national polls, Americans rated the QAnon movement at 21 in July 2019, 25 in March 2020, 24 in June 2020, 16 in October 2020, 19 in February 2021, and 16 in May 2021, on average. These findings are sharply incongruent with the proposition that QAnon support has grown over time. To add context to these ratings, "white nationalists" were rated 15 and "antifa" 18 on the October 2020 poll in which the QAnon movement was rated 16. QAnon finds no more support than other fringe groups. Simply put, QAnon is relatively unpopular – and stably so – over time.

The only temporal change that our data reveal is an increase in the proportion of respondents choosing to rate the QAnon movement (regardless of how they rated it): 42 percent of respondents chose not to respond to the question in August 2018, but only 10 percent chose not to respond in May 2021. We suspect that the sharp increase in QAnon coverage – particularly over the course of 2020 – made nonfollowers more aware of the group and therefore better equipped to register their feelings. This interpretation is supported by the results of a March 2020 poll of Americans by the Pew Research Center, which found that only 3 percent of Americans knew much about QAnon, and only 24 percent knew a little; of those who knew at least a little, most had heard of it from mainstream (and presumably negative) news reporting.

Still, one might wonder how many people really "belong" to the QAnon movement, which cannot be inferred with precision from the feeling thermometers. To answer this question, we look to polls that specifically ask people to what extent they believe in or support QAnon. Table 9.1 contains the results of reputable national polls of Americans conducted between 2019 and 2021. As we should expect given the trend found above, these measures reveal meager support for QAnon. Across the slightly different question wordings, belief in and support for QAnon never exceeds about 8 percent of American adults. Moreover, the partisan and ideological differences in QAnon support are considerably weaker than the conventional wisdom suggests, which we explore at greater length below.

Some might wonder whether our polling evidence is subject to social desirability bias, thereby leading survey respondents to hide their support for QAnon out of fear of reprisal. If QAnon were growing as claimed, then our measurements would have picked up that growth regardless of such

Table 9.1 *Sample of polls about QAnon beliefs.*

Poll	Question	Result
Emerson College Polling n = 1,458 US registered voters August 24–26, 2019	Are you a believer in QAnon?	"Yes": 5% (6% Democrats; 6% Republicans)
ISD/Brian Schaffner n = 4,057 US adults September 18–20, 2020	Overall, do you have a favorable or unfavorable impression of QAnon?	"Very" or "Somewhat Favorable": 7% (4% Democrats; 13% Republicans)
Qualtrics/Joseph Uscinski n = 2,015 US adults October 8–21, 2020	I am a believer in QAnon	"Strongly Agree" and "Agree": 6.8% (5% Democrats; 11% Republicans)
Lucid/Adam Enders n = 1,100 US adults February 9–11, 2021	Do you support the QAnon movement?	"Strongly Support" and "Support": 8% (10% Democrats; 7% Republicans)
Suffolk University/USA Today n = 1,000 US adults February 15–20, 2021	Is your opinion of QAnon generally favorable or generally unfavorable?	"Favorable": 4% (4% liberal; 5% conservative)
Civiqs n = 19,831 US registered voters September 10–February 22, 2021	Are you a supporter of QAnon?	"Yes": 5% (1% Democrats; 10% Republicans)
Qualtrics/Joseph Uscinski n = 2,021 US adults April 30–May 19, 2021	Are you a believer in QAnon?	"Yes": 6% (7% Democrats; 6% Republicans)

biases, even if our baseline measurements did indeed undercount support. Furthermore, our survey respondents were quite willing to express belief in other equally taboo conspiracy theories, such as those about school shootings, Barack Obama's birth certificate, and the Holocaust. In fact, QAnon finds less support than most conspiracy theories that are regularly polled on. In our May 2021 national survey (bottom row of Table 9.1) QAnon found less support than *all but one* of forty-three conspiracy theories we asked about; conspiracy theories about government mind control, the dangers of 5G cellular technology, and the nefarious plans of George Soros are all more popular than QAnon.

Who and What Counts as QAnon?

Thus far, we have focused our efforts on survey questions about "QAnon" or "the QAnon movement." Yet, QAnon is associated with countless specific beliefs about satanists, sex traffickers, and the impending mass arrest of government and Hollywood elites. This conundrum highlights one difficulty in measuring QAnon support: Which individuals and beliefs count as QAnon? Surely questions asking directly about QAnon strike to the heart of the matter, but what about questions regarding Donald Trump's supposed battle against the Deep State, for example?

Table 9.2 contains information about the percentages of Americans who believe in various conspiracy theories associated with QAnon, as well as the correlation between each belief and general QAnon support. Importantly, each specific belief is positively and statistically significantly correlated with QAnon support to approximately the same degree – in some sense, each of these beliefs is similarly indicative of QAnon support. However, there is additional nuance to this story. Whereas only 7 percent of Americans either "agreed" or "strongly agreed" with the statement "I am a believer in QAnon," many more expressed belief in theories that the QAnon movement also seems to have adopted (e.g. about satanic sex traffickers, Donald Trump's battle with the Deep State, and Hillary Clinton's arrest for human trafficking). Indeed, two of these beliefs – about the Deep State and a massive child sex-trafficking racket – receive four to five times more support than the general QAnon belief question. These discrepancies undermine the claim that our more basic operationalizations of QAnon support might be yielding biased estimates (underestimates in particular) of the size of QAnon. Given that respondents have no problem expressing belief in other similar ideas on our surveys, we think our estimates specifically of QAnon support are likely not *under*estimates.

Many conspiracy theories associated with QAnon either predate QAnon, exist outside the confines of the QAnon milieu, or both. Take, for example, conspiracy theories about ritualized child abuse and satanism. We can trace these back to the "Satanic Panic" of the 1980s, the Salem witch trials, and countless older conspiracy theories that targeted Jews and other social, racial, and religious outsiders that even predate the American founding (see Chapter 16 of this volume for comparisons between QAnon and other movements). Simply put, conspiracy theories alleging child abuse are millennia old. Likewise, theories about the Deep State and nefarious government officials were focal talking points of the Trump 2016 presidential campaign, which, of course, predated the first Q-drop in 2017. This explains not only why these theories find more support than QAnon does, but also the moderate correlations between such beliefs and partisanship, which appear in the final column of Table 9.2. To believe

Table 9.2 *Distribution of QAnon-related conspiracy theory beliefs and correlations with QAnon support and partisanship (October 2020 data).*

QAnon conspiracy theory belief question	% agree	Correlation with QAnon support	Correlation with political party
Satanic sex traffickers control the government	14	0.492	0.085
Elites, from government and Hollywood, are engaged in a massive child sex-trafficking racket	35	0.463	0.152
Donald Trump is battling the Deep State	33	0.418	0.389
Hillary Clinton has been arrested for crimes involving human trafficking	11	0.452	0.197

Note: n = 2,015. All correlations are significant at $p < 0.001$ (two-sided *t*-test).

that Donald Trump is battling the Deep State is not necessarily to believe that an anonymous government official codenamed Q is communicating with the public on 8kun about a secret government operation to take down corrupt leaders – the only tenet of the QAnon movement that seems to be canonical. One could believe Trump is battling the Deep State simply because they believe Trump when he – very frequently – asserts that there is a Deep State and that he is battling it. Moreover, one could have held a belief about the Deep State (albeit by another term perhaps) decades before Q began posting or even before Trump entered politics.

This problem cuts both ways. For example, some of the ideas most unique to QAnon, such as the idea that John F. Kennedy, Jr. is still alive, appear quite controversial among Q followers. The idea that the moon landings were faked, which is an important belief for some vocal QAnon supporters, was specifically denounced by Q in a Q-drop. Thus, if we were to poll on any such idea, it would be difficult to determine how to appropriately interpret the connections between particular beliefs and support for QAnon. Given these theoretical and methodological difficulties, we argue that referring to some beliefs as "Q-adjacent," as many observers do, is frequently inappropriate, serving only to confuse who is a QAnon supporter and who is not; many people with such "Q-adjacent" beliefs are not supporters of QAnon and might never have even heard of it (at least not before late 2020).

Explaining QAnon Support

On the one hand, support for and belief in QAnon appears to be fairly scant and stable over time, in both the absolute sense and when compared to other conspiracy theories. On the other hand, the group became salient during the 2020 presidential election, and some followers have shown the propensity to engage in violent action. It is therefore important to understand who believes in QAnon and why, regardless of its size. The conventional wisdom points to political orientations (e.g. being "far-right") as perhaps the primary factor guiding support for QAnon (see Chapters 3, 4, and 5 of this volume for more on the characteristics of QAnon supporters). A cursory examination of QAnon suggests that this is a reasonable inference: Most of the 2020 congressional candidates affiliated in some way with QAnon ran as Republicans; other visible Republicans, like General Michael Flynn, support QAnon; and QAnon supporters, many of whom have lionized Trump, were visibly present at the January 2021 Capitol riot, which occurred in the wake of Trump's "Save America" rally.

Compelling as these insights might seem, we also see reason to be skeptical about the partisan and ideological composition of the QAnon movement. First, there is a glaring logical contradiction in labeling QAnon both "extreme" or "far-right" and, at the same time, "mainstream." Extremist groups and ideologies are, somewhat tautologically, no longer extreme once they come to be "mainstream," whatever that means. Extremity aside, it is also worth separating Donald Trump – an individual politician – from the Republican Party or conservatism more generally. While most QAnon followers are supporters of Donald Trump given the centrality of his role in canonical QAnon beliefs, not all Trump supporters identify as Republicans or conservatives. Indeed, QAnon is a movement premised on a Manichean struggle to recapture a corrupt, evil political establishment – this hardly sounds like traditional political conservatism or the musings of people deeply committed to an entrenched political party. Most importantly, in QAnon lore both Democrats (e.g. Hillary Clinton) and Republicans (e.g. the Bush family) are said to be targets of human-trafficking investigations that will end with their imprisonment, trial, and eventual execution. In short, there is nothing about QAnon theories suggesting a strong commitment to the Republican Party or to conservative values.

Theoretical arguments aside, claims about the partisan and ideological foundations of QAnon support remain largely unevidenced. In fact, the polling data presented above refute this narrative. First, support for or belief in QAnon (Table 9.1) is not limited to people self-identifying as Republicans or conservatives. For example, equal percentages of Republicans and Democrats claim to believe in QAnon in the Emerson Poll (top row of Table 9.1). When differences between Republicans/conservatives and Democrats/liberals exist, they tend to be quite small. This is to be expected given that so few people are supporters of or believers in QAnon. Regardless, the polling in Table 9.1 is, at best, inconsistent regarding the connection between the "far-right" and QAnon.

Explaining QAnon Support

In this section, we examine the conventional explanations about the sources of QAnon support. We do this in a multivariate regression framework where we can pit several potential explanations for QAnon support – including partisanship and ideology – against each other to determine which explanations exhibit the strongest relationships with QAnon support. Our dependent variable is responses to the statement "I am a believer in QAnon," which were measured on a scale ranging from "strongly disagree" to "strongly agree." Political orientations are operationalized in several ways. First, we include measures of partisanship (Democrat vs. Republican) and ideology (liberal vs. conservative). If QAnon support is primarily born of Republicanism and conservatism, both variables should be strong, positive, and significant predictors. We separately include the strength of partisan and ideological attachments, as previous work shows that, in some instances, conspiracy beliefs are fueled by political extremists (Enders & Uscinski, 2021a). In a similar vein, we include support for Donald Trump, which is measured using a 101-point feeling thermometer, just as feelings toward the QAnon movement were above. The coefficient associated with Trump support should be large, positive, and significant.

We also move beyond political orientations and preferences in attempting to explain QAnon support. Perhaps the most important addition to the conventional wisdom is antiestablishment orientations (Enders & Uscinski, 2021b). Antiestablishment orientations, as theorized by Uscinski et al. (2021), are a combination of populist (e.g. "the people, not politicians, should make our most important policy decisions"), Manichean (e.g. "politics is a battle between good and evil"), and conspiracy (e.g. "much of our lives are being controlled by plots hatched in secret places") thinking. Stronger antiestablishment views signify a detachment from the political system writ large and a deep-seated disillusionment with and suspicion of the established political order. As we understand QAnon supporters to be political outsiders in this vein, we expect antiestablishment orientations to play a substantial role in fueling attraction to QAnon.

We also consider the role of antisocial personality traits – namely, the dark triad. The dark triad is a general dimension of personality composed of three traits: narcissism (e.g. "I tend to want others to admire me"), psychopathy (e.g. "I tend to be unconcerned with the morality of my actions"), and Machiavellianism (e.g. "I tend to manipulate others to get my way"; Furnham et al., 2013). Dark-triad traits have long been linked to antisocial behaviors and beliefs, including various conspiracy theories (Enders et al., 2021). Because QAnon "true believers" have adopted beliefs that are both outside the mainstream and accuse innocent individuals of heinous crimes and because they frequently attempt to convert others through interpersonal connections, online activity, and rallies, we expect individuals who exhibit dark-triad traits to be more attracted to QAnon than those who do not, all else being equal.

The final substantive explanatory variable of interest that we consider is beliefs about the prevalence of child sex trafficking in the USA. If we were to liken QAnon to other political movements, we might think of concerns about sex trafficking as the political "issue" with which the movement is most concerned. We measured this concern vis-à-vis a question asking respondents how many children they believe currently fall victim to sex trafficking in the USA compared to a benchmark value of 300,000 (Uscinski & Enders, 2021); response options, on a five-point scale, ranged from "much less than 300,000" to "much higher than 300,000." Response options are anchored to the 300,000 number because it is both widely touted by politicians and has been repeatedly determined by fact checkers to be a gross exaggeration (Kessler, 2015). In other words, people who agree that the true number is 300,000 or more are vastly overestimating the scope of human trafficking in the USA.

We also include in our model respondent demographics (e.g. gender, race, age), social media use (e.g. frequency of time spent on Twitter and Facebook), and religiosity (e.g. how frequently they attend religious services). We present the effects of key variables of interest from this model – in descending order of effect size – in Figure 9.2. The points represent the coefficients from our model (i.e. estimated strength of that variable's effect on belief in QAnon) and the black horizontal lines represent 95 percent confidence intervals. Points falling to the right of the vertical dashed line at 0 signify a positive effect; when confidence intervals overlap with the dashed line, effects are nonsignificant.

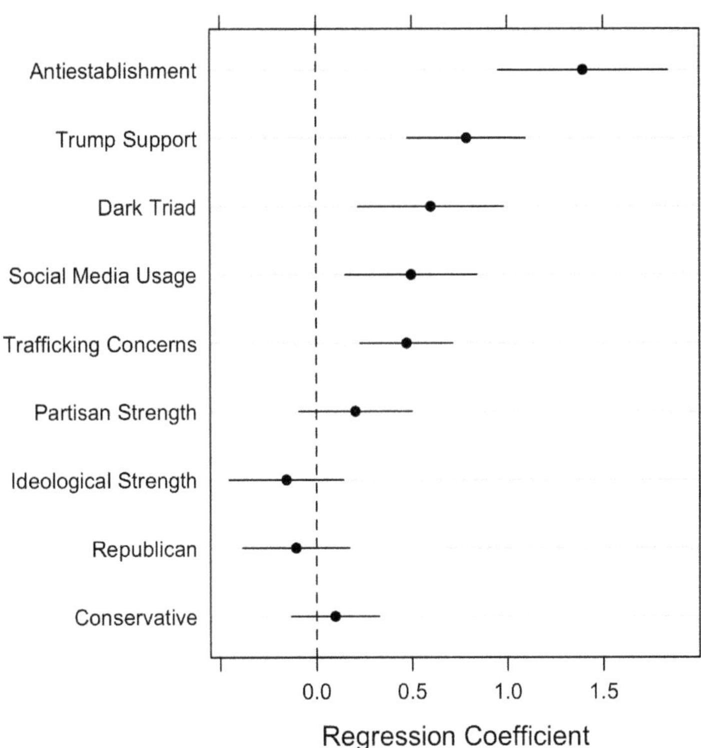

Figure 9.2 Standardized coefficients (with 95 percent confidence bands) from a regression of QAnon support on potential explanatory factors (October 2020 data).

While antiestablishment sentiment, dark-triad personality traits, support for Donald Trump, and overestimations of child sex trafficking significantly predict support for QAnon, ideological and partisan identities – in terms of both strength and direction – do not. These findings not only severely undercut conventional wisdom that QAnon support is "far-right" in some way, but also suggest that support is more associated with nonpartisan and prepartisan personality traits and worldviews regarding the broader political establishment (presumably including the parties, as Uscinski et al., 2021 find). Thus, even though some high-profile Republicans and conservatives support (or once supported) QAnon, neither party allegiances and ideological preferences nor the strengths of those orientations inherently dispose individuals to believe that a secret agent is posting coded clues about a battle between satanic sex traffickers and the President on a fringe website. To be clear, ideology of some sort likely factors into QAnon support, but this ideology is likely to be more anti-governmental in nature than liberal/conservative or Democrat/Republican. Given the reported behaviors of QAnon supporters, their calls for mass executions, and the vivid, violent imagery shared in their online posts, it is no surprise that they tend to share dark-triad personality traits as well.

The Role of Social Media

The final piece of conventional wisdom about QAnon we examine involves the spread of QAnon beliefs – the mechanism by which unwitting individuals are converted into disciples. According to many accounts, the primary culprit is social media – after all, the QAnon movement was born on a social media platform. We have already argued that support for QAnon is quite weak and stably so over time; thus, we merely remind the reader that the visibility and increase of available QAnon material online do not appear to have translated into an increase in followers. Still, it seems reasonable to assume that social media play some role in fueling QAnon beliefs.

Those who sympathize with this argument typically propose that incidental or unintentional online exposure to QAnon content (or any conspiracy theories for that matter), perhaps due to social media algorithms, causes people to adopt conspiracy theory beliefs. Intuitive as this argument might be, it is sharply at odds with well-evidenced theories of media effects, public opinion formation, and cognitive dissonance (Iyengar & Hahn, 2009; Lodge & Taber, 2013; Stroud, 2010). Simply put, people do not uncritically accept all information they encounter. Instead, information acceptance – especially when it comes to political information – is conditional on the congruence between said information and previously held beliefs, values, identities, and predispositions. For example, Democrats are unlikely to tune into Fox News or otherwise accept information produced by that network, though Republicans are more likely to do both. In the former case, Democrats selectively avoid incongruent information, whereas Republicans selectively expose themselves to congruent information.

The same psychological processes are at play with respect to conspiratorial information online. Those who are least disposed to seeing the world in conspiratorial terms are less likely to seek out or believe conspiratorial information, while those who are prone to interpreting salient events and circumstances as products of conspiracies are more likely to seek out conspiratorial content, or at least accept conspiratorial information when

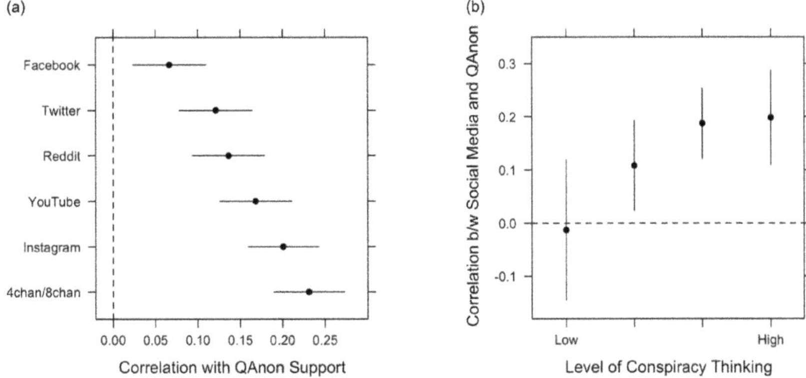

Figure 9.3 Left: Correlation between social media use and QAnon support. Right: Correlation between social media use (scale of all platforms) and QAnon support at different levels of conspiratorial thinking (October 2020 data).

incidentally exposed. Here, we present support for this proposition. In the left-hand panel of Figure 9.3, we report the correlations between support for QAnon and the frequency with which individuals visit each of six social media platforms (measured on five-point scales ranging from "never" to "every day"). QAnon support is significantly and positively correlated with usage of each platform, albeit differentially so in terms of strength. QAnon beliefs are most strongly associated with 4chan/8chan use; this makes perfect sense given that these platforms welcome anonymous posts about fringe topics and that QAnon got its start on these platforms. This finding is supportive of the conventional wisdom about the role of social media in promoting QAnon beliefs.

The right-hand panel of Figure 9.3 tells a different story. This panel depicts the correlation between QAnon support and a scale of all the social media platforms in the left-hand panel by the level of one's predisposition toward conspiratorial thinking – the general propensity to interpret events and circumstances as products of conspiracies (Uscinski et al., 2020). At the lowest levels of conspiratorial thinking, there is no significant correlation between QAnon beliefs and frequency of social media use. As one's disposition toward conspiratorial thinking increases, so too does the correlation between social media use and QAnon support. Thus, time spent on social media is a necessary but not sufficient condition for the promotion of QAnon beliefs. Social media could facilitate the spread of conspiratorial information, but this does not translate into belief unless one is already disposed to viewing the world through a conspiratorial lens.

Conclusion

Lacking any governing experience or recognizable ideology, Donald Trump entered the race for president in 2015 as an unconventional candidate. He used his outsider status to rhetorically dismantle his more experienced and traditional "insider" opponents. Interestingly, Trump attacked not only the opposing party, but his own party as well. For example, Trump regularly accused fellow Republicans of rigging the nominating contests against him. Once nominated, Trump made clear his intention to "drain the swamp" of all insiders regardless of their ideology or partisan ties. Trump's outsider persona made him appeal not only to voters looking for a fresh candidate, but also to voters who harbored a deep-seated distrust of the political establishment. At the extreme edge of that group of supporters were Americans possessing a combination of antiestablishment views, antisocial personality traits, and profound anxieties about child sex trafficking – the same individuals that QAnon appealed to. While both Trump and QAnon preached to the converted, appealing to people with uncharitable views of the government, society, and elites, Trump cast a larger, slightly more palatable net than did QAnon.

Our findings underscore that whatever growth QAnon experienced was concentrated among a small number of people who already possessed amenable characteristics. Generally speaking, for individuals to accept media messages, those messages must comport with their existing identities, worldviews, and beliefs. In other words, media messages are best at persuading people already inclined to believe those messages. This is especially the case for conspiracy theories: People must be inclined toward conspiracy theories and toward demonizing the villain in the particular theories in question in order to seek them out (Bessi et al., 2015) or believe them (Uscinski et al., 2020). Thus, while some people have been turned on to QAnon via social media activity, such individuals were not unwittingly pulled "down the rabbit hole" (see also Chapter 2 of this volume). Instead, they were likely already comfortably bunkered at the bottom. Put simply, QAnon messaging online did little to convert people who did not already share conspiratorial, antiestablishment worldviews; this partially explains the lack of growth in the QAnon movement over time.

Nevertheless, repeated journalistic claims about QAnon eventually took hold among the mass public and policymakers alike. Even some Republican Congresspeople – who we would expect to disavow the connection between QAnon and the political right – have accepted the idea that the QAnon movement is expansive and mainstream. This newfound attention matters: Bills designed to alter or remove section 230 of the Communications Decency Act have been introduced in Congress, lawmakers are considering a wide variety of methods to monitor and regulate internet activity, and social media companies are altering policies in response to the conventional wisdom about QAnon. We are not necessarily arguing that these steps should not be taken, but rather that they are based on false pretexts. Perhaps we should first try to understand why journalists and other observers got QAnon so wrong.

As previously mentioned, news reports about QAnon in 2020 often relied on inadequate polling and anecdotes (e.g. the number of people with QAnon T-shirts or signs at rallies). For example, many polls fielded in 2020 and early 2021 contained poorly worded survey questions that combined numerous conspiracy theories into "double-barreled" survey items (Halvorsen, 2021) or even failed to ask about QAnon belief specifically (PRRI, 2021). Along similar lines, many journalists confused belief in or support for QAnon with belief in other conspiracy theories supposedly associated with QAnon in some way (e.g. Deep State theories). Interpretation of even properly executed polling proved problematic. Finally, there has been a tendency among journalists and other observers to infer from retweets of QAnon-related accounts on the part of President Trump and his allies that QAnon beliefs are pervasive. While the use of conspiracy theories by politicians is certainly disconcerting, it is not necessarily the case that those messages persuade the mass public. If QAnon were indeed "mainstream," why did Trump and the vast majority of QAnon-linked candidates lose in the elections of 2020 and 2022?

Although our investigations failed to produce evidence supportive of conventional wisdom regarding the size, scope, and foundations of support for QAnon, the movement is still worthy of serious attention. Future studies should continue to track support for QAnon and other fringe groups over time using national polling, both in the USA and abroad. Indeed, little is known about the life cycles of conspiracy theory beliefs and related movements – continued polling, even when a given conspiracy theory seems less salient than it once was, can help fill this void. Relatedly, scholars should continue to investigate the proper ways to poll on conspiracy theories: How should questions be worded, what are appropriate response options, and what does general agreement with conspiratorial notions on surveys tell us? These questions lie at the heart of disagreements about the size and scope of QAnon and will presumably fuel similar confusion with conspiracy theories in the future if not carefully investigated now. Finally, researchers must also expend more effort in connecting individual-level (social) media habits with expressed beliefs. The scholarly and journalistic treatment of QAnon showcases how the results of media studies are oftentimes at odds with inferences made by polling work – how, when, and why this is the case must be better understood.

Even small groups can engage in troubling actions and have a measurable political impact. Trump, his associates inside and outside of government, and various other political allies used both overt messaging and dog whistles to attract distrusting, antiestablishment, and generally conspiratorial people to their cause and to keep them motivated, donating, and participating. The power of the conspiratorial narratives wielded by Trump and his allies was never clearer than on January 6, 2021, when voter fraud conspiracy theories fueled a riot in which many QAnon supporters participated. In this light, the QAnon movement might be more of a political cudgel – an idea to be strategically weaponized – than a natural threat in its own right.

REFERENCES

Bessi, A., Coletto, M., Davidescu, G. A., Scala, A., Caldarelli, G., & Quattrociocchi, W. (2015). Science vs conspiracy: Collective narratives in the age of misinformation. *PLoS ONE*, *10*(2), e0118093.

Bump, P. (2019, March 28). The murder of an alleged gangster on Staten Island loops in an unexpected figure: QAnon. *The Washington Post*. www.washingtonpost.com/politics/2019/03/28/murder-an-alleged-gangster-staten-island-loops-an-unexpected-figure-qanon/

Collins, B. (2020, August 14). How QAnon rode the pandemic to new heights – and fueled the viral anti-mask phenomenon. *NBC News*. www.nbcnews.com/tech/tech-news/how-qanon-rode-pandemic-new-heights-fueled-viral-anti-mask-n1236695

Enders, A., & Uscinski, J. (2021a). Are misinformation, anti-scientific claims, and conspiracy theories for political extremists? *Group Processes & Intergroup Relations*, *24*(4), 583–605.

(2021b). The role of anti-establishment orientations in the Trump presidency. *The Forum*, *19*(1), 47–76.

Enders, A., Uscinski, J., Klofstad, C., Premaratne, K., Seelig, M., Wuchty, S., Murthi, M., & Funchion, J. (2021). The 2020 presidential election and beliefs about fraud: Continuity or change? *Electoral Studies*, *72*, 102366.

Enders, A., Uscinski, J., Klofstad, C., Wuchty, S., Seelig, M., Funchion, J., Murthi, M., Premaratne, K., & Stoler, J. (2022). Who supports QAnon? A case study in political extremism. *Journal of Politics*, *84*(3), 1844–1849.

Furnham, A., Richards, S. C., & Paulhus, D. L. (2013). The dark triad of personality: A 10 year review. *Social and Personality Psychology Compass*, *7* (3), 199–216.

Gabbatt, A. (2020, October 16). Trump refuses to disavow QAnon conspiracy theory during town hall. *The Guardian*. www.theguardian.com/us-news/2020/oct/15/qanon-trump-refuses-disavow-conspiracy-theory-town-hall

Halvorsen, M. (2021, June 28). Not every QAnon believer's an antisemite. But there's a lot of overlap between its adherents and belief in a century-old antisemitic hoax. *Morning Consult*. https://morningconsult.com/2021/06/28/qanon-antisemitism-right-wing-authoritarianism-polling/

Ingram, M. (2020, August 13). The QAnon cult is growing and the media is helping. *Columbia Journalism Review*. www.cjr.org/the_media_today/the-qanon-conspiracy-cult-is-growing-and-the-media-is-helping.php

Iyengar, S., & Hahn, K. S. (2009). Red media, blue media: Evidence of ideological selectivity in media use. *Journal of Communication*, *59*(1), 19–39.

Kessler, G. (2015, May 28). The bogus claim that 300,000 U.S. children are "at risk" of sexual exploitation. *The Washington Post*. www.washingtonpost.com/news/fact-checker/wp/2015/05/28/the-bogus-claim-that-300000-u-s-children-are-at-risk-of-sexual-exploitation/

Lamoureux, M. (2020, July 29). QAnon has gone global. *Vice News*. www.vice.com/en/article/pkym3k/qanon-conspiracy-has-gone-global

Lodge, M., & Taber, C. S. (2013). *The rationalizing voter*. Cambridge University Press.

Marcotte, A. (2020, August 13). Is QAnon the new Christian right? With evangelicals fading, a new insanity rises. *Salon.com*. www.salon.com/2020/08/13/is-qanon-the-new-christian-right-with-evangelicals-fading-a-new-insanity-rises/

Moorhouse, D., & Malone, E. (2020, September 4). Here's why BuzzFeed News is calling QAnon a "collective delusion" from now on. *Buzzfeed*. www.buzzfeednews.com/article/drumoorhouse/qanon-mass-collective-delusion-buzzfeed-news-copy-desk

Musgrave, P. (2018, August 2). Conspiracy theories are for losers. QAnon is no exception. *The Washington Post*. www.washingtonpost.com/news/posteverything/wp/2018/08/02/conspiracy-theories-are-for-losers-qanon-is-no-exception/

PRRI. (2021, May 27). Understanding QAnon's connection to American politics, religion, and media consumption. *PRRI.org*. www.prri.org/research/qanon-conspiracy-american-politics-report/

Roose, K. (2020, August 20). Think QAnon is on the fringe? So was the Tea Party. *The New York Times*. www.nytimes.com/2020/08/13/technology/qanon-tea-party.html

Samuels, B., & Rodrigo, C. M. (2020, August 19). Trump praises QAnon supporters: They "love our country." *The Hill*. https://thehill.com/homenews/administration/512821-trump-praises-qanon-supporters-they-love-our-country

Seetharaman, D. (2020, August 13). QAnon booms on Facebook as conspiracy group gains mainstream traction. *Wall Street Journal*. www.wsj.com/articles/qanon-booms-on-facebook-as-conspiracy-group-gains-mainstream-traction-11597367457

Shammas, B. (2020, January 8). A mother teamed up with QAnon followers to kidnap her son from protective custody, police say. *The Washington Post*. www.washingtonpost.com/crime-law/2020/01/08/mother-teamed-up-with-qanon-followers-kidnap-her-son-protective-custody-police-say/

Steck, E., & Andrew, K. (2021, January 26). Marjorie Taylor Greene indicated support for executing prominent Democrats in 2018 and 2019 before running for Congress. *CNN*. www.cnn.com/2021/01/26/politics/marjorie-taylor-greene-democrats-violence/index.html

Stelter, B. (2020, August 15). QAnon is conspiratorial, dangerous, and growing. And we're talking about it all wrong. *CNN*. www.cnn.com/2020/08/14/media/qanon-news-coverage/index.html

Stroud, N. J. (2010). Polarization and partisan selective exposure. *Journal of Communication*, *60*(3), 556–576.

Uscinski, J., & Enders, A. (2021, March 9). Unfounded fears about sex trafficking did not begin with QAnon and go far beyond it. *LSE USAPP Blog*. https://bit.ly/3qx9keU

Uscinski, J., Enders, A., Seelig, M. I., Klofstad, C. A., Funchion, J. R., Everett, C., Wuchty, S., Premaratne, K., & Murthi, M. N. (2021). American politics in two dimensions: Partisan and ideological identities versus anti-establishment orientations. *American Journal of Political Science*, *65*(4), 877–895.

Uscinski, J., Enders, A. M., Stefan, W., Klofstad, C., Seelig, M., Funchion, J., Murthi, M., Premaratne, K., & Everett, C. (2020). Why do people believe COVID-19 conspiracy theories? *The Harvard Kennedy School (HKS) Misinformation Review*, *1*, 1–12.

Zadrozny, B., & Collins, B. (2020, August 21). QAnon looms behind nationwide rallies and viral #SavetheChildren hashtags. *NBC News*. www.nbcnews.com/tech/tech-news/qanon-looms-behind-nationwide-rallies-viral-hashtags-n1237722

CHAPTER 10

The QAnon Conspiracy Narrative
Understanding the Social Construction of Danger

David G. Bromley and James T. Richardson

Because humans are social and cultural animals, across time and cultures there have been countless forms of symbolic communication and social organization. One important and pervasive narrative form that emerges at moments when a sense of endangerment arises is what we term "conspiracy narratives" (CNs). Using the case of QAnon in the USA, the broader argument to be developed here is that: (1) the emergence of CNs can be traced to moments of major social dislocation, which we shall refer to as "deterritorialization–reterritorialization" (DR); (2) irrespective of the time period, they have presented a distinctive set of characteristics that together project a sense of imminent, catastrophic danger; and (3) the QAnon narrative is distinctive because it has emerged with the advancement of globalization, incorporated a broad range of issues and advocacy groups, and organized in an online environment (see Chapter 14 of this volume for more on QAnon narratives).

As Felstiner et al. (1980–1981, p. 633) have pointed out, "[t]rouble, problems, personal and social dislocation are everyday occurrences [in social life]." Because the social order within which humans live is socially constructed, most social troubles are integral to the nature of that order. At an institutional level, religion is a major social form through which human groups self-regulate by envisioning supranatural entities and forces that could independently intervene in human affairs, creating or resolving troubling circumstances. In the everyday social world, symbolic responses to perceived disorder and danger – both religious and secular – are often analyzed as rumor, gossip, or urban legend; corresponding social movements are typically termed "scares" or "moral panics" (Bromley, 2010; Bromley & Shupe, 1981; Richardson & Introvigne, 2007).

We shall argue that the CN is a regulatory form that falls between formal institutional religious/spiritual narratives and informal gossip/urban legend narratives. The QAnon narrative is such a danger narrative. This is not a narrative about a secret attack by a hostile invading force. Rather, it is a narrative of ultimate betrayal in which the major protagonists are insiders who were trusted to be committed to the best interests of the group and its membership but have instead organized secretly to appropriate power and now intentionally and collectively use that power to exploit and victimize their fellows. In its strongest form, the threat is imminent and of apocalyptic proportions; there is an urgent need for restorative action. CNs therefore might incorporate elements of both institutional and informal narratives. The conspiratorial force is to be found outside of everyday life experience (and might include religious elements) and until now has been unrecognized for what it actually is.

The Emergence of Conspiracy Narratives

While minor CNs and their social transmission have been perennial features of the American social environment, more major episodes have been less common. QAnon presents an important and informative case as the narrative has achieved a more advanced level; conflict now ranges across a large number of issues, network communication is frenetic, and disputation has reached a high level of intensity. QAnon thus offers insight into a distinctive and fully developed CN form. These more developed forms are most likely to emerge during moments of thoroughgoing transformation of the social order, described by Gilles Deleuze and Félix Guattari (1977) as "deterritorialization–reterritorialization."

Territorialization is not simply a geographic concept; rather, it refers to the complex integration of place and sociocultural structures. At moments of deterritorialization, traditional social and cultural moorings are upended and power relations across the social and institutional landscape are reconfigured. Groups experiencing this process frequently conceptualize the precipitating forces as transcending their immediate life domain, draw on relevant cultural imagery from their own culture (Deutsch & Bochantin, 2020), and depict the source of trouble as ultimate evil (such as "Satan" or "the Devil"). A key element of this process is that impacted people are essentially living in two opposed social worlds, with the former order disintegrating and the emerging order enveloping their lives. Traditional ways of living and coping lose their legitimacy and effectiveness, and, at least for the most highly impacted segment of the social order, the connection between day-to-day life and the larger social order becomes more remote. The result is a sense of chaos and loss of control. As is shown herein, CNs function both as symbolic means of communicating a sense of danger and as danger control mechanisms (Bromley, 1994).

In American history, two important earlier episodes in which DR has been attributed to satanic forces are the outbreak of witchcraft allegations at Salem Village, Massachusetts, in 1692 and what has been called the "Satanism Scare" in the 1980s. The current QAnon episode, which also includes a major satanic theme, continues a pattern of major dislocation, this time emanating from the impacts of globalization, translating into conspiracy accusations.

Seventeenth-Century Salem

The 1692 Salem outbreak of witchcraft allegations began when several adolescent girls in Salem Village began exhibiting alarming psychological symptoms; the narrative constructed by parents soon attributed the apparently external influence over their children to witchcraft (bewitchment). Once the witchcraft theme was enunciated, accusations spread rapidly from a small group of Salem Village neighbors (who were particularly vulnerable people) to a broad range of geographically dispersed people (Erikson, 2004). The episode ultimately produced hundreds of charges and twenty executions. However, the outbreak was contained fairly rapidly, in part due to accusations threatening powerful people, including the wife of the Massachusetts Bay Colony's governor (Shupe & Bromley, 1981).

The events of 1692 actually were several decades in the making. There were several destabilizing events around the same time (lingering fears of Native American attacks on the community, the aftermath of war with the British several years earlier, and an epidemic of smallpox), as well as other witchcraft outbreaks. However, the 1692 episode in Salem erupted out of rural–urban conflict that began with commercial development and continued later with the advent of industrialization. There was constant tension and conflict between small, more agrarian Salem Village and larger, more commercial Salem Town. The latter was rapidly growing, becoming the second-largest seaport in Massachusetts Bay Colony with commercial ties to Boston and internationally to London (Nash, 1979). Salem Village was continually engaged in a struggle for financial and ecclesiastical autonomy from Salem Town. As Boyer and Nissenbaum (1974, p. 180) summarized this period and the conflict dynamics, the crux of the matter was

> ... the resistance of back-country farmers to the pressures of commercial capitalism and the social style that accompanied it; the breaking away of outlying areas from parent towns; difficulties between ministers and their

> congregations; the crowding of third-generation sons from family lands; the shifting locus of authority within individual communities and society as a whole; the very quality of life in an unsettled age.

1980s Satanism Scare

About three centuries later in the USA, another CN emerged; it has been widely referred to as the "Satanism Scare" or the "Satanic Panic" (Bromley, 1991; Richardson, 1997; Richardson et al., 1991; Victor, 1993). As in the case of the Salem episode, there were other stressors in the environment during this period, a number of which were related to children (fears about widespread kidnapping of children and malicious Halloween treat contamination, reports of scary killer clowns preying on children). However, the CN in this case more fundamentally grew out of tensions between family and economy that had been intensifying for several decades. The conventional division of responsibility within the family coming out of the 1950s and 1960s (husband/father as "breadwinner" and wife/mother as "homemaker") gave way with increasing rapidity to dual-career families. Both gender role expectations and wage stagnation during this period produced a sharp increase of married women in the labor force. Greater family labor force participation triggered a corresponding need to purchase what previously had been family-provided services. One result was a rapid growth of daycare provider services, which were both expensive and of variable quality. Children were now increasingly being entrusted to stranger-managed, for-profit businesses during their critical formative years (Bromley, 1991).

In late twentieth-century America, the imagery of ultimate evil became a group of satanists who, for their own power, pleasure, and profit, exploited the vulnerability of American families and the trust placed in them as surrogate parents by abusing and murdering children (Bromley, 1991, p. 69). This satanism episode, which began in the USA and spread to other nations as well, gradually declined as an array of powerful institutions mobilized against claims of "recovered memories" of sexual abuse on which many allegations rested (Mulhern, 1991).

Contemporary QAnon

Like its predecessor CNs in American history, the roots of QAnon can be found in a major episode of DR, with the expansion of globalization, which began its rapid ascension and impact in the USA during the early 1980s. Put simply, the process of globalization involves the increasing interdependence of the world as a whole. While globalization is often defined in terms of technology and economy, it actually reshapes every institutional arena and the territories on which they are situated. Earlier in American history, it was possible for local communities to coexist in parallel fashion with the developmental trajectory of national organization. Numerous groups that created networks of organizations that sought to empower local communities were created. This was particularly visible in conservative Christian America (e.g. incorporation of creationist doctrine and Christian prayer in public schools, construction of Christian bookstores, establishment of the Christian music industry, religiously affiliated homeschooling, adoption of fundamentalist theology, covenantal marriage laws).

The continued advance of globalization has made a parallel-worlds solution less viable. In a globalized social order, humanity is in control of its own destiny through a program of rational action in search of "progress." As Thomas (2007, p. 37) notes, "[t]echnology, bureaucratic formal organization, science, and professionalization are ritualized means of action that promises progress," and this rationalized environment "creates, stabilizes, and legitimates corporations, states, associations, and individuals to rationally pursue interests and goals." These various types of global organization are isomorphic with one another (DiMaggio & Powell, 1983) in the public sphere and also seek similar consistency in the private sphere. As a result, "globalization must be spread even at the expense of traditional knowledge and practice" (Thomas, 2007, p. 38). Traditional local communities are therefore increasingly subsumed by the logic and organization of globalism, and these populations experience a greater disconnection between the everyday lives they seek to sustain and the larger global order. For transnational corporations, geographic reallocation of production facilities to control labor costs is rational policy and the responsibility is to corporate shareholders; however, for local communities, this transnational logic means the abandonment of sometimes long-standing community partnerships, undermining of the viability of local economies.

In a globalizing world, population movement and diversification are integral dynamics, and borders that once functioned as points of separation now become connection points. For local communities, the issue is often fashioned as undesired immigrants who, by their presence, challenge established racial/ethnic, religious, and linguistic/cultural hierarchies. In a global environment, key power resources (financial, educational, technological, political) shift from local independent communities to internationally oriented metropolitan centers. A number of the themes in the QAnon CN are related to tensions that have evolved out of expanding globalism.

Prior to the emergence of Q, there were people who claimed to be knowledgeable "Deep State" insiders who posted on message boards using names like FBIAnon and CIAAnon. However, it was the QAnon CN post by "Q Clearance Patriot" (Q is the designation for top secret, highly restricted government data), who claimed to be a high-ranking intelligence officer, on October 28, 2017, on the 4chan message board that is widely credited with igniting QAnon. That initial post asserted that former presidential candidate Hillary Clinton was about to be arrested for her orchestration of the Deep State pedophilia ring, and that military units were being mobilized to deal with an anticipated violent reaction. Q subsequently predicted that Donald Trump would reveal the identities of the satanic cult members and prosecute them for their crimes. Following public recognition of the conspiracy, called "The Great Awakening," a successful confrontation, called "The Storm," would restore the nation to its naturally intended order (Beverly, 2020, p. 31). QAnon is currently in an advanced formative stage and therefore offers a unique case through which to examine the core characteristics of a CN in the global age.

The Structure of the QAnon Conspiracy Narrative

CNs possess a distinctive narrative structure, with various levels of development and emphasis possible. Most CNs remain at lower levels of organization and transmission and therefore have limited visibility and impact at a societal level. In their most fully developed form, CNs assert evil and transgression so dangerous that mutual occupancy of the same social space is held to be impossible. If a carrier social movement exists, a moment of dramatic denouement might ensue (Bromley, 2002). The QAnon CN has developed considerably in terms of size, complexity, and impact and therefore manifests the defining characteristics of such narratives. These characteristics include revelatory framing, mythic themes, an insurgent media network, and narrative radicalization.

Revelatory Framing

The QAnon narrative is framed as revelatory and deterministic; this combination of a stunning revelation and the imperviousness of narrative truth to disconfirmation is critical to the strength and resilience of the QAnon narrative. Indeed, advocates of the QAnon CN do not present it as a theory but rather as a revelation or a manifesto. It is a foundational assertion of truth, the basis on which the merit of other claims is measured. In short, narrative truth drives facts rather than facts driving truth. The narrative is a saga of subversion and restoration. It shares certain characteristics with Christian apocalyptic narratives, as one segment of the movement – Christian evangelicals – draws heavily on biblical imagery. As one observer put the matter, "QAnon is a train that runs on the tracks that religion has already put in place" (Rogers, 2021). In the narrative, the first-order problem is that Americans have been deceived; all is not as it seems. There has been a deliberate subversion of the natural order of things, and the most urgent priority becomes restoration of that natural order. The book *QAnon: An Invitation to the Great Awakening* asserts that:

> ... the world is not how we think it is and sure enough, with each revelation, each clue, each rabbit hole, we get further away from the fake reality that was created for us, and a bit closer to the truth. Everything we thought was real is fake, and everything we thought was fake, is real. (Beverly, 2020, p. 37)

The world has been corrupted by evil forces, and the goal of QAnon is restoration of the natural order of things, although that order is rarely described. As one Anon (people who identify with QAnon and actively participate in the online networks often refer to themselves simply as "Anons") wrote: "Fellow slaves. It's time to buckle your seatbelts, recognize your true enemy, and embrace a new future that we all owe to the brave patriots who risked their lives to achieve victory against the greatest force of evil the world has ever known" (Beverly, 2020, p. 35). The revelation that the book announces is referred to as "The Great Awakening," and advocates regard Q as allowing them "for the first time ever [to] stand together and start spreading only one simple thing – the truth" (Beverly, 2020, p. 31). There also is no need to lay out a plan or vision as a reversal of fortunes in what is described since "The Storm" is already certain, and Anons are enjoined to simply "trust the plan" and "enjoy the show."

Some QAnon predictions are religiously themed. Indeed, in March 2020, a series of three posts from Q linked the QAnon predictions to a deity: The first post shared Trump's tweet from the night before and repeated, "Nothing Can Stop What Is Coming." The second said: "The Great Awakening is Worldwide." The third was simple: "GOD WINS"

(LaFrance, 2020). An August 2020 post compared the Democratic Party National Convention logo to the satanic Baphomet and asserted that Republicans discuss God while Democrats discuss "darkness" (Thomas, 2020). In other versions, the promised revolution is not expected to emanate directly from a supranatural source, as a mysterious patriot within the government (Q) and a messianic figure fighting on behalf of true Americans (Donald Trump) will win in an Armageddon-style confrontation. At least some Anons expect the process to be nonviolent: "No war. No civil unrest. Clean and swift" (QAnon News, 2017).

As a revelatory thought system, the QAnon narrative is highly resistant to disconfirmation. Confronted with opposition and allegations of supporting a closed thought system, QAnon followers typically respond by rejecting counterarguments and engaging in their own "research" to discover the "Truth." As in other such revelatory narratives, opposition and apparent disconfirmation might actually intensify belief. As one supporter commented:

> No. If it were a cult, it would be the only one in history that brainwashes you to think for yourself! No one has met the leader. It promotes nonviolence and truth. Its sole weapons are logic, research, and information. (Beverly, 2020, p. 37)

Indeed, there have been a number of apparently invalidating events (e.g. the predictions that then-President Trump would be reelected on March 4, 2021, and then later that he would be reinstated in office in August 2021), but, as in the case of apocalyptic religious groups, disconfirmation has not reduced support for its guiding narrative, at least for a time (Dawson, 1999).

Mythic Themes

CNs typically incorporate several loosely coupled themes (Zald & Useem, 1982) – at least initially – that might share in common only a mistrust of established institutions and a sense of chaos and loss of control. The more profound the mistrust, the broader the array of narrative truths that might be proposed. The most central theme is likely to be one that overlaps with others sufficiently as to be plausible to those nominating other themes.

The overarching theme in the QAnon CN does not begin with suspicions about neighbors as have previous satanic CNs, such as the colonial Salem and 1980s episodes. Rather, the imminent threat is posed by the "Deep State," which is themed through the envisioning of a highly organized satanic cult that has infiltrated and coopted the federal government. The narrative of an organized, secret group that represents itself as serving the public interest intentionally using its delegated authority to harm and scar innocent children creates an evil of the highest order. This cult allegedly includes primarily Democratic politicians (Hillary Clinton, Barack Obama) and wealthy supporters (George Soros), along with Hollywood celebrities (Ellen DeGeneres, Tom Hanks, Oprah Winfrey). Religious leaders are also sometimes included (the Dalai Lama, Pope Francis). The names of Republican political figures and local political leaders are rarely invoked (see Chapter 9 of this volume for more on the political nature of QAnon). This satanic cult network allegedly abuses and sexually molests children to whom they have gained access, and these satanists murder and drink the blood of these children in order to extract "adrenochrome" (oxidized adrenaline), which is believed to increase personal power and life expectancy, from their blood. If the children are terrified during the extraction, the blood is believed to be even more salubrious and powerful. Former President Trump is revered as a messianic-style figure who has secretly been combating this satanic conspiracy, and he ultimately will expose it and organize the arrest of the conspirators.

This updated QAnon version of the 1980s satanic cult narrative raises the danger level of the putative satanists to an apocalyptic degree. No longer a story of satanic pedophiles simply gaining control over local daycare centers to secretly carry out their nefarious activities, now the conspiracy allegedly has penetrated the Deep State and is led by powerful politicians and celebrities. The figures in the QAnon narrative are of mythic proportions. Q is a patriotic whistleblower who uses his position inside the Deep State to publicly warn of the ongoing mayhem. Donald Trump is the messianic figure who leads the secret coalition (which includes Special Counsel Robert Mueller, who was supposedly secretly working with Trump and not investigating him) into battle with the satanists. QAnon followers believe that the satanists will be purged and punished. The mythic nature of the narrative is demonstrated by its avoiding linking the accused politicians and celebrities to specific, verifiable offenses and, at the same time, carefully excluding from the narrative any of the substantial number of cases in which politicians and celebrities have actually been convicted on charges of sexual abuse of children.

There are numerous satellite narratives (Beverly, 2020). These are significant because they had preexisting supporters and communication networks that were at least potentially receptive to the QAnon narrative.

These preexisting networks include white nationalist groups, militia and antigovernment groups, and antivaccination groups. Since the QAnon narrative network is loosely coupled and oppositionally focused, it has been able to accommodate these improbable allies and conflicting positions. Indeed, QAnon has actively solicited followers of other narratives, and this is at once QAnon's greatest strength and weakness.

For example, one set of satellite narratives builds on the child endangerment theme. QAnon supporters have attempted to play off of the well-respected, charitable Save The Children Fund (which has pushed back against cooptation) by using #SaveTheChildren, which buttresses their satanic cult network argument and attracts potential participants to their ranks. Dickson (2020) reported that "[o]n Facebook alone, the hashtag has garnered more than three million interactions in the past month [September], according to Crowdtangle data, in part due to the proliferation of #SaveTheChildren rallies in cities across the country ..." Similarly, Rahn and Patterson (2021) reported that, according to the Associated Press, #SaveTheChildren was mentioned more than 800,000 times on Twitter in August 2020. There have also been online urban legend-style narratives, such as that children are being smuggled into the USA for nefarious purposes in industrial furniture constructed by Wayfair.

Another set of satellite narratives has formed around the antivaccination group theme (Dickson, 2020). For example, one narrative is that COVID-19 is not simply a hoax, but that government-sponsored vaccinations contain tracking chips. Through these chips and with the advent of 5G transmission technology, people can be monitored by the government. This narrative thus ties together rejection of both scientific/medical and governmental authority and leads to opposition to community lockdowns and mask and vaccination mandates. Related narratives warn that the government is trying to cover up the link between vaccines and autism, which draws interest from families concerned about multiple childhood vaccinations. Finally, already circulating urban legend-style narratives, such as the 9/11 "truther" movement, are accommodated under the QAnon narrative umbrella.

Insurgent Media Network

Fifty years ago, three major networks distributed daily news using a one-way broadcast model in which professional journalists selected "news" and provided a receiver audience with those facts and interpretations. Throughout American history, activist groups have resisted established media with insurgent media forms (Robé & Charbonneau, 2020). There have been two important developments influencing information production, distribution, and reception in recent years. First, American public trust in the media is currently at a low level: "Four in 10 U.S. adults say they have 'a great deal' (9%) or 'a fair amount' (31%) of trust and confidence in the media to report the news 'fully, accurately, and fairly,' while six in 10 have 'not very much' trust (27%) or 'none at all' (33%)." The trust level among Republicans is at the lowest level on record, at 32 percent (Brenan, 2020). These numbers, of course, reflect the impetus to seek alternative sources of information. Second, global internet access through easily constructed, low-cost websites and online messaging systems, such as Facebook and Twitter, has facilitated the formation of multimedia information-sharing networks of various kinds (see Chapter 12 of this volume for more about QAnon and social media).

QAnon narratives have flourished in this new information-sharing environment (Beverly, 2020). While the initial messages from Q appeared on 4chan (and then moved to 8chan and 8kun), the network quickly expanded to thousands of individuals' accounts on internet message board platforms, and active participation was generated through retweets, sharing, likes, and remixing. The distinguishing feature of QAnon messaging is resistance to institutionally controlled news sources as posted material is CN themed, and participants have adopted the role of "citizen journalists" who conduct their own "research" and report their findings.

Initially, the most important posts were from Q (who has not posted since the beginning of 2021); of course, whether Q is an individual or set of individuals remains shrouded in mystery and controversy. Q's anonymity might well strengthen QAnon, as none of the potential Q nominees appear to have the charismatic qualities to equal those of the mysterious figure(s). Nonetheless, a network of ancillary roles has gradually developed around the Q postings, which creates a self-contained, independent "alternative facts" network (Marwick & Partin, 2020). The "Q-drops" are cryptic bits of information ("crumbs"). The people who adopt a "scientistic self" to examine the crumbs and produce "bread" (agreed-upon facts) are known as "bakers." This is a critical process, as many participants believe that Donald Trump is sending them secret messages. For example, because Q is the seventeenth letter in the alphabet, when Trump has mentioned that number in public, bakers will attempt to decode this as a secret message.

There are also "teachers" who instruct others within the network and "citizen journalists" who broadcast relevant information. The various posts are sometimes combined into "evidence collages," diagrammatic presentations of evidentiary links between posts that represent research results (Krafft & Donovan, 2020). The formation of this role set has allowed QAnon participants – "Anons" – to pursue and expand their discovery and dissemination of information somewhat independently of Q's involvement. People who seek to manipulate the network for personal purposes (such as making money) are referred to as "trolls" (Marwick & Partin, 2020).

Regarding to the overall QAnon online network, there is little doubt that there are thousands of accounts and millions of followers – the ongoing removal of accounts deemed inflammatory by hosting platforms, such as Facebook and Twitter, notwithstanding. It is also clear that activity across the network is intense. For example, Graphika reported that when it first mapped the QAnon network in 2018, it was the densest network of its kind that it had ever encountered (Smith, 2020). Graphika's examination of the nearly 14,000 most concentrated accounts in January and February of that year yielded 41,000,000 tweets; that number rose to 62,500,000 for July and August. Despite these impressive numbers, there is also evidence of QAnon's limited reach. In his survey, Schaffner (2020) found that just over 20 percent of those interviewed were aware of the allegation that "[a] global network tortures and sexually abuses children in Satanic rituals." The profile of the QAnon network that emerges is one of both a large number of loosely connected online participants, with a much smaller more radical and active core, and connections to other networks that have continued to supply potential new participants (see Chapter 13 of this volume for other perspectives on measuring the QAnon network).

Narrative Radicalization

Conspiracy is a conclusion about the source and meaning of a series of troubling events; the process could dissipate or gather momentum at any point (Felstiner et al., 1980–1981). When what are perceived as troubling or dangerous events initially occur, the first response is "naming," as creating a symbolic meaning for events is a preliminary means of control. A second step is moving from experiencing such events as random to "identifying a pattern" that connects them, which is followed by "identifying the source" of that pattern. Because the globalization process has been accelerating for several decades, so has associated explanatory narrative formation. From this perspective, many QAnon participants had already been experiencing the impact of DR in the form of globalization for some time, and they were deeply suspicious of a range of major institutions. They had already reached the point of "blaming," identifying those institutions for what they experienced as growing dislocation.

The QAnon narrative created the master narrative for linking the various issues. Most importantly, QAnon created the basis for "claiming," assigning responsibility to specific individuals and alleging intentionality for their transgressive actions – in this case, high-profile political and Hollywood figures. Claiming represents a critical point in the development of CNs, as it sets the stage for initiating claims-making forums with sanctioning capacity. In the QAnon case, there have been public calls for the arrest and imprisonment of public figures such as Hillary Clinton, and there have been instances of insurrection activity at both the state and federal levels. To date, these responses lack only a forum and process through which claims might be processed, which would complete the conspiracy response sequence. Other initiatives (political gerrymandering and voter suppression, limited insurrection activity, proposals for secession) that are independent of but compatible with the QAnon narrative indicate sufficient alienation to support the kind of redress forums that have occurred in other conspiracy episodes, which would be the final stage of the naming, blaming, claiming process.

Conclusions and Future Research

We have argued that various kinds of disorder and troubling circumstances are commonplace in human groups and that there are various informal and formal means of signifying and controlling perceived social danger. CNs are most likely to emerge when major social and cultural dislocations moments, which we refer to as DR, occur. There have been several notable episodes of this kind throughout American history, with QAnon being the most recent. QAnon is a particularly informative case as its narrative formation is quite advanced, and we have identified core characteristics of such a CN.

The QAnon narrative and the organized activity associated with it will continue to develop, but the direction and degree of that development remain contingent on both future societal conditions and support and opposition from numerous sources. The changes that occur should be apparent in the core narrative components that we have identified. One of the most important issues for future research, therefore, is analyzing the developmental trajectory of this major CN as it takes place (see Chapter 17 of this volume for more on the future of QAnon). While there are multiple possibilities, several seem plausible (Bromley & Shupe, 1983). One is that

QAnon will go the way of most past rumors and urban legends and gradually dissipate (Heffernan, 2021). This does not mean that the narratives and allegations will completely disappear; there are, for example, continuing isolated flare-ups of witchcraft and local satanic cult abuse narratives (Reichert & Richardson, 2012). Such circumstances are met with established, institutionalized constraints, such as mental health treatment and criminal prosecution. A second possibility is that one component of QAnon will separate from the larger coalition and launch an aggressive initiative based on its selected set of grievances. In this case, the most likely candidate would seem to be white nationalist groups like those that participated in the US Capitol insurrection. Numerous governmental agencies have warned of this possibility. However, as dangerous as such incidents might be, they are likely to take a form for which existing law enforcement responses already exist. The most destabilizing possibility would be for the QAnon narrative to transform into an organized social movement. A key to that kind of transformation is the development of a process for creating victims, such as witches and abuse survivors, and the establishment of a forum and process through which allegations can be refereed and sanctions imposed. To date, there have been "escape" and "rescue" narratives, but those have not yet been linked to forums with sanctioning authority. Future events and scholarship on these developments will constitute the next chapter in the history of QAnon.

In this chapter, we have sought to make the case that troubling, dangerous circumstances and the narratives about them are commonplace in human groups. CNs, like the QAnon narrative, are much more rare. These occur under circumstances of exceptional social and cultural disruption, which we have examined through the concepts of deterritorialization and reterritorialization and have linked to the contemporary forces of globalization. A highly developed CN, such as the QAnon narrative, contains a number of key elements: a shared perception of danger, agreement on the nature and source of the danger, formation of a communication network, and attribution of intentionality for the dangerous circumstances to specific individuals or groups. There is one additional element that has yet to develop in the QAnon episode: the incorporation of the narrative into the mission of a group with sanctioning capacity. Because the social and cultural context within which the QAnon narrative has developed and the narrative formation dynamics remain contingent, there are a number of potential future developments that could occur. Whatever outcomes eventuate, the QAnon episode offers an extraordinary window into the ongoing tension between order and disorder in human groups.

REFERENCES

Barnes, J. (2020). *QAnon: The Awakening begins: The most complete report on the great conspiracy against the United States*. Published independently.

Beverly, J. (2020). *The QAnon deception: Everything you need to know about the world's most dangerous conspiracy theory*. EqualTime Books.

Boyer, P., & Nissenbaum, S. (1974). *Salem possessed: The social origins of witchcraft*. Harvard University Press.

Brenan, M. (2020, September 30). Americans remain distrustful of mass media. *Gallup Organization*. https://news.gallup.com/poll/321116/americans-remain-distrustful-mass-media.aspx

Bromley, D. G. (1991). Satanism: The new cult scare. In J. T. Richardson, J. Best, & D. Bromley (Eds.), *The satanism scare* (pp. 49–72). Aldine De Gruyter.

(1994). The social construction of subversion: A comparison of anti-religious and anti-satanic cult narratives. In A. Shupe & D. Bromley (Eds.), *Anti-cult movements in cross-cultural perspective* (pp. 49–76). Garland.

(2002). Dramatic denouements. In D. G. Bromley & J. G. Melton (Eds.), *Cults, religion and violence* (pp. 11–41). Cambridge University Press.

(2010). Moral panics. In G. Ritzer & J. Ryan (Eds.), *Concise encyclopedia of sociology* (pp. 412–413). Wiley.

Bromley, D. G., & Shupe, A. (1981). *Strange gods: The great American cult scare*. Beacon Press.

(1983). Repression and the decline of social movements: The case of new religions. In J. Freeman (Ed.), *Social movements of the sixties and seventies* (pp. 333–347). Longman.

Dawson, L. (1999). When prophecy fails and faith persists: A theoretical overview. *Nova Religio*, *3*(1), 60–82.

Deleuze, G., & Guattari, F. (1977). *Capitalism and schisophrenia*. Viking.

Deutsch, J., & Bochantin, L. (2020, December 7). The folkloric roots of the QAnon conspiracy. *Folklife*. https://folklife.si.edu/magazine/folkloric-roots-of-qanon-conspiracy

Dickson, E. (2020, September 3). The birth of QAnon. *Rolling Stone*. www.rollingstone.com/culture/culture-features/qanon-mom-conspiracy-theory-parents-sex-trafficking-qamom-1048921/

DiMaggio, P., & Powell, W. (1983). The iron cage revisited: Institutional isomorphism and collective rationality in organizational fields. *American Sociological Review*, *48*(2), 147–160.

Erickson, K. (2004). *Wayward puritans*. Allyn and Bacon.

Felstiner, W., Abel, R., & Sarat, A. (1980–1981). The emergence and transformation of disputes: Naming, blaming, claiming . . . *Law & Society Review*, *15* (3/4), 631–654.

Heffernan, V. (2021, June 11). Reports of QAnon's death aren't exaggerated. *Los Angeles Times*. www.latimes.com/opinion/story/2021-06-11/qanon-jan-6-ron-watkins-sidney-powell

Jenkins, J. (2021, May 27). Survey: White evangelicals, Hispanic Protestants, Mormons most likely to believe in QAnon. *Religious News Service*. https://religionnews.com/2021/05/27/survey-white-evangelicals-hispanic-protestants-and-mormons-most-likely-believe-in-qanon/

Krafft, P. M., & Donovan, J. (2020). Disinformation by design: The use of evidence collages and platform filtering in a media manipulation campaign. *Political Communication*, *37*(2), 194–214.

LaFrance, A. (2020, June). The prophecies of Q: American conspiracy theories are entering a dangerous new phase. *The Atlantic*. www.theatlantic.com/magazine/archive/2020/06/qanon-nothing-can-stop-what-is-coming/610567/

Marwick, A., & Partin, P. (2020, October). The construction of alternative facts: "QAnon" researchers as scientistic selves. Paper presented at the 21st Annual Conference of the Association of Internet Researchers. Virtual Event: AoIR. http://spir.aoir.org

Mulhern, S. (1991). Satanism and psychotherapy: A rumor in search of an inquisition. In J. T. Richardson, J. Best, & D. Bromley (Eds.), *The satanism scare* (pp. 145–172). Aldine de Gruyter.

Nash, G. (1979). *The urban crucible: Social change, political consciousness, and the origins of the American Revolution*. Harvard University Press.

QAnon News. (2017, November 1). Bread crumbs – Q Clearance Patriot. *QAnon News*. https://qanonnews.wordpress.com/2017/11/01/bread-crumbs-q-clearance-patriot/

Rahn, W., & Patterson, D. (2021, March 29). What is the QAnon conspiracy theory? *CBS News*. www.cbsnews.com/news/what-is-the-qanon-conspiracy-theory/

Reichert, J., & Richardson, J. T. (2012). Decline of a moral panic: A social psychological and socio-legal examination of the current status of satanism. *Nova Religio*, *16*(2), 48–63.

Richardson, J. T. (1997). The social construction of satanism: Understanding an international social problem. *Australian Journal of Social Issues*, *32*(1), 61–86.

Richardson, J. T., & Introvigne, M. (2007). New religious movement, countermovements, moral panics, and the media. In D. Bromley (Ed.), *Teaching new religious movements* (pp. 91–111). Oxford University Press.

Richardson, J. T., Bromley, D., & Best, J. (1991). *The satanism scare*. Aldine de Gruyter.

Robé, C., & Charbonneau, S. (2020). *Insurgent media from the front*. Indiana University Press.

Rogers, K. (2021, March 4). Why QAnon has attracted so many white evangelicals. *FiveThirtyEight*. https://fivethirtyeight.com/features/why-qanon-has-attracted-so-many-white-evangelicals/

Schaffner, B. (2020, October 5). QAnon and conspiracy beliefs (paras. 4–7). Report supported by the Institute for Strategic Dialogue and funded by Luminate. www.isdglobal.org/isd-publications/qanon-and-conspiracy-beliefs/

Shupe, A., & Bromley, D. G. (1981). Witches, Moonies, and accusations of evil. In T. Robbins & D. Anthony (Eds.), *In gods we trust: New patterns of religious pluralism in America*. Routledge.

Smith, M. (2020, August). Interpreting social Qs: Implications of the evolution of QAnon. *Graphika*. https://public-assets.graphika.com/reports/graphika_report_interpreting_social_qs.pdf

Taylor, B. (1999). *Thanks for the memories . . . the truth has set me free! The memoirs of Bob Hope's and Henry Kissinger's mind-controlled slave*. Brice Taylor Trust.

Thomas, G. (2007). The cultural and religious character of world society. In P. Byer & L. Beaman (Eds.), *Religion, globalization, and culture* (pp. 35–66). Brill.

Thomas, P. (2020, October 20). How QAnon uses satanic rhetoric to set up a narrative of "good vs. evil." *The Conversation*. https://theconversation.com/how-qanon-uses-satanic-rhetoric-to-set-up-a-narrative-of-good-vs-evil-146281

Tuathail, G., & Luke, T. (1994). Present at the (dis)integration: Deterritorialization and reterritorialization in the New Wor(l)d Order. *Annals of the Association of American Geographers*, *84*(3), 381–398.

Victor, J. (1993). *Satanic Panic: The creation of a contemporary legend*. Open Court Press.

Zald, M., & Useem, B. (1982). *Movement and countermovement: Loosely coupled conflict*. Working Paper No. 276. Center for Research on Social Organization.

CHAPTER 11

The Need to Belong
The Appeal, Benefits, and Dangers of QAnon and Similar Groups

Kelly-Ann Allen, Zoe A. Morris, Margaret L. Kern, Christopher Boyle, and Caomhan McGlinchey

> As Robert's interest in politics increased across Donald Trump's presidency, Robert's family and friends noticed something different about him. He increasingly ignored calls by family members, spending all his spare time online. His online posts became more radical. As the COVID-19 pandemic and associated lockdown swept the nation, he worked from home, rarely leaving the house. He became increasingly paranoid and struggled to perform well in his work. As lockdown restrictions eased, his close family members hoped to support him. But often, their conversations would turn to the politics of vaccines, lockdowns, and COVID-19, ending in explosive rows. His family believed his views became outlandish and frightening. They later identified Robert had joined QAnon.

What would draw well-meaning people like Robert to a group that spreads health misinformation and creates a risk to public safety? In this chapter, we discuss the human need for belonging and how struggles to belong contribute to participation in antisocial groups such as gangs, cults, and conspiracy groups, including the group at the heart of this book: QAnon. We argue that conspiracy groups provide a sense of belonging, as people find and create meaning around shared and constructed identities. But the need for belonging can be fulfilled in ways that are valued and beneficial to society as well as in harmful and detrimental ways, both for the people involved and for society. By exploring belongingness and the QAnon phenomenon, we illustrate both the benefits and risks of social identity in the modern era.

What Is Belonging?

Belonging has been defined and described in a variety of ways, with various theories, frameworks, and studies contributing to understanding its meaning, predictors, correlates, and consequences (Allen, 2020b). Some theorists have conceptualized belonging as a person's involvement in an environment or system and the subsequent feeling of being a part of that system or environment (Hagerty et al., 1992). Others have proposed a need to belong as something that drives people to form and maintain positive relationships (Baumeister & Leary, 1995; Pillow et al., 2015). Belonging as a need that motivates behavior appears across multiple theories (Allen et al., 2021b). For instance, Maslow (1943, 1970) suggested that belongingness is a need that is so necessary that when it is not fulfilled, we struggle to feel fully human. Ryan and Deci's (2000) theory of basic psychological needs suggests that relatedness is essential to motivate behavior, drive performance, and experience well-being.

Although a sense of belonging can be developed for a place, an event, and/or a period (Allen et al., 2021a), belonging is commonly felt with people, and especially within one or more groups (Baldwin & Keefer, 2020). Group belonging can improve a person's social standing and influence, grant access to material resources, provide information, offer various forms of social support, and provide acceptance and a sense of meaning and identity (Leary & Allen, 2011).

The social aspects of a group are particularly important, with such bonds being essential for psychological growth (Over, 2016; Wagle et al., 2021). However, as a subjective feeling, one's sense of belonging is largely dependent on person-specific factors, such as a person's character, social background, perceptions, emotions, culture, and experiences (Allen et al., 2017, 2021b; Peter et al., 2015), such that being a part of a group might or might not provide a sense of belonging (Lambert et al., 2013). Positive relationships are more likely to develop as part of a cascade of positive interactions, beginning with a positive introduction and unfolding through a dynamic relationship over time that might or might not remain positive in nature (Baumeister & Leary, 1995). Like a dance, the feeling of belonging is delicate and complex, with many possible ways in which it can be derailed.

Unfulfilled Belonging

The need for belonging drives the desire to connect with others. Akin to other unfulfilled desires, the failure to belong can lead to undesirable outcomes (Allen, 2020b; Allen et al., 2021a). A lack of belonging can generate negative emotions, including embarrassment, jealousy, anxiety, and depression (Leary & Guadagno, 2011). *Sociometer theory* suggests that this is because interpersonal rejection threatens one's self-esteem

(Leary & Baumeister, 2000; Schmidt et al., 2021). The self is constructed intrapersonally and interpersonally. Across most cultures and communities, social institutions and groups define and reinforce the values and norms of the people, often defined by the majority and those with influence or power (Kern et al., 2020). But when a person's own values, beliefs, or actions differ or are sanctioned by the majority culture, the need and desire for belonging remains.

Common responses to threats to one's sense of self can include altering one's behaviors to better align with others, finding alternative groups where they better belong, blaming others (van Orden et al., 2010), emphasizing one's own perceived positive characteristics to others (Aronson et al., 1995), or engaging in risky behaviors (Baumeister et al., 1993; Twenge & Campbell, 2008). The need for belongingness has been linked to membership in antisocial and potentially harmful groups, such as gangs (Howell & Griffiths, 2018) and nonconventional religious groups and cults (Melton, 2014; Yakovleva, 2018). Notably, people experiencing a lack of belongingness might not only seek alternative sources of belongingness, but they might also denigrate others, inflate their own self-importance, and engage in risky behaviors while doing so (Arslan, 2021).

Actions that align with socially valued behaviors are of little concern and illustrate how lacking belonging can positively motivate people to find and create connection with others. However, when one's actions counter social expectations and norms (e.g. gang-related behavior), a person might be punished or socially reprimanded, reinforcing the perception that one is an outsider, and often resulting in further escalation of problematic behaviors. And then there are those who find connection with a significant minority group that holds beliefs and acts in ways that are counter to existing cultural paradigms. Groups like QAnon might offer a supportive environment, providing a sense of identity and meaning to people who feel lost or disconnected. Social sanctions by mainstream society become irrelevant as the person finds acceptance within a group through inspiring messages, condemning messages toward the majority that a person has been rejected by, and camaraderie with seemingly like-minded others.

The Draw of the Alternative

Rejection, sanction, and threat by the majority culture can make membership in gangs, cults, and fringe groups more attractive. Gang members have repeatedly highlighted the "companionship and a sense of belonging" that can be found within the gang environment (Garduno & Brancale, 2017, p. 767; see also Brown, 1977; Hochhaus & Sousa, 1987). Studies find that a "lack of attachment to school" is an important contributing factor (Gebo & Sullivan, 2014, p. 193; see also Howell & Egley, 2005; Klein & Maxson, 2006). Interestingly, when it comes to gang membership and belongingness within a family, research is more mixed (Eitle et al., 2004; Hill et al., 1999; Young et al., 2014). For example, while it is true that difficult family relationships can lead to a need for belonging that is satisfied by joining a gang, some people with good family relationships also join gangs. In some cases, this is because their family already has a positive view of gangs, or their family members are already active gang members themselves. Similarly, some QAnon members are exposed to QAnon-based beliefs by others in their real-world social spheres.

Other parallels appear with nontraditional religious groups and cults. Indeed, several commentators have highlighted the similarities between QAnon and religious cults (Diresta, 2018; Sommer, 2018). People can be drawn into such groups for various reasons. For some, it is about an unmet need for belonging. Levine (1986) has argued that new cult members seek belongingness in the cult because they have enjoyed fewer meaningful relationships with peers before joining. Melton (2014) observed that most new cult members came from religious families but were inactive within their family's religious tradition. For others, feelings of ostracism and rejection make one particularly susceptible to cult recruiters (Wesselmann & Williams, 2010). QAnon has been compared to religious cults not only because it recruits ostracized and vulnerable people, but also because it draws potential members in with the promise of increasingly colorful secrets (Diresta, 2018; see Chapter 16 of this volume for more on QAnon as a new religious movement).

Regardless of what draws people into gangs, cults, fringe institutions, and other such groups, social isolation, loneliness, rejection by others, and a search for meaning can make people vulnerable, which such groups prey upon (Lim et al., 2021). Notably, numerous scholars have highlighted a growing *epidemic of loneliness* in parts of the world, including the USA, Germany, Australia, and the UK (e.g. Allen, 2020a; Allen & Furlong, 2021; Hari, 2018; Holt-Lunstad, 2017; Snell, 2017). If this so-called epidemic of loneliness is not only a sad reality but one that is growing, then it might be expected that people will look for new communities in which to belong.

A Social Appeal

What would draw people specifically to groups such as QAnon? Does QAnon provide a sense of belonging? There is clearly no doubt that through shared ideologies QAnon provides its members with a feeling of connectedness and perhaps a collective sense of purpose to uncover and decode cryptic messages. However, on close examination, those who identify with such groups have links that extend beyond the mere sharing of common beliefs or ideas. Indeed, according to van Prooijen (2016), social concern is one psychological process that can lead to beliefs in conspiracy theories, although some researchers have argued that conspiracy theorists might also show higher concern for themselves than for others (Hornsey et al., 2021). In the case of social concern, some might identify themselves with a particular group of people who have been threatened or negatively impacted by one or more adverse events. In doing so, they develop strong feelings of inclusion with that specific group, such that any further event or situation that specifically threatens that group is likely to be viewed as a conspiracy against them. For instance, some Americans who have traditionally been the majority but now find their religious, political, and other beliefs threatened by various minority groups have found like-minded people among other QAnon followers. This is particularly obvious in the case of closely knit but marginalized groups whereby societal conditions not only provide a common platform for developing a sense of belongingness but also form the basis of conspiracy beliefs, especially when members of such groups feel discriminated against (Mazzocchetti, 2012; Poon et al., 2020; van Prooijen & Acker, 2015).

Interest in and subsequent adherence to QAnon beliefs might also occur through psychosocial processes such as pattern perception (Shermer, 2011; van Prooijen & van Vugt, 2018). Recognizing patterns is, in fact, a key feature of human ability, which helps to associate events to identify causes and effects. However, as people try to understand the world around them, especially when faced with complex events, they might wrongly identify patterns that do not exist, thereby leading to irrational beliefs. Therefore, van Prooijen (2016) identified subjective uncertainty as a second process that can cause people to adopt conspiracy theories as they try to make sense of things that might be beyond their understanding. Scholars have also proposed the concept of *conspiracy thinking*, in which those who believe in such theories are more likely to adopt new ones, even though the latter might be unrelated to previous beliefs (Douglas et al., 2019; Imhoff & Bruder, 2014; Uscinski & Parent, 2014).

These psychological processes are not the only reasons people adopt conspiracy theories, but they do highlight that seeking belongingness is not the sole purpose behind adherence to QAnon. As described above, belonging has been conceptualized as a need whose fulfillment motivates our actions. Joining QAnon or other similar groups might not be naturally driven (e.g. a person is groomed or persuaded by others), and thus it can only provide pseudo-connection while undermining actual belonging. Furthermore, adopting conspiracy beliefs can often be associated with disruptive behavior as well as feelings of anxiety or depression (De Coninck et al., 2021; Smith & Santiago, 2021), whereas satisfying one's sense of belonging is, instead, more commonly associated with positive outcomes.

Sinatra and Hofer (2021) suggest that at the core of science denial is social identity, a sense of value and meaning that people ascribe to group membership. For QAnon members, it is likely that the group provides a social identity that is unfulfilled in other areas of life. QAnon serves as an example of collective science denial in which the social elements of critical thinking (or the lack thereof) are central to membership involvement. As Greene and Yu (2015) emphasize, thinking is hard, and critical thinking is harder. Whereas most people rely on the collective to facilitate their social thinking, what is the result when the collective demonstrates flawed thinking and a reliance on misinformation?

Critical Thinking and the Psychology of Believing

For many people outside the QAnon phenomenon, one of its most striking features is the extravagance of its claims. It has been suggested by Carl Sagan (2011), among others, that extraordinary claims require extraordinary evidence. One might therefore have assumed that QAnon supporters would have solid grounds for believing that Hollywood actors, Democratic politicians, and high-ranking government officials are part of a satanic cult. However, this is not the case (Sommer, 2018).

Researchers interested in how incredible beliefs are sustained have highlighted the role of critical thinking (Greene et al., 2019; McIntyre, 2018; Prado, 2018), with Barzilai and Chinn (2020) outlining four main hypotheses to explain deficiencies in critical thinking. First, the skills hypothesis states that people desire accurate information to justify their beliefs, but many lack the media and digital literacy skills to evaluate sources of information (i.e. they do not know how to fact-check online claims or recognize bias in each source; Hobbs, 2017; Journell & Clark, 2019; Wardle & Derakhshan, 2017).

Second, the rationality hypothesis suggests that humans are beset by cognitive fallibilities that make thinking rationally an especially challenging endeavor (Greene & Yu, 2015; Haidt, 2001; Kahneman, 2011; Nickerson, 1998; Stanovich, 2011). For instance, with the illusory-truth effect, a person gives more credence to information they have been repeatedly exposed to rather than to novel information even if the repeated information is implausible (Dechêne et al., 2010; Pennycook et al., 2018). Similarly, the confirmation bias suggests that a person might favor information that confirms preexisting beliefs (Chinn & Brewer, 1993; Lord et al., 1979; Nickerson, 1998).

Third, the subordination hypothesis suggests that people are not led to their beliefs by rational consideration of the data, but rather they *cherry-pick* their data to support their social, economic, religious, and/or political beliefs (McIntyre, 2018). Whereas the rationality argument suggests that humans believe irrational things because of flaws in their cognitions, the subordination hypothesis suggests that it might be rational to hold irrational beliefs when these beliefs are consonant with those of an in-group, signaling commitment to the group and the benefits from group membership (Pennycook & Rand, 2019).

Fourth, the epistemology argument suggests that there are different ways of knowing that something is true and therefore sources of information that prioritize one way of knowing can be dismissed by certain people and groups. For example, a QAnon supporter might value information shared by a trusted fellow-subscriber over information produced by *science*. Indeed, science might be dismissed because it is tied to powerful financial or corporate interests (Hansson, 2017; Scheufele & Krause, 2019; Waisbord, 2018). In the case of QAnon, science might even be dismissed because it is under the control of the same sinister forces that QAnon aims to expose, such as the control of individual liberties by the government.

Intersections with the Online Space

Over the past decade, the various psychological, cognitive, and social aspects of alternative groups that might appeal to disconnected people have been accentuated, preyed upon, and altered through the rapid development of the online space. From its inception, the internet was designed to facilitate communication (Manasian, 2003), and the potential for people to find a sense of belonging and social connectedness online has long been recognized (Bargh & McKenna, 2004; Ryan et al., 2017). Research exploring whether users experience increased social connectedness online is mixed; while some studies suggest that social media users can experience an increase in social connectedness, they also highlight that social connectedness can be undermined on social networking sites (SNSs; Ahn & Shin, 2013; Allen et al., 2014; Grieve et al., 2013; Seabrook et al., 2016; Sheldon et al., 2011). Despite ongoing concerns about the potential negative impacts of social media, including superficial connections, cyberbullying, addiction, and disinformation, the proliferation of SNSs suggests that the appeal of these platforms is relatively undiminished. For example, current estimates indicate that as many as 2.8 billion people, or approximately 35.44 percent of the world's population, are active on the SNS Facebook at least once each month (Facebook, 2021). A growing number of SNSs are available, each providing different communities, options, and points of connection (see Chapter 12 of this volume for more on QAnon and social media).

Recent research has highlighted that a variety of emotions can prompt a person to seek social connectedness online. Kimmel (2017), for example, has suggested that a sense of entitlement and victimization among certain demographic groups – in Kimmel's case, white males in the USA – has led to feelings of anger and a desire for solidarity, which can be more easily accessed online. While SNSs are appealing to people who enjoy a shared interest that is relatively uncommon offline (i.e. in *real life*; McKenna et al., 2002), Bargh and McKenna (2004) have also shown that when a person's feelings and views are felt to be socially unacceptable offline, then they will seek like-minded people online.

Online platforms can be especially attractive for people who feel lonely (Amichai-Hamburger & Ben-Artzi, 2003), whether this loneliness is a consequence of geographical isolation, reduced mobility, and/or a sense that one does not belong in the groups that are available offline. Moreover, this appeal is enhanced when a person experiences social anxiety (Lee et al., 2012; Saunders & Chester, 2008), discrimination (Miller et al., 2021), or trauma (Zhong et al., 2021). With the combination of the COVID-19 pandemic, numerous national disasters, intense political events and movements, and strong and vocal personalities, anxiety levels worldwide have increased, discrimination against both majority and minority groups has occurred, and people worldwide have experienced various degrees of individual and collective trauma (see Chapters 8 and 9 of this volume for more on how the events of 2020 contributed to the growth of QAnon). The online space intersects with these vulnerabilities, with groups such as QAnon meeting people's frustration and unmet needs and providing answers, purpose, and connection.

Future Directions

Alternative groups such as QAnon come and go over the years, but they can have a significant impact on both vulnerable people and larger aspects of society. What draws people into groups such as QAnon? We have considered various psychological, social, and technological aspects, which have been particularly accentuated through the events of 2020 and beyond. The need for belonging most likely plays a role, but this intersects with various other aspects for people and their environments. It is unlikely that the fulfillment of a sense of belonging is the sole driver of QAnon membership, but the role it plays should be subject to further research. Certainly, social drivers as identified in this chapter are central to QAnon involvement, and without the presence of other people it is unlikely QAnon would exist.

Further research is needed to provide greater insight into people's perceptions and experiences of alternative groups, including those who are part of groups such as QAnon, those contemplating membership of these groups, and those who might be vulnerable to grooming and propaganda by these groups. Little is known about the processes involved (including the role of belonging), the sustainability of beliefs, and the ways to engage in harm minimization and prevention for persons, families, communities, and society.

Conclusion

Humans have a deep need for connection, purpose, and coherence to life. We long for a place to belong. Society, including norms, cultural values, groups, and social institutions, helps define and provide places to fulfil that need. And yet, as times of change, uncertainty, and chaos occur, these needs have been deeply disrupted. This chapter demonstrates how the need for belonging intersects with various other factors in potentially beneficial or detrimental ways. Accentuated by rapid technological change, political instability, disruption of traditional structures and norms, and charismatic people with strong agendas that run counter to majority values and norms, groups such as QAnon seemingly provide order, common identity, and a sense of belonging, but the individual, collective, and societal consequences, both in the short and long term, are unknown, including in terms of appeals, opportunities, and dangers.

REFERENCES

Ahn, D., & Shin, D. (2013). Is the social use of media for seeking connectedness or for avoiding social isolation? Mechanisms underlying media use and subjective well-being. *Computers in Human Behaviour*, *29*(6), 2453–2462.

Allen, K.-A. (2020a). Commentary: A pilot digital intervention targeting loneliness in youth mental health. *Frontiers in Psychiatry*, *10*, 959.

(2020b). *The Psychology of belonging*. Routledge (Taylor and Francis Group).

Allen, K.-A., & Furlong, M. (2021a). Leveraging belonging in response to global loneliness special issue: Belonging and loneliness. *Australian Journal of Psychology*, *73*, 1–3.

Allen, K.-A., Gray, D., Baumeister, R., & Leary. M. (2021b). The need to belong: A deep dive into the origins, implications, and future of a foundational construct. *Educational Psychology Review*, *34*, 1133–1156.

Allen, K.-A., Kern, M. L., Rozek, C. S., McInereney, D., & Slavich, G. M. (2021). Belonging: A review of conceptual issues, an integrative framework, and directions for future research. *Australian Journal of Psychology*, *73*(1), 87–102.

Allen, K.-A., Ryan, T., Gray, D. L., McInerney, D., & Waters, L. (2014). Social media use and social connectedness in adolescents: The positives and the potential pitfalls. *The Australian Educational and Developmental Psychologist*, *31*(1), 18–31.

Allen, K.-A., Vella-Brodrick, D., & Waters, L. (2017). School belonging and the role of social and emotional competencies in fostering an adolescent's sense of connectedness to their school. In E. Frydenberg, A. J. Martin, & R. J. Collie (Eds.), *Social and emotional learning in Australia and the Asia-Pacific: Perspectives, programs and approaches* (1st ed., pp. 83–99). Springer.

Amichai-Hamburger, Y., & Ben-Artzi, E. (2003). Loneliness and internet use. *Computers in Human Behaviour*, *19*(1), 71–80.

Aronson, J., Blanton, H., & Cooper, J. (1995). From dissonance to disidentification: Selectivity in the self-affirmation process. *Journal of Personality and Social Psychology*, *68*, 986–996.

Arslan, G. (2021). Social ostracism in school context: Academic self-concept, prosocial behaviour, and adolescents' conduct problems. *Educational and Developmental Psychologist*, *38*(1), 24–35.

Baldwin, M., & Keefer, L. A. (2020). Being here and now: The benefits of belonging in space and time. *Journal of Happiness Studies*, *21*(8), 3069–3093.

Bargh, J. A., & McKenna, K. Y. A. (2004). The internet and social life. *Annual Review of Psychology*, *55*(1), 573–590.

Barzilai, S., & Chinn, C. A. (2020). A review of educational responses to the "post-truth" condition: Four lenses on "post-truth" problems. *Educational Psychologist*, *55*(3), 107–119.

Baumeister, R. F., & Leary, M. R. (1995). The need to belong: Desire for interpersonal attachments as a fundamental human motivation. *Psychological Bulletin*, *117*(3), 497–529.

Baumeister, R. F., Heatherton, T. F., & Tice, D. M. (1993). When ego threats lead to self-regulation failure: Negative consequences of high self-esteem. *Journal of Personality and Social Psychology*, *64*, 141–156.

Brown, W. K. (1977). Black female gangs in Philadelphia. *International Journal of Offender Therapy and Comparative Criminology*, *21*(3), 221–228.

Chinn, C. A., & Brewer, W. F. (1993). The role of anomalous data in knowledge acquisition: A theoretical framework and implications for science instruction. *Review of Educational Research*, *63*(1), 1–49.

De Coninck, D., Frissen, T., Matthijs, K., d'Haenens, L., Lits, G., Champagne-Poirier, O., Carignan, M. E., David, M. D., Pignard-Cheynel, N., Salerno, S., & Généreux, M. (2021). Beliefs in conspiracy theories and misinformation about COVID-19: Comparative perspectives on the role of anxiety, depression and exposure to and trust in information sources. *Frontiers in Psychology*, *12*, 646394.

Dechêne, A., Stahl, C., Hansen, J., & Wänke, M. (2010). The truth about the truth: A meta-analytic review of the truth effect. *Personality and Social Psychology Review*, *14*(2), 238–257.

Diresta, R. (2018, November 13). Online conspiracy groups are a lot like cults. *Wired*. www.wired.com/story/online-conspiracy-groups-qanon-cults

Douglas, K. M., Uscinski, J. E., Sutton, R. M., Cichocka, A., Nefes, T., Ang, C. S., & Deravi, F. (2019). Understanding conspiracy theories. *Political Psychology*, *40*(Suppl. 1), 3–35.

Eitle, D., Gunkel, S., & Van Gundy, K. (2004). Cumulative exposure to stressful life events and male gang membership. *Journal of Criminal Justice*, *32*(2), 95–111.

Facebook (2021, January 27). Facebook reports fourth quarter and full year 2020 results. *Meta*. https://investor.fb.com/investor-news/press-release-details/2021/Facebook-Reports-Fourth-Quarter-and-Full-Year-2020-Results/default.aspx

Garduno, L. S., & Brancale, J. M. (2017). Examining the risk and protective factors of gang involvement among Hispanic youth in Maryland. *Journal of Community Psychology*, *45*(6), 765–782.

Gebo, E., & Sullivan, C. J. (2014). A statewide comparison of gang and non-gang youth in public high schools. *Youth Violence and Juvenile Justice*, *12*(3), 191–208.

Greene, J. A., & Yu, S. B. (2015). Educating critical thinkers: The role of epistemic cognition. *Policy Insights from the Behavioural and Brain Sciences*, *3*(1), 45–53.

Greene, J. A., Cartiff, B. M., Duke, R. F., & Deekens, V. M. (2019). A nation of curators: Educating students to be critical consumers and users of online information. In P. Kendeou, D. H. Robinson, & M. T. McCrudden (Eds.). *Misinformation and fake news in education* (pp. 187–206). Information Age Publishing.

Grieve, R., Indian, M., Witteveen, K., Tolan, G. A., & Marrington, J. (2013). Face-to-face or Facebook: Can social connectedness be derived online? *Computers in Human Behaviour*, *29*(3), 604–609.

Hagerty, B. M. K., Lynch-Sauer, J., Patusky, K., Bouwseman, M., & Collier, P. (1992). Sense of belonging: A vital mental health concept. *Archives of Psychiatric Nursing, 6*, 172–177.
Haidt, L. (2001). The emotional dog and its rational tail: A social intuitionist approach to moral judgment. *Psychological Review, 108*(4), 814–834.
Hansson, S. O. (2017). Science denial as a form of pseudoscience. *Studies in History and Philosophy of Science, 63*, 39–47.
Hari, J. (2018). *Lost connections: Uncovering the real causes of depression and unexpected solutions*. Bloomsbury.
Hill, K. G., Howell, J. C., Hawkins, J. D., & Battin-Pearson, S. R. (1999). Childhood risk factors for adolescent gang membership: Results from the Seattle Social Development Project. *Journal of Research in Crime and Delinquency, 36*(3), 300–322.
Hobbs, R. (2017). Teaching and learning in a post-truth world. *Educational Leadership, 75*(3), 26–31.
Hochhaus, C., & Sousa, F. (1987). Why children belong to gangs: A comparison of expectations and reality. *The High School Journal, 71*(2), 74–77.
Holt-Lunstad, J. (2017). The potential public health relevance of social isolation and loneliness: Prevalence, epidemiology, and risk factors. *Public Policy & Aging Report, 27*(4), 127–130.
Hornsey, M. J., Chapman, C. M., Alvarez, B., Bentley, S., Casara, B., Crimston, C. R., Ionescu, O., Krug, H., Selvanathan, H. P., Steffens, N. K., & Jetten, J. (2021). To what extent are conspiracy theorists concerned for self versus others? A COVID-19 test case. *European Journal of Social Psychology, 51*(2), 285–293.
Howell, J. C., & Egley, A. (2005). Moving risk factors into developmental theories of gang membership. *Youth Violence & Juvenile Justice, 3*(4), 334–354.
Howell, J. C., & Griffiths, E. (2018). *Gangs in America's communities*. Sage.
Imhoff, R., & Bruder, M. (2014). Speaking (un-)truth to power: Conspiracy mentality as a generalised political attitude. *European Journal of Personality, 28*(1), 25–43.
Journell, W., & Clark, C. H. (2019). Political memes and the limits of media literacy. In W. Journell (Ed.), *Unpacking fake news: An educator's guide to navigating the media with students* (pp. 109–125). Teachers College Press.
Kahneman, D. (2011). *Thinking, fast and slow*. Penguin Books.
Kern, M. L., Williams, P., Spong, C., Colla, R., Sharma, K., Downie, A., Taylor, J. A., Sharp, S., Siokou, C., & Oades, L. G. (2020). Systems informed positive psychology. *Journal of Positive Psychology, 15*(6), 705–715.
Kimmel, M. (2017). *Angry white men: American masculinity at the end of an era*. Bold Type Books.
Klein, M. W., & Maxson, C. L. (2006). *Street gang patterns and policies*. Oxford University Press.
Lambert, N. M., Stillman, T. F., Hicks, J. A., Kamble, S., Baumeister, R. F., & Fincham, F. D. (2013). To belong is to matter: Sense of belonging enhances

meaning in life. *Personality and Social Psychology Bulletin, 39*(11), 1418–1427.

Leary, M. R., & Allen, A. B. (2011). Belonging motivation: Establishing, maintaining, and repairing relational value. In D. Dunning (Ed.), *Social motivation* (pp. 37–55). Psychology Press.

Leary, M. R., & Baumeister, R. F. (2000). The nature and function of self-esteem: Sociometer theory. In M. P. Zanna (Ed.), *Advances in experimental social psychology* (pp. 1–62). Academic Press.

Leary, M. R., & Guadagno, J. (2011). The sociometer, self-esteem, and the regulation of interpersonal behaviour. In K. D. Vohs & R. F. Baumeister (Eds.), *Handbook of self-regulation: Research, theory, and applications* (pp. 339–354). Guilford Press.

Lee, Z. W. Y., Cheung C. M. K., & Thadani, D. R. (2012). An investigation into the problematic use of Facebook. Presented at: *2012 45th Hawaii International Conference on System Sciences* (pp. 1768–1776). https://doi.org/10.1109/HICSS.2012.106

Levine, S. (1986). *Radical departures: Desperate detours to growing up*. Harcourt.

Lim, M. H., Allen, K.-A., Furlong, M. J., Craig, H., & Smith, D. C. (2021). Introducing a dual continuum model of belonging and loneliness. *Australian Journal of Psychology, 73*, 81–86.

Lord, C. G., Ross, L., & Lepper, M. R. (1979). Biased assimilation and attitude polarization: The effects of prior theories on subsequently considered evidence. *Journal of Personality and Social Psychology, 37*(11), 2098–2109.

Manasian, D. (2003). Digital dilemmas: A survey of the internet society. *Economist, 25*, 1–26.

Maslow, A. H. (1943). A theory of human motivation. *Psychological Review, 50* (4), 370–396.

(1970). *Motivation and personality*. Harper & Row.

Mazzocchetti, J. (2012). Feelings of injustice and conspiracy theory. Representations of adolescents from an African migrant background (Morocco and sub-Saharan Africa) in disadvantaged neighbourhoods of Brussels. *Brussels Studies, 63*(63), 1–10.

McIntyre, L. (2018). *Post-truth*. MIT Press.

McKenna, K. Y. A., Green, A. S., & Gleason, M. E. J. (2002). Relationship formation on the internet: What's the big attraction? *Journal of Social Issues, 58*(1), 9–31.

Melton, J. G. (2014). *Encyclopaedic handbook of cults in America*. Routledge.

Miller, G. H., Marquez-Velarde, G., Williams, A. A., & Keith, V. M. (2021). Discrimination and Black social media use: Sites of oppression and expression. *Sociology of Race and Ethnicity, 7*(2), 247–263.

Nickerson, R. S. (1998). Confirmation bias: A ubiquitous phenomenon in many guises. *Review of General Psychology, 2*(2), 175–220.

Over, H. (2016). The origins of belonging: Social motivation in infants and young children. *Philosophical Transactions of the Royal Society B: Biological Sciences, 371*(1686), 20150072.

Pennycook, G., & Rand, D. G. (2019). Lazy, not biased: Susceptibility to partisan fake news is better explained by lack of reasoning than by motivated reasoning. *Cognition*, *188*, 39–50.

Pennycook, G., Cannon, T. D., & Rand, D. G. (2018). Prior exposure increases perceived accuracy of fake news. *Journal of Experimental Psychology General*, *147*(12), 1865–1880.

Peter, M. Z., Peter, P. F. J., & Catapan, A. H. (2015). Belonging: Concept, meaning, and commitment. *US–China Education Review*, *5*(2), 95–101.

Pillow, D. R., Malone, G. P., & Hale, W. J. (2015). The need to belong and its association with fully satisfying relationships: A tale of two measures. *Personality and Individual Differences*, *74*(1), 259–264.

Poon, K. T., Chen, Z., & Wong, W. Y. (2020). Beliefs in conspiracy theories following ostracism. *Personality & Social Psychology Bulletin*, *46*(8), 1234–1246.

Prado, C. G. (Ed.). (2018). *America's post-truth phenomenon: When feelings and opinions trump facts and evidence*. Praeger.

Ryan, R. M., & Deci, E. L. (2000). Self-determination theory and the facilitation of intrinsic motivation, social development, and well-being. *American Psychologist*, *55*(1), 68–78.

Ryan, T., Allen, K.-A., Gray, D., & McInerney, D. (2017). How social are social media? A review of online social behaviour and connectedness. *Journal of Relationships Research*, *8*, E8.

Sagan, C. (2011). *The demon-haunted world: Science as a candle in the dark*. Ballantine Books.

Saunders, P. L., & Chester, A. (2008). Shyness and the internet: Social problem or panacea? *Computers in Human Behaviour*, *24*, 2649–2658.

Scheufele, D. A., & Krause, N. M. (2019). Science audiences, misinformation, and fake news. *Proceedings of the National Academy of Sciences of the United States of America*, *116*(16), 7662–7669.

Schmidt, A., Dirk, J., Neubauer, A. B., & Schmiedek, F. (2021). Evaluating sociometer theory in children's everyday lives: Inclusion, but not exclusion by peers at school is related to within-day change in self-esteem. *European Journal of Personality*, *35*(5), 736–753.

Seabrook, E. M., Kern, M. L., & Rickard, N. S. (2016). Social networking sites, depression, and anxiety: A systematic review. *JMIR Mental Health*, *3*(4), e5842.

Sheldon, K. M., Abad, N., & Hinsch, C. A. (2011). Two-process view of Facebook use and relatedness need-satisfaction: Disconnection drives use, and connection rewards it. *Journal of Personality and Social Psychology*, *100* (4), 766–775.

Shermer, M. (2011). *The believing brain: From ghosts and gods to politics and conspiracies – how we construct beliefs and reinforce them as truths*. Henry Holt.

Sinatra, G., & Hofer, B. (2021). *Science denial: Why it happens and what to do about it*. Oxford University Press.

Smith, R. J., & Santiago, A. M. (2021). The storming of Washington, DC: The city of love against the city of white supremacy. *Journal of Community Practice, 29*(1), 1–10.

Snell, K. D. M. (2017). The rise of living alone and loneliness in history. *Social History, 42*(1), 2–28.

Sommer, W. (2018, March 20). What is QAnon? The craziest theory of the Trump era, explained. *The Daily Beast*. www.thedailybeast.com/what-is-qanon-the-craziest-theory-of-the-trump-era-explained

Stanovich, K. E. (2011). *Rationality and the reflective mind*. Oxford University Press.

Twenge, J. M., & Campbell, W. K. (2008). Increases in positive self-views among high school students: Birth cohort changes in anticipated performance, self-satisfaction, self-liking, and self-competence. *Psychological Science, 19*(11), 1082–1086.

Uscinski, J. E., & Parent, J. M. (2014). *American conspiracy theories*. Oxford University Press.

van Orden, K. A., Witte, T. K., Cukrowicz, K. C., Braithwaite, S. R., Selby, E. A., & Joiner, T. E., Jr. (2010). The interpersonal theory of suicide. *Psychological review, 117*(2), 575–600.

van Prooijen, J. W. (2016). Sometimes inclusion breeds suspicion: Self-uncertainty and belongingness predict belief in conspiracy theories. *European Journal of Social Psychology, 46*(3), 267–279.

van Prooijen, J. W., & Acker, M. (2015). The influence of control on belief in conspiracy theories: Conceptual and applied extensions. *Applied Cognitive Psychology, 29*(5), 753–761.

van Prooijen, J. W., & van Vugt, M. (2018). Conspiracy theories: Evolved functions and psychological mechanisms. *Perspectives on Psychological Science, 13*(6), 770–788.

Wagle, R., Dowdy, E., Nylund-Gibson, K., Sharkey, J. D., Carter, D., & Furlong, M. J. (2021). School belonging constellations considering complete mental health in primary schools. *Educational and Developmental Psychologist, 38*(2), 173–185.

Waisbord, S. (2018). Truth is what happens to news. *Journalism Studies, 19*(13), 1866–1878.

Wardle, C., & Derakhshan, H. (2017, September 27). Information disorder: Toward an interdisciplinary framework for research and policymaking. *Council of Europe*. https://firstdraftnews.org/wp-content/uploads/2017/11/PREMS-162317-GBR-2018-Report-de%CC%81sinformation-1.pdf?x56713

Wesselmann, E. D., & Williams, K. D. (2010). The potential balm of religion and spirituality for recovering from ostracism. *Journal of Management, Spirituality & Religion, 7*(1), 31–49.

Yakovleva, M. G. (2018). Developmental characteristics of adolescents that increase risk of joining anti-social cults. *Russian Education & Society, 60*(3), 269–277.

Young, T., Fitzgibbon, W., & Silverstone, D. (2014). A question of family? Youth and gangs. *Youth Justice*, *14*, 171–185.

Zhong, B., Huang, Y., & Liu, Q. (2021). Mental health toll from the coronavirus: Social media usage reveals Wuhan residents' depression and secondary trauma in the COVID-19 outbreak. *Computers in Human Behavior*, *114*, 106524.

PART IV

The Role of Communication in Promoting and Limiting QAnon Support

CHAPTER 12

QAnon and Social Media

Tatyana Kaplan

Introduction

This chapter begins with an overview of QAnon's origin and rise on social media. In the chapter, I explore the strategies used by conspiracy groups such as QAnon to manipulate media and spread disinformation and how social media platforms initially aided in QAnon's proliferation (see also Chapter 13 of this volume for more on disinformation and QAnon). I also examine the potential consequences of exposure to QAnon and widespread disinformation on social media as related to conspiratorial beliefs and potentially harmful behavior. Though it does not appear that exposure to QAnon-related social media content necessarily engenders conspiratorial thoughts and behaviors, exposure to some conspiracy-related disinformation (e.g. regarding COVID-19) can be associated with potentially harmful behaviors. The chapter concludes with recommendations for future research on the consequences of social media use and exposure to conspiracy theories.

The Rise of QAnon on Social Media

The figure of "Q" first appeared on an anonymous message board forum called 4chan in 2017 (Zadrozny & Collins, 2018). Q alluded to being a government official with high-level governmental clearance ("Q" clearance). Consequently, 4chan users appeared to believe that posts by Q were composed of government intelligence tidbits. The bits of information shared by Q on 4chan were referred to as "crumbs." These crumbs were often presented by Q in the form of leading questions, fostering a sort of game whereby 4chan readers would try to decode the posts through "research." Q posts then moved to a different message board called 8chan, and eventually the conversation surrounding the QAnon conspiracy moved to more mainstream social media sites such as Facebook, Twitter, and YouTube.

The first post by Q on 4chan stated that extradition agreements with other countries were in motion in case Hillary Clinton tried to flee the USA. The second post stated that Hillary Clinton would be arrested on October 30, 2017. The posts became more cryptic over time, and conversation surrounding the posts morphed into a scavenger hunt-type game wherein followers would try to figure out the persons, places, or events that they believed Q was referencing. Soon, a cohesive conspiracy emerged: Donald Trump was leading a secret fight against prominent members of the Democratic Party and Hollywood elites who were engaged in a satanic child-trafficking ring. The portion of the conspiracy referencing a satanic child-trafficking ring originated with the Pizzagate conspiracy, which prompted a man to enter a pizza restaurant in Washington, DC, carrying an assault rifle because he believed that children were being held in the restaurant's basement (Siddiqui & Svrluga, 2016). There would be 1,800 posts by Q by August 2018 and more than 4,000 by August 2020. Though Q posted only on 4chan (eventually 8chan/8kun), much of the conspiracy decoding and conversation took place on social media forums such as Reddit, Facebook, Twitter, and YouTube.

The first step in the progression of the QAnon movement from obscurity to mainstream social media was a social media platform called Reddit. Q was not the first 4chan poster to suggest their possession of high-level government clearance. At least four other 4chan accounts had previously claimed to have access to high-level government intelligence before the account known as Q posted on 4chan in October 2017. Each of these accounts also posted conspiratorial information related either to the Clinton Foundation or to high-profile forthcoming events that would shed light on illicit activities conducted by persons involved with the US Democratic Party (Zadrozny & Collins, 2018). Unique to Q was the interest that the original post sparked among three people who would coordinate their efforts to propel Q-related content to a more mainstream audience (Zadrozny & Collins, 2018). These efforts gave rise to the movement known as QAnon.

Initially, one of the group members who worked to create a following for Q posted a video discussing the Q conspiracy on a subreddit for politically incorrect content. The video garnered 250,000 views as of August 2018 (Zadrozny & Collins, 2018). Given the large amount of engagement with the video, the group then created a new subreddit called CBTS_Stream (CBTS = Calm Before the Storm) as a dedicated space for Q conspiracy discussion on the Reddit social media platform. This Reddit board eventually obtained 20,000 subscribers (Tiffany, 2020; Zadrozny &

Collins, 2018). The Reddit moderators who created CBTS_Stream grew in popularity, gaining followers and increasing viewership of their YouTube videos. After Reddit shut down the board for inciting violence and sharing personally identifying information and banned the creators of the board, the group's efforts to propagate Q-related content did not end. One of the creators started a YouTube streaming channel that ran Q-related content twenty-four hours a day, seven days a week. In August 2018, the streaming channel had 46,000 subscribers (Zadrozny & Collins, 2018).

Although 2018 does not boast the largest numbers for the QAnon movement (see Chapter 8 of this volume for an account of QAnon's growth during COVID-19), both Reddit and Facebook had tens of thousands of QAnon-related groups in 2018. For example, in addition to CBTS_Stream, Reddit also had a subreddit called "r/TheGreatAwakening." This subreddit had 70,000 members as of August 2018 (Tiffany, 2020). Though Reddit banned a significant portion of subgroups related to Q and QAnon in September 2018 (Timberg & Dwoskin, 2020), it would be years before Twitter, YouTube, and Facebook would take the necessary steps to curb the spread of the conspiracy theory on their respective social media platforms.

In 2020, QAnon followers began to share conspiracies about COVID-19 on social media, including a conspiracy that the virus was planned by a secret cabal of elitists to control the population at large. The conspiracy also suggested that mask wearing "triggers" the virus and that vaccines were designed to monitor those who become inoculated. A thirty-minute video entitled "Plandemic" encapsulated these theories and was shared and viewed widely on social media platforms. The video garnered some 8 million views (Frenkel et al., 2020).

As the QAnon movement grew, it also captured the media's attention. Twitter accounts associated with the Trump administration retweeted posts by users who frequently posted or shared QAnon-related content. President Trump was asked by a journalist to denounce the theory during a televised town hall (Vazquez, 2020). The QAnon movement appeared to have gained a substantial amount to traction, despite its inauguration on a fringe message board, due to its spread to mainstream social media.

The Spread of Conspiracy Theories in the Age of Social Media

Boasting users in the billions, social media platforms have the potential for an incredibly wide reach. Moreover, the structure of social media platforms allows users to share content with others in their network with unprecedented speed. As such, the structure and reach of social media warrant examination regarding the extent to which social media platforms play a role in the spread of conspiracy theories and the rise of movements such as QAnon.

Social Media Reach

Facebook has approximately 2.85 billion active users (Tankovska, 2021c). YouTube has approximately 2.1 billion users (Tankovska, 2021b). Twitter has approximately 290.5 million global users (Tankovska, 2021a). In 2020, Reddit disclosed that it had 52 million daily users (Sahil, 2020). It is not clear how many unique users each social media platform has; however, research suggests that some 72 percent of American adults uses some type of social media (Pew Research Center, 2021). People between the ages of eighteen and twenty-nine years are more likely to use social media (81 percent) than people who are sixty-five years of age or older (45 percent). These older adults tend to use Facebook (50 percent) and YouTube (49 percent) more than other social media platforms, though YouTube and Facebook are the most widely used social media platforms in general. Younger people are more likely to use a wide variety of social media websites, including YouTube (95 percent), Instagram (71 percent), Facebook (70 percent), Snapchat (65 percent), TikTok (48 percent), and Twitter (42 percent), than those approximately thirty years of age or older. A majority of Facebook (71 percent), Instagram (59 percent), Snapchat (59 percent), and YouTube (54 percent) users say they visit these platforms every day, many of whom visit these platforms several times per day (Auxier & Anderson, 2021).

Social Media Structure

Most social media platforms require that a user signs up or registers to utilize the platform in a meaningful or engaging way, such as posting or sharing content, providing commentary, joining groups, or subscribing to content. Once registered, social media platforms might ask if the person signing up wants to import a list of their contacts from other sites, such as Google, so that they can interact with their acquaintances, friends, coworkers, or family members who already have accounts on the platform. After a user signs up, the social media platform's algorithm kicks in to show the user content that they might be interested in based on their engagement with other content or groups or content that has been shared or engaged with by those in their network.

Each social media platform has its own algorithm or algorithms that is uses to promote content or groups. Often, the algorithms incorporate content that friends or family have engaged with in conjunction with a user's past activity (e.g. Koumchatzky & Andryeyev, 2017). In this way, social media users are not always in control of the information they are exposed to, and social media algorithms have the potential to drive the extensive growth of content and groups related to conspiracy theories, or disinformation in general, among its users.

In 2020, Facebook had thousands of groups and pages related to the Q conspiracy and QAnon movement (Sen & Zadrozny, 2020). In total, QAnon-related groups comprised some 3 million members. It appears that QAnon-related groups were recommended by Facebook's algorithm to its users, though the extent to which the recommendation system contributed to QAnon's growth is unclear (McNamee, 2020; Sen & Zadrozny, 2020; Wong, 2020). In 2016, a Facebook employee's internal presentation indicated that more than two-thirds of all joins to extremist groups on Facebook were attributed to the algorithmic recommendation system employed by Facebook (Horwitz & Seetharaman, 2020). Additionally, a 2020 internal memo at Facebook indicated that a Facebook team discovered that the company had accepted 185 pro-QAnon or QAnon-related ads on its platform, which had generated approximately 4 million impressions (Sen & Zadrozny, 2020).

In October 2020, Facebook announced that it would ban all groups and pages representing QAnon on Facebook and Instagram (Albert, 2020). As a result, some 1,700 pages and 5,600 groups related to QAnon were removed as of August 2020 (Frenkel, 2020). On Instagram, which is owned by Facebook, approximately 18,700 QAnon-related accounts were removed (Binder, 2020). Also, in October 2020, YouTube announced that QAnon- and Pizzagate-related content targeting individual persons or groups would no longer be allowed on its platform. Just one of the videos impacted by this policy included a QAnon-related film that had over 15 million views (Zadrozny & Collins, 2020).

Twitter is less centralized than Facebook. A user can follow accounts on Twitter and see the content that these accounts engage with if they like or retweet content, but Twitter does not host formalized groups like Facebook. Twitter relies more on the use of hashtags, which are phrases or words preceded by the "#" sign. Hashtags communicate a tweet's relevance to a specific topic. For example, if a user were to tweet about how much they love tacos on a Tuesday, the user would add #TacoTuesday to the tweet. Hashtags that garner engagement among users are ranked, and popular hashtags (i.e. "trending" hashtags) appear on the "Trending" tab on the website and mobile application. There were more than 22 million tweets with a QAnon-related hashtag on Twitter in 2019. In comparison, there were about 5 million tweets related to the MeToo movement in 2019 on Twitter (Haimowitz, 2020). Also, by 2019, the QAnon movement on Twitter was an international phenomenon, with QAnon-related tweets originating from accounts in the UK, Canada, Australia, and Germany, in addition to the USA (Haimowitz, 2020).

In July 2020, Twitter announced that it had placed restrictions on QAnon-related content and links (Albert, 2020; BBC News, 2021). The restrictions included the discontinuation of QAnon-related account, trend, and content recommendations, which suggests that Twitter's algorithm had also made such recommendations to its users. Twitter stated that the restrictions would impact 150,000 accounts (Collins & Zadrozny, 2020). In an attempt to evade being banned or censored by social media platforms, some QAnon followers removed the word "Q" from their accounts, posts, or hashtags and instead used "17" (Q is the seventeenth letter in the alphabet) or "CUE" to signal membership in the QAnon movement (Teh, 2021). Shortly after the US Capitol attack, Twitter announced that it had suspended some 70,000 accounts related to QAnon (Twitter Safety, 2021). The fact that approximately 70,000 QAnon-related accounts were detected by Twitter after the initial restrictions in July 2020 suggests that Twitter was still widely used by QAnon followers at the beginning of 2021 despite Twitter's efforts.

Social Media and Media Manipulation

Groups that propagate inflammatory content or disinformation on social media platforms, like the QAnon movement, engage in strategies that can help promote their messages by garnering attention and visibility. These strategies can also manipulate news frames and alter the prominence of topics covered by news organizations, which is referred to as agenda setting (Marwick & Lewis, 2017).

One strategy that a group can engage in to promote their messages and ideas is through involvement of participatory culture, whereby group members both consume and produce content relevant to the group's messages or ideas (Fuchs, 2014). A participatory culture has been defined as one with low barriers to expression and engagement, strong support for creating and sharing original content with others, informal mentorship, a sense that members believe that contributions matter, and a sense of social connection with other members (Jenkins, 2009). This definition certainly applies to the QAnon movement. The movement relied heavily on followers connecting the dots of "crumbs" in posts by Q. In fact, the QAnon movement explicitly encouraged followers to conduct their own "research." This research and decoding often included followers producing content such as memes, maps, videos, and other graphics (Morrish, 2020) to connect or illuminate pieces of the Q conspiracy puzzle. Participatory culture allows followers to identify others who share their views and to work in a coordinated fashion to produce and disseminate group-related information (Marwick & Lewis, 2017). Group members are motivated to produce content that is likely to resonate with others in the group as the content can generate status and praise through likes, shares, and comments (Fisher, 2021; Marwick & Lewis, 2017). QAnon followers on Twitter often used hashtags such as #WWG1WGA (Where We Go One, We Go All) to signal membership in the group and to share QAnon-related Twitter and Facebook posts. In this way, QAnon followers on Twitter could have their content shared widely among fellow followers and receive attention and praise quickly from a large number of people, including accounts with large followings, known as influencers. On YouTube, QAnon content garnered millions of views and a substantial number of subscribers, making it a potentially profitable venture.

Another way in which groups can manipulate media is through the use of hashtags on social media platforms such as Twitter. Coordinated efforts to get a hashtag trending can expose a message associated with that hashtag to a much wider audience, as trending hashtags can be seen by Twitter users regardless of whether or not they follow accounts that share this type of content. In some cases, groups will coopt or hijack popular hashtags, such as #BlackLivesMatter (Marwick & Lewis, 2017), and share it widely to get the hashtag trending. As a possible by-product of the attempt to avoid detection by Twitter or Facebook, QAnon followers began using #SaveTheChildren in their posts and tweets, ostensibly to shed light on child trafficking. This hashtag began appearing on Twitter circa June 2020 and was used some 800,000 times in one week (Seitz, 2020). Across social media platforms, the hashtag garnered engagement in the millions. Marches took place in the USA as part of the Save The Children movement, which also garnered media attention (Seitz, 2020). Some have suggested that the hashtag was a more palatable way for the QAnon movement to introduce the conspiracy to a new and broader audience, especially women (Greenspan, 2020b).

The use of bots is another strategy employed by groups such as QAnon. Bots are defined as automated social media accounts, which can be used for a variety of reasons, including amplifying content and spreading misleading propagandistic information on social media platforms (Ferrara, 2020). Unless someone is well-versed in identifying bot-like behavior, it can be difficult for people utilizing social media platforms to determine whether viral or trending content has legitimate grassroots support or whether the support is manufactured. In May 2020, a group of researchers suggested that approximately 45 percent of all accounts tweeting about coronavirus were bots, and much of the content that the bots disseminated was related to misinformation (Allyn, 2020). Prior investigation into bot activity on Twitter in 2020 found that approximately 13 percent of accounts that tweeted or retweeted conspiracy-related hashtags, including those associated with the QAnon movement, were bots (Ferrara, 2020). Bots have been successful in garnering engagement from real users to spread conspiracy-related content and help it trend, as was the case with the Pizzagate conspiracy.

One reason why bots pose a potential problem regarding the spread of misinformation on social media is that social media algorithms select content that has higher engagement when determining which content to prioritize and share with or recommend to users. Additionally, some social media platforms, like Twitter, display topics or hashtags that are trending on the website. Theoretically, to the extent that bots can amplify misinformation enough to get it trending, they can drive substantial growth of or exposure to conspiratorial content.

Trending topics on social media platforms like Twitter catch the eye of organizations that produce more mainstream news-related content, as they rely on fresh and sometimes sensationalistic content to drive traffic to their website (Marwick & Lewis, 2017). In some cases, entire stories on news-related blogs are composed of a topic trending on social media and the way in which it unfolded through tweets or Facebook posts. In this way, groups who intentionally seek to manipulate media get to frame the way in which a story unfolds. There are also cases of the news media covering stories about celebrities who have been harassed on social media by the followers of a conspiracy theory (e.g. Dickson, 2021; Greenspan, 2020a), and in some cases celebrity figures receive news coverage when they promote or indicate support for a conspiracy group or theory (e.g. Raju, 2020). Moreover, the public might place undue prominence on topics that receive frequent media attention (Marwick & Lewis, 2017). For example, the NBC News journalist who interviewed Donald J. Trump during a televised town hall thought that the QAnon movement was important enough to include in the televised discussion. Events such as these foster subsequent media coverage (e.g. Vazquez, 2020) that dictates the content to which the public devotes time and attention. As such, media manipulators who drive media attention through the use of participatory culture, hashtags, and bots get to dictate the agenda for the public (Marwick & Lewis, 2017) and create a wide-reaching platform for spreading conspiratorial content.

Social Media's Impact on Conspiracy Theorizing and Adoption

Many news organizations and journalists have produced stories related to QAnon's presence on social media. Given the volume with which such stories are produced, it might seem logical to conclude that QAnon and misinformation more generally would not exist if it were not for the internet or social media. At the very least, considering the sheer vastness and structure of social media, it is possible to surmise that social media has unprecedented potential to expose a large portion of the population to conspiracy theories. But does this mean that the internet and social media platforms give rise to conspiratorial belief? According to some researchers, the likely answer is no.

To be sure, conspiratorial support, dissemination, and endorsement are not unique to the QAnon movement. There is also no substantive evidence to support the notion that conspiratorial belief has increased over time (Uscinski & Parent, 2014). Indeed, conspiracy theorizing existed before the advent of the internet (e.g. regarding the assassination of John F. Kennedy, McCarthyism). In fact, conspiracy theory endorsement is believed to have been prevalent throughout human history (see van Prooijen & Douglas, 2017).

Although it might seem intuitive to believe that the internet and the structure and reach of social media could foster an increase in conspiratorial thinking, Uscinski and Parent (2014) surmise that the internet simply replaced the functionality of other forms of communication, such as word of mouth. Put simply, though social media likely allows for conspiracy theories to reach a wide audience at a much faster rate than other more traditional forms of communication, conspiracy theories had the potential for an equally wide reach before the internet.

Overall, research in conspiratorial theorizing and adoption suggests that people who believe in conspiracy theories are already predisposed to conspiratorial views, which can be understood as a tendency to see powerful and secretive agents and organizations conspiring to do harm to society for their own benefit (Goertzel, 1994; van Prooijen, 2018). There are motives and explanations that elucidate participation in conspiracy-supporting groups like QAnon. For example, some research suggests that people seek out and adopt conspiracies in an attempt to fulfill existential, epistemic, and social needs (see Chapter 3 of this volume). Moreover, people are social animals with a strong need for belonging (see Chapter 11 of this volume). Group membership can alleviate isolation and feelings of loneliness, as well as provide a sense of safety, survival, and purpose. Who is likely to be susceptible to conspiratorial views and the QAnon movement? Chapter 5 in this volume discusses the role of moral cognitions in the growth of QAnon, while Chapter 4 discusses traits such as lower levels of education and narcissism that might be associated with QAnon followers. Chapter 4 also reviews the roles that cognitive process such as delusional ideation, a need for closure, and confirmation bias might play in increasing the likelihood of QAnon association. There is also research suggesting that people are more likely to adopt politically laden conspiracies that color "the other side" negatively (see Douglas et al., 2019). For example, Republicans are more likely to endorse conspiracies that involve Democrats, and vice versa (e.g. Miller et al., 2016). Unsurprisingly, this relationship extends to the endorsement of fake news, such that conspiracy ideation and political identity are strongly related to judgments of the truthfulness of politically congruent conspiratorial fake news (Anthony & Moulding, 2019).

QAnon and Gamification

In journalistic circles, QAnon has been referred to as both a cult (e.g. Blazakis, 2021; Rogers, 2020) and a new religious movement (Nyce, 2020). Though it is beyond the scope of this chapter to compare the QAnon movement to other religious movements (see Chapters 8 and 16 of this volume), it is worth exploring how QAnon differs from religious groups and other conspiracy groups in its social media use.

QAnon social media use resembled religious social media use in both content and purpose. For example, several posts by Q contained Christian scripture, and this scripture was circulated by QAnon followers on social media platforms (Burke, 2020). This is unsurprising given that the QAnon theory contains religious elements such as a prophet (i.e. Q) and an apocalyptic fight between good and evil. Additionally, religious followers who use social media like Facebook often do so to build relationships with others who share similar beliefs, and they share content others might find uplifting or reaffirming (Brubaker & Haigh, 2017). In this way, QAnon social media use resembled religious-based social media use such that QAnon followers could use social media to identify others who also endorsed the theory and provide support to others if their belief in the conspiracy or faith in Q was waning.

As mentioned previously, the QAnon movement was steeped in participatory culture, such that consumers produced much of the information that was shared and engaged with across social media platforms. The culture surrounding belief in a flat Earth appears to function similarly. On YouTube, flat-Earth conspiracy followers create content advocating for the idea of a flat Earth, which is then consumed by other followers. Also, the content of social media posts surrounding both QAnon and belief in a flat Earth can include suggestions that followers should question what they believe (e.g. about science) or what they have been told by scientific or governmental institutions (de Melo et al., 2020). However, QAnon differed from religious or other conspiracy-endorsing groups in its social media use due to its extreme reliance on and incorporation of gamification, which is the use of gaming elements to increase engagement in nongaming contexts (Robson et al., 2015).

It is not difficult to conceive of the QAnon movement as a game. In fact, the movement has been identified as resembling an MMORPG (massively multiplayer online role-playing game), a live action role-playing game (LARP), and an alternate-reality game (ARG; Berkowitz, 2020; Daly, 2020; Warzel, 2020). ARGs are designed as scavenger hunts whereby clues are left by the game designers in the real world across platforms. Once a clue is uncovered, it often leads to additional clues. Players work together to share their interpretations of the clues and uncover new clues. The QAnon movement sounds very similar to this. Followers worked together on social media platforms to unravel cryptic messages and connect clues in prior and new posts by Q. Posts or tweets that seemed to be the "correct" interpretation of some clue or puzzle would be widely shared and lauded. For QAnon, the "live action" part took place on social media, and in real time, but clues were often searched for by followers outside of social media platforms in images, published stories, or maps.

In short, though QAnon social media posts contained content that was similar to that of other groups, these other groups do not rely on social media users to seek out clues or unravel cryptic messages to keep the movement circulating and engaging on social media platforms. The gaming elements inherent to the QAnon movement made the movement somewhat unique in its use of social media.

Consequences of QAnon, Disinformation, and Social Media

Although the presence of QAnon on social media might not increase belief in conspiratorial thinking, there are negative consequences related to the spread of disinformation and QAnon. Indeed, the news media have published several stories about the negative impacts QAnon can have on families (Chabria, 2021; Gilbert, 2021) and alleged criminal acts associated with QAnon followers (Brewster, 2021), which are discussed more in Chapter 5 of this volume. Outside of these topics, the news media and researchers have devoted a considerable amount of time and resources to investigating the prevalence of disinformation on social media.

Around the time of the 2016 US presidential election, Facebook began garnering negative media attention that suggested that fake news was prevalent on the platform (Ohlheiser, 2016). Twitter did not fare better (Isaac & Ember, 2016). As recently as March 2021, representatives of Google (which owns YouTube), Facebook, and Twitter were interviewed by Members of Congress about the proliferation of disinformation on each respective social media platform (Wakefield, 2021). This hearing followed on the heels of the attack on the US Capitol, and it built up the perception that social media is rampant with disinformation regarding many topics, including COVID-19.

In January 2021, the Pew Research Center published the results of a survey examining the use of social media for news gathering among Americans. Approximately half of Americans in the Pew study reported getting news from social media sources at least some of the time (Shearer & Mitchell, 2021). Approximately a third (36 percent) reported that they got news from Facebook, and approximately a quarter (23 percent) reported visiting YouTube for news. Although only 15 percent of respondents reported getting news from Twitter, 59 percent of those respondents indicated that they get their news from Twitter on a regular basis. Interestingly, a majority of respondents (60 percent) who gathered news from social media platforms indicated their belief that news on social media is largely inaccurate. Though there has been a good deal of media attention given to the prevalence of disinformation on social media platforms, the extent to which fake news and disinformation are pervasive on social media and the harm associated with disinformation and social media use are not clear. On the one hand, news consumption in general appears to make up only a small fraction (4.2 percent) of total media consumption (Allen et al., 2020). Moreover, though fake news is more likely to be encountered on social media, fake news in total makes up only a small fraction (1 percent) of total media consumption overall. Television appears to dominate all other sources of news by a large margin.

On the other hand, some research suggests that social media use exposes people to conspiracy theories and disinformation to a greater extent than other forms of media. For example, American adults who depended on social media for political news were more likely to be aware of the "Plandemic" conspiracy theory related to COVID-19 than American adults who relied on network and cable television, news websites, and radio for political news (Mitchell et al., 2020). At the same time, it appears that people who consume political news from social media platforms are less engaged in political news and discourse than American adults who get their political news from other media platforms. For example, a majority of American adults who relied on social media for political news (57 percent) were categorized as having low political knowledge and only 17 percent were categorized as having high political knowledge compared to adults who rely on news websites (45 percent), radio (42 percent), and print media (41 percent) for political news (Mitchell et al., 2020). It is not clear whether these results are related to exposure to disinformation on social media or a general lack of engagement with politics.

There is a growing body of evidence that suggests that social media use and/or exposure to conspiracy theories related to COVID-19 can have a negative impact on private and public health outcomes. For example, Allington et al. (2020) found that people who reported a preference for social media use rather than other forms of media were also more likely to report holding conspiratorial views about COVID-19. In turn, these conspiratorial views were negatively related to self-reports of health-protective behaviors, such as handwashing often and practicing social distancing. The same study found a negative association between using social media platforms as a source of information on COVID-19 and self-reported engagement in health-protective behaviors. Jolley and Douglas (2014) found that belief in and exposure to antivaccine conspiracy theories negatively impacted vaccination intentions. The authors reported that antivaccine conspiracy theories appear to increase suspicion regarding vaccine safety and feelings of powerlessness and disillusionment while simultaneously decreasing trust in authorities.

Taken together, the research suggests that exposure to conspiracy theories and disinformation is more likely to occur on social media platforms than other forms of media. However, people appear to be mostly skeptical of the authenticity of news encountered on social media, even when they are the consumers of such news, and increased exposure does not necessarily translate to increased conspiratorial belief. Regardless, in some contexts (e.g. COVID-19), conspiracy theories and misinformation might play a role in potentially harmful behavior or a lack of protective behavior.

Given the likelihood that social media use increases exposure to conspiracy theories, it is worth investigating the effect that simple exposure might have on other outcomes, such as perceived accuracy of information. This line of reasoning is rooted in the mere exposure effect, which suggests that exposing people to some stimulus, especially if they do not consciously register the stimulus, results in more positive attitudes toward the stimulus (Zajonc, 1968). Building on a phenomenon referred to as the illusory-truth effect, Pennycook et al. (2018) examined the effect of prior exposure of fake news headlines on the likelihood of judging subsequent fake news headlines as accurate. The researchers found that even a single prior exposure to a fake news headline increased ratings of accuracy of the headline, and that additional exposure compounded this effect. Exposure did not have to reach participant awareness to have an effect. Implausibility played an interesting role in the study, such that repetition did not increase perceived accuracy of extremely implausible fake news headlines, suggesting that plausibility might play a role in the extent to which conspiracy theories have the potential to impact attitudes, behavioral intent, or behavior.

Future Directions

Several motives have been proposed for why users share conspiracy-related information and misinformation on social media platforms. For example, people can be motivated to share potentially false, conspiratorial, misleading, or inflammatory information to increase their followers (Pennycook et al., 2021) or to share content that generates likes and shares (Fisher, 2021; Pennycook et al., 2021). But the consequences of the widespread sharing of such information is still unclear. Put differently, there is a solid understanding of who is sharing conspiratorial or misinformation content and why, but less is known about the consequences of the spread of this information. Additionally, much of the research related to social media, fake news, and conspiracy theories is correlational or cross-sectional, which is certainly helpful but limits our knowledge regarding causality and long-term effects. Although not an easy undertaking, longitudinal study and analyses (e.g. diary studies) on conspiratorial content and social media use could parse out differences in the amount and content of conspiratorial exposure and consumption and the potential impact these factors have on a variety of outcomes, including behavior, which is not often researched or studied systematically outside of the context of sharing conspiratorial content on social media.

Especially intriguing was the finding by Pennycook et al. (2018) on implausibility and the potential barrier that implausibility might play in curbing belief in conspiracy theories and misinformation. This line of research could help explain why some conspiracies are widely believed and some are not, despite widespread sharing on social media. For example, this chapter highlighted a fraction of social media's impact on COVID-19-related health intentions and self-reported behaviors (e.g. Allington et al., 2020; Jolley & Douglas, 2014). However, the research seems to point to a consistent finding that exposure to COVID-19 conspiracy theories or misinformation, often found on social media, can have potentially harmful effects. Less is known about the systematic impact of QAnon, but some research suggests that QAnon was not a widely supported phenomenon (see Chapter 9 of this volume). It might be that COVID-19 conspiracy theories are more plausible to the public or to certain subpopulations and therefore more impactful. Relatedly, the research by Pennycook et al. (2018) indicates that simple exposure (and repetition) to fake news headlines can impact judgments about a headline's accuracy. This then begs the question of whether or not mainstream media coverage of QAnon might do harm to the public overall, especially for those who might rely on news from sources other than social media. Additional research on the extent to which mainstream media coverage might somehow legitimize conspiracy-related content would be welcomed.

Conclusion

In a relatively short amount of time, the QAnon movement appears to have exploded on social and mainstream media. Through the use of participatory culture and gamification, the movement rose on social media platforms and potentially fostered the exposure of conspiracy-laden content to millions of people both in the USA and abroad. This chapter sought to identify the consequences of such exposure and engagement.

All in all, QAnon's presence on social media might have increased its exposure to a wide audience, but the negative consequences associated with that exposure appear to be limited to those who were already predisposed to hold conspiratorial views (see Douglas et al., 2019) and the extent to which QAnon adherents spread specific conspiracy information such as that related to COVID-19. Moreover, this exposure might have had more impactful consequences for people who rely solely on social media for information and perhaps avoid other forms of media, though additional research into this is warranted.

REFERENCES

Albert, V. (2020, October 7). Facebook bans QAnon pages, groups, and Instagram accounts. *CBS News*. www.cbsnews.com/news/facebook-bans-qanon-platforms-pages-groups-instagram-accounts/

Allen, J., Howland, B., Mobius, M., Rothschild, D., & Watts, D. J. (2020). Evaluating the fake news problem at the scale of the information ecosystem. *Science Advances*, *6*(14), eaay3539.

Allington, D., Duffy, B., Wessely, S., Dhavan, N., & Rubin, J. (2020). Health-protective behaviour, social media usage and conspiracy belief during the COVID-19 public health emergency. *Psychological Medicine*, *51*(10), 1–7.

Allyn, B. (2020, May 20). Researchers: Nearly half of accounts tweeting about Coronavirus are likely bots. *NPR*. www.npr.org/sections/coronavirus-live-updates/2020/05/20/859814085/researchers-nearly-half-of-accounts-tweetin g-about-coronavirus-are-likely-bots

Anthony, A., & Moulding, R. (2019). Breaking the news: Belief in fake news and conspiracist beliefs. *Australian Journal of Psychology*, *71*(2), 154–162.

Auxier, B., & Anderson, M. (2021, April 7). Social media use in 2021. *Pew Research Center*. www.pewresearch.org/internet/2021/04/07/social-media-use-in-2021/

BBC News. (2021, January 12). Twitter suspends 70,000 accounts linked to QAnon. *BBC News*. www.bbc.com/news/technology-55638558

Berkowitz, R. (2020, September 30). A game designer's analysis of QAnon. *Medium*. https://medium.com/curiouserinstitute/a-game-designers-analysis-of-qanon-580972548be5

Binder, M. (2020, October 28). Facebook shares specifics on how many QAnon accounts it banned. *Mashable*. https://mashable.com/article/facebook-qanon-account-takedowns

Blazakis, J. (2021, February 21). Op-Ed: Why QAnon's similarity to other cults makes it a significant national security threat. *Los Angeles Times*. www.latimes .com/opinion/story/2021-02-21/qanon-cults-capitol-attack-trump-threat

Brewster, J. (2021, May 27). QAnon believers committed nearly 80 conspiracy-motivated crimes, report finds. *Forbes*. www.forbes.com/sites/jackbrewster/ 2021/05/27/qanon-believers-committed-nearly-80-conspiracy-motivated-crimes-report-finds/?sh=6ddf2d971840

Brubaker, P. J., & Haigh, M. M. (2017). The religious Facebook experience: Uses and gratifications of faith-based content. *Social Media + Society*, *3*(2), 2056305117703 72.

Burke, D. (2020, October 15). How QAnon uses religion to lure unsuspecting Christians. *CNN*. www.cnn.com/2020/10/15/us/qanon-religion-churches/index.html

Chabria, A. (2021, March 18). QAnon's "collateral damage": Families struggle to pull loved ones back from the brink. *Los Angeles Times*. www.latimes.com/california/story/2021-03-18/post-trump-qanon-conspiracy-side-effects-divide-families

Collins, B., & Zadrozny, B. (2020, July 21). Twitter bans 7,000 QAnon accounts, limits 150,000 others as part of broad crackdown. *NBC News*. www.nbcnews.com/tech/tech-news/twitter-bans-7-000-qanon-accounts-limits-150-000-others-n1234541

Daly, K. (2020, August 18). Twitter bans 7,000 QAnon accounts, limits 150,000 others as part of broad crackdown. *NBC News*. www.nbcnews.com/tech/tech-news/twitter-bans-7-000-qanon-accounts-limits-150-000-others-n1234541

de Melo, L. W. S., Passos, M. M., & Salvi, R. F. (2020). Analysis of "Flat-Earther" posts on social media: Reflections for science education from the discursive perspective of Foucault. *Revista Brasileira de Pesquisa em Educação em Ciências*, *20*, 295–313.

Dickson, E. J. (2021, March 25). Did QAnon drive Chrissy Teigen from Twitter? *Rolling Stone*. www.rollingstone.com/culture/culture-news/chrissy-teigen-deletes-twitter-qanon-1143259/

Douglas, K. M., Uscinski, J. E., Sutton, R. M., Cichocka, A., Nefes, T., Ang, C. S., & Deravi, F. (2019). Understanding conspiracy theories. *Political Psychology*, *40*(Suppl. 1), 3–35.

Ferrara, E. (2020, October 28). On Twitter, bots spread conspiracy theories and QAnon talking points. *The Conversation*. https://theconversation.com/on-twitter-bots-spread-conspiracy-theories-and-qanon-talking-points-149039

Fisher, M. (2021, May 7). "Belonging is stronger than facts": The age of misinformation. *The New York Times*. www.nytimes.com/2021/05/07/world/asia/misinformation-disinformation-fake-news.html

Frenkel, S. (2020, December 18). QAnon is still spreading on Facebook, despite a ban. *The New York Times*. www.nytimes.com/2020/12/18/technology/qanon-is-still-spreading-on-facebook-despite-a-ban.html

Frenkel, S., Decker, B., & Alba, D. (2020, May 21). How the "Plandemic" movie and its falsehoods spread widely online. *The New York Times*. www.nytimes.com/2020/05/20/technology/plandemic-movie-youtube-facebook-coronavirus.html

Fuchs, C. (2014). Social media as participatory culture. In *Social media: A critical introduction* (pp. 52–68). SAGE.

Gilbert, D. (2021, March 31). How QAnon is tearing families apart. *Vice*. www.vice.com/en/article/dy8ayx/how-qanon-is-tearing-families-apart

Goertzel, T. (1994). Belief in conspiracy theories. *Political Psychology*, *15*(4), 731–742.

Greenspan, R. E. (2020a, May 28). Hilary Duff appeared to respond to baseless QAnon conspiracy theories saying that she was involved in child trafficking. *Insider*. www.insider.com/hilary-duff-responds-to-qanon-conspiracy-theories-about-child-trafficking-2020-5

(2020b, December 18). Trump's description of QAnon as being "against pedophilia" follows its insidious takeover of the "Save The Children" movement. *Insider*. www.insider.com/qanon-save-the-children-pedophilia-sex-trafficking-paranoia-2020-9

Haimowitz, I. (2020, December 17). No one is immune: The spread of Q-anon through social media and the pandemic. *Center for Strategic & International Studies*. www.csis.org/blogs/technology-policy-blog/no-one-immune-spread-q-anon-through-social-media-and-pandemic

Horwitz, J., & Seetharaman, D. (2020, May 26). Facebook executives shut down efforts to make the site less divisive. *The Wall Street Journal*. www.wsj.com/articles/facebook-knows-it-encourages-division-top-executives-nixed-solutions-11590507499

Isaac, M., & Ember, S. (2016, November 8). For election day influence, Twitter ruled social media. *The New York Times*. www.nytimes.com/2016/11/09/technology/for-election-day-chatter-twitter-ruled-social-media.html

Jenkins, H. (2009). *Confronting the challenges of participatory culture: Media education for the 21st century*. MIT Press.

Jolley, D., & Douglas, K. M. (2014). The effects of anti-vaccine conspiracy theories on vaccination intentions. *PLoS ONE*, *9*(2), e89177.

Koumchatzky, N., & Andryeyev, A. (2017, May 9). Using deep learning at scale in Twitter's timelines. *Twitter*. https://blog.twitter.com/engineering/en_us/topics/insights/2017/using-deep-learning-at-scale-in-twitters-timelines

Marwick, A., & Lewis, R. (2017). Media manipulation and disinformation online. *Data & Society Research Institute*. https://datasociety.net/pubs/oh/DataAndSociety_MediaManipulationAndDisinformationOnline.pdf

McNamee, R. (2020, September 30). Op-Ed: Facebook drove QAnon's mad growth and enhanced its power to poison elections. *Los Angeles Times*. www.latimes.com/opinion/story/2020-09-30/facebook-qanon-conspiracy-social-media-election

Miller, J. M., Saunders, K. L., & Farhart, C. E. (2016). Conspiracy endorsement as motivated reasoning: The moderating roles of political knowledge and trust. *American Journal of Political Science*, *60*(4), 824–844.

Mitchell, A., Jurkowitz, M., Oliphant, J. B., & Shearer, E. (2020, July 30). Americans who mainly get their news on social media are less engaged, less knowledgeable. *Pew Research Center*. www.journalism.org/2020/07/30/americans-who-mainly-get-their-news-on-social-media-are-less-engaged-less-knowledgeable/

Morrish, L. (2020, December 3). How QAnon content endures on social media through visuals and code words. *First Draft*. https://firstdraftnews.org/articles/how-qanon-content-endures-on-social-media-through-visuals-and-code-words/

Nyce, C. M. (2020, May 14). The Atlantic daily: QAnon is a new American religion. *The Atlantic*. www.theatlantic.com/newsletters/archive/2020/05/qanon-q-pro-trump-conspiracy/611722/

Ohlheiser, A. (2016, November 11). Mark Zuckerberg denies that fake news on Facebook influenced the elections. *The Washington Post*. www.washingtonpost.com/news/the-intersect/wp/2016/11/11/mark-zuckerberg-denies-that-fake-news-on-facebook-influenced-the-elections/

Pennycook, G., Cannon, T. D., & Rand, D. G. (2018). Prior exposure increases perceived accuracy of fake news. *Journal of Experimental Psychology. General*, *147*(12), 1865–1880.

Pennycook, G., Epstein, Z., Mosleh, M., Arechar, A. A., Eckles, D., & Rand, D. G. (2021). Shifting attention to accuracy can reduce misinformation online. *Nature (London)*, *592*(7855), 590–595.

Pew Research Center. (2021, April 7). Social media fact sheet. *Pew Research Center*. www.pewresearch.org/internet/fact-sheet/social-media/

Raju, M. (2020, December 3). Trump praised QAnon during meeting about keeping the Senate. *Insider*. www.cnn.com/2020/12/03/politics/donald-trump-qanon/index.html

Robson, K., Plangger, K., Kietzmann, J. H., McCarthy, I., & Pitt, L. (2015). Is it all a game? Understanding the principles of gamification. *Business Horizons*, *58*(4), 411–420.

Rogers, K. (2020, December 1). QAnon has become the cult that cries wolf. *FiveThirtyEight*. https://fivethirtyeight.com/features/qanon-has-become-the-cult-that-cries-wolf/

Sahil, P. (2020, December 1). Reddit claims 52 million daily users, revealing a key figure for social-media platforms. *The Wall Street Journal*. www.wsj.com/articles/reddit-claims-52-million-daily-users-revealing-a-key-figure-for-social-media-platforms-11606822200

Seitz, A. (2020, October 28). QAnon's "Save The Children" morphs into popular slogan. *Associated Press*. https://apnews.com/article/election-2020-donald-trump-child-trafficking-illinois-morris-aab978bb7e9b89cd2cea151ca13421a0

Sen, A., & Zadrozny, B. (2020, August 10). QAnon groups have millions of members on Facebook, documents show. *NBC News*. www.nbcnews.com/tech/tech-news/qanon-groups-have-millions-members-facebook-documents-show-n1236317

Shearer, E., & Mitchell, A. (2021, January 12). News use across social media platforms in 2020. *Pew Research Center*. www.pewresearch.org/journalism/2021/01/12/news-use-across-social-media-platforms-in-2020/

Siddiqui, F., & Svrluga, S. (2016, December 5). N.C. man told police he went to D.C. pizzeria with gun to investigate conspiracy theory. *The Washington*

Post. www.washingtonpost.com/news/local/wp/2016/12/04/d-c-police-respond-to-report-of-a-man-with-a-gun-at-comet-ping-pong-restaurant/

Tankovska, H. (2021a, February 10). Number of Twitter users worldwide from 2019 to 2024. *Statista.* www.statista.com/statistics/303681/twitter-users-worldwide/

(2021b, April 29). YouTube: Statistics & facts. *Statista.* www.statista.com/topics/2019/youtube/#:~:text=As%20of%202020%2C%20there%20was, up%20on%20the%20latest%20news

(2021c, May 21). Facebook: Number of monthly active users worldwide 2008–2021. *Statista.* www.statista.com/statistics/264810/number-of-monthly-active-facebook-users-worldwide/

Teh, C. (2021, May 27). Big tech cracked down on QAnon but its followers are still diving into online rabbit holes to connect and spread dangerous conspiracies. *Business Insider.* www.businessinsider.com/big-tech-cracked-down-qanon-followers-finding-rabbit-holes-conspiracies-2021-5

Tiffany, K. (2020, September 23). Reddit squashed QAnon by accident. *The Atlantic.* www.theatlantic.com/technology/archive/2020/09/reddit-qanon-ban-evasion-policy-moderation-facebook/616442/

Timberg, C., & Dwoskin, E. (2020, October 3). As QAnon grew, Facebook and Twitter missed years of warning signs about the conspiracy theory's violent nature. *The Washington Post.* www.washingtonpost.com/technology/2020/10/01/facebook-qanon-conspiracies-trump/

Twitter Safety. (2021, January 12). An update following the riots in Washington, DC. *Twitter.* https://blog.twitter.com/en_us/topics/company/2021/protecting–the-conversation-following-the-riots-in-washington–

Uscinski, J. E., & Parent, J. M. (2014). *American conspiracy theories.* Oxford University Press.

van Prooijen, J. W. (2018). *The psychology of conspiracy theories.* Routledge.

van Prooijen, J. W., & Douglas, K. M. (2017). Conspiracy theories as part of history: The role of societal crisis situations. *Memory Studies*, *10*(3), 323–333.

Vazquez, M. (2020, October 15). Trump again refuses to denounce QAnon. *CNN.* www.cnn.com/2020/10/15/politics/donald-trump-qanon-town-hall/index.html

Wakefield, J. (2021, March 25). Google, Facebook Twitter grilled in US on fake news. *BBC News.* www.bbc.com/news/technology-56523378.

Warzel, C. (2020, August 4). Is QAnon the most dangerous conspiracy theory of the 21st century? *The New York Times.* www.nytimes.com/2020/08/04/opinion/qanon-conspiracy-theory-arg.html

Wong, J. C. (2020, June 25). Down the rabbit hole: How QAnon conspiracies thrive on Facebook. *The Guardian.* www.theguardian.com/technology/2020/jun/25/qanon-facebook-conspiracy-theories-algorithm

Zadrozny, B., & Collins, B. (2018, August 14). How three conspiracy theorists took "Q" and sparked QAnon. *NBC News.* www.nbcnews.com/tech/tech-news/how-three-conspiracy-theorists-took-q-sparked-qanon-n900531

(2020, October 15). YouTube bans QAnon, other conspiracy content that targets individuals. *NBC News*. www.nbcnews.com/tech/tech-news/youtube-bans-qanon-other-conspiracy-content-targets-individuals-n1243525

Zajonc, R. B. (1968). Attitudinal effects of mere exposure. *Journal of Personality and Social Psychology*, *9*(2 Pt. 2), 1–27.

CHAPTER 13

Social Network Analysis Techniques Using NodeXL for Analyzing Disinformation Related to QAnon

Wasim Ahmed and Marc Smith

Introduction

Chapter 12 of this volume argued that many social media platforms enabled QAnon conspiracy beliefs to gain traction and widespread acceptance in ways that would not have been possible prior to social media. This chapter provides an overview of social network analysis (SNA) and content analysis methods that are demonstrated using a tool known as NodeXL (Ahmed & Lugovic, 2019), which retrieves and analyzes network and text data from social media (Smith, 2015). This method is used to study QAnon, which is the focus of this chapter. Academics researching a particular topic could be interested in using SNA to discover the leaders of social media discussions, subgroups and segments, the most shared posts, key websites, key hashtags, and the overall social network structure of the group. In this chapter, we will show how these insights can be gained through the use of NodeXL and SNA methods. We apply this method to a collection of tweets containing the term "QAnon" and generate a rich data analysis and visualization that reveal the social structure and thought leaders driving the topic. This process is relatively easy to replicate, so scholars can apply the tool to a wide range of discussions over time. The results are detailed maps and reports that can be used to contrast topics with one another or over time. Scholars can also use social media data and link them to more traditional sources of data – for instance, comparing online discussions of mandatory vaccinations to case numbers and uptake (Olszowski et al., 2022).

Background

Over the past two decades, a number of social networking platforms built on internet technologies have allowed people from all around the world to connect with one another. In academia, for instance, many scholars now connect with each other in the online world (Jordan, 2020). Not all of these platforms have been a success. However, a small number of platforms have gone on to be immensely popular, with massive user populations measuring in the hundreds of millions to billions of people. As people connect in the online world they leave behind "footprints" that generate vast amounts of data. When users of social media write a post, like a post, reshare it, and react to it, they generate data that can be analysed for insights by academics and marketing professionals. For instance, marketing professionals may analyze the social media activity generated during the launch of a new product or TV show and use this information as intelligence (Ahmed et al., 2022). In aggregate, these collections of connections can be analyzed using social network methods to generate micro-level metrics that describe the location of each individual social media user within a web of connections. SNA metrics also allow researchers to describe the meso-level (the size and shape of groups) as well as the macro-level (the size and shape of whole networks). These metrics reveal the leaders and shapes of conversations, enabling them to be studied empirically and at scale. In contrast to attempting to read thousands (or hundreds of thousands) of messages, SNA can quickly identify the people, messages, groups, URLs, words, and hashtags that most define the content. Network metrics are used to guide scholars to use their scarce and precious capability to read, understand, and interpret only the most salient content. While many social media topics generate tens or hundreds of thousands of messages each day, SNA methods help scholars focus on the small nucleus of active contributors who have a proven ability to engage other users. Segmentation of the network into subgroups based on patterns of connections also can be used to quickly identify issue stakeholders and their orientations.

Scholars seek to efficiently monitor and observe streams of social media content related to key topics and issues. Rather than trying to manually read and analyze huge volumes of content, preprocessing social media data through network and content analysis enables the rapid identification of the key people and groups leading the discussion. This higher-level representation of social media content is like seeing the forest rather than the leaves and branches of individual trees. Multiple social media network maps and reports for the same topic over time or two topics contrasted with one another can quickly reveal key insights into the structure and dynamics of the content stream.

Many tools have been developed to allow marketing professionals to analyze social media data. These tools have powerful features, but they may lack the ability to export and analyze the data using advanced methods. Marketing-based tools can also be very costly, and academics may lack the budget needed to use them. A number of tools used to research social media are evaluated by an academic researcher in a popular blog post series aimed at academics for the London School of Economics and Political Science Impact Blog (Ahmed, 2021). One leading software package to study social media is NodeXL.

A search on Google Scholar reveals many thousands of academic outputs that mention and/or cite "NodeXL." NodeXL was designed to make it easy to collect, analyze, and generate insightful social media reports by analyzing the patterns revealed among the collections of connections created in many types of social media platforms (Himelboim et al., 2017). Previously, retrieving and analyzing social media data required knowledge of software development and programming skills. A key strength of NodeXL is that it can be used by social scientists with no programming experience, and it is built within the familiar Microsoft Excel spreadsheet software application. If users are comfortable making a pie chart, NodeXL enables them to now make a network chart and report. A wide range of disciplines have utilized NodeXL to extract insights from social media datasets. Social media represent just one type of network that can be analyzed with NodeXL, but we will focus in this chapter on applying network analysis to Twitter discussions. Other platforms, as well as network data that were not generated by computer-mediated interactions, can also be analyzed (Cline, 1993).

NodeXL was recently used to study disinformation topics during the COVID-19 pandemic. One particular study utilized NodeXL to identify the thought leaders and network structure found in discussions of an alleged conspiracy linking the 5G communications network to COVID-19 (Ahmed et al., 2020b). In another study, NodeXL was used to study discussions of the alleged conspiracy that argued that the COVID-19 pandemic was a hoax and encouraged users to film their local hospitals to show that they were "empty" (Ahmed et al., 2020a). In both of these studies, NodeXL was able to identify the thought leaders of the discussion as well as the key narratives, topics, and hashtags that were most active. Network analysis of social media often reveals that only very few people have high numbers of connections to others. Further, an even smaller number of people have a pattern of connection that crosses many subgroups and communities. These observations guide researchers to quantitatively identify the leaders and factions within any social media message stream. The next section will describe the steps needed to analyze social media discussion topics, including disinformation topics, using SNA.

Mapping Disinformation Topics

Many actively discussed topics across social media platforms can attract disinformation. Disinformation topics may arise in connection with politics, public health, policy, and conflicts. In politics, those against a particular candidate and/or political party may draw upon disinformation techniques and tactics to spread incorrect and potentially damaging information across online spaces (see Chapter 12 of this volume for more on the harms of disinformation). In public health, the recent COVID-19 pandemic has seen discussions of many alleged conspiracies shared, including disinformation campaigns around vaccines (Das & Ahmed, 2022). Disinformation has also been shared in previous infectious disease outbreaks such as swine flu and Ebola (Ahmed et al., 2018).

Generating disinformation is a low-cost strategy to persuade or even just confuse the general public. It is important to make a distinction between misinformation and disinformation. Misinformation is driven by error and ignorance while disinformation is intentional and will have malicious purposes (Hameleers et al., 2022). Studying disinformation topics requires tools and methods that can organize social media data into a structure that can highlight key people, groups, divisions, topics, and URLs. SNA of social media data is a useful approach for collecting, analyzing, visualizing, and revealing social structures, leaders, and content. Applying social media network analysis tools to disinformation topics is a powerful way to reveal the relatively small group of influential users who most amplify and propel the distribution of low-quality information. Data visualizations often reveal interesting patterns, shapes, and structures that can be more easily conveyed as compared to textual descriptions of the data.

In this section, we describe the step-by-step operations needed to collect, analyze, visualize, and interpret collections of annotated connections from social media data sources. We use the example of QAnon. These methods require no advanced technical and/or programming skills and can be used by researchers across a wide range of domains. Twitter is a common social media platform that has hosted many disinformation discussions and is the focus of this chapter. Twitter also provides more generous access to its data compared to other platforms, which makes it easier to analyze. It is also the case that these methods can be applied to other social media data sets if the data can be obtained. Twitter hosts many disinformation topics such as QAnon, #WWG1WGA, Plandemic, hydroxychloroquine, and ivermectin, among many others. Twitter's search application programming interface (API) is widely accessible and is a simple way to connect to Twitter in order to retrieve data. This API does limit direct access to topics from the past seven or eight days. However, as of very recently, academics can now apply directly to Twitter for special access to the "Academic Track," which provides much more generous historical access. The work presented in this chapter did not use the Academic Track API and accessed data only through the public API. While this API has limits, it remains a valuable source of data. Further, network methods are robust because they can generate useful metrics despite missing data.

Twitter allows for the collection of any tweet if the user already has the tweet ID, and tweet ID archives can be found widely on the internet. These can be found simply by searching on Google – for instance, using the query "COVID-19 tweet IDs" to find potential IDs related to COVID-19 on the web. NodeXL can import tweet IDs lists, which allows for access to much older data than can be accessed via the public Twitter API. In this chapter, we will demonstrate both a search query against the recent activity on Twitter and the use of a list of tweet IDs obtained from a web-hosted archive.

From either data source, we will be collecting the data that Twitter provides and then processing them into a collection of "edges" that represent connections among the users in the discussion. Connections are created in Twitter whenever a user mentions, replies to, or retweets another user. The collection of connections forms a network that can be mathematically analyzed to reveal key people, divisions, groups, or sub-communities and the overall social structure of the discussion.

To collect data from the current time period, NodeXL offers a data importer that connects to the Twitter search API. In this chapter, we will use NodeXL Pro to perform a Twitter search query for the search term "QAnon." Those interested in learning more about how Twitter search terms work may be interested in the Twitter Developer Labs documentation (https://developer.twitter.com/en/docs/labs).

Figure 13.1 provides an overview of the Microsoft Excel desktop application after the NodeXL plugin is installed. NodeXL provides the ability to retrieve and analyze network data. It also creates a general overview of the data and can zoom into and filter them, all while providing on-demand displays of the details of relationships and display message contents.

Once the data are collected and analyzed, the NodeXL workbook is composed, consisting of a series of worksheets each with the following information:

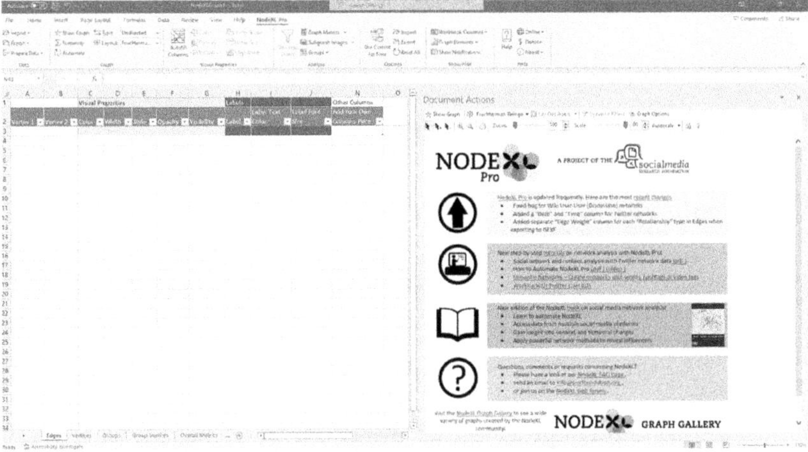

Figure 13.1 Overview of the NodeXL plugin within Microsoft Excel.

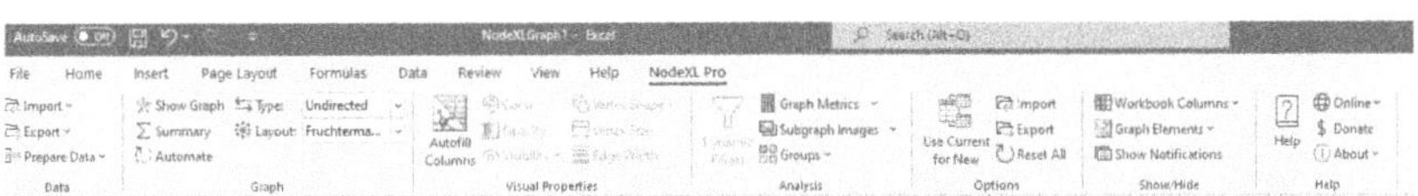

Figure 13.2 NodeXL Pro ribbon in the Excel menu.

- *Edges:* Lists all of the connections among vertices (users) as well as the metadata associated with each connection.
- *Vertices:* Lists all of the vertices (users) within the data alongside metrics that describe each entity's network and platform attributes (e.g. the count of followers for each user).
- *Overall metrics:* Lists a summary of the important metrics that describe the network as a whole.
- *Words and word pairs:* Lists the most commonly occurring words as well as the top word pairs (words that appear together frequently).
- *Network top items:* Gives insights into the influential users, websites, hashtags, words, and word pairs.
- *Time series:* Provides the ability to create a chart that visualizes tweets in a data set over time.

Figure 13.2 displays the NodeXL Pro ribbon in the Excel menu.

By navigating to the NodeXL "Data>Import" menu and then selecting "From Twitter Search Network," a dialogue box will appear (as shown in Figure 13.3). Figure 13.3 provides an overview of the Twitter Network

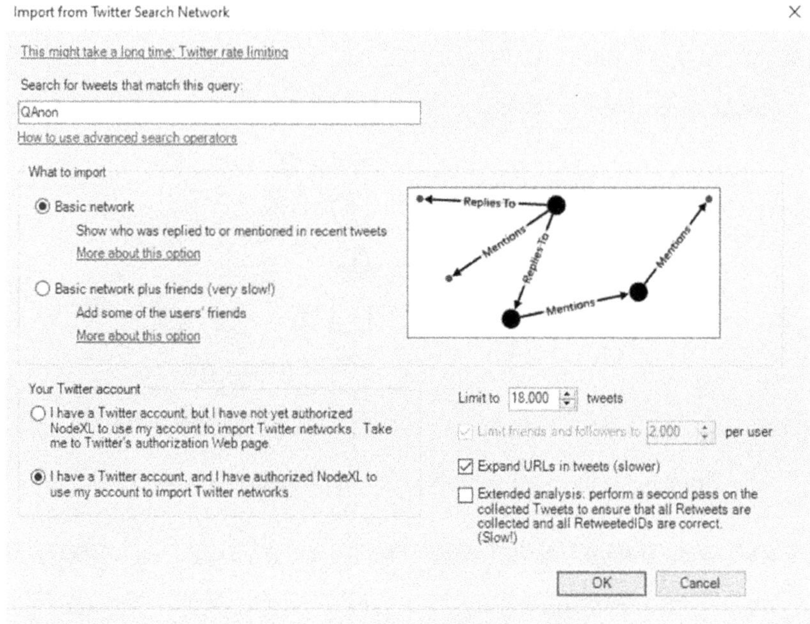

Figure 13.3 Twitter Search Network Importer.

Search Importer. Search terms can be entered here to search for tweets that match the query provided. There are also a number of options that can be selected. In our example, we limit our network to a "basic network," limited to 18,000 tweets (the maximum Twitter can return from a single search), and we want to expand URLs (resolve URLs to show the original rather than the shortened URL). Although Twitter's search API has an 18,000 limit, depending on the RAM memory of a machine, NodeXL can potentially handle more tweets.

In the above example, we retrieved Twitter data using the Twitter Search Network Importer. However, it is also possible to import data using a collection of tweet IDs. Each tweet has a unique ID number, and NodeXL can also import network data from Twitter via lists of these ID numbers. Lists of Twitter tweet IDs can be found in a variety of repositories. A tweet ID repository is simply a website that collects and stores tweet IDs. One example is the "tweetsets" repository, maintained by The George Washington University library (https://tweetsets.library.gwu.edu), which contains a host of data sets and their associated tweet IDs.

Table 13.1 *Sample tweet IDs related to #WWG1WGA.*

1125590029491793921
1125590065642725376
1125590230118039552
1125590360116408320
1125590670897496070
1125590773943025664
1125590806927224832
1125590851399368704
1125590865865510918
1125590917996531713
1125591063660453891
1125591067506696195
1125591089862152192
1125591157369602048
1125591190953451522
1125591284293558272
1125591299439124480
1125591330430652417

In an effort to provide historical archives of critical discussions and topics, scholars have compiled a variety of tweet IDs grouped by a wide range of topics and query terms.

At the Internet Archive, we found millions of tweet IDs that contained the hashtag #WWG1WGA, a term used frequently by users who also mentioned QAnon (https://archive.org/details/wwg1wga-tweets). The hashtag refers to the phrase "Where We Go One, We Go All," a common expression of solidarity among "Q" discussion participants. We selected 50,000 tweet IDs and pasted them into the NodeXL Pro > Data > Import > Import from Twitter Tweet ID List importer. Table 13.1 provides an example of a list of tweet IDs.

Figure 13.4 provides an overview of the dialogue box related to importing tweet IDs.

Figure 13.5 provides an overview of the network visualization based on the 51,058 tweet IDs that were entered. However, due to there being a number of deleted tweets, 14,596 out of 51,058 tweets were collected and analysed.

Network visualizations, such as that shown in Figure 13.5, provide a visual representation of the activity and connections taking place on Twitter. There are various ways to lay out a network visualization, and a network can be represented visually in multiple ways. The layout will

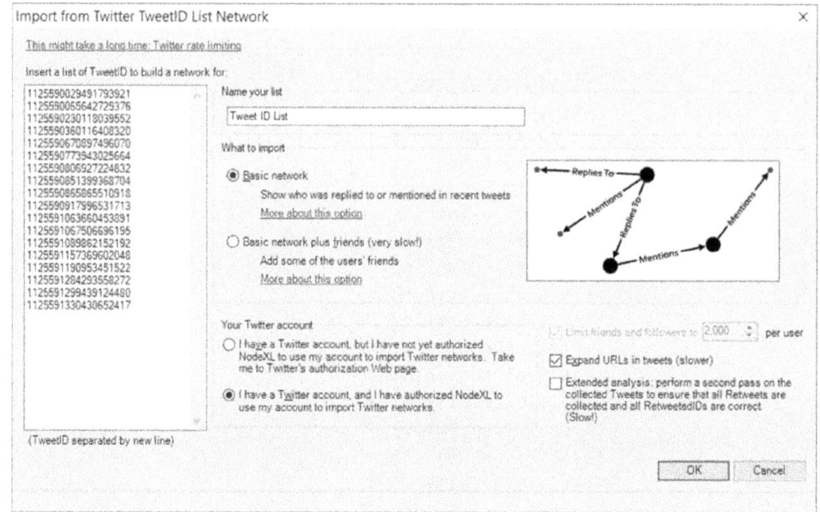

Figure 13.4 NodeXL Pro import from a Twitter tweet ID list network importer.
Note: When a list of tweet IDs is collected, it is very possible that some of the tweets will no longer be available. Tweets can be deleted by the author or in some cases by Twitter. Deleted tweets will not be collected or analyzed. A count of deleted or missing tweets is included in the results generated by NodeXL.

depend on the type of layout algorithm selected within NodeXL as well as the grouping or clustering algorithm applied to the data. In this particular visualization, the groups were clustered based on the Clauset–Newman–Moore (Clauset et al., 2004) cluster algorithm, and they were laid out using the Harel–Koren fast multiscale (Koren & Harel, 2003) layout algorithm.

The full network visualization and report can be found on the NodeXL Graph Gallery (https://nodexlgraphgallery.org/Pages/Graph.aspx?graphID=257293). The NodeXL Graph Gallery is a searchable interface for a collection of NodeXL datasets and visualizations.

NodeXL also provides a list of "overall" metrics associated with the data that will be of particular interest to academics. Network metrics related to the #WWG1WGA analysis are listed below:

- Vertices: 7,092
- Unique edges: 9,513
- Edges with duplicates: 12,093
- Total edges: 21,606
- Number of edge types: 3

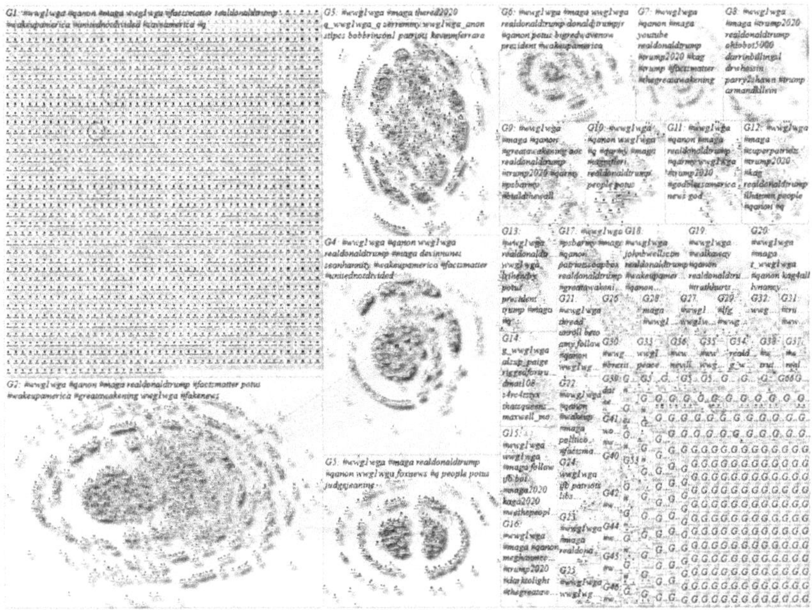

Figure 13.5 #WWG1WGA Twitter network, Monday, March 18, 2019, at 00:47 UTC to Sunday, March 24, 2019, at 01:38 UTC.

- Tweet: 8,557
- Mentions: 9,918
- Replies to: 3,131
- Self-loops: 8,557
- Graph density: 0.000184452492268148
- Modularity: 0.386533
- NodeXL version: 1.0.1.445

The "vertices" metric refers to the number of Twitter users and the "unique edges" aspect refers to the number of unique relationships between users – for instance, a mention and/or a reply. The "edges with duplicates" aspect counts the number of connections between users that occur more than once. The "total edges" count provides insights into the overall number of connections among all users in the network. There are also a number of metrics that provide insights into the frequency and type of edges between users. More specifically, there were three types of edges, ranging from tweets, mentions, and replies.

Table 13.2 *Overview of the most popular links within tweets.*

Rank	Title/source (if still available)	Link	Count
1	Deleted tweet	https://twitter.com/realDonaldTrump/status/1107462671614570496	47
2	"Nunes sues Twitter, some users, seeks over $250M alleging anti-conservative 'shadow bans,' smears" (*Fox News*)	www.foxnews.com/politics/nunes-files-bombshell-defamation-suit-against-twitter-seeks-250m-for-anti-conservative-shadow-bans-smears	23
3	"Follow live updates from the #PutItToThePeople Brexit march in London" (tweet from *The Independent*)	https://mobile.twitter.com/Independent/status/1109527242613448704	22
4	Deleted tweet	https://twitter.com/realDonaldTrump/status/1107276504415854592	21
5	"We Must Fight – President Reagan (Long Version)" (YouTube video)	www.youtube.com/watch?v=JDVT-8tUfiE&feature=youtu.be	21
6	Deleted source	https://ps247.link/ThePlanToSaveTheWorld	21
7	Deleted source	https://threadreaderapp.com/thread/1107433362736594944/error	21
8	No title	https://qanon.pub/	20
9	Deleted tweet	https://twitter.com/realDonaldTrump/status/1107771030385426432	20
10	Tweet from Devin Nunes	https://twitter.com/DevinNunes/status/1107788111407284224	19

Table 13.2 provides an overview of the most popular links shared during this time. Users can share links to any website or even other tweets. It is important to note that as tweets can be deleted and accounts suspended, this may mean that the most shared links to popular tweets may no longer be available. This is a limitation of online digital research more generally. Encountering deleted tweets and websites may be more prevalent when retrieving historical Twitter data than more recent topics.

Table 13.3 provides an overview of the popular hashtags tweeted in the QAnon discussion during this time period. The rank column provides insights into the popularity of the hashtag overall and the count column shows the specific amount of times that the hashtag was used.

Table 13.3 *Overview of popular hashtags.*

Rank	Hashtag	Count
1	WWG1WGA	11,582
2	qanon	4,572
3	MAGA	4,257
4	FactsMatter	2,070
5	WakeUpAmerica	1,854
6	UnitedNotDivided	1,409
7	SaveAmerica	1,293
8	QArmy	1,164
9	GreataWakening	1,044
10	q	824

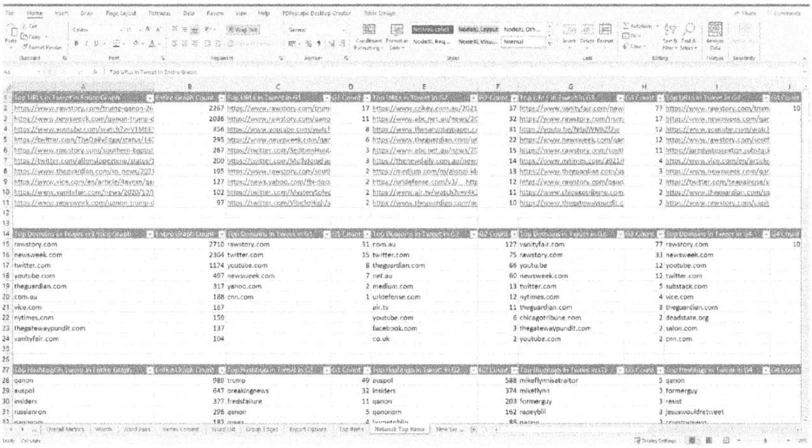

Figure 13.6 Network Top Items worksheet.

Table 13.3 highlights how three hashtags were more frequently used compared to others. These included WWG1WGA (n=11,582), qanon (n=4,572), and MAGA (n=4,257).

In NodeXL, details about the content present in each group are displayed in a worksheet called "Network Top Items." As is shown in Figure 13.6, this worksheet makes it easy to contrast such content from different groups. Some groups in the QAnon discussion have distinct topics that are present in one group but not any of the others. Some topics do appear in almost all groups (e.g. MAGA, #WWG1WGA), whereas others are distinct to their group (e.g. WakeUpAmerica).

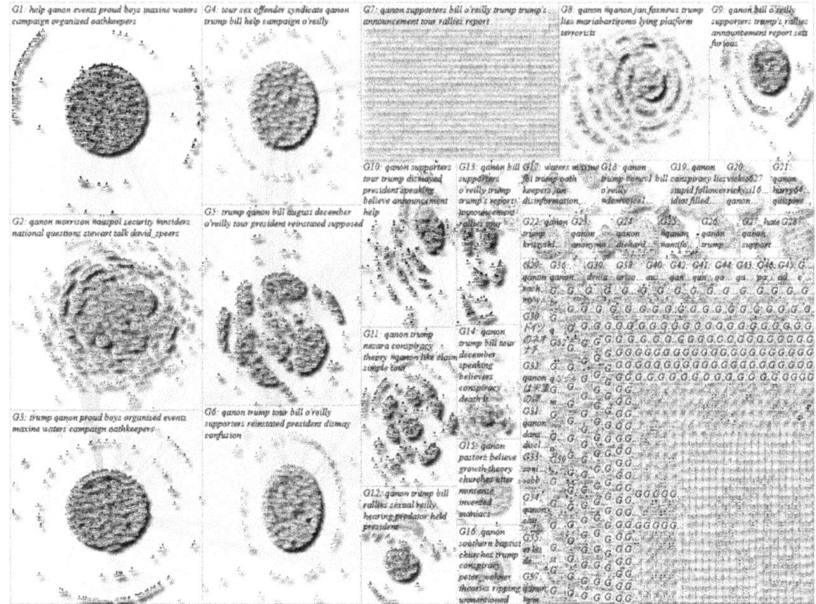

Figure 13.7 QAnon Twitter NodeXL social network analysis map and report for Sunday, June 20, 2021, at 23:03 UTC.

A similar report was created for QAnon, but this dataset is drawn directly from the Twitter search API rather than a list of tweet IDs. The resulting visualization is shown in Figure 13.7. The Twitter search API has a different set of limits, primarily the constraint to seven or eight days of data and not any older tweets. We used the NodeXL Pro > Data > Import > Import from Twitter Search Importer to request recent tweets that contained "QAnon." This generated a dataset and network (the full data set can be located on the NodeXL Graph Gallery, which can be accessed here: https://nodexlgraphgallery.org/Pages/Graph.aspx?graphID=257332).

Measures and visualizations of networks allow researchers to draw insights by interpreting these images. A network visualization is a graphical representation of the members of a population and the set of relationships among them. Sometimes called "node–link" diagrams, network visualizations provide a bird's-eye view of a population and their interconnections over a period of time. These diagrams have emergent structures that have been classified into a taxonomy using empirical research. This taxonomy is a set of classifications for different social media network structures that are commonly observed. Guidance on the interpretation and classification of social media network graphs has been published and is available for readers interested in learning more about the major structural shapes of network graphs (Smith et al., 2015).

This taxonomy of Twitter social media network visualizations has six basic categories:

- *Polarized:* Two dense groups with minimal cross-connection. Many political and controversial topics display this structure.
- *Tight crowd/in-group:* One dense group with little to no "out-group." Many online "communities" such as academic conferences or other esoteric professional topics display this structure.
- *Brand/public topic:* Populated by users with zero connections to other users. These "isolates" indicate the presence of a "brand" topic or widely disseminated popular story.
- *Clustered communities:* Similar to the brand structure above, but with the addition of many smaller clustered groups. Many global media topics have this type of network structure, which forms when multiple news outlets develop audiences of their own.
- *Broadcast:* A "hub-and-spoke" network structure with a celebrity, thought leader, or "influencer" at the hub and a large group of "audience" members who link to the hub, but not to one another. News outlets and famous users have this type of network structure.
- *Support:* A "hub-and-spoke" structure with a business or customer service account at the center that replies to a larger group of other users who do not themselves connect to one another. Customer support for airlines, computer companies, and other public services that may reply to a large number of otherwise disconnected users often have this network pattern.

Specific research objectives or exploratory analysis can be performed by collecting and mapping social media networks. Network analysis results can be used to quickly identify the very small number of users who occupy very rare positions within the network. These are the leaders, influencers, and celebrities who have a dramatically higher level of engagement than the average user. Network analysis also organizes the population into clusters based on their strength of interconnection, which reveals the internal segmentation of the population as people who contribute to the discussion form clusters or subgroups.

In this chapter, our insights into the QAnon Twitter social media network, as shown in Figures 13.5 and 13.7, reveal that a very small number of participants set the agenda. The structure of these networks is largely the "broadcast network" structure containing a "hub-and-spoke" pattern in which a large set of accounts form an audience centered around only about a dozen highly influential user accounts. The hub-and-spoke network structure contrasts with the network structure of "communities," which require the presence of reciprocity and density, patterns of reply, and interconnectivity. The absence of reciprocity excludes the presence of discussion or "community." These networks are dominated by retweets and replies that are themselves not reciprocated. QAnon Twitter populations are structured as audiences or rebroadcasters, most of whom get no retweets themselves. Moreover, these network data sets reveal that only a small number of web domains (URLs) are present in the content. By examining the list of the websites frequently linked to in the QAnon tweets, we found that these domains do not include nonpartisan or scientific organizations. Many partisan websites contain disputed information that lacks support from the institutions and organizations usually tasked with validating and endorsing information. While it is certainly possible that well-intentioned people can disagree with a particular organization, the QAnon data show that the URLs used in these tweets link to no institutions with scientific or medical authority.

Future Research Ideas Related to QAnon

QAnon is like many other groups that make claims that do not use recognized sources of authority for support. For example, diet and nutrition topics are routinely dominated by discussions of fad diets and medically dangerous practices and products. These discussions rarely link to medical or scientific resources, and the leading contributors do not display credentials or claim associations with institutions with a reputation for validating information. One suggestion is, therefore, for professional and trained practitioners in many topics to "patrol" and intervene in discussions that are dominated by disinformation.

Furthermore, the results of this study include related words and hashtags that can guide further investigations. For example, our data show that the term "QAnon" is often accompanied by the terms #WWG1WGA, #qanon, and #MAGA. These topics can, in turn, be mapped to ensure that the complete social phenomenon of QAnon is captured and studied.

Our key findings revealed that QAnon tweets link to low-quality information sources, that QAnon is mostly a "broadcast" phenomenon, and that QAnon has a very small number of "leaders." These leaders do not link to sources that would be recognized as medical or scientific authorities. Most QAnon users exclusively retweet existing content from a very small number of contributors.

It is also noted that the Twitter QAnon network is similar to that of other conspiracy groups on Twitter that arose during the COVID-19 pandemic. For instance, Ahmed et al. (2020b) found similar insights when analyzing a conspiracy theory network linking 5G to COVID-19. Specifically, users in the network contained a small number of leaders and were linking to low-quality information sources. Similarly, QAnon is not a "community" in that it lacks reciprocity (people do not interact with one another; i.e. reply and generate conversations) and density (people link only to a central account but not to one another). These observations can guide interventions that focus on the small core of influential QAnon contributors.

Conclusion

In a world in which a topic of public interest can generate thousands of tweets per minute, automated analysis of social media content is critical to facilitate scalable situational awareness. Analysts need tools to enhance their limited human data collection and analysis capabilities. With augmentation, analysts can shift focus from the processing of hundreds of thousands of elements to the interpretation of a few dozen images and reports. In this chapter, we provided an overview of how academics can use the software application NodeXL to easily retrieve and analyze social media network data sets. In the financial and commercial sectors, accounting and auditing are common practices that help manage issues such as manipulation, fraud, and deception. Social media can be thought of as a "marketplace of ideas," and tools such as NodeXL are akin to the accounting tools used in the commercial sector. Social media accounting tools enable audits of social media discussions that pinpoint and identify the influences and connections among users. These results highlight how SNA and NodeXL can identify the small groups of sources of disinformation, such as those found in QAnon tweets, which can help guide interventions to minimize low-quality information dissemination.

REFERENCES

Ahmed, W. (2021, May 18). Using Twitter as a data source: An overview of social media research tools (updated for 2021). *Impact of Social Sciences Blog*.

https://blogs.lse.ac.uk/impactofsocialsciences/2021/05/18/using-twitter-as-a-data-source-an-overview-of-social-media-research-tools-2021/

Ahmed, W., & Lugovic, S. (2019). Social media analytics: Analysis and visualisation of news diffusion using NodeXL. *Online Information Review*, *43*(4), 149–160.

Ahmed, W., Bath, P. A., Sbaffi, L., & Demartini, G. (2018). Moral panic through the lens of Twitter: An analysis of infectious disease outbreaks. In *Proceedings of the 9th International Conference on Social Media and Society* (pp. 217–221). Association for Computing Machinery.

Ahmed, W., Fenton, A., Hardey, M., & Das, R. (2022). Binge watching and the role of social media virality towards promoting Netflix's *Squid Game*. *IIM Kozhikode Society & Management Review*, *11*(2), 222–234.

Ahmed, W., Seguí, F. L., Vidal-Alaball, J., & Katz, M. S. (2020a). COVID-19 and the "Film Your Hospital" conspiracy theory: Social network analysis of twitter data. *Journal of Medical Internet Research*, *22*(10), e22374.

Ahmed, W., Vidal-Alaball, J., Downing, J., & Seguí, F. L. (2020b). COVID-19 and the 5G conspiracy theory: Social network analysis of Twitter data. *Journal of Medical Internet Research*, *22*(5), e19458.

Clauset, A., Newman, M. E. J., & Moore, C. (2004). Finding community structure in very large networks. *Physical Review E*, *70*, 066111.

Cline, D. H. (1993). Six degrees of Alexander: Social network analysis as a tool for ancient history. www.ancienthistorybulletin.org/subscribed-users-area/wp-content/uploads/2015/04/DIANE-HARRIS-CLINE-Six-Degrees-of-Alexander-Social-Network-Analysis-as-a-Tool-for-Ancient-History-Volume-26-59-70.pdf

Das, R., & Ahmed, W. (2022). Rethinking fake news: Disinformation and ideology during the time of COVID-19 global pandemic. *IIM Kozhikode Society & Management Review*, *11*(1), 146–159.

Hameleers, M., Brosius, A., Marquart, F., Goldberg, A. C., van Elsas, E., & de Vreese, C. H. (2022). Mistake or manipulation? Conceptualizing perceived mis- and disinformation among news consumers in 10 European countries. *Communication Research*, *49*(7), 919–941.

Himelboim, I., Smith, M. A., Rainie, L., Shneiderman, B., & Espina, C. (2017). Classifying Twitter topic-networks using social network analysis. *Social Media + Society*, *3*(1), 2056305117691545.

Jordan, K. (2020). Imagined audiences, acceptable identity fragments and merging the personal and professional: How academic online identity is expressed through different social media platforms. *Learning, Media and Technology*, *45* (2), 165–178.

Koren, Y., & Harel, D. (2003). Axis-by-axis stress minimization. In *International Symposium on Graph Drawing* (pp. 450–459). Springer.

Olszowski, R., Zabdyr-Jamróz, M., Baran, S., Pięta, P., & Ahmed, W. (2022). A social network analysis of tweets related to mandatory COVID-19 vaccination in Poland. *Vaccines*, 10(5), 750.

Smith, M. A. (2015). Catalyzing social media scholarship with open tools and data. *Journal of Contemporary Eastern Asia*, *14*(2), 87–96.

Smith, M. A., Himelboim, I., Rainie, L., & Shneiderman, B. (2015). The structures of Twitter crowds and conversations. In S. A. Matei, M. G. Russell, & E. Bertino (Eds.), *Transparency in social media* (pp. 67–108). Springer.

CHAPTER 14

QAnon, Folklore, and Conspiratorial Consensus

A Case Study in the Computational Analysis of Conspiracy Theory Narratives

Timothy R. Tangherlini, Shadi Shahsavari, Pavan Holur, and Vwani Roychowdhury

Introduction

Conspiracy theories have long been part of narrative tradition, fueled by a broad range of fears both real and imagined, and, in turn, inciting real-world actions (van Prooijen & Douglas, 2017). The remarkably capacious QAnon conspiracy theory is the most recent and most visible of many such narrative complexes (Bodner et al., 2020). Stories of shady cabals working clandestinely to achieve some sort of malevolent goal are commonplace in both oral and written traditions dating back hundreds if not thousands of years (Barzilay, 2016; Burns, 2003; Fay, 2019; Gray-Fow, 1998). A feature of these complex narratives is the linking of various stories and story parts, along with the attendant discussions surrounding those stories, that, over time, converge on a group consensus detailing the contours of the conspiracy theory. Because the majority of the stories that contribute to the overarching conspiracy theory are straightforward threat narratives in which an outside threat agent disrupts the safety of the inside group (almost always a representation of the storytellers' own community), the linking of stories creates a metanarrative explanatory framework that reveals a coordinated yet hidden effort of these otherwise independent threat agents to undermine society (van Prooijen, 2020). In this chapter, we briefly describe a pipeline of interlocking computational methods used to uncover the underlying generative narrative framework undergirding social media discussions, apply that pipeline to a large corpus of QAnon-related social media posts, and present the narrative graph driving these conversations. We explore the dynamics of this changing narrative graph and consider how the interpretation of "Q-drops" engenders a negotiated process of narrative alignment that creates an expanding series of linked domains that result in a totalizing narrative framework.

Folklorists have long recognized that many stories-told-as-true, such as legends and rumors, have a simple structure consisting of three main features: (1) an orientation, which identifies the "insiders" and details the who, where, and when of the story; (2) a complicating action composed of two main parts – a threat or disruption aimed at the insiders and a strategy settled upon by the insiders to countermand that threat; and (3) a resolution that provides retrospective commentary on the success of a particular strategy for dealing with a particular threat (Nicolaisen, 1987; Tangherlini, 2018). Unlike rumors or legends (stories that are told as true but that have their own independent existence in folk traditions; Dégh, 2001; Tangherlini, 1990), conspiracy theories operate at the level of metanarrative, aligning stories from these other genres while creating a totalizing narrative framework of their own (Bennet, 2007). Through conspiracy theorizing, the threat agent from one legend (e.g. a murderous thief who eats children's hearts to gain extraordinary strength) is shown to be an ally of an otherwise unconnected threat agent (e.g. a wealthy landowner who terrorizes his workers from another story), and so on (Tangherlini, 2021). As a consequence of these alignments, a conspiracy theory becomes a master narrative explaining how the world works and thus encapsulates the cultural ideology of the group in which the conspiracy theory emerges (Dean, 2000; Goertzel, 1994). Unlike most other folklore narrative genres, conspiracy theories are rarely told in their entirety, existing more as an "immanent" narrative whole (Clover, 1986). Because of this, one needs to aggregate discussions from a broad range of sources if one hopes to determine the scope of a conspiracy theory's narrative framework (see Chapter 10 of this volume for more on the social construction of QAnon narratives).

Unlike many earlier conspiracy theories, QAnon leverages the internet-based information age, including the illusion of community that emerges on social media and the extraordinary speed and reach of communication that are key features of the internet (Anderson, 2006; Bak-Coleman et al., 2021; O'Connor & Weatherall, 2019; see also Chapter 12 of this volume for more about social media and QAnon). Its precursor, Pizzagate, also relied on social media for its spread, reach, and contributors, and it can be seen as a dress rehearsal for the narratively voracious QAnon conspiracy theory (Tangherlini et al., 2020). In contrast to that earlier manifestation, however, the QAnon conspiracy theory does not aim for completion. Instead, a notable feature of it is its open-ended nature, characterized by an ongoing process of fitting new narratives into the overarching framework, even in the absence of additional "Q-drops" (Papasavva et al., 2022).[1]

Because of the scope and penetration of social media, the scale of the materials available – the stories, story parts, and conversations – that contribute to the increasingly broad contours of the QAnon conspiracy theory dwarfs that of most other conspiracy theories. Because the social media forums where QAnon resides are notoriously unmediated, including image boards and forums renowned for the trolling behavior of their members (Phillips, 2019), the QAnon data are remarkably noisy (Kahneman et al., 2016). This noisiness is exacerbated by the limited context presented in individual posts – often as responses to longer exchanges – that either cryptically reference QAnon themes or entirely avoid explicitly mentioning the theory. Computational methods can cut through this noise, and they allow us to identify and aggregate the main actants and their relationships as they are "discovered" by the QAnon "bakers" working with "crumbs," developing "proofs" as they "do their own research" (Zuckerman, 2019). Our methods allow us to distill these conversations and present a dynamic series of network graphs modeling the narrative frameworks of the different parts of the conspiracy theory as it comes together. These graphs, in turn, capture the shifting features of the conspiracy theory over time.

Related Work

Conspiracy theories proliferate when people are confronted with crises that challenge their understanding of how the world works – or should work – and when access to reliable information is compromised, either because access has been constrained, trust in the available information resources is low, or because of a combination of the two (Fine, 2007; Rosnow, 1980). In response, people reach out to their local community for understanding and explanations. It is in this environment that legends, rumors, and broader conspiracy theories can take root and thrive. These stories not

[1] The open-ended nature of QAnon coupled with the predominance of online conversations negotiating the contours of the conspiracy theory have led some to interpret it as an MMORPG or massive multiplayer online role-playing game. As with rumor, conspiracy theory often pushes decision-making out of the narrative realm and into the realm of real-world action, a process redolent of the creeping suspicion among even some QAnon adherents that the conspiracy theory had taken on aspects of a live-action role-playing game (LARP; Ellis, 1989; Mullen, 1972; Zuckerman, 2019). In these forums, it is not enough to discuss what one would like to do. Instead, there is an implicit exhortation to real-world action that can, in its most extreme form, lead to events such as, in the case of QAnon, support for the storming of the US Capitol on January 6, 2021 (Munn, 2021).

only provide explanations of what is going on, detailing the various threats confronting a society, their source, and the reasons for those threats, but also offer an opportunity for community members to discuss and settle on a strategy or series of strategies for dealing with those threats. In some cases, the stories can create an information cascade, gaining adherents and crowding out other possible explanations, irrespective of convincing arguments that countermand the explanations proffered by the story (Bikchandhani et al., 1992), an apt description for the dynamic evolution of QAnon over recent years. This effect is particularly pronounced in social media and the internet in general (Bak-Coleman et al., 2021).

Conspiracy theories are predicated on monological thinking and, as a result of this thinking, conspiracy theorists are motivated to tie up all the loose ends of the multivalent stories and story parts circulating in a community into a single, interlocking totalizing narrative (Goertzel, 1994). In the most comprehensive examples, such as QAnon, a conspiracy theory connects all of the stories circulating in a group, thereby creating at least the illusion of coherence. The process is both dynamic and messy – stories and story parts are either accepted and told anew, over time accruing new features and shedding others, or are rejected in part or in whole. This negotiated process of "puzzling out" the broader conspiracy theory – the interlinked actants, their relationships, and the events that comprise the narrative foundations of the conspiracy theory – can be seen as a form of consensus building within the group. The conversations in these forums are vigorous but work within the constraints of the members' internalization of the expectation of bounded disagreement (Kahneman et al., 2021). In preinternet times, this process would take place in face-to-face interactions or during occasional meetings of like-minded people, thereby imposing constraints on both the speed with which a conspiracy theory could grow and its reach. The impact of social censure during such interactions would prevent the proliferation of the most unlikely claims, or at least relegate those claims to "fringe" status, to which earlier conspiracy theorizing was often consigned (Hofstadter, 1964; O'Connor & Weatherall, 2019). In the contemporary social media world, these social constraints are largely gone. Well-known network effects such as homophily and preferential attachment quickly allow groups of like-minded people to form, thereby creating the illusion of community but without many of the social controls of actual communities (Andersen, 2006; Bak-Coleman et al., 2021; McPherson et al., 2001; Newman, 2001). These communities can, in turn, be easily manipulated to amplify certain messages (O'Connor & Weatherall, 2019). Importantly, the interlocking stories and story parts that comprise these complex narrative cycles are not innocuous flights of fancy, but rather can have real-world impact, encouraging people to take action to protect themselves against the various threats presented by those behind the conspiracy theory.

The computational study of social media and the attendant emergent social and communication structures are active areas of research across many disciplines. In the context of conspiracy theories and the circulation of misinformation on social media platforms, O'Connor and Weatherall (2019) provide a comprehensive overview of various network phenomena that allow ideologically motivated actors to considerably influence the circulation of misinformation. The Observatory on Social Media (Davis et al., 2016) provides a series of easy-to-use computational tools to monitor such discussions as well as the circulation of ideas in mainstream media (Shao et al., 2016). Other research has presented methods for exploring the impact of distortion and automation (e.g. bots) on Twitter during the 2020 US presidential election (Ferrarra et al., 2020). Computational work centering on QAnon specifically reveals the main topics of these discussions, how Q-drops enter into the "canon," how they are disseminated, as well as shifts in the style of the Q-drops over time (Papasavva et al., 2022). Additional work has explored QAnon through topic-modeling and word-embedding methods (Papasavva et al., 2021).

Data

Data collection for this project were biased toward sources known to harbor conversations related to the QAnon conspiracy theory. Q's initial "drops" were made on the imageboard 4chan starting in October 2017. Since then, the location of the cryptic "drops" migrated from 4chan to 8chan, and later to 8kun. At the same time, discussions of these drops proliferated on various social media platforms, including Twitter, Facebook, Parler, Voat, Telegram, and Reddit, as well as video platforms such as YouTube. The most consistent discussions of the Q-drops and the interpretation of these posts occurred on Reddit's subreddits, /pol and /qresearch, and on the less stable 4chan/8chan/8kun platforms (Papasavva et al., 2022). We created a comprehensive QAnon data set by including crawls from the discussion forums on Reddit and the comment sections on YouTube, both of which have been active loci for the ongoing debate over the various actants and their relationships in the expansive QAnon realm. As of June 15, 2021, we had collected approximately 2 million posts from these sources over the course of twelve months of data collection; we augmented these data resources with early comprehensive data collections of 4chan, 8chan, Reddit, and YouTube QAnon discussion forums (Hagen et al., 2020). The fleeting nature of these discussions due to platform instability or the banning of the discussions required a flexible data collection strategy for social media.

When the COVID-19 pandemic gripped the world in March 2020, conspiracy theories about the origin of the virus along with suggestions that the virus was a hoax quickly spread on these platforms as well. Given the expansive nature of the QAnon conspiracy theory, we began observing overlap between it and the emerging COVID-19 conspiracy theories, thereby providing additional resources for studying the dynamics of QAnon (Shahsavari et al., 2020). At the same time as QAnon adherents were developing the conspiracy theory across social media, reporting on this increasingly complex narrative appeared with regularity on a wide range of news platforms. To account for this, we include crawls of the news aggregator site GDelt.

To collect all of these data, we devised a web crawler that captured comprehensive data from the various chan/kun channels noted above, along with queries specifically tuned to terms related to conspiracy theories, COVID-19, Q, QAnon, WWG1WGA, and other QAnon-specific terms directed at numerous Reddit forums, Twitter, and YouTube comment sections. We also devised a similar set of queries for the GDelt news aggregation platform. These news sources often recap and/or provide additional context to a few subplots that appear in the broader narrative framework graphs. All of these crawls are currently performed daily.[2]

Methods

In the current work, we refine an existing computational pipeline for the discovery of the underlying narrative frameworks initially devised for work on vaccine hesitancy discussions (Tangherlini et al., 2016) and conspiracies and conspiracy theories (Tangherlini et al., 2020), including conspiracy theories that emerged during the COVID-19 pandemic (Shahsavari et al., 2020). We build on earlier structural models of personal experience narrative (Labov & Waletzky, 1967; Nicolaisen, 1987) by expanding on the concept of the complicating action to include both a delineation of the threat or disruption as well as the proposal of a potentially efficacious

[2] While our sources are diverse, it is important to note that the model's performance relies on the data sources themselves and, as new platforms emerge, these will be appended to the source list.

strategy for dealing with that (Tangherlini, 2018). We integrate this structural model with a model of inter-actant relationships based on the narratological theories of Algirdas J. Greimas (1968).

We model narratives as generated by an underlying graphical model where the actants (characters, things, or places) are the nodes, while the relationships between actants are the edges. In this model, a user creates a social media post by drawing a set of nodes and edges from the underlying narrative framework network graph with some probability. Our task is to reconstruct the entire narrative network by aggregating the subnetworks expressed by these posts. The pipeline takes as input the noisy data scraped from social media and news data sources. First, each sentence is processed to extract relationships that constitute our final nodes and edges. A joint estimation step discovers the actants and their context-dependent relationships and represents them as "subnodes" and context-based edges. The actant discovery begins with grouping co-occurrent words that tend to appear within the same context. We then aggregate their corresponding set of phrases and use word-embedding approaches to cluster these large collections of phrases into groups with similar meanings, allowing us to condense this network space considerably. A further step aggregates these context-dependent subnodes into supernodes, with edges collapsed into smaller categories as well. A final community-detection step determines the various narrative domains that exist in this narrative framework graph. Importantly, these weak links are most often created by the conspiracy theorists' interpretation of the various Q-drops in the context of the existing narrative, allowing them to continuously update the cast of actants and their relationships and link in additional narrative frameworks into the growing graph.

Traversing these narrative (sub)graphs provides a clearer understanding of the otherwise noisy conversations that characterize the QAnon social media space. It is worth noting that one can interrogate the graph at various levels of granularity. Focusing on the broader graph communities, their constituent actants, and within-community connections offers, for example, an understanding of how the domain "Justice Department" is understood by the conspiracy theorists. Focusing on the links between communities, such as the link between "Democrats" and "child trafficking," provides insights into the fundamental narrative pieces of the much broader puzzle. Finally, focusing on subnodes, such as "Anthony Fauci" in the context of COVID-19 drug development, can reveal more nuanced perspectives on the complexity of the narrative. Since the data collection includes time stamps, one can also explore the changes in the graph over time, which reveals, for example, how independent rumors and conspiracy theories about the COVID-19 pandemic become aligned with the broader QAnon conspiracy theory (Shahsavari et al., 2020).

Results and Discussion

The earliest features of the QAnon conspiracy theory mirrored closely the Pizzagate narrative framework, with the obvious addition of Donald Trump playing a leading role in the effort to expose and ultimately defeat the pedophilic satanic cabal of largely Democratic operatives proposed in Pizzagate (Tangherlini et al., 2020). The Q-drops additionally provided ongoing fodder for the emerging group of "bakers" to extend the scope of the narrative and, because these drops came allegedly from an insider with considerable access to the workings of the Trump White House, also bolstered the idea that there was a "plan" or a strategy for addressing the threat of the "Deep State," of which the Democratic cabal was one manifestation. Additional threat agents and groups quickly expanded to include: the "Illuminati," a long-standing object of conspiracism and only vaguely related to the Enlightenment-era Bavarian secret society from which it takes its name; the "globalists," echoing the anti-Semitic use of the term from far-right groups; and Hollywood, a shorthand for social decadence. In these three groups can be found threats not only to transparency and democratic traditions, but also to free markets and, from the perspective of the storytellers, morality (Zimmer & Reich, 2018). In very short order, then, the QAnon conspiracy theory narrative framework had expanded beyond the relatively modest scope of Pizzagate to include components of many preexisting conspiracy theories through simple additions of already accessible narrative frameworks. The evidence for the links between one domain, such as that of the Illuminati, and the Democrats could be found in the interpretation of the Q-drops and the "research" of the "bakers."

As additional drops were made and as the news cycle developed, it was not difficult for conspiracy theorists to add additional actants, such as Jeffrey Epstein, to the expanding narrative framework graph. Indeed, Epstein, with his contacts to wealthy members of the financial elite including numerous Democrats, "globalists," and Hollywood, was an ideal candidate for playing a central network role by bridging certain regions of the narrative framework graph. Additional actants such as George Soros, whose endorsement of global markets, extraordinary wealth, and Jewish heritage, and Bill Gates, whose support for global health projects as well as

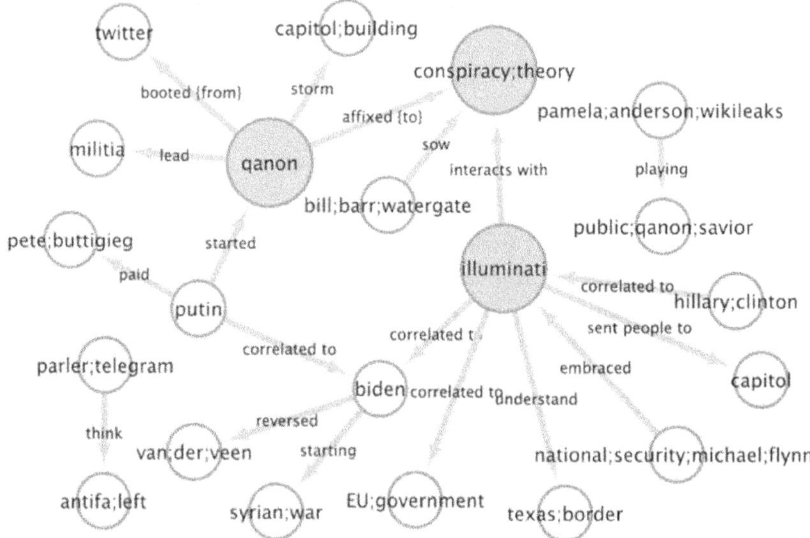

Figure 14.1 This abbreviated graph is extracted from a larger cumulative narrative network estimated from conversations between January 1, 2021, and March 31, 2021. Popular conspiracy-theoretic actors included in this graph are the QAnon poster Bill Barr, the Illuminati, Putin, Biden, Parler, antifa, Clinton, and WikiLeaks. Among the relationships between these actants, we find the following interesting chain: Putin >> paid >> Pete Buttigieg, Putin >> started >> QAnon, Illuminati >> Biden >> starting >> Syrian war. This small subgraph proposes a close relationship between Putin and Buttigeig, a causal relationship between Biden and the Syrian war, and support for Biden by the Illuminati, thereby presenting an almost impenetrable wall of threatening relations.

his control of the one of the largest technology companies in the world, were similarly easy narrative targets, whose inclusion in the expanding graph brought with them discussions of chemtrails, the JFK assassination, the faked moon landing, discussions about UFOs and that JFK, Jr. was still alive, and other earlier conspiratorial thinking about similarly wealthy families such as the Rothschilds, who were already embedded in existing conspiracy theories such as the age-old anti-Semitic blood-libel conspiracy theory.

An early high-level graph from our extractions on the later QAnon data reveals the persistence of these core components in the conspiracy theory narrative framework (Figure 14.1). Other peripheral nodes, such as Pamela Anderson, who appears as a proponent of Q (endorsing the QAnon poster as a public savior), provide a strong link to the otherwise maligned realm of Hollywood, where Chrissy Teigen, for example, was an early target of

Pizzagate and, subsequently, QAnon for her alleged links to Jeffrey Epstein and her trolling behavior on Twitter. The Illuminati figure prominently in the graph and have a strong connection to the European Union, another target of antiglobalist rhetoric in the QAnon space. Other long-standing actants in the space include Hillary Clinton, who appears as a villain in Pizzagate (in which she controls a satanic child-trafficking ring), and the QAnon stalwart Michael Flynn, who both narratively and in real life acts as a proxy for Trump in battling these malign forces. Because this specific snapshot of the graph is from early 2021, it includes a suggestion that Joe Biden started the war in Syria, an allegation that Vladimir Putin made payments to Pete Buttigeig, and discussion of the storming of the Capitol, which is not seen as a bad thing, but rather as an attempt to preserve democracy.

The COVID-19 pandemic was also the subject of conspiracy theorizing as the virus gathered steam in mid-2020 and as states began shutting down in the face of unfettered spread of the disease. The preexisting narrative frameworks related to disease and vaccination – already a subject of considerable discussion on the same broader social media forums where Q was making their drops – were easily brought into these conversations. We identified two main narrative frameworks competing for space in the COVID-19 conspiracy theorizing space. On the one hand were narratives presenting the virus as a hoax and not a threat to health at all, but rather an operation intended to support various globalist agendas. Most prominent among these subnarratives was one linking Bill Gates' earlier philanthropic work on worldwide vaccination efforts, his interest in developing prophylaxis for malaria, and the Bill & Melinda Gates Foundation's broader interest in women's health to the suggestion that his real and heretofore hidden interest was the development a global surveillance system to support his quest for absolute power. In these narratives, the push for a vaccine against the virus was a cover operation for an effort to inject the global population with monitoring chips that could then be triggered by the 5G cellular networks that were being rolled out at that time (Figure 14.2).

As the conspiracy theorizing progressed, a degree of ambiguity emerged as to whether the virus was an actual threat or not. In turn, this ambiguity allowed these narratives to be aligned with the "virus-as-hoax" narratives that also gained considerable traction as the virus continued to spread. Not surprisingly, given various "attachment points" in the initially disconnected narrative frameworks surrounding the pandemic, connections to core actants in the QAnon narrative framework precipitated the process of aligning disparate subgraphs of the COVID-19 narrative space with the QAnon conspiracy theory.

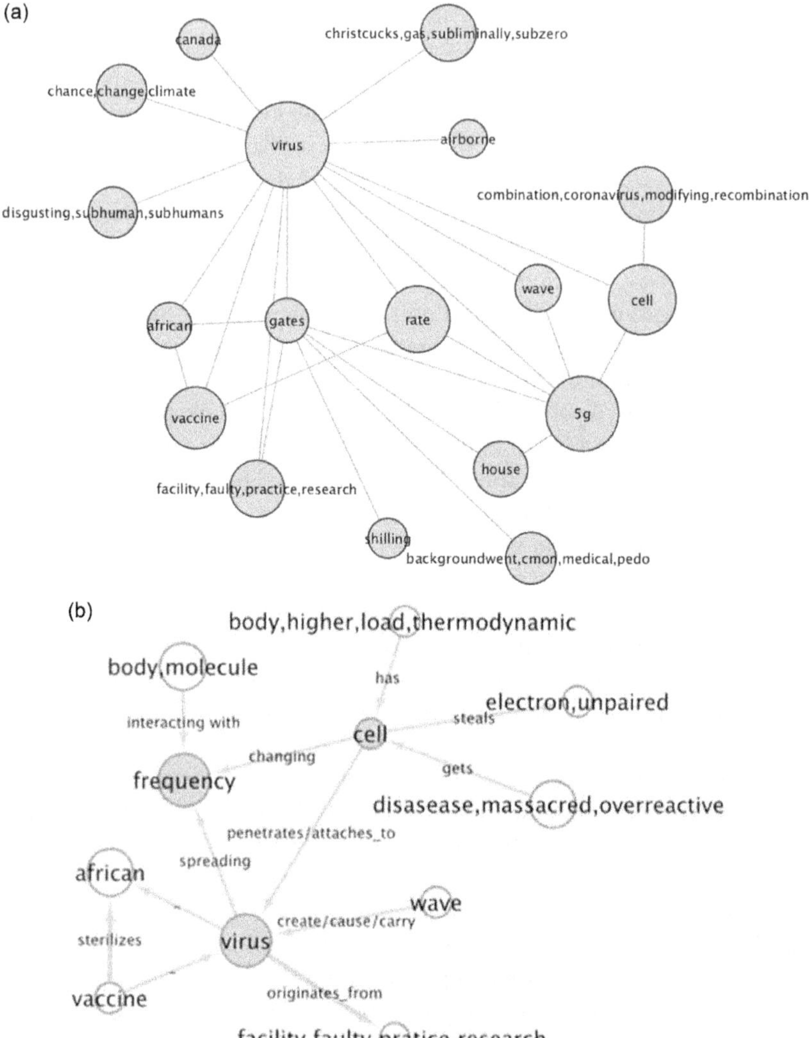

Figure 14.2 (a) A subnetwork of the overarching COVID-19 conspiracy theory narrative space, in which Bill Gates and 5G are linked to vaccination. In a broader view of the network space, QAnon figures prominently in linking this subgraph to other graphs related to the virus as a bioweapon and the virus as a hoax, two directly contradictory phenomena that nonetheless were held in play in the narrative space. (b) A subnetwork of the QAnon graph from fall 2020, showing changes in the 5G/Bill Gates narrative, but also revealing the persistence of this portion of the narrative in the overall conspiracy theory space. It also elaborates on how the alleged implantation of chips would work.

A similar phenomenon occurred as the Black Lives Matter (BLM) movement gained momentum in the aftermath of the murder of George Floyd in Minneapolis in May 2020 (see Chapters 8 and 9 of this volume for more on QAnon in 2020). As demonstrations and protests took hold in many parts of the USA, a refiguration of the BLM movement as a threat to democracy took hold in the QAnon narrative space, aligning the movement with an ad hoc grouping of self-proclaimed antifascists represented as a coordinated and clandestine force, antifa. Speculations concerning the connection between, for example, George Soros and the antifa BLM protesters (he was alleged to be paying for pallets of bricks to be delivered to protest sites for use as projectiles) attached the protests and the movement to existing discussions of globalists, the Illuminati, and a host of other narrative fragments that had been nestled into the larger narrative framework. Consequently, actants such as antifa and BLM began to emerge not only in the COVID-19 narrative space, but also in the QAnon narrative space, the latter space having largely subsumed the former.

The QAnon narrative framework also brought in new narrative nucleations such as the emerging stories about the origins of the SARS-CoV-2 virus in China as a bioweapon deliberately (or unintentionally) released from a laboratory. Trump's anti-Chinese stance was then seen as a bulwark against this global threat, which Anthony Fauci was characterizing improperly. It also incorporated preexisting conspiracy theories, forming links to other narrative frameworks as noted above. This feature of the QAnon conspiracy theory further emphasizes our original description of the theory as *narratively voracious*. Because of this voraciousness, the complete network can be difficult to understand, particularly when it includes contradictory narratives such as the pandemic being a hoax, which gave rise to the #filmyourhospital movement and fueled antimask and antivaccination sentiment, and the pandemic representing a deliberate release of a dangerous bioweapon by the Chinese Communist Party. Subnetworks, or smaller parts of the overarching graph, can instead provide more interpretable views regarding the QAnon narrative communities with increasing granularity. Rather than trying to understand the entire graph, subgraph views provide insight into the components of the overarching narrative.

Because of the dynamic nature of the evolving narrative space, we developed a graphical web-based user interface to work with the narrative graphs extracted from the target data sets with a rolling time window. The changes in the actants and their relationships reveal both the open-endedness and the adaptiveness of the overarching conspiracy theory. Again, small neighborhoods of the graph (or subgraphs) provide the most

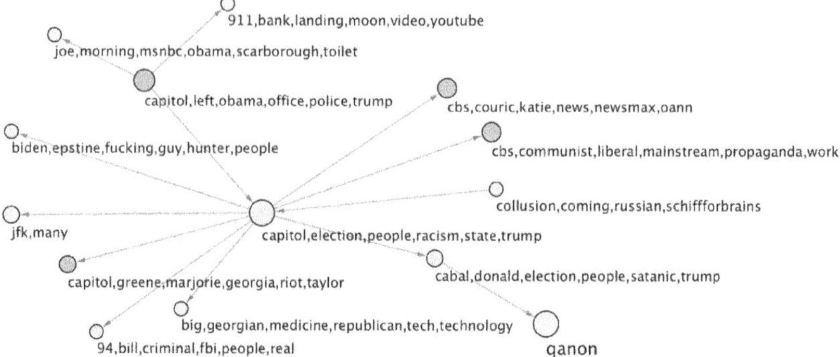

Figure 14.3 An inter-actant subgraph from a rolling time window of QAnon-related discussions around January 18, 2021, that includes nodes related to a satanic Democratic cabal and the presidential election, the Jeffrey Epstein pedophilia scandal, the attack on the Capitol, the JFK assassination, 9/11, and the moon landing.

information as to how and where the conspiracy theory is growing. For example, a narrative network graph drawn from discussions from January 18, 2021, includes nodes related to well-known conspiracy theories such as ones suggesting that the Apollo moon landing was faked, that the JFK assassination was the result of hidden sinister forces, that satanic Democratic cabals trafficked children in underground tunnels in Washington, DC and New York, and that the January 6 riots at the Capitol were an antifa "false flag" operation. The graph also includes notable actant nodes for the media conglomerate Newsmax and Jeffrey Epstein (Figure 14.3).

Interestingly, the "QAnon" node exists as a peripheral pendant node in this subgraph, as opposed to the central node of the Capitol, Trump, and the election. The peripheral nature of the QAnon node is in fact a common feature of many of the networks we derive from these data, providing clear support for the observation that Q rarely tells an entire story in a drop. Instead, the conspiracy theorizing relies on the "bakers" to shape and detail the drop into a more fully formed narrative and on the community discussing these propositions to reach, over time, consensus on what is and is not included in the underlying narrative framework.

Conclusion and Future Work

While some observers have predicted a rapid decline for the QAnon conspiracy theory as the Trump presidency fades and other pundits believe that the alleged "unmasking" of Q will have similar effects, the ongoing discussion of the conspiracy theory and its myriad subtheories (i.e. narrative communities in the broader framework graph) on various social media forums suggests that the rumors of the end of QAnon are greatly exaggerated (Holt & Rizzuto, 2021). Our work reveals how the conspiracy theory, rather than simply going dormant in the face of various challenges to its ability to explain, changes through several notable processes: The conspiracy theorists incorporate new narrative nucleations, they align the expanding narrative framework with additional network communities representing independent narrative frameworks, and they allow other parts of the graph to recede into a less active state. Indeed, it is worth noting that the community discussing Q is still actively shaping and reshaping the contours of the conspiracy theory's narrative framework even in the absence of additional Q-drops (Papasavva et al., 2022). This change in the transmission state of various parts of the conspiracy theory narrative graph is not surprising and tracks closely other conspiracy theories, as well as the relationship between rumor and legend, where rumor often presents as a hyperactive transmission state of legend (Tangherlini, 1990). With complex narrative cycles such as QAnon, it is quite likely that components of the narrative space exist in a steady state, creating a context for additional discussions. Other parts of the graph have receded in their prominence but act as a narrative reservoir that can be relied on both as background for the ongoing discussions about the conspiracy theory and as models for other emerging narrative components of the broader theory. And finally, new information from the news cycle as well as reinterpretations of Q-drops provide additional narrative material to be fit into the narrative framework graph.

The current social media environment raises numerous challenges to the circulation of truthful information, as the rise, spread, and persistence of the far-reaching QAnon conspiracy theory attest (Rosenblum & Muirhead, 2020). News stories are immediately mediated and transformed by social media, with millions of people letting their opinions be known and various communities, such as those that coalesced around Q, reaching negotiated consensus within their self-limiting echo chambers. The internet has a nanosecond heartbeat that, when coupled with its vast scale, acts as a binding voting machine. As was the case of Pizzagate, out of the millions of Democratic National Committee emails dumped on WikiLeaks, an otherwise innocuous set of emails referring to a pizzeria and a handkerchief became a lightning rod. In turn, these messages became the source of hidden knowledge that formed the cornerstone of the conspiracy theory. Similarly, the broader QAnon framework has proven to be a powerful generative engine to drive social media and the folkloric process of narrative consensus building. Social media continually highlight different current events, however innocuous, and present them to the community for further interpretation. Self-appointed interpreters then explore the ways in which these current events form links to the narratives with which they are already familiar and that reflect their existing cultural ideology. Users react and the narrative "winners" (i.e. those stories and story parts that persist) get selected through the tipping point phenomenon of consensus building. Given the complex beliefs underlying the different groups engaged in this dynamic process, coupled with an inherent randomness, it is difficult to predict how these narratives will develop. The cycle of aggregation, selection, and elimination, of course, does not stop. Although the broader conspiracy theorizing process is akin to a natural selection process, the claws and the stronger muscles of the natural world are replaced by imaginative thinking, mental gymnastics, a vast reservoir of existing narrative models, and a certain degree of randomness.

Our methods are broadly applicable to any textual data and, while currently limited to English-language materials, could theoretically be adopted to work with any language for which there are robust natural language processing models for sentence parsing and transformer-based word embedding. Therefore, the methods and interface could also be used to interrogate historical data, perhaps providing support to investigations into whether conspiracy theories share certain network topological features across time or whether conspiracy theories developed on the internet and in social media are fundamentally different from earlier conspiracy theories. As we showed in earlier work on pandemic-related conspiracy theories, which comprise only a small portion of QAnon discussions, the methods we develop here are good at capturing dynamic change in the overall discussion space, identifying both the nucleations of emerging stories as well as the alignment of new and existing narrative frameworks into more comprehensive ones (Shahsavari et al., 2020). In this work, we have shown how the QAnon conspiracy theory aligns numerous preexisting conspiracy theories, such as the age-old anti-Semitic "blood-libel" stories and stories about the clandestine machinations of the "Illuminati," with more recent narratives, including the Pizzagate conspiracy theory and a raft of emerging conspiracy theories surrounding the COVID-19 pandemic and Jeffrey Epstein, to name but two of the most notable examples (Dundes, 1991; Tangherlini et al., 2020). Finally, our current interface promotes understanding of the real-time negotiation of the ever-changing narrative framework. Working with this interface, one can easily monitor new suggestions made by community members, trace the various relationships being established between actants as well as narrative domains, and explore the conversational reinforcement of existing parts of the narrative framework, providing, as it were, a front row seat to the "Great Awakening."

REFERENCES

Anderson, B. (2006). *Imagined communities: Reflections on the origin and spread of nationalism.* Verso Books.

Bak-Coleman, J. B., Alfano, M., Barfuss, W., Bergstrom, C. T., Centeno, M. A., Couzin, I. D., & Weber, E. U. (2021). Stewardship of global collective behavior. *Proceedings of the National Academy of Sciences of the United States of America, 118*(27), e2025764118.

Barzilay, T. (2016). Well *p*oisoning *a*ccusations in *m*edieval Europe: 1250–1500 (Doctoral dissertation, Columbia University).

Bennett, B. (2007). Hermetic histories: Divine providence and conspiracy theory. *Numen, 54*(2), 174–209.

Bikhchandani, S., Hirshleifer, D., & Welch, I. (1992). A theory of fads, fashion, custom, and cultural change as informational cascades. *Journal of Political Economy, 100*(5), 992–1026.

Bodner, J., Welch, W., & Brodie, I. (2020). *Covid-19 conspiracy theories: QAnon, 5G, the New World Order and other viral ideas.* McFarland.

Burns, W. E. (2003). *Witch hunts in Europe and America: An encyclopedia.* Greenwood Publishing Group.

Clover, C. (1986). The long prose form. *Arkiv för nordisk filologi, 101*, 10–39.

Davis, C. A., Ciampaglia, G. L., Aiello, L. M., Chung, K., Conover, M. D., Ferrara, E., Flammini, A., Fox, G. C., Gao, X., Gonçalves, B., Grabowicz, P. A., Hong, K., Hui, P.-M., McCaulay, S., McKelvey, K., Meiss, M. R., Patil, S., Kankanamalage, C. P., Pentchev, V., . . . Menczer, F. (2016). OSoMe: The IUNI Observatory on Social Media. *PeerJ Computer Science, 2*, e87.

Dean, J. (2000). Theorizing conspiracy theory. *Theory & Event, 4*(3). https://muse.jhu.edu/article/32599

Dégh, L. (2001). *Legend and belief: Dialectics of a folklore genre.* Indiana University Press.

Dundes, A. (Ed.). (1991). *The blood libel legend: A casebook in anti-Semitic folklore.* University of Wisconsin Press.

Ellis, B. (1989). Death by folklore: Ostension, contemporary legend, and murder. *Western Folklore, 48*(3), 201–220.

Fay, B. (2019). The Nazi conspiracy theory: German fantasies and Jewish power in the Third Reich. *Library & Information History, 35*(2), 75–97.

Ferrara, E., Chang, H., Chen, E., Muric, G., & Patel, J. (2020). *Characterizing social media manipulation in the 2020 US presidential election*. First Monday.

Fine, G. A. (2007). Rumor, trust and civil society: Collective memory and cultures of judgment. *Diogenes*, *54*(1), 5–18.

Goertzel, T. (1994). Belief in conspiracy theories. *Political Psychology*, *15*(4), 731–742.

Gray-Fow, M. J. (1998). Why the Christians? Nero and the great fire. *Latomus*, *57* (Fasc. 3), 595–616.

Greimas, A. J. (1968). Sémantique structurale, Paris, 1966. Archiv Orientální, *36*, 150–152.

Hagen, S., Peeters, S., Jokubauskaitė, E., & de Zeeuw, D. (2020, April 20). Cross-platform mentions of the QAnon conspiracy theory [Data set]. *Zenodo*. http://doi.org/10.5281/zenodo.3758479

Hofstadter, R. (1964, November). The paranoid style in American politics. *Harper's Magazine*. https://harpers.org/archive/1964/11/the-paranoid-style-in-american-politics/

Holt, J., & Rizzuto, M. (2021, May 26). QAnon's hallmark catchphrases evaporating from the mainstream internet. *Digital Forensic Research Lab*. https://medium.com/dfrlab/qanons-hallmark-catchphrases-evaporating-from-the-mainstream-internet-ce90b6dc2c55

Kahneman, D., Rosenfield, A. M., Gandhi, L., & Blaser, T. (2016). Noise: How to overcome the high, hidden cost of inconsistent decision making. *Harvard Business Review*, *94*, 38–46.

Kahneman, D., Sibony, O., & Sunstein, C. R. (2021). *Noise: A flaw in human judgment*. Little, Brown.

Labov, W., & Waletzky, J. (1967). Narrative analysis. In J. Helm (Ed.), *Essays on the verbal and visual arts* (pp. 12–44). University of Washington Press. Reprinted in *Journal of Narrative and Life History*, *7*, 3–38 (1997).

McPherson, M., Smith-Lovin, L., & Cook, J. M. (2001). Birds of a feather: Homophily in social networks. *Annual Review of Sociology*, *27*(1), 415–444.

Mullen, P. B. (1972). Modern legend and rumor theory. *Journal of the Folklore Institute*, *9*(2/3), 95–109.

Munn, L. (2021). *More than a mob: Parler as preparatory media for the US Capitol storming*. First Monday.

Newman, M. E. (2001). Clustering and preferential attachment in growing networks. *Physical Review E*, *64*(2), 025102.

Nicolaisen, W. F. (1987). The linguistic structure of legends. *Perspectives on Contemporary Legend*, *2*(1), 61–67.

O'Connor, C., & Weatherall, J. O. (2019). *The misinformation age*. Yale University Press.

Papasavva, A., Blackburn, J., Stringhini, G., Zannettou, S., & De Cristofaro, E. (2021). "Is it a qoincidence?": A first step towards understanding and characterizing the QAnon movement on Voat. In J. Leskovec, M. Grobelnik, M. Najork, J. Tang, & L. Zia (Eds.), *Proceedings of the Web Conference 2021* (pp. 460–471). Association for Computing Machinery.

Papasavva, A., Aliapoulios, M., Ballard, C., De Cristofaro, E., Stringhini, G., Zannettou, S., & Blackburn, J. (2022). The gospel according to Q: Understanding the QAnon conspiracy from the perspective of canonical information. In C. Budak, M. Cha, & D. Quercia (Eds.), *Proceedings of the International AAAI Conference on Web and Social Media* (vol. 16, pp. 735–746). AAAI Press.

Phillips, W. (2019). It wasn't just the trolls: Early internet culture, "fun," and the fires of exclusionary laughter. *Social Media + Society*, *5*(3), 2056305119849493.

Rosenblum, N. L., & Muirhead, R. (2020). *A lot of people are saying*. Princeton University Press.

Rosnow, R. L. (1980). Psychology of rumor reconsidered. *Psychological Bulletin*, *87*(3), 578–591.

Shahsavari, S., Holur, P., Wang, T., Tangherlini, T. R., & Roychowdhury, V. (2020). Conspiracy in the time of corona: Automatic detection of emerging COVID-19 conspiracy theories in social media and the news. *Journal of Computational Social Science*, *3*(2), 279–317.

Shao, C., Ciampaglia, G. L., Flammini, A., & Menczer, F. (2016). Hoaxy: A platform for tracking online misinformation. In *Proceedings of the 25th International Conference Companion on World Wide Web* (pp. 745–750). IW3C3.

Tangherlini, T. R. (1990). "It happened not too far from here...": A survey of legend theory and characterization. *Western Folklore*, *49*(4), 371–390.

(2018). Toward a generative model of legend: Pizzas, bridges, vaccines, and witches. *Humanities*, *7*(1), 1.

(2021). A conspiracy of witches. In J. Glauser & P. Hermann (Eds.), *Myth, magic, and memory in early Scandinavian narrative culture* (pp. 181–193). Brepols.

Tangherlini, T. R., Roychowdhury, V., Glenn, B., Crespi, C. M., Bandari, R., Wadia, A., Falahi, M., Ebrahimzadeh, E., & Bastani, R. (2016). "Mommy blogs" and the vaccination exemption narrative: Results from a machine-learning approach for story aggregation on parenting social media sites. *JMIR Public Health and Surveillance*, *2*(2), e6586.

Tangherlini, T. R., Shahsavari, S., Shahbazi, B., Ebrahimzadeh, E., & Roychowdhury, V. (2020). An automated pipeline for the discovery of conspiracy and conspiracy theory narrative frameworks: Bridgegate, Pizzagate and storytelling on the web. *PLoS ONE*, *15*(6), e0233879.

van Prooijen, J. W. (2020). An existential threat model of conspiracy theories. *European Psychologist*, *25*(1), 16–25.

van Prooijen, J. W., & Douglas, K. M. (2017). Conspiracy theories as part of history: The role of societal crisis situations. *Memory Studies*, *10*(3), 323–333.

Zimmer, F., & Reich, A. (2018). What is truth? Fake news and their uncovering by the audience. In V. Cunnane & N. Corcoran (Eds.), *Proceedings of the 5th European Conference on Social Media* (pp. 374–381). Academic Conferences and Publishing International.

Zuckerman, E. (2019). QAnon and the emergence of the unreal. *Journal of Design and Science*, *6*, 1–14.

CHAPTER 15

Debunking and Preventing Conspiracies
Special Challenges of QAnon

John A. Banas and Elena Bessarabova

Introduction

According to an NPR poll published on December 30, 2020, in response to the statement, "A group of Satan-worshipping elites who run a child sex ring are trying to control our politics and media," 17 percent of Americans polled believed the statement to be true, with an additional 37 percent indicating that they did not know if it was true or false (Rose, 2020). That only 44 percent of Americans polled in this survey on misinformation correctly identified the central tenet of the QAnon conspiracy theory as false is an alarming sign that conspiracy theories and other misinformation campaigns have effectively undermined our society's grasp on reality. As QAnon-supporting politicians like Marjorie Taylor Greene and Lauren Boebert ascend to the halls of power in the USA while repeatedly spouting easily discredited nonsense (e.g. Congresswoman Greene claimed that wildfires in California were the result of Jewish space lasers; Lee, 2021), it seems pertinent to examine whether there are effective ways to combat or even prevent the spread of misinformation and conspiracy theories like QAnon.

This chapter reviews the empirical research regarding communication strategies aimed at correcting and preventing misinformation and conspiracy theories. The chapter begins with an examination of why misinformation and conspiracy theories can be dangerous, followed by a description of the scholarship regarding debunking of misinformation. Next, the theoretical research on inoculating against or "prebunking" conspiracy theories is detailed, followed by a discussion of how critical thinking and media literacy can combat conspiratorial ideation. Finally, a brief discussion of how QAnon is different from other conspiracies is offered, along with some research questions for the future study of QAnon specifically.

Although the terms "misinformation" and "conspiracy theories" share considerable conceptual overlap, we use misinformation to describe instances in which people believe information that was presented as true but actually is false (Lewandowsky et al., 2017). Some scholars see conspiracy theories as part of misinformation (e.g. Roozenbeek et al., 2019), and we certainly agree that conspiracy theories incorporate false information, but we distinguish between simply believing in false information (e.g. vaccines cause autism) and attributing the cause of that information to a nefarious cabal of people (e.g. the pharmaceutical companies are conspiring with doctors to unleash diseases on the public so that they can profit off these dangerous vaccines that cause autism). Although there is some disagreement about these terms (see Vraga & Bode, 2020), regardless of terminology, misinformation and conspiracy theories function similarly in terms of their harmful effects and their resistance to correction.

Dangers of Conspiracy Theories and Misinformation

Although conspiracy theory beliefs have sometimes been framed as harmless eccentricities or normal rationalizations of intergroup representation (Sapountzis & Condor, 2013), the QAnon phenomenon aptly demonstrates many of the dangers of conspiratorial belief systems. It is important to distinguish between conspiracy theories that are laughable but generally only harm one's credibility regarding basic science (e.g. Flat Earth) from the more pernicious conspiracy theories that cause widespread societal harm, including death, such as conspiracy theories against vaccinations and climate science and QAnon. We explore why conspiracy theories can be so harmful next.

QAnon, as with other conspiracy theories (e.g. 9/11 Truth), is predicated on misinformation, and misinformation is harmful to optimal decision-making for both individual people and society. Democracy relies on a well-informed public (Kuklinski et al., 2000); if people are pervasively misinformed, societal choices will be suboptimal. For example, various QAnon groups on social media focused their indignation and anger on coronavirus vaccines in March 2021 (Dwoskin & Timberg, 2021; see Chapter 12 of this volume for more on social media and disinformation related to QAnon). The misinformation that the coronavirus is a hoax and that the coronavirus vaccines are unsafe or contain tracking devices persisted, and it is the basis for people to choose not to socially distance or be immunized against the coronavirus, which increases the spread of this vaccine-preventable virus and decreases the ability of society to achieve herd immunity. The USA has far and away the largest death toll from the coronavirus, even though Americans had ample time to prepare for the virus and witness the devastation as it swept through Asia and Europe before the pandemic reached its shores. In short, misinformation about coronavirus vaccines has literally cost people their lives.

Another danger of conspiracy theories is that they "distract public attention from other more pragmatically important political issues and prevent constructive approaches to whatever issues they do address" (Banas & Miller, 2013, p. 186). Indeed, at a time in history when collective action is required to deal with record economic inequality, environmental catastrophe due to climate change, and crumbling infrastructure, investing cognitive resources in a belief system espousing that a secret group of Satan-worshipping, cannibalistic pedophiles is running a global child sex-trafficking ring while conspiring against Donald Trump impedes progress not only by focusing attention away from real problems but also by undermining faith in the governmental structures that are necessary to deal with large-scale problems. When people are exposed to conspiratorial narratives, they are less likely to accept official accounts of events, even if the conspiracy theory claims are refuted (Jolley & Douglas, 2014; Raab et al., 2013).

Beyond distraction and loss of faith in governmentally sanctioned accounts of events, one of the more pernicious side effects of the prevalence of misinformation and conspiracy theorizing is how they erode confidence that the truth can be knowable at all. As Lewandowsky et al. (2017) explained, "misinformation doesn't just misinform. There is evidence that it stops people from believing in facts altogether" (p. 7). Conspiracy theories contribute to a sense that the world is too confusing to be properly understood and that "facts" are just terms used in support of an argument. Scholars have found that exposure to and belief in conspiracy theories contribute to feelings of personal turmoil and uneasiness driven by a sense that the social world is essentially unknowable (e.g. Douglas et al., 2017).

A final harmful outcome of conspiracy theories and misinformation is that they can lead to physical violence. The paranoid worldview espoused by conspiracy theories can fuel dangerous extremism (Pfau, 2005). This can be seen with the QAnon conspiracy theory in the insurrectionist behavior of January 6, 2021, which moved beyond free speech on internet platforms to physical aggression at the Capitol Building of the USA. Fueled by misinformation that the election had been "stolen" from Trump by evil Democrats in league with powerful pedophiliac satanists, QAnon believers used violence against the police protecting the Capitol. Five people died during the attack, dozens of others were injured (Healy,

2021), and the videos of hundreds of misinformed people battling police at the Capitol is a chilling reminder of the dangerous consequences of misinformation campaigns like QAnon.

This section has detailed how conspiracy theories and other misinformation campaigns can be dangerous, leading to a range of maladaptive outcomes, including poor decision-making, distraction from real issues, a belief that truth and facts cannot actually be known, and even physical violence. Given the negative consequences of misinformation and conspiracy theories, there has been a great deal of theoretical and practical research examining potential solutions to the problem of misinformation. We review the effectiveness of various communication strategies for dealing with misinformation and conspiracy theories next.

Dealing with Misinformation and Conspiracy Theories

One of the challenges of dealing with misinformation is that humans are inclined toward accepting information that they encounter as true, a phenomenon known as "truth bias" (Levine, 2019). Because of truth bias, misinformation is seldom recognized as such without considerable effort, knowledge, and assistance. Indeed, misinformation is typically presented as factual information, and humans rarely perceive that any claim or piece of evidence they encounter as false or incorrect unless they are alerted to its lack of veracity, typically through something like a retraction or correction (Lewandowsky et al., 2012).

Suspension of belief, although possible, is cognitively effortful (Hasson et al., 2005). Research indicates that suspending belief requires heightened awareness, the recognition of something improbable in the message, or increased suspicion during message processing (Schul et al., 2008). Providing additional information through retractions or debunking efforts could help people suspend belief enough to recognize misinformation. Furthermore, preemptive communication strategies like inoculation may also inhibit belief in false or misleading content. Finally, increased critical thinking and media literacy could also help people to identify misinformation.

Debunking

Debunking, or correcting misinformation, seems so easy at first glance. Conventional logic suggests that if the problem is that people are misinformed about an issue, then we simply need to provide them with the correct information. Human message processing and the accompanying belief structures and attitudes are not so simple that merely retracting false claims or correcting erroneous information erases their influence. The seminal research on misinformation (Johnson & Siefert, 1994; Wilkes & Leatherbarrow, 1988) was conducted using a neutral topic (e.g. a warehouse fire), and one piece of misinformation was introduced (e.g. a wiring cabinet contained oil paints and pressured gas cylinders) to those in the misinformation experimental condition, which was subsequently explicitly and clearly corrected later in the story (e.g. the wiring cabinet was, in fact, empty). Those in the control condition read the same story about the warehouse fire, but they never received a correction, as they had been informed that the wiring cabinet was empty from the beginning of the study. All participants were then given a comprehension test to recall basic facts and whether a retraction was provided. The key outcome was the participant responses to the indirect questions about the event (e.g. "What caused the black smoke?"). Despite understanding and remembering the retraction, the misinformation was frequently referenced as a cause of the smoke.

In a review of research using the classic misinformation paradigm described above, Lewandowsky et al. (2012) summarize that "retractions rarely, if ever, have the intended effect of eliminating the reliance on misinformation" (p. 114). The persistence of misinformation, even after retractions or debunking efforts, is known as the "continued-influence effect," and it endures even when people remember the retraction and believe in its accuracy (e.g. Ecker et al., 2011a; Johnson & Siefert, 1994, 1998, 1999; van Oostendorp & Bonebakker, 1999; Wilkes & Reynolds, 1999). Retraction research reveals the best outcome to be a 50 percent reduction in references to misinformation, again accounting for noticing and remembering the retraction (e.g. Ecker et al., 2011b), and some studies reveal retractions to be completely ineffective at decreasing reliance on misinformation (e.g. Johnson & Siefert, 1994).

It is noteworthy that the persistence of misinformation in these studies occurred despite optimal conditions being present – namely, the laboratory setting was free from distraction and participants were motivated to be as accurate as possible, and the topic chosen was not one with which participants would be ego-involved, which could motivate them to defend a particular attitudinal position. This is crucial as corrections that contradict a person's worldviews are even less likely to be successful and could even increase belief in misinformation (Lewandowsky et al., 2012).

Although the research literature on correcting misinformation portrays the process in a rather dismal light, there are three communication techniques that have been empirically demonstrated to boost the effectiveness of retractions: (1) repeated retractions; (2) providing an alternative account in the correction that assists in filling in the narrative gap left by the retraction; and (3) warnings during the initial misinformation exposure. We briefly review and explain these helpful communication techniques below.

One way to enhance the effectiveness of retractions is through repetition. Ecker et al. (2011b) found that, when participants were repeatedly exposed to erroneous claims, repeated retractions helped reduce, but not eradicate, the continued-influence effect. Repetition needs to be handled carefully, as some research has found that repeated corrections could arouse suspicion and cause people to question the accuracy of the correction (Bush et al., 1994). Additionally, repeating the misinformation in the correction could actually cause the faulty information to be remembered better (Schwarz et al., 2007). For this reason, corrections should avoid repeating the myth as much as possible and instead emphasize the correct factual information instead.

A second – and more promising – approach to correcting misinformation involves providing an alternative account of the misinformation in order to fill in the narrative coherence gap in the recipient's comprehension of an occurrence (Lewandowsky et al., 2012). For example, in the warehouse fire example described above, people who received a retraction could still rely on misinformation because there was now a gap in the story (e.g. "If it wasn't the oil or gas cylinders, then what else could it be?"). The continued-influence effect of misinformation can actually be eliminated if an alternative account explains *why* the initial information was wrong (e.g. "The wiring closet did not contain oil paints and gas cylinders, but there were arson materials recovered at the scene"; Johnson & Seifert, 1994; Tenney et al., 2009). Alternative accounts should explain the causal factors in the misinformation, and they will be more effective still if they can also explain why the misinformation was reported to be correct initially (e.g. Rapp & Kendeou, 2007). Additionally, the most effective corrections also provide for a motivation behind an erroneous reporting of facts. Finally, simple alternative explanations are preferable to complex ones (e.g. Lombrozo, 2006, 2007).

A third method for enhancing corrections of misinformation is explicitly warning people that they are about to encounter false claims (e.g. Ecker et al., 2010). Ecker et al. (2010) found that warnings are most effective when they are delivered *prior* to misinformation exposure. Preemptive warnings are thought to at least temporarily promote a skeptical state of message processing, thereby allowing people to better distinguish between truthful and misleading information (Lewandowsky et al., 2012).

The warning strategy was widely implemented by social media companies like Facebook and Twitter in 2020 to address misinformation about the US presidential election and coronavirus. Recent research findings suggest that warning labels on online stories containing misinformation substantially inhibited behavioral intentions to share those stories online (Mena, 2020; Vraga et al., 2020). Warning labels may not completely erase misinformation effects, but they appear to make users question the information and substantially reduce sharing of misinformation.

Correcting misinformation is extremely challenging under the best of circumstances (e.g. with neutral topics in a laboratory setting), and misinformation that challenges a person's worldview is particularly resistant to correction through debunking efforts (Cook et al., 2017). Conspiracy theories like QAnon, which has been likened to a cult or a religion, certainly fit this description. Conspiracy theories are so challenging to debunk because evidence or people who contradict the conspiracy theory are cast as part of the conspiracy (Lewandowsky et al., 2013b). Once the paranoid mindset of a conspiracy like QAnon is adopted, it is difficult to accept evidence that contradicts the conspiracy theory narrative. The general lack of success with debunking conspiracy theories and other misinformation campaigns has led researchers to examine ways to prevent conspiracy theories from taking hold. One promising theoretical approach on this front is known as "prebunking," which is based on inoculation theory (see Banas, 2020 for an overview).

Inoculation

Introduced by McGuire in the early 1960s, inoculation theory is predicated on the idea that stimulating resistance to persuasion is analogous to medical vaccination. Medical inoculations typically[1] work by introducing weakened viruses into an uninfected person, causing the body to produce antibodies that enable resistance to subsequent exposure to that virus. Similarly, attitudinal inoculation exposes people to weakened arguments contrary to their current attitudinal position, triggering a range of

[1] mRNA vaccines, like many Western coronavirus vaccines, do not contain a weakened form of the virus.

resistance-promoting actions that confer resistance to subsequent exposure to persuasive attacks (Banas, 2020; Compton, 2013; McGuire, 1964).

Contemporary inoculation treatments contain two key message elements: explicit forewarning and refutational preemption, designed to trigger the theoretical mechanisms of perceived threat and counterarguing (Compton, 2013). Explicit forewarning has been conceptualized as a statement that attitudinal positions or beliefs may be vulnerable to subsequent challenges. The refutational preemption embodies the process of counterarguing, and it typically involves using two-sided messages that raise and then refute counterattitudinal arguments (Compton, 2013).

Inoculation has been successfully utilized against conspiracy theories (Banas & Miller, 2013; Banas & Richards, 2017; Banas et al., 2015; Cook et al., 2017). Banas and Miller (2013) examined the effectiveness of inoculation messages on inducing resistance to the 9/11 Truth propaganda film *Loose Change: Final Cut*. The 9/11 Truth conspiracy claims that the terrorist attacks on September 11, 2001, were an "inside job" in which agents of the US government coordinated and carried out the attacks and then covered up their crimes in order to engage in war in the Middle East. Study participants were first presented with a warning that the *Loose Change: Final Cut* film would promote an unsubstantiated conspiracy theory and that they were vulnerable to being persuaded by their deceptive messaging. Participants were then given either a fact-based or a logic-based inoculation treatment that introduced and refuted arguments made in the film. The fact-based inoculation treatment focused on dispelling some of the factual errors in the film, and the logic-based inoculation treatment attempted to demonstrate that the 9/11 Truth conspiracy theory was not logically sound. After reading the messages, participants watched about forty minutes of the *Loose Change: Final Cut* film, featuring the section in which it is argued that the Twin Towers collapsed due to controlled demolition. Compared to control participants, who read an unrelated essay about the history of sushi, both inoculation messages were effective at preventing attitude change toward the conspiracy theories advocated for in the film, with the fact-based message performing substantially better than the logic-based message.

In another 9/11 Truth study using the methodology from Banas and Miller (2013), Banas et al. (2015) examined how inoculation – or prebunking – messages affected the emotional responses to the film and how those responses related to conspiracy theory ideation. Participants exposed to the inoculation messages felts less fear while they were watching *Loose Change: Final Cut* compared to participants who read the control message. This is important because fear can inhibit adaptive responses like clear and rational thinking, especially when there is not a clear sense of what someone can do to effectively deal with the threatening event (Cialdini, 2016). The Banas et al. (2015) study also examined whether inoculating participants against the 9/11 Truth conspiracy theory would extend to conspiracy theories about the New World Order. The researchers found that the inoculation messages about 9/11 Truth, although effective against the 9/11 Truth conspiracy theory, had no effect on attitudes toward the other conspiracy theory, providing evidence that the protection provided by the inoculation against one conspiracy theory does not extend to other conspiracy theories. This was true even for the logic-based message, which the researchers had hoped the participants would be able to apply to subsequent conspiracist messaging. The results were quite disappointing in terms of inoculation's ability to provide a broader level of the protection against conspiracist ideation, and they led the researchers to speculate that perhaps the logic-based inoculation treatment provided logic lessons that were not easily grasped by the participants, and hence they were not able to apply the logic lessons during subsequent exposure to other conspiracy theories.

Another example of using inoculation to combat misinformation and conspiracy theories comes from Cook et al.'s (2017) study on climate change. Although their study focused on deceptive argumentation techniques rather than conspiracy theories per se, they noted that research has correlated the rejection of climate change with conspiratorial thinking (Lewandowsky et al., 2013a), and among those who reject climate science, advocating for conspiracy theories to explain scientific consensus regarding climate change is the most common response (Smith & Leiserowitz, 2012). The strong connection between misinformation about climate science and conspiracy theories regarding climate change makes Cook et al.'s (2017) study particularly relevant to our discussion of inoculating against conspiracy theorizing.

In the Cook et al. (2017) study, inoculation was effective against disinformation attempts by deniers of climate science by exposing their misleading argumentation tactics. The researchers presented participants first with a warning about efforts to undermine beliefs in the scientific consensus about climate change motivated by politics and then with a description of a common disinformation tactic that utilizes "fake experts" to mislead people into doubting that there is a legitimate scientific consensus regarding climate science. Further, the inoculation treatment also connected the deceptive argumentation strategy to prior misinformation campaigns, including the "fake expert" testimonials used by major tobacco companies to undermine the scientific consensus about the dangers of smoking. The inoculation group and a comparison group then received information utilizing the "fake expert" strategy by referencing the so-called 31,000 scientists who signed the Oregon Petition. The results of the study were impressive, with inoculated participants (who received misinformation) scoring equally well on an assortment of climate-related questions when compared to a control group who did not receive *any* misinformation about the scientific consensus. However, for those who did not receive an inoculation treatment, the misinformation involving "fake experts" had a substantial and negative effect on a variety of climate science measures.

Although inoculation theory has been successfully applied to a wide range of influence topics (see Banas & Rains, 2010 for a meta-analysis), inoculation research has traditionally been limited by a need to address particular arguments against specific persuasion topics, which essentially is an issue of intervention scalability. In the context of inoculating against misinformation campaigns, this requires anticipating specific claims or arguments and then preemptively refuting these specific examples of misinformation. Banas et al. (2015) attempted to show that exposing the logical problems of one conspiracy theory would inoculate against the logical fallacies of other conspiracy theories, but they found such inoculation to be limited to the conspiracy theory targeted in the message. Further, inoculation research is typically conducted by passively supplying participants with preemptive refutation evidence and arguments instead of allowing participants to generate their own resistance to the misinformation (Roozenbeek et al., 2020). As Roozenbeek et al. (2020) explained, the premise of their research program "is that fake news stories themselves constantly change and evolve so building immunity against the underlying tactics of misinformation is a more durable strategy" (p. 3).

To address previous limitations with scalability, Roozenbeek and van der Linden (2019) applied the inoculation metaphor of enhancing the generation of "mental antibodies" in their online game *Bad News*. Their clever innovation is an internet-based game in which users play the role of applying for the "position of disinformation and fake news tycoon," and the theoretical rationale behind the game is that having people actively engage in learning about the various popular misinformation tactics utilized in the production and dissemination of fake news can successfully create "broad-spectrum" inoculation against misinformation. In this way, the *Bad News* game builds on the intention to teach participants to spot the faulty logic behind conspiracy theories and misinformation campaigns from Banas et al. (2015) and the exposure of deceptive argumentation techniques from Cook et al. (2017). The goal of the game is to learn about and use various deceptive tactics to increase social media followers, thereby earning "badges" representing mastery of the six commonly used misinformation techniques, specifically, "impersonating people or organizations online; using emotional language to evoke fear or anger; using divisive language to drive groups in society apart (polarization); spreading conspiracy theories; discrediting opponents by using gaslighting and red herrings; and baiting people into responding in an exaggerated manner (trolling)" (Roozenbeek et al., 2020, p. 7).

This research program has produced impressive results in terms of participants rating fake news headlines as less reliable without affecting the reliability ratings of true headlines, and these findings are consistent regardless of ideology (Roozenbeek & van der Linden, 2019). Furthermore, scholars have also shown that playing *Bad News* increases confidence in detecting misinformation, which is associated with resisting persuasion (Basol et al., 2020).

Subsequent studies of the *Bad News* research program have replicated and extended it to examine issues of culture and effect decay. Roozenbeek et al. (2020) found the gameplay to be effective at reducing the reliability ratings of manipulative fake news Twitter posts among participants in Sweden, Poland, Greece, and Germany. Further, the ability to identify misinformation did not significantly differ across demographic variables such as age, gender, or ideology in those countries. Maertens et al. (2021) examined the long-term effectiveness of *Bad News* active inoculation and found the inoculation effects to last at least three months, as long as the game was played at regular intervals. When they followed up with participants in a separate experiment in which the researchers did not check in with the participants regularly, the inoculation effects were no longer significant two months after the gameplay intervention.

Media Literacy/Critical Thinking

Thematically relevant to the preceding review of inoculation research, scholars have argued that media literacy and critical thinking are key elements in preventing misinformation and conspiracist ideation (Lewandowsky et al., 2017). Media literacy and critical thinking share conceptual overlap, as media literacy is about "understanding of the role of media in society as well as essential skills of inquiry and self-expression necessary for citizens of a democracy" (Center for Media Literacy, 2021, para. 1).

Explicitly connecting critical thinking to media news literacy, Lutzke et al. (2019) tested two types of brief critical thinking interventions: one in which participants read guidelines for evaluating online information and another in which participants both read and rated each guideline in terms of importance. Compared to a control group who received no guidance, participants in both intervention conditions reported diminished likelihood to trust, like, and share misinformation about climate change via social media. It is noteworthy that the critical thinking intervention did not diminish perceptions of legitimate news about climate change. Relevant to QAnon, Craft et al. (2017) found that news literacy inhibited acceptance of low-quality information, including believing political conspiracy theories. Furthermore, in a recent survey using a nationally representative sample, Vraga and Tully (2021) found that people with high levels of news literacy were more skeptical of the quality of information presented on social media, and they also found that being knowledgeable about media structures resulted in exposing oneself to less online information and sharing less content via social media.

Special Challenges Posed by QAnon

As both a conspiracy theory and misinformation vector, QAnon presents a range of challenges for those who wish to engage in debunking or prebunking in order to reduce the negative effects associated with it. One difficulty is that, unlike other conspiracy groups (e.g. Flat Earthers), QAnon is tied to political identity, and when misinformation is connected to elements of a person's worldview, it is particularly resistant to change. Another challenge is that QAnon is constantly shifting to introduce new claims or incorporate other conspiratorial ideas. Other conspiracy theories focus on a single issue (e.g. 9/11 Truth is singularly focused on the "inside job" that resulted in the 9/11 attacks), making them less influential as a movement as the public moves on to other issues. QAnon's ability to adapt and to continue to gain influence makes it a particularly persistent problem. Finally, unlike many other conspiracy theories, many of QAnon's ideas (e.g. the stolen election) receive a great deal of support from right-wing media. Constant repetition of misinformation makes it especially difficult to dislodge (see Chapter 9 of this volume for more on the politics of QAnon). Aside from highly partisan news channels like Fox News or OAN, mainstream news presents stories using "false balance" framing, which facilitates belief in misinformation (Lewandowsky et al., 2013a).

Conclusion

Conspiracy theories such as QAnon contribute to a variety of negative outcomes, including suboptimal decision making, undermining democracy, and even violence. Debunking efforts are largely ineffective in dealing with conspiracy theories and other misinformation campaigns, although repeated corrections, warnings about misinformation, and alternative accounts to misinformation do increase the effectiveness of debunking efforts. A contrast to debunking is "prebunking," or trying to *prevent* conspiracies rather than *counter* them. Prebunking is based on inoculation theory, which has been effective at targeting specific conspiracy propaganda as well as the general tactics of conspiracy groups. Recent developments regarding prebunking and gamification have shown promising results related to inhibiting misinformation. Misinformation often is presented as legitimate news, so critical thinking and media news literacy are important factors in preventing misinformation. Future research should continue to explore how gamification and inoculation can be applied to QAnon conspiracy misinformation, particularly regarding the robustness of their effects. Critical thinking and media news literacy variables need to be incorporated into future research about QAnon, particularly when exposing the misinformation techniques used on social media. Overall, the research outlined in this chapter demonstrates that preventative communication strategies are key to stopping the spread of QAnon and other conspiracy theories. People are generally poor at resisting influences against which they are unprepared. Without forewarning and a critical understanding of the manipulation used in conspiracy theory rhetoric, QAnon and other conspiracy theories will continue to proliferate.

REFERENCES

Banas, J. A. (2020). Inoculation theory. In *The International Encyclopedia of Media Psychology* (pp. 1–8). John Wiley & Sons.

Banas, J. A., & Miller, G. (2013). Inducing resistance to conspiracy theory propaganda: Testing inoculation and meta-inoculation strategies. *Human Communication Research*, *40*, 1–24.

Banas, J. A., & Rains, S. A. (2010). A meta-analysis of research on inoculation theory. *Communication Monographs*, *77*, 281–311.

Banas, J. A., & Richards, A. (2017). Apprehension or motivation to defend attitudes? Exploring the underlying threat mechanism in inoculation-induced resistance to persuasion. *Communication Monographs*, *84*, 164–178.

Banas, J. A., Bessarabova, E., Adame, B., & Robertson, K. (2015). The role of emotion in inoculating against conspiracy media. Paper presented at the *65th Annual Conference* of the *International Communication Association*, San Juan, Puerto Rico, May 21–25.

Basol, M., Roozenbeek, J., & van der Linden, S. (2020). Good news about *Bad News*: Gamified inoculation boosts confidence and cultivates cognitive immunity against fake news. *Journal of Cognition*, *3*, 1–9.

Bush, J. G., Johnson, H. M., & Seifert, C. M. (1994). The implications of corrections: Then why did you mention it? In A. Ram & K. Eiselt (Eds.), *Proceedings of the 16th Annual Conference of the Cognitive Science Society* (pp. 112–117). Erlbaum.

Center for Media Literacy. (2021). Media literacy: A definition and more. *Center for Media Literacy.* www.medialit.org/media-literacy-definition-and-more

Cialdini, R. (2016). *Pre-suasion: A revolutionary way to influence and persuade.* Simon and Schuster.

Compton, J. (2013). Inoculation theory. In J. P. Dillard & L. Shen (Eds.), *The SAGE handbook of persuasion: Developments in theory and practice* (2nd ed., pp. 220–236). SAGE.

Cook, J., Lewandowsky, S., & Ecker, U. K. (2017). Neutralizing misinformation through inoculation: Exposing misleading argumentation techniques reduces their influence. *PLoS ONE*, *12*, e0175799.

Craft, S., Ashley, S., & Maksl, A. (2017). News media literacy and conspiracy theory endorsement. *Communication and the Public*, *2*(4), 388–401.

Douglas, K. M., Sutton, R. M., & Cichocka, A. (2017). The psychology of conspiracy theories. *Current Directions in Psychological Science*, *26*, 538–542.

Dwoskin, E., & Timberg, C. (2021, January 16). Misinformation dropped dramatically the week after Twitter banned Trump and some allies. *The Washington Post.* www.washingtonpost.com/technology/2021/01/16/misinformation-trump-twitter/

Ecker, U. K. H., Lewandowsky, S., & Apai, J. (2011a). Terrorists brought down the plane! – No, actually it was a technical fault: Processing corrections of emotive information. *Quarterly Journal of Experimental Psychology*, *64*, 283–310.

Ecker, U. K. H., Lewandowsky, S., Swire, B., & Chang, D. (2011b). Correcting false information in memory: Manipulating the strength of misinformation encoding and its retraction. *Psychonomic Bulletin & Review*, *18*, 570–578.

Ecker, U. K. H., Lewandowsky, S., & Tang, D. T. W. (2010). Explicit warnings reduce but do not eliminate the continued influence of misinformation. *Memory & Cognition*, *38*, 1087–1100.

Hasson, U., Simmons, J. P., & Todorov, A. (2005). Believe it or not: On the possibility of suspending belief. *Psychological Science*, *16*, 566–571.

Healy, J. (2021, January 11). These are the 5 people who died in the Capitol riot. *The New York Times.* www.nytimes.com/2021/01/11/us/who-died-in-capitol-building-attack.html

Johnson, H. M., & Siefert, C. M. (1994). Sources of the continued influence effect: When misinformation in memory affects later inferences. *Journal of Experimental Psychology: Learning, Memory, and Cognition*, *20*, 1420–1436.

(1998). Updating accounts following a correction of misinformation. *Journal of Experimental Psychology: Learning, Memory, and Cognition*, *24*, 1483–1494.

(1999). Modifying mental representations: Comprehending corrections. In H. van Oostendorp & S. R. Goldman (Eds.), *The construction of mental representations during reading* (pp. 303–318). Erlbaum.

Jolley, D., & Douglas, K. M. (2014). The effects of anti-vaccine conspiracy theories on vaccination intentions. *PLoS ONE*, *9*, e89177.

Kuklinski, J. H., Quirk, P. J., Jerit, J., Schwieder, D., & Rich, R. F. (2000). Misinformation and the currency of democratic citizenship. *Journal of Politics*, *62*, 790–816.

Lee, B. Y. (2021, January 30). Did Rep. Marjorie Taylor Greene blame a "space laser" for wildfires? Here's the response. *Forbes*. www.forbes.com/sites/brucelee/2021/01/30/did-rep-marjorie-taylor-greene-blame-a-space-laser-for-wildfires-heres-the-response/?sh=7db907a1e44a

Levine, T. R. (2019). *Duped: Truth-default theory and the social science of lying and deception*. University Alabama Press.

Lewandowsky, S., Ecker, U. K. H., & Cook, J. (2017). Beyond misinformation: Understanding and coping with the "post-truth" era. *Journal of Applied Research in Memory and Cognition*, *6*(4), 353–369.

Lewandowsky, S., Ecker, U. K. H., Seifert, C. M., Schwarz, N., & Cook, J. (2012). Misinformation and its correction: Continued influence and successful debiasing. *Psychological Science in the Public Interest*, *13*(3), 106–131.

Lewandowsky, S., Gignac, G. E., & Oberauer, K. (2013a). The role of conspiracist ideation and worldviews in predicting rejection of science. *PLoS ONE*, *8*(10), e75637.

Lewandowsky S., Oberauer, K., & Gignac, G. E. (2013b). NASA faked the moon landing, therefore, (climate) science is a hoax. An anatomy of the motivated rejection of science. *Psychological Science*, *24*, 622–633.

Lombrozo, T. (2006). The structure and function of explanations. *Trends in Cognitive Sciences*, *10*, 464–470.

(2007). Simplicity and probability in causal explanation. *Cognitive Psychology*, *55*, 232–257.

Lutzke, L., Drummond, C., Slovic, P., & Arvai, J. (2019). Priming critical thinking: Simple interventions limit the influence of fake news about climate change on Facebook. *Global Environmental Change*, *58*, 101964.

Maertens, R., Roozenbeek, J., Basol, M., & van der Linden, S. (2021). Long-term effectiveness of inoculation against misinformation: Three longitudinal experiments. *Journal of Experimental Psychology: Applied*, 27(1), 1–16.

McGuire, W. J. (1964). Inducing resistance to persuasion. Some contemporary approaches. In L. Berkowitz (Ed.), *Advances in experimental social psychology* (pp. 191–229). Academic Press.

Mena, P. (2020). Cleaning up social media: The effect of warning labels on likelihood of sharing false news on Facebook. *Policy & Internet, 12*, 165–183.

Pfau, M. W. (2005). Evaluating conspiracy: Narrative, argument, and ideology in Lincoln's "House Divided" speech. *Argumentation and Advocacy, 42*, 57–73.

Raab, M. H., Ortlieb, S., Auer, N., Guthmann, K., & Carbon, C. C. (2013). Thirty shades of truth: Conspiracy theories as stories of individuation, not of pathological delusion. *Frontiers in Psychology, 4*, 406.

Rapp, D. N., & Kendeou, P. (2007). Revisiting what readers know: Updating text representations during narrative comprehension. *Memory & Cognition, 35*, 2019–2023.

Roozenbeek, J., & van der Linden, S. (2019). The fake news game: Actively inoculating against the risk of misinformation. *Journal of Risk Research, 22*, 570–580.

Roozenbeek, J., van der Linden, S., & Nygren, T. (2020). Prebunking interventions based on "inoculation" theory can reduce susceptibility to misinformation across cultures. *The Harvard Kennedy School Misinformation Review, 1*, 1–23.

Rose, J. (2020, December 30). Even if it's "bonkers," poll finds many believe QAnon and other conspiracy theories. *NPR.* www.npr.org/2020/12/30/951095644/even-if-its-bonkers-poll-finds-many-believe-qanon-and-other-conspiracy-theories

Sapountzis, A., & Condor, S. (2013). Conspiracy accounts as intergroup theories: Challenging dominant understandings of social power and political legitimacy. *Political Psychology, 34*, 731–752.

Schul, Y., Mayo, R., & Burnstein, E. (2008). The value of distrust. *Journal of Experimental Social Psychology, 44*, 1293–1302.

Schwarz, N., Sanna, L. J., Skurnik, I., & Yoon, C. (2007). Metacognitive experiences and the intricacies of setting people straight: Implications for debiasing and public information campaigns. *Advances in Experimental Social Psychology, 39*, 127–161.

Smith N., & Leiserowitz A. A. (2012). The rise of global warming skepticism: Exploring affective image associations in the United States over time. *Risk Analysis, 32*, 1021–1032.

Tenney, E. R., Clearly, H. M. D., & Spellman, B. A. (2009). Unpacking the doubt in "beyond a reasonable doubt": Plausible alternative stories increase not guilty verdicts. *Basic and Applied Social Psychology, 31*, 1–8.

van Oostendorp, H., & Bonebakker, C. (1999). Difficulties in updating mental representations during reading news reports. In H. van Oostendorp & S. R. Goldman (eds.), *The construction of mental representations during reading* (pp. 319–339). Erlbaum.

Vraga, E. K., & Bode, L. (2020). Defining misinformation and understanding its bounded nature: Using expertise and evidence for describing misinformation. *Political Communication, 37*, 136–144.

Vraga, E. K., & Tully, M. (2021). News literacy, social media behaviors, and skepticism toward information on social media. *Information, Communication, & Society*, *24*, 150–166.

Vraga, E. K., Kim, S. C., Cook, J., & Bode, L. (2020). Testing the effectiveness of correction placement and type on Instagram. *International Journal of Press/Politics*, *25*, 632–652.

Wilkes, A. L., & Leatherbarrow, M. (1988). Editing episodic memory following the identification of error. *Quarterly Journal of Experimental Psychology Section A: Human Experimental Psychology*, *40*, 361–387.

Wilkes, A. L., & Reynolds, D. J. (1999). On certain limitations accompanying readers' interpretations of corrections in episodic text. *Quarterly Journal of Experimental Psychology Section A: Human Experimental Psychology*, *52*, 165–183.

PART V

The Future of QAnon

CHAPTER 16

Categorizing QAnon
Is This a New Religious Movement?

Amarnath Amarasingam, Marc-Andre Argentino, Dakota Johnston, and Sharday Mosurinjohn

Introduction

Over the course of 2020, QAnon repeatedly captured the news media's attention more than ever as the group started to move its activities from online chat boards into the offline world. With increased public attention, political commentators (expert and lay) increasingly refer to QAnon as a "cult" (Blazakis, 2021; Hassan, 2021). What is missing in the growing literature on QAnon is: (1) an examination of the movement within the context of the substantial academic literature on new religious movements (NRMs); and (2) use of this research to see whether labeling QAnon a "cult" or "new religious movement" makes sense in a comparative context. In order to do this, we discuss QAnon's fit with two widely used NRM definitions, its fit with definitions of conspiracy from religious studies literature, and its differences from and similarities to other related types of organizations, including terrorist groups, social movements, and even multilevel marketing (MLM) companies. It is this latter comparison that we spend the most time on, using the example of the company NXIVM (pronounced "NEX-ee-um")[1] to test out the NRM criteria with two loosely defined groups that have recently come to public attention and therefore do not neatly fit into the NRM discourse. This exploratory analysis is of particular importance in the case of QAnon, not only because the use of the terms "cult," "religion," and "conspiracy" by the public is usually divorced from academic research, but also because the terms are often used as weapons to tarnish movements that are considered to be deviant in some way.

In the past, panic around cults was related to mass deaths, accusations of brainwashing and thought control, and charges by loved ones that their

[1] We appreciate the work of Quinn Finlay on NXIVM in her essay "Reorganizing the Field of New Religious Movement Studies" (unpublished [2019]).

family members were being held against their will. Even as claims of brainwashing by cults have never held empirical muster (Dawson, 2001; Richardson, 2003), "deprogramming" experts like Rick Alan Ross and Steven Hassan continue to push the narrative in the public discourse around QAnon. QAnon, as it stands today, represents an amalgamation of virtually every popular conspiracy theory under a single interpretive frame. This is what Michael Barkun dubs a *superconspiracy*. Superconspiracies are "conspiratorial constructs in which multiple conspiracies are believed to be linked together hierarchically" (Barkun, 2013, p. 6). In superconspiracies, Barkun argues that "event-based and systemic conspiracies are joined in complex ways so that conspiracies come to be nested within one another. At the summit of the conspiratorial hierarchy is a distant but all-powerful evil force manipulating lesser conspiratorial actors. These master conspirators are almost always . . . invisible and operat[e] in secrecy" (Barkun, 2013, p. 6). Yet, is it possible – and academically beneficial – to talk about this superconspiracy as a kind of NRM for its followers?

One thing that is clear is that the QAnon message is certainly resonating with some religious communities. As discussed in the Chapter 1 of this volume, at the behest of both anonymous poster "Q" and influential members of the movement, QAnon supporters watch out for purported secret clues from President Trump, "deciphering" cryptic, often religiously charged "Q-drops" (online posts by "Q") to learn more about the underground cabal of QAnon's focus. This deciphering process goes beyond the level of the individual person. For example, Russ Wagner, an independent congregation pastor, and Kevin Bushey, a retired military officer, started hosting weekly Bible studies broadcast on YouTube to decode the biblical language used in "Q-drops," preaching Neo-charismatic interpretations to affirm the legitimacy of their conspiracy theories (Argentino, 2020). In other words, QAnon supporters often decode these Q-drops collectively.

While the other chapters in this book primarily treat QAnon as a conspiracy group, this chapter encourages future research on QAnon as a religious movement as well. In this chapter, we examine the ways in which QAnon has evolved substantially since its ignominious beginnings as a fringe online community to an established, offline political and religious movement with a shared sense of purpose, agency, and belonging – combined with an overwhelming desire for social change. United by a shared belief that the American way of life is under siege, QAnon supporters feel a moral duty to uncover the truth about the supposed cabal and fight back – in effect, creating a decentralized violent ideology that has materialized into a possible threat to domestic security (Amarasingam & Argentino, 2020).

What Are Cults and New Religious Movements?

To disassociate new religions and religious movements from the pejorative connotations of the term "cult," scholars generally prefer the more neutral terms "new religion" or "new religious movement" to describe emerging fringe religious groups (Dillon & Richardson, 1991). The term "cult" initially served as an extension to the famous Weberian church–sect typology, offering a new analytic concept to distinguish the traditional (albeit socially deviant) beliefs and practices of sects from the radically reformed, deviant beliefs and practices of cults. During the "cult panic" of the 1960s and 1970s across the USA, the term was increasingly employed as a social weapon to reinforce the claims that all religious movements deemed "cults" are violent and manipulative with a charismatic ringleader, preying on the emotionally weak through deception, brainwashing, and/or fraud (Richardson, 1993). While it is true that some former cult members describe their participation as one born from deception and maintained through indoctrination, this is not the case for all members, nor should it be portrayed as such (see Chapter 7 of this volume for more on other NRMs).

However unorthodox NRMs might be, painting all NRMs with the same brush undermines members' rationality, agency, and freedom of religion. Oftentimes, determinations that a group is a "cult" depend on the degree of deviance the group exhibits from mainstream norms. Whether or not the group is accused of brainwashing (itself a debunked concept) or scamming its members, these standards misrepresent reality and gratuitously diminish legitimate – albeit perhaps strange – religious experiences and practices (Dawson, 2013). NRMs grow out of a desire to fulfill spiritual needs and maintain themselves by regularly satisfying the needs of their members. Oftentimes, converts were already susceptible to certain beliefs or worldviews but, for a wide range of reasons, might have struggled to articulate themselves or did not feel comfortable expressing those ideas in their previous environment before joining an NRM (see Chapter 7 of this volume for more on recruitment to NRMs).

Despite the best efforts of many religious studies scholars, there is no "one-size-fits-all" definition or classification of cults. It should also be noted that which groups are considered "cult-like" varies drastically from country to country. The problem arises, in part, from the diversity of NRMs. In other words, scholars have been unable to identify a singular set of definitional characteristics that apply to all NRMs. Normative NRM definitions seek to identify a set of mandatory characteristics to establish a "norm" that distinguishes NRMs from other forms of religions (Dawson, 2013).

However, these sorts of definitions are often problematic as they are too specific to be useful, and they generally lack impartiality by imposing value judgments within their criteria (for a discussion of normativity in scholarship, see Martin, 2016). Thus, many normative definitions of NRMs construct NRMs as inherently problematic or dangerous, producing practical consequences such as the stigmatization or dehumanization of NRM members (Gallagher, 2007). That said, identifying shared characteristics among a set of NRMs, though limited, can be fruitful for cross-case comparative analysis. However, defining and classifying various cults exclusively on their shared characteristics has proven insufficient as such definitions fail to adequately account for and reconcile the diversity facing those same groups (Melton, 2004).

Another significant difficulty in classifying NRMs is their tendency to fluctuate and adapt over time. Studies have found that as they grow in size some NRMs tend to adopt similar modes of membership and organization to sects and churches (Dawson, 2013; Gallagher, 2007). Definitions proposed by the anticult movement[2] are also not helpful, as Dawson (2013) states, for two reasons: There is a value judgment associated with NRMs that is not present when judging other religions; and, relatedly, they leave a variety of other religious groups unclassified. For the purposes of this chapter, though, there remains a need to settle on some definitional parameters or typologies in order to make sense of QAnon in a comparative context.

For Dawson (2006, p. 374), NRMs share at least a few characteristics:

(1) They are more concerned than churches or sects with meeting the needs of their individual members.
(2) They lay claim to some esoteric knowledge that has been lost, repressed, or newly discovered.
(3) They offer their believers some kind of ecstatic or transfiguring experience that is more direct than that provided by traditional modes of religious life.
(4) Unlike established faiths, they often display no systematic orientation to the broader society and usually are loosely organized.
(5) They are almost always centered on a charismatic leader and face disintegration when the leader dies or is discredited.

[2] The Anti-Cult Crisis of the 1960s and 1970s saw the development of numerous national and transnational Anti-Cult Coalitions that were determined to remove "cults" and "cult activity" from their society as they presented a "threat to the safety of families and the social order" (Feltmate, 2016, p. 84).

Dawson readily notes that his typology does not necessarily apply to some of the more infamous NRMs, such as the Church of Scientology or Krishna Consciousness. Instead, he suggests that some of these groups have moved into other categories along the church–sect–cult continuum.

Using mode of membership and the consequent form of NRMs' social organization as a guiding criterion, scholars William Bainbridge and Rodney Stark further divided NRMs into three categories: audience cults, client cults, and cult movements (Bainbridge & Stark, 1980). Audience cults, they argue, are the least organized but the most prevalent in North America. These are not formal organizations, and "the great majority of persons who take in audience cults do so entirely through mass media: books, magazines, newspapers, TV, astrology columns, and the like" (p. 199). Into this category fit UFO enthusiasts, flat-Earth believers, and New Agers. Next, client cults are movements that most closely resemble "the consultant/client or therapist/patient model" with "short-term exchanges with relatively specific aims" (p. 199). Many of the followers of these kinds of NRMs may remain members of different and more established religions but use their relationship with these NRMs' leaders for specific needs like remembering past lives, meditation, or healing traumatic memories. Finally, according to Bainbridge and Stark, cult movements represent "organized religious entities that attempt to satisfy all the needs of their adherents" (Saliba, 2003, p. 141). Examples of cult movements include Raëlians and Krishna Consciousness (see Clarke, 2006 for descriptions).

For the purposes of this chapter, we use a combination of Dawson's (2006) and Bainbridge and Stark's (1980) typologies discussed above to elucidate the salient features of QAnon as a movement. We do this by comparing QAnon to NXIVM, the controversial MLM company/self-improvement group. These two phenomena, QAnon and NXIVM, make an illuminating comparison because they both have religious elements but do not self-identify as religions. No one is born into them, as are some members of minority religious groups. Instead, they perpetuate themselves by seeking to convince adults that they have the keys to some hidden truths about the world. The "deviance" of both has come to the forefront of public consciousness when they have convinced followers to break laws with serious penalties in the name of uncovering those hidden truths. And it has been at this point that both have been labeled as "cults" in mainstream discourse. It therefore helps to have another "quasi-religious" (Franks et al., 2013) example in mind when evaluating QAnon against NRM criteria so that conventionally theistic NRMs do not implicitly serve as the anchoring examples of the category.

Case Comparison: NXIVM

NXIVM was a MLM self-improvement company promoting workshops and success programs for business executives. Emerging in the late 1990s in Albany, New York, thousands of students signed up for NXIVM workshops over the span of two decades, including a number of high-profile actors, businesspeople, and politicians. Some estimates put the number of people who have taken NXIVM courses at 16,000 – many NXIVM leaders brought in upwards of 2,000 students during their time – but only around 50–100 people have ever constituted the core of the group at any given time (Meier, 2017).

For participants, NXIVM offered a lifestyle framed around personal and career growth. At seminars, participants were led through self-help exercises, such as "Rational Inquiry" to overcome self-limiting beliefs and "Exploration of Meaning" to figure out why something elicited a strong emotional reaction in them. NXIVM offered no accreditation to students who completed training, but the program was often described as a "practical MBA," with a strict internal hierarchy existing among students and leadership. Because NXIVM was nominally a self-help business, the vast majority of participants were not formally part of the organization, and the relationship between leaders and clients was similar to that of a therapist/patient relationship, NXIVM can be described in Bainbridge and Stark's (1980) terms as a client cult.

As an MLM, NXIVM reproduced itself primarily by recruiting members with a promise of payments or services for enrolling others into the scheme rather than supplying investments or sale of products. Thus, the organization did not need to introduce any policy on children, families, and generational transmission in order to ensure its viability. However, NXIVM leadership still strictly regulated the sexuality and relationships of core women members. For these women, NXIVM leader Keith Raniere was a spiritual leader to whom obedience was ultimate. NXIVM did indeed "attempt to satisfy all the religious needs" of these converts and demanded their whole lives in return (Stark & Bainbridge, 1985, p. 29).

At its core, then, NXIVM can be understood as a cult movement organized around the "charismatic leader" Keith Raniere, who socialized a subgroup of women into practices of so-called self-realization and transformation, gradually destroying their ability to approach their lives outside of the NXIVM framework. These facts were made clear as NXIVM disintegrated after the highly publicized 2018 arrest and 2020 conviction of Raniere on counts of sex trafficking, racketeering, forced labor conspiracy, wire fraud conspiracy, and more. Raniere, aged sixty at the time, was sentenced to 120 years in prison and ordered to pay a $1.75 million fine.

Presently, a web search of "NXIVM" yields hundreds of news articles, op-eds, videos, and TV episodes that deems NXIVM specifically a "sex cult." Beyond general NXIVM programming concerned with sexuality and sex differences, Raniere's women-only subprogram called JNESS featured a two-hour lecture outlining men's biological disposition to polygyny and emphasizing that "the female sex" was infected with parasitic characteristics (Bloch et al., 2018). NXIVM leadership deemed these women as *parasites* – suggesting that their inability to overcome suffering, harm, discomfort, sickness, pain, or insecurity on their own is an intentional means of imposing one's needs on other people (Freedman, 2003). Moreover, NXIVM leadership maintained that *parasites* create problems where none exist and "crave attention"; *parasitic strategies* lower self-esteem, destroying a person's value. NXIVM's intent was thus to rid the world of things that destroy value, including the purported "parasitism" of women, through the modeling of strategies and helping others learn to use them (Burton, 2018).

In addition to JNESS, another more exclusive women-only program sought to purify women's parasitism. This group was called "DOS" for "*Dominus Obsequious Sororium*," translating approximately to "Master Over the Slave Women." Members of DOS were required to adopt master–slave designations, where the "slaves" would turn over highly damaging collateral to their "masters." Leaders explained this act of surrender to member women as necessary to ensure their accountability to the program and, ultimately, to their own personal goal of truly reaching their full potential (Meier, 2017). "Masters" always had control over "slaves," requiring them to be available by phone twenty-four hours a day, systematically testing their availability by waking them up multiple times a night, and requiring six hours per week of labor. Failure to comply with these requirements resulted in heavy penalties: imposed fasting, more work, paddling, and other physical punishments. According to the highest-ranking members of DOS, the group was an exclusive "secret society aimed at empowering women," built by and for NXIVM women, totally independent of Raniere's influence. As NXIVM unraveled due to DOS-related legal action, this characterization was shown to be patently false.

In 2017, Canadian actor Sarah Edmondson, who had long been involved in NXIVM, went to the *New York Times* to break the story of DOS. According to Edmonson, the "secret sorority" began when three women offered up damaging collateral to Raniere himself to seal lifetime vows of commitment and obedience to their leader (Meier, 2017). Edmonson maintains that DOS was originally marketed to her as the pinnacle of self-development as well as a "source of good, that could grow into a network that could potentially influence elections" (Meier, 2017).

Edmonson felt motivated to leave NXIVM following an incident of ritual branding, which also received ample attention in news media coverage of the story. The ritual, which had been introduced to Edmondson as a small tattoo, entailed an almost hour-long unanesthetized branding with a cauterizing pen. Edmondson felt that the resulting mark was much larger than initially described. Furthermore, in the days following the event, Edmondson realized that the mark she had received were Raniere's initials. According to Edmonson, this realization motivated her to leave the group and go to the press with her story. Notably, she began publicly using the charged term "cult" to describe NXIVM, which served as a means to delegitimize NXIVM as a business and encourage intervention to ensure no one else experienced the same abuses she had.

The requisite secrecy, collateral, and investment in DOS were not unique to DOS. In fact, all NXIVM participants had to sign a nondisclosure agreement upon enrollment and vowed to never share what they learned in the programming (Freedman, 2003); and "Executive Success Program" (ESP) participants paid as much as $10,000 for a five-day course consisting of thirteen-hour cram sessions and intense emotional probing. Edmondson reports that, over her twelve-year involvement with the group, she spent $100,000 on NXIVM programming (Bloch et al., 2018).

NXIVM's doctrine emphasized that all people are responsible for everything that happens in their lives – successes, failures, thoughts, feelings – and through sharing one's deepest thoughts and secrets they wholly "own" their personhood and identify their emotional limitations (Bloch et al., 2018). During introductory classes, participants underwent "Explorations of Meaning," where teachers "plumbed" students' beliefs and backgrounds, looking for emotional buttons, encouraging students to share their negative habits and think about why they were so attached to them. From there, participants were encouraged to pledge to change and replace those behaviors with something more productive (Bloch et al., 2018; Freedman, 2003). The intensity of these sessions was such that participants had been reported to have psychotic episodes afterward (Freedman, 2003). Whether members were targeted for deliberate master–slave relationships or subjected, as some were, to psychological experiments that exposed them to graphic and disturbing images of violence, their adverse reactions were framed as personal limitations that required identification and correction.

Venerating Raniere represented an essential part of NXIVM's program, and participants were taught on day one to say "thank you" to his image on the wall and only to refer to him by his epithet, "Vanguard" (Bloch et al., 2018). Though NXIVM is nontheistic and does not self-describe itself as a religion, some members described Raniere as a spiritual leader. In almost messianic terms, Raniere himself proclaims that he is one of the smartest and most ethical people in the world who is riding a "new wave into the future" where he will "reorder human existence" (Odato & Gish, 2012). (In contrast, former members describe Raniere as a manipulator who regularly had sex with his adherents and encouraged the women close to him to adhere to near-starvation diets to achieve the physique he finds appealing.) In equally religious terms, Raniere consistently characterized NXIVM as a program for transcending ordinary consciousness and achieving enlightenment through the sacred value of self-empowerment, which participants develop via economic growth and social climbing. Based on Bainbridge and Stark's (1980) typology of cults, we can conceptualize NXIVM's core as a cult movement and its periphery as a client cult.

In turn, Dawson's (2006) five characteristics of NRMs become apparent in NXIVM:

(1) *More concerned than churches or sects with meeting the needs of their individual members:* In its concentrated focus on developing the self-realization and transformation of members, NXIVM seeks to directly meet the needs of its members. Members join programs seeking to better manage their emotions, overcome their limits, and achieve greater success in personal or business affairs. These programs are explicitly practical rather than symbolic.

(2) *Claiming esoteric knowledge that has been lost, repressed, or newly discovered:* NXIVM purports to have access to knowledge that allows for the self-actualization of members. Access to this knowledge is limited to the inner core of NXIVM who organize workshops and to members who pay exorbitant sums of money to gain access to this esoteric knowledge via seminars. NXIVM leaders portray this esoteric knowledge in pseudo-psychological terms, borrowing language from popular psychology and self-help books, but they present their knowledge as uniquely effective for achieving personal success. Access to higher levels of esoteric knowledge increases with closer

identification with the group and more personal investment. Members of JNESS and DOS, for example, gain increasing access to knowledge about the so-called parasitic behaviors purportedly inherent to women and how to overcome them.

(3) *Offering believers some kind of ecstatic or transfiguring experience that is more direct than that provided by traditional modes of religious life:* NXIVM offers participants direct, transfiguring experiences in several ways. For seminar participants, experiences in these seminars are intended to be transformational, allowing participants to overcome self-limiting beliefs or negative emotions. As noted above, many of these sessions are intensely emotional for participants. For DOS and JNESS members, other ritualized, transfiguring experiences, such as the branding described by Edmonson, also take place.

(4) *Displaying no systematic orientation to the broader society and usually loosely organized:* While Raniere may have had world-changing aspirations (as evidenced in his view that he will "reorder human existence"), he spoke to contemporary cultural anxieties only to the extent that he could use them to market NXIVM courses as means to overcome participants' personal unhappiness. Rather than pursuing societal transformation, Raniere offered individual transformation, setting participants' self-interest as paramount. Similarly, recruiters sought to grow the organization primarily in terms of paying participants rather than inner-core members. As noted, up to 16,000 people might have participated in NXIVM's seminars. These members, however, had no formal role in the organization. Roughly 50–100 members constituted the more formal "core" of NXIVM. This leadership core exhibited a more formal, hierarchical organization.

(5) *Centered on a charismatic leader and face disintegration when the leader dies or is discredited:* Clearly, Raniere played the role of a charismatic leader for NXIVM members. This fact emerges both in the requisite veneration of "Vanguard" at the conclusion of seminars by participants and in the extreme degree of control Raniere wielded over inner-core members in DOS particularly. Though NXIVM is now largely defunct as an organization, Raniere has wielded his charisma to rally his supporters and to continue recruiting.

NXIVM, then, not only seeks to meet the needs of its members through programs designed to help them overcome their limitations, manage their emotions, and so on, but also presents them with an opportunity to eventually enter the inner core of the organization, wherein greater insights are available (for a price). Below, we are not necessarily comparing NXIVM to QAnon but only using NXIVM as another quasi-religious example so that we may evaluate QAnon's potential religious qualities with more comparative clarity.

Is QAnon a New Religious Movement?

There are many ways to connect religion and conspiracy theories, as both are "typically seen as involving specific patterns of thought and ideas, and ... both relate in complicated ways to social power" (Robertson et al., 2019, p. 3). Belief in QAnon conspiracies has many similarities with religious belief, epistemologically, psychologically, or socially. Epistemologically, religion and conspiracy theory discourse share a common function: Both permit the development of symbolic resources that enable humans to define and address the problem of evil. In this vein, Stephen O'Leary writes that defining this problem in conspiracist and religious contexts is not about secular evidence but about theodicy (O'Leary, 1994).

At a psychological level, as Uscinski and Parent (2014, p. 131) state, "conspiracy theories are essentially alarm systems and coping mechanisms to help deal with threats." Conspiracy theories and religions can both be frightening, as they magnify the power of evil and offer a dualistic struggle between light and darkness. Simultaneously, both can provide reassurance to their adherents as they present a world that is meaningful, not arbitrary. The assimilation of threatening events into a religious or conspiratorial scheme offers meaning from chaos by conjuring something to fight against: "Not only are events nonrandom, but the clear identification of evil gives the conspiracist a definable enemy against which to struggle, endowing life with purpose" (Barkun, 2013, p. 4). For both religions and conspiracy theories, this struggle against evil offers a path to salvation, whether personal or societal. Finally, at a social level, belief in QAnon helps create an in-group identity and maintains group cohesion by attributing evil deeds and effects to an out-group while providing adherents with feelings of individual existential importance. Religious communities similarly produce us versus them dynamics, as members often share beliefs about cosmology and morality (see Part II of this volume for more on the psychology of conspiracy theories).

QAnon, however, differs in a significant way from traditional "world religions": QAnon filters its understanding of "ultimate concern" by assembling a bricolage of elements from popular culture. QAnon cosmology (what the world and universe appear to be like, its characteristics, and the types of creatures that populate it) and QAnon anthropology (ideas about human beings, their origin, and their destiny) are rooted in a mélange of conspiracy theories, historical facts, and mythical history from film and popular culture. For example, QAnon followers often reference scenes from Terry Gilliam's film *Fear and Loathing in Las Vegas* as evidence of the effects of adrenochrome, a substance that satanic elites ostensibly extract from children to ensure their immortality (Friedberg, 2020). Similarly, QAnon followers reference *The Matrix*'s blue pill/red pill scene to frame the choice to either be a part of the Great Awakening, becoming aware of how the world is run by satanic pedophiles, or to remain "asleep," ignorant of the extensive influence of these elites. Another popular slogan used by QAnon followers, "Where We Go One, We Go All," comes from the film *White Squall*, whose official YouTube trailer's comments section is filled with QAnon followers. The top-rated comment, with over 5,000 upvotes, reads: "Thumbs up if Q sent you here." Finally, "Q," the prophetic leader of QAnon, also regularly references movies in their Q-drops; these pop culture references play a central role in establishing meaning for the movement.

The centrality of popular culture in QAnon narratives distinguishes it from the traditional "world religions." As such, we argue that the current iteration of the QAnon movement is better understood as a NRM and, specifically, as a "hyperreal religion." According to Adam Possamai, who coined the term, a hyperreal religion is "a simulacrum of a religion created out of, or in symbiosis with, commodified popular culture which provides inspiration at a metaphorical level and/or is a source of beliefs for everyday life" (Possamai, 2012, p. 20). Possamai's definition describes movements such as QAnon that rely heavily on references to films or books to articulate their beliefs, as evidenced above. As a movement in a perpetual state of evolution, QAnon constantly blurs the boundaries between popular culture and everyday life as its members continue to incorporate QAnon into their online and offline behaviors.

In his book *Authentic Fakes: Religion and American Popular Culture*, David Chidester argues that popular culture is not only permeated by religion, but popular culture essentially embodies the characteristics and roles of faith in its mutual mimetic play method. Both religion and pop culture play with what it means to be human, be part of a community, possess a body, and have desires (Chidester, 2005). Both are "an arena of human activity marked by the concerns of the transcendent, the sacred, the ultimate – concerns that enable people to experiment with what it means to be human" (Chidester, 2005, p. 1).

QAnon, we argue, is a hyperreal religion, with QAnon adherents making meaning from Q-drops, often in relation to popular culture references. QAnon adherents are not passive consumers of content; they generate memes, videos, texts, music, films, and social media material based on the information provided in Q-drops, in turn feeding further interaction by other members and shaping how the community collectively engages with new Q-drops. As Henry Jenkins writes on convergence culture in new media: "This new vernacular culture encourages broad participation, grassroots creativity, and a bartering or gift economy. This is what happens when consumers take media into their own hands" (Jenkins, 2006, p. 136).

For example, when "Q" posts a new drop, adherents interpret it by juxtaposing it with old Q-drops or tweets from Trump to collectively decipher its meaning. Following this, they create YouTube videos, Twitter threads, Facebook posts, blog posts, livestreams, and memes, disseminating these interpretations for others in the community to consume or expand upon. Moreover, "Q" themself will reference or adapt community-created material in following Q-drops. This echoes Possamai's (2012) notion of a hyperreal religion, in which the popular culture (here, user-generated content regarding Q-drops) forms the basis for the beliefs of the religious group. These dynamics of interrelated consumption and production have material consequences for personal engagement with the movement: "[C]ontemporary expressions of religion are likely to be consumed and individualized, and thus have more relevance to the self than to a community and/or congregation" (Clarke & Beyer, 2009, p. 489). This feature of QAnon recalls characteristics 1 (meeting individual needs) and 4 (loosely organized) in Dawson's (2006) definition of NRMs.

Since QAnon's inception, news media organizations have largely focused on the outlandish or absurd elements of its conspiracy narratives. We argue, however, that there is an urgent need to move beyond sensational representations of the movement and toward a more robust analysis of its dynamics. One has to look no further than the Capitol Hill insurrection on January 6, 2021, to see why taking seriously QAnon as a social movement is important, especially with respect to how the movement contributes to ideologically motivated extremism and violence. Applying the notion of hyperreal religion to QAnon permits scholars to move beyond crude caricatures of the movement and better understand how and why QAnon adherents incorporate the QAnon conspiracies into their online and offline behaviors, as well as the interrelated digital dynamics that shape these behaviors.

We now turn to placing QAnon in the context of Dawson's (2006) five characteristics of NRMs:

(1) *More concerned than churches or sects with meeting the needs of their members:* QAnon adherents are offered an interpretive scheme that assimilates confusing life and political events into a relatively simple grand narrative: that of a global pedophilic elite. For example, political events interpreted as losses, such as Trump's loss in the 2020 election, can be reinterpreted simultaneously as evidence of nefarious actors who rigged the election, as well as being part of a broader, longer-term plan by Trump to overthrow the cabal. As described, these processes of meaning making are profoundly social for members of QAnon, as they rely on videos, tweets, posts, and memes to collectively work toward meaning. QAnon thus also meets social needs for many of its members by creating a close-knit sense of community oriented around this secret knowledge.

(2) *Claiming esoteric knowledge that has been lost, repressed, or newly discovered:* The central feature of QAnon narratives is that followers are being let in on secret military operations via posts by "Q." In fact, the moniker "Q" itself makes reference to the designation for high-level security clearance in the USA. Moreover, followers use other forms of esoteric knowledge, such as intelligence techniques, kabbalah symbolism, gematria, cryptography, and gnosis, available only to "true" decoders, to gain access to what "Q" is trying to tell them. QAnon members also believe that the esoteric knowledge posted by Q is being actively repressed by members of the cabal, who seek to cover up their operations.

(3) *Offering believers some kind of ecstatic or transfiguring experience that is more direct than that provided by traditional modes of religious life:* The knowledge offered by "Q" to followers ostensibly results in a radical transformation in their ability to accurately perceive reality. Again, the concept of getting "red-pilled," a term borrowed from *The Matrix* to describe the moment in which nonbelievers become believers and finally understand how the world works, represents a transfiguration of the self by way of new knowledge. Similarly, the oft-referred to "Great Awakening" – a moment in the future when all of the knowledge gathered by "Q" and adherents will be verified and lead to mass conversion – speaks to the epistemological, psychological, and

social transformations QAnon adherents go through (Anti-Defamation League, 2019). Finally, the "Storm," which has been mentioned by "Q" and followers, refers to the apocalyptic moment in which the "Deep State" will be destroyed, and "Q," along with Donald Trump, will usher in a golden age of peace and prosperity free from the influence of a global satanic cabal.

(4) *Displaying no systematic orientation to the broader society and usually loosely organized:* As a movement, QAnon is amorphous by nature as there is no leader or hierarchy in a traditional sense. Instead, "Q" acts as an oracle sharing the secret knowledge necessary for decoding information, while Trump serves as a messianic figure that would bring about salvation. The movement's closest resemblance to leadership has come from influencers in the movement who have gained authority due to their longevity or capacity to interpret Q-drops. Since 2020, Republican politicians have shown their ability to influence and amplify QAnon narratives, but they do not act as leaders, nor do they provide any type of guidance for the movement.

(5) *Centered on a charismatic leader and face disintegration when the leader dies or is discredited:* This feature is where QAnon is different from other NRMs. As noted, the movement has no official "charismatic" leader, despite the groups' affinity for "Q" and Trump. While "Q" served as the main distributor of top-secret information since 2017, they have not posted since December 2020. Trump himself has never explicitly associated himself with QAnon, so it is difficult to assign the "charismatic" leader role to him. Further, following Trump's repeated allegations of election fraud on Twitter, he was banned from the platform. In effect, this has limited his capacity to amplify QAnon narratives and communicate support for the movement. Despite this, QAnon as a movement remains active. Influencers continue to promulgate conspiratorial narratives for adherents, filling the gap left by Q and Trump. Relatedly, followers hold on to the hope that "Q" will return to posting and that Trump will return to power at a later date. Finally, QAnon adherents have 4,953 Q-drops to which they can turn and use to reinterpret current and future sociopolitical and geopolitical events. These drops have turned into a quasi-sacred text, representing an authority for determining whether a current event was predicted by "Q" as part of the "plan." Although not a leader, these drops act as sacred texts that can lead followers to interpret new political and social developments.

Conclusion

Notwithstanding the fact that QAnon began as a fringe convergence of conspiracy theories, the evolution of the movement has reached a critical point. As a movement, QAnon is no longer confined to dark corners of the internet, nor is it contained within the USA. In a matter of a few years, QAnon has transformed into a potentially violent, extremist religio-political ideology, with no signs of the movement slowing down (see Chapter 17 of this volume for more on the future of QAnon).

While the other chapters in this book primarily treat QAnon as a conspiracy group, this chapter encourages future research on QAnon as a religious movement as well. As we have argued throughout this chapter, QAnon sufficiently meets Lorne Dawson's (2006) five characteristics of a NRM. Furthermore, it shares many features with other religious movements: apocalypticism, good–evil dualisms, and sacred texts. By classifying QAnon as a NRM as opposed to a mere conspiracy theory, it is possible to gain significant insight into the movement, its followers, and its goals. In other words, understanding QAnon in this way allows researchers to take it seriously as a movement with potentially wide-reaching ramifications. Regardless of how absurd some of QAnon's narratives might appear to those outside the movement, its members genuinely believe its narratives to be true. This belief is starting to pose a significant threat to public safety (Amarasingam & Argentino, 2020), public health (with respect to rampant COVID-19 vaccine conspiracism) and democracy at large (as evidenced by the January 6 insurrection; see Argentino & Amarasingam, 2021).

Moreover, we argue that QAnon should be understood according to Adam Possamai's (2012) concept of hyperreal religion. This classification allows for a more robust analysis of the complex dynamics that animate QAnon. QAnon believers borrow frequently from pieces in popular culture, such as famous films, to produce systems of meaning that explain their world, despite their artificial or fictional origins. In complex, intertwined loops of digital media production and consumption, QAnon followers cocreate new interpretations of unfolding political events or Q-drops with references to popular culture. We argue that these dynamics distinguish QAnon from and relate it to the traditional "world religions" and other NRMs. However, a great deal of work remains to be done in the area of conspiracy groups and NRMs, such as synthesizing method and theory in the study of NRMs with work from the philosophy of religion – for example, reading Dawson's (2006) five-criteria definition of NRMs together with Kevin Schilbrack's (2018) five-criteria anchored polythetic definition of religion. It would be a welcome development to link these areas of religious studies that seldom speak to each other.

There are many future directions for research regarding QAnon specifically. Having classified QAnon as a NRM, researchers can begin to employ analytic frameworks to quantify and qualify QAnon as a social problem worthy of review. There is a legitimate danger in prematurely dismissing QAnon as a simple conspiracy theory, particularly given the overwhelming evidence that QAnon has already produced ideologically motivated extremist violence (Amarasingam & Argentino, 2020). By using existing scholarly tools and frameworks that describe the complex dynamics of NRMs, researchers can become more prepared to address the potentially far-reaching social and political consequences that QAnon poses.

Following David Robertson's (2017) proposal that religious studies needs to pay more attention to conspiracy thinking, conspiracy (e.g. when there are actually conspiratorial plots like the experiments at Fort Detrick),[3] and conspiracism (a worldview that sees conspiracy as a motivating force of history), researchers should track how QAnon develops through time, both online and offline. Future research directions on this topic include theorizing the emergence and differentiation of conspiracy theories within this "superconspiracy" with respect to their mainstream plausibility compared to their fringe uptake (e.g. COVID-19 as a hoax generally versus COVID-19 as a creation of Bill Gates in order to inject mind-control devices through fake vaccines specifically) as well as emic disagreements and schisming. There are also important insights to be gleaned about the ways in which QAnon-related ideas are seeping into more established far-right organizations and movements. There is a wealth of data available through social media platforms and online forums such as Reddit and 4chan for researchers to pursue quantitative and qualitative analysis and to determine what online social pressures and offline material structures lead to participating in the QAnon movement – and leaving it.

In sum, the other chapters in this book primarily treat QAnon as a conspiracy group; however, this chapter encourages future research on QAnon as a religious movement as well. Doing so will broaden researchers' understanding of this group and its influence on modern society and help us to predict how the group will evolve in the future.

[3] QAnon conspiracists claim that the coronavirus originated from the US Army biological research facility at Fort Detrick in Frederick, Maryland, and was brought to Wuhan, China, during the 2019 Military World Games by a US Army reservist (Schafer, 2021).

REFERENCES

Amarasingam, A., & Argentino, M.-A. (2020, August 20). The QAnon conspiracy theory: A security threat in the making? *Combating Terrorism Center at West Point*. https://ctc.usma.edu/the-qanon-conspiracy-theory-a-security-threat-in-the-making/

Anti-Defamation League. (2019, November 6). The extremist medicine cabinet: A guide to online "pills." *Anti-Defamation League*. www.adl.org/blog/the-extremist-medicine-cabinet-a-guide-to-online-pills

Argentino, M.-A. (2020, July 8). QAnon conspiracy theory followers step out of the shadows and may be headed to Congress. *The Conversation*. https://theconversation.com/qanon-conspiracy-theory-followers-step-out-of-the-shadows-and-may-be-headed-to-congress-141581

Argentino, M.-A., & Amarasingam, A. (2021). They got it all under control: QAnon, conspiracy theories, and the new threats to Canadian national security. In L. West, T. Juneau, & A. Amarasingam (Eds.), *Stress tested: The COVID-19 pandemic and Canadian national security* (pp. 15–32). University of Calgary Press.

Bainbridge, W. S., & Stark, R. (1980). Client and audience cults in America. *Sociological Analysis*, *41*(3), 199–200.

Barkun, M. (2013). *Culture of conspiracy: Apocalyptic visions in contemporary America*. University of California Press.

Blazakis, J. (2021, February 21). Why QAnon's similarity to other cults makes it a significant national security threat. *Los Angeles Times*. www.latimes.com/opinion/story/2021-02-21/qanon-cults-capitol-attack-trump-threat

Bloch, J., Goldhar, K., Elash, A., & Pizer, D. (2018, September 12). Escaping NXIVM: Inside the secretive world of leader Keith Raniere. *CBC News*. https://newsinteractives.cbc.ca/longform/the-making-of-the-vanguard

Burton, T. I. (2018, July 24). Seagram's heiress arrested for role in controversial "sex cult." *Vox News*. www.vox.com/platform/amp/2018/4/25/17275930/allison-mack-smallville-actress-sex-cult-nxivm-dos-prison-arrest-sex-trafficking-keith-raniere

Chidester, D. (2005). *Authentic fakes: Religion and American popular culture*. University of California Press.

Clarke, P. B. (2006). *Encyclopedia of new religious movements*. Routledge.

Clarke, P. B., & Beyer, P. (2009). *The world's religions: Continuities and transformations*. Routledge.

Dawson, L. L. (2001). Raising Lazarus: A methodological critique of Stephen Kent's *Revival of the brainwashing model*. In B. Zablocki & T. Robbins (Eds.), *Misunderstanding cults: Searching for objectivity in a controversial field* (pp. 379–400). University of Toronto Press.

(2006). New religious movements. In R. A. Segal (Ed.), *The Blackwell companion to the study of religion* (pp. 369–384). Blackwell.

(2013). *Comprehending cults: The sociology of new religious movements*. Oxford University Press.

Dillon, J., & Richardson, J. (1991). *A politics of representation analysis of social construction of the term "cult."* Society for the Scientific Study of Religion Conference.

Feltmate, D. (2016). Rethinking new religious movements beyond a social problems paradigm. *Nova Religio 20*(2), 82–96.

Franks, B., Bangerter, A., & Bauer, M. W. (2013). Conspiracy theories as quasi-religious mentality: An integrated account from cognitive science, social representations theory, and frame theory. *Frontiers in Psychology*, *4*, 424.

Freedman, M. (2003, October 13). Cult of personality. *Forbes*. www.forbes.com/sites/willyakowicz/2019/05/15/keith-raniere-the-leader-of-the-nxivm-sex-cult/?sh=6a7987ff35a9

Friedberg, B. (2020, July 31). The dark virality of a Hollywood blood-harvesting conspiracy. *Wired*. www.wired.com/story/opinion-the-dark-virality-of-a-hollywood-blood-harvesting-conspiracy/

Gallagher, E. V. (2007). "Cults" and "new religious movements." *History of Religions*, *47*(2/3), 205–220.

Hassan, S. (2021, February 4). I was a member of a cult. Here's how to bring QAnon believers back to reality. *CNN*. www.cnn.com/2021/02/04/perspectives/qanon-cult-truth/index.html

Jenkins, H. (2006). *Convergence culture: Where old and new media collide*. New York University Press.

Martin, C. (2016, July 22). Disambiguating normativity. *Craig Martin Blog*. https://craigmartinreligion.wordpress.com/2016/07/22/disambiguating-normativity/

Meier, B. (2017, October 17). Inside a secretive group where women are branded. *The New York Times*. www.nytimes.com/2017/10/17/nyregion/nxivm-women-branded-albany.html

Melton, J. G. (2004). Perspective: Toward a definition of "new religion." *Nova Religio*, *8*(1), 73–87.

O'Leary, S. D. (1994). *Arguing the apocalypse a theory of millennial rhetoric*. Oxford University Press.

Odato, J. M., & Gish, J. (2012, February 11). Secrets of NXIVM. *Times Union*. www.timesunion.com/local/article/Secrets-of-NXIVM-2880885.php

Possamai, A. (2012). *Yoda goes to Glastonbury: An introduction to hyper-real religions*. Brill.

Richardson, J. T. (1993). Definitions of cult: From sociological-technical to popular-negative. *Review of Religious Research*, *34*(4), 348–356.

(2003). A critique of "brainwashing" claims about new religious movements. In L. L. Dawson (Ed.), *Cults and new religious movements: A reader* (pp. 160–166). Blackwell Publishing.

Robertson, D. G. (2017). The hidden hand: Why religious studies need to take conspiracy theories seriously. *Religion Compass 11*(3–4).

Robertson, D. G., Asprem, E., & Dyrendal, A. (2019). Introducing the field: Conspiracy theory in, about, and as religion. In D. G. Robertson, E. Asprem, & A. Dyrendal (Eds.), *Handbook of conspiracy theories and contemporary religion* (pp. 1–20). Leiden.

Saliba, J. (2003). *Understanding new religious movements*. Altamira Press.

Schafer, B. (2021, July 9). China fires back at Biden with conspiracy theories about Maryland lab. *Foreign Policy*. https://foreignpolicy.com/2021/07/09/china-fires-back-at-biden-with-conspiracy-theories-about-maryland-lab/

Schilbrack, K. (2018). Mathematics and the definitions of religion. *International Journal for Philosophy of Religion*, *83*(2), 145–160.

Stark, R., & Bainbridge, W. S. (1985). *The future of religion: Secularization, revival, and cult formation*. University of California Press.

Uscinski, J. E., & Parent, J. M. (2014). *American conspiracy theories*. Oxford University Press.

CHAPTER 17

The Future of QAnon
Emergent Patterns of Social Movement Adaptation and Change

Jared M. Wright and Stuart A. Wright

Introduction

QAnon is a conspiracy theory that has taken hold across the internet since 2017. It is based on an ongoing series of online posts by its alleged leader "Q," who claims to use insider knowledge to make political predictions. "Q" frequently communicates through riddles and puzzles, calling on their followers to engage in their own "research" to solve them. QAnon has also been compared to a "cult" for the feverish devotion of its members (Ingram, 2020). It has shown a particular ability to reinvent itself in the face of failed predictions, "frame bridging" (Snow et al., 1986) or brokering ties with existing social networks and movements including lifestyle and wellness communities, antivaxxers, Deep State conspiracists, radical religious right factions, Patriot and militia movement actors, and other conspiracy-minded groups. While the formal literature on the QAnon community remains sparse, we take the approach of examining this phenomenon from the perspective of social movement adaptation and change, exploring possible trajectories of QAnon in the near future. Drawing on the themes of the previous chapters, this chapter considers the future of QAnon.

In the wake of the 2020 US presidential election, some observers think that Trump's failed efforts to win another term will not hurt the conspiracy-laden, pro-Trump, virtual movement (see also Chapters 8 and 9 of this volume for more on QAnon in 2020). They point out that QAnon predictions have failed before (e.g. Hillary Clinton was not arrested in 2017; JFK Jr. didn't return on October 17, 2020; high-profile elites have not been killed or sent to Guantanamo) and it did not prevent the movement from growing (Amarasingam & Argentino, 2020). And, of course, there is a significant body of research to show that social and religious movements can survive failure of prophecy (Festinger et al., 1956; Stone, 2000; Tumminia & Swatos, 2011). Some also point out that Trump could use QAnon's popularity to help position himself as a "resistance fighter" for a 2024 presidential bid or use his influence to mobilize an array of right-wing political forces.

In the meantime, QAnon has evolved and become a movement with a life of its own, independent of Trump. While Trump embraced conspiracy theories promulgated by QAnon such as the existence of a "Deep State" intent on sabotaging the former president's policies, the range of conspiratorial ideas expand well beyond Trump. In this chapter, we explore patterns of post-Trump-era trajectories of QAnon, examining preliminary evidence of movement adaptation and change to shifting political conditions. These conditions include the political pressure exerted on major social media platforms such as Facebook and Twitter to tamp down on misinformation freely circulated by QAnon followers, the election of Joe Biden and the transition to a new administration in the White House, the emergence of a QAnon religion, and the spreading influence of QAnon abroad, adapted and revised for different political environments.

Social Media Bans and the Presidential Election

Bans on QAnon from major social media platforms like Facebook, Twitter, and YouTube (starting in mid- to late 2020) have been effective in curtailing its spread in the mainstream (see Chapter 12 of this volume for more about QAnon and social media). Analyzing data from Google, we find searches for "QAnon" decreased significantly in the months and weeks leading up to the 2020 presidential election (see Figure 17.1). There was also decreased activity by QAnon's leader: Evidently, Q only made one post in December 2020, which is quite low compared to previous months, and they did not post at all in 2021.[1] In the wake of the 2020 electoral defeat, it would not be surprising to see the movement enter a brief nascent phase, retreating into "abeyance structures" (Taylor, 1989). Trump's election loss and the extended silence of Q in concert may result in a loss of faith or "identity crisis" for some (Harwell & Timberg, 2020).

On the other hand, the dogged persistence of Trump and his most loyal followers to claim election fraud and declare Trump the winner in the face of overwhelming evidence to the contrary ("Stop the Steal") has been a sustaining meme among QAnon adherents and other pro-Trump groups. Some critics have suggested that Trump's stubborn refusal to acknowledge

[1] An account claiming to be Q began posting again on the far-right message board 8kun in June 2022, but it is disputed who is behind this new series of posts.

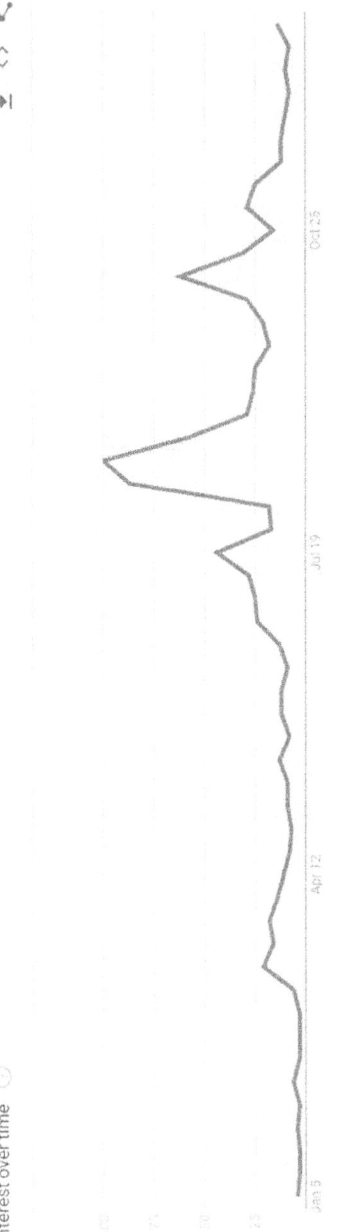

Figure 17.1 Google searches for QAnon, January–December 2020.

defeat is largely a political ploy to bolster a following among his base in the future. By continuing to play to this conspiracy narrative, it is possible that the movement will not only withstand the election loss but be fueled by the perceived plot of a sophisticated, widely coordinated collusion effort by the Deep State (Waldman, 2021; see also Chapters 10 and 14 of this volume for more on the narratives of QAnon). In effect, Trump's devastating loss by more than 7 million votes to Democrat Joe Biden becomes "proof" of the putative conspiracy. As Marc-Andre Argentino (2020b) pointed out before the presidential election, "[i]f Trump loses, it will be attributed to the Deep State Luciferian cabal and they [QAnon] will have a role to play in fighting against the fake government that's replaced Donald Trump."

Indeed, on January 6, 2021, a Trump rally to protest Congress's certification of the electoral college results turned into a riot as Trump supporters, including QAnon followers, stormed the Capitol Building, breaking through barriers and forcing their way into the House and Senate chambers and offices of elected officials while looting and destroying property. Five people died during or shortly after the violence as Capitol Police were joined by DC city police and the National Guard to quell the riot (Byrnes & Marcos, 2021; Kanno-Youngs et al., 2021). In the days following the violence, reports surfaced that the insurrection has been carefully planned in advance with some possible help from insiders in the Capitol (Fuller, 2021; Timberg et al., 2021). News reports also suggested that QAnon played a significant role in radicalizing believers and fermenting online organizing ahead of the assault on the Capitol (Harwell et al., 2021).

QAnon has been linked to violence and networking with violent extremist groups. A report in May 2020 by the Rutgers Miller Center for Community Protection and Resilience and the Network Contagion Research Institute at Rutgers University found that QAnon conspiracy ideas had become more militarized, evolving with more militia-like themes and promoting insurgent zeal across web platforms during the COVID-19 quarantine (Finkelstein et al., 2020). "In the face of COVID-19," the report states, "QAnon now witnesses massive growth and appears to militarize, like the boogaloo, with revolutionary and apocalyptic themes in a more militant and global mode of inciting revolt" (p. 10). Hence, the report cautioned that QAnon had "found an increasing participation with both anti-government groups and militia members" (p. 10). Evidence of militarization in QAnon was also seen in references to a "Q-army," complete with military-style badges both across social media and among protestors on the ground.

Even if the conditions of sustained opposition prevail, however, the movement is likely to undergo change, and perhaps already has. "Deplatforming" certain accounts and groups from major social media sites like Facebook and Twitter may help reduce the spread of QAnon content; however, research shows that such efforts can lead to the emergence of "alternative social media ecologies" (Rogers, 2020), whereby users flock to different platforms or appropriate existing hashtags from other campaigns. For example, QAnon did not become widespread on Facebook until after it was first banned from Reddit in 2018. When the Facebook bans began in 2020, QAnon content then began to flood into platforms like Instagram, Telegram, Gab, and Parlor. It now appears that "influencers" or individuals with large followings (e.g. Tracy Diaz [aka Tracy Beanz], David Hayes, Mark Taylor, Kevin Bushy, Russ Wagner) are most aggressively pushing the conspiracy narrative, suggesting the potential for new fissions and trajectories. It is they who are moving QAnon beyond its creators to fill the void left behind by prominent figures like Trump and Q. As Argentino (2020b) fittingly articulates, the "movement [is] in a constant state of mutation."

QAnon as a New Religious Movement

One such example of transmutation is the emergence of a QAnon religion (LaFrance, 2020; see also Chapter 16 of this volume). According to Argentino (2020b), a faction within the movement has evolved to interpret the Bible through QAnon conspiracies. A Charismatic/Pentecostal QAnon church in Indiana now broadcasts religious services through the Omega Kingdom Ministry (OKM) on Zoom. OKM is part of a network of independent house churches or congregations called Home Congregations Worldwide (HCW). HCW's spiritual advisor is Mark Taylor, a self-appointed Trump prophet (Taylor & Colbert, 2017) and QAnon "influencer" with a large social media following on Twitter and YouTube.

The HCW website links to QAnon conspiracy theories and resources, including a documentary called *Fall Cabal* by Dutch conspiracy theorist Janet Ossebaard, which serves as an introduction to the QAnon religion in a ten-part video series. Argentino (2020a) notes that Kevin Bushy and Russ Wagner, the leaders of OKM, are operating with the objective to "train congregants to form their own home congregations in the future and grow the movement." He also notes that OKM references and utilizes the language of Christian Dominionism, a theology that advocates for a theocracy and a government reconstructed to align with biblical law (see also

Ingersoll, 2017). "Its goal is to attain sociopolitical and economic transformation through the gospel of Jesus in what it calls the seven mountains or spheres of society: religion, family, education, government, media, entertainment and business. This blends QAnon's apocalyptic desire to destroy society 'controlled' by the deep state with the need for the Kingdom of God on Earth" (Argentino, 2020a).

Not surprisingly, some researchers have observed a link between QAnon and Christian nationalism (Djupe & Burge, 2020; O'Donnell, 2020). Djupe and Burge (2020) conducted a national survey and found a "very strong" link between Christian nationalists and QAnon. Among the most ardent, "politically interested" Christian nationalists, nearly 80 percent said they believed in Q. Among the less politically interested Christian nationalists, approximately 55 percent believed in QAnon.

O'Donnell (2020) points out that Trump's putative battle against the Deep State took on cosmic meaning for QAnon followers. The Deep State is central to QAnon believers because it depicts an embedded cabal of Satan-worshipping pedophiles and corrupt politicians working behind the scenes to destroy the Republic. Hence, it overlaps with the notion of "spiritual warfare" espoused by Christian nationalists to "save America," even if it requires violence (Argentino, 2020b; Gjelten, 2021). A *warfare* framing in a religious context is a common pattern used by extremists to legitimate violence (Juergensmeyer, 2017). Indeed, linking religion to warfare and the framing of political conflict in terms of a "sacred struggle" can elevate violence to a moral imperative (Wright, 2009). Argentino (2020b) warned in May 2020 that QAnon "provides an analytical framework to quantify and qualify QAnon-inspired acts of ... ideologically motivated violent extremism." Andrew Whitehead, a sociologist at Indiana University–Purdue University Indianapolis, told the *New York Times* after the insurrection on January 6 that "[y]ou can't understand what happened today without wrestling with Christian Nationalism" (Dias & Graham, 2021). QAnon believers have been tied to other violent acts in recent years, including threats to elected officials, an armed standoff near the Hoover Dam, breaking into the residence of the Canadian prime minister, two kidnappings, and at least one murder (Becket, 2020).

Kristian (2020) finds a less violent strain in QAnon, stating that "QAnon builds on apocalyptic thinking common in parts of evangelical and fundamentalist Christianity in America." Q-drops can include Bible references that adherents perceive as having hidden prophetic meaning for interpreting current events. According to LaFrance (2020), "[p]eople are expressing their faith through devoted study of Q drops as installments of a foundational text, though the development of Q-worshipping groups ..." True believers experience a "feeling of rebirth" and "an arousal to existential knowledge." As such, QAnon is propelled not merely by populism and paranoia, "but is also propelled by religious faith."

Employing a term coined by sociologist Adam Possamai, Argentino (2020b) views QAnon as a "hyperreal religion." Possamai (2012, p. 1) defines a hyperreal religion as "a simulacrum of a religion, created out of, or in symbiosis with, popular culture, which provides inspiration for believers/consumers." Based on Jean Baudrillard's work on hyperreality simulations, hyperreal religion draws on the notion that pop culture shapes and constructs our actual reality. The development of a consumer culture involves the proliferation of signs and symbols ready to be used for one's own religious or spiritual meanings and pursuits. Baudrillard's notion of hyperreality, says Possamai (2018), views everything in terms of simulacra being exchanged constantly for other signs and symbols.

Possamai notes that religious consumers since the late twentieth century have adopted what sociologists of religion term the "bricolage" approach, which combines religious and philosophical or popular traditions, such as Catholicism with astrology, or Protestantism with tarot card readings. Specific to the twenty-first century, Possamai (2005) points to an innovative style of spirituality that mixes religious tradition with popular culture. For example, he refers to surveys that show that "close to 71,000 people in Australia reported being Jedi by religion" (Possamai & Lee, 2011, p. 229). A significant number of people also reported "Matrixism," a hyperreal religion appropriated from the *Matrix* trilogy. It is in this postmodernist framework that a QAnon religion can be understood as a customized religiosity with spiritual meanings attributed to Q and Q-drops, along with an eschatology and a Manichean vision of good and evil.

A similar religious trajectory of QAnon may trend toward what Ward and Voas (2011) call "conspirituality." Conspirituality is a hybrid of alternative/New Age spirituality and conspiracy theory. It comprises two core convictions: (1) belief in a secret group covertly controlling the social and political order; and (2) the idea that humanity is undergoing a "paradigm shift" in consciousness or awareness such that solutions lie in acting in accordance with this emergent worldview (Ward & Voas, 2011, p. 104). Ward and Voas observe that some "awakenings," such as those expressed by well-known author, lecturer, and New Age conspiracist David Icke, involve becoming "aware of the shadow government." Icke has denied the existence of COVID-19, falsely linked the virus to 5G networks, and claimed that people with healthy immune systems are safe from contracting the virus. Twitter suspended Icke's account in November 2020 for violating the platform's rules on COVID-19 misinformation. Icke has published twenty books that blend conspiracy theory with spirituality, including *Children of the Matrix*, which claims that "interdimensional" shape-shifting reptilian creatures secretly control the planet. A popular website for conspiritual devotees, Project Camelot, offers a platform for "shadow government whistle-blowers" to expose the global conspiracy. The global conspiracy tends to be linked to the idea of a New World Order or, in some cases, secret societies of the "Illuminati." Project Camelot claims to have garnered 10 million hits since it was formed in 2006 (Ward & Voas, 2011, p. 111). Such New Age conspirituality groups have proven to be fertile ground for QAnon due to their similar tendency toward paranoia and apocalyptic prophecies and their deep skepticism of mainstream science and medicine (Walker, 2021).

As these developments involving the fusion of QAnon and religion suggest, multiple movement trajectories are evident going forward. Which of these generative mutations will remain viable is still to be determined, but it deserves the attention of scholars and students of social movements.

QAnon as a Global Movement

Just as QAnon has spread into the realm of religion, it has also diffused across the world. What originated as a primarily US-centric phenomenon has now taken root in at least seventy-one nations, including Canada, the UK, France, Germany, Australia, Japan, and Brazil (Farivar, 2020). And while some American followers of QAnon have been deeply shaken by the electoral defeat of Trump, their international counterparts continue to grow, spurred on largely by anxieties over the COVID-19 global pandemic. Historically, major crises have often led to an increased prevalence of conspiracy theories as people search for meaning in the uncertainty (Moscovici, 1987; van Prooijen & Douglas, 2017). In this sense, QAnon was primed at just the right time to benefit from the international wave of fear and confusion resulting from the coronavirus. A joint report from the Institute for Strategic Dialogue (ISD) and NewsGuard shows that the biggest growth in QAnon groups outside of the USA occurred in late 2019 and early 2020, especially after the pandemic began to take hold in March 2020 (O'Conner et al., 2020).

These international nodes of the QAnon movement further reveal its flexibility and adaptability to new contexts. They tend to focus less on

Trump as their "savior," instead espousing narratives of local leaders arising to combat their own "Deep State." According to the ISD/NewsGuard report, prior to the ban, members of QAnon Facebook groups in the UK proposed that Prime Minister Boris Johnson was working in concert with Trump to "drain the swamp" in Britain, as supposedly evidenced by his support of Brexit and banning of the Chinese company Huawei from the UK's 5G networks. Italian QAnon supporters similarly extolled their far-right former interior minister Matteo Salvini. Meanwhile, in Germany and France, users posted about their own leaders, Chancellor Angela Merkel and President Emmanuel Macron, as being "puppets" or "pawns" who must be overthrown in order to free the people. The report shows that many of these groups had grown their ranks to number in the tens of thousands by mid-2020, identifying a total of 448,760 followers or members of European QAnon groups prior to the Twitter and Facebook bans.

The spread of QAnon outside of the USA appears to show that it is no longer reliant only on Trump as its leading figure. QAnon discourse has managed to "resonate" (Benford & Snow, 2000; Snow, 2004) with anti-elitist sentiment in a wide variety of cultures and ideologies by adapting to local vocabularies and practices. The multiplicity and flexibility of beliefs under the QAnon umbrella is especially advantageous for "frame bridging" with other existing networks and movements (Snow et al., 1986). For instance, Facebook groups supporting France's Yellow Vests or *Gilets Jaunes* movement, which have engaged in highly contentious protests against Macron's administration since 2018, have become hotbeds for Q narratives (John, 2020). In Germany, members of the antistate and anti-Semitic *Reichsbürger* or "Citizens of the Reich" movement were among the first to pick up on QAnon narratives, and in late August 2020 they joined forces with other German antivaxxers and antilockdown protesters for a massive rally in Berlin (Ruahala & Morris, 2020).

Meanwhile, one of the most highly active QAnon networks outside of the USA is in Japan, organized through the hashtags like #J-Anon and #QArmyJapanFlynn. These followers particularly idolize Michael Flynn, a former US national security adviser in the Trump administration and an open advocate for QAnon. They draw from a diverse ecosystem of Japanese far-right, ultranationalist, and anticommunist groups; anti-US base activists in Okinawa; human rights activists supporting democracy in Hong Kong or opposing the persecution of Uyghurs in China; and fringe religious groups including Happy Science, the Sanctuary Church, and Falun Gong (Thompson, 2021). Moreover, many such QAnon networks outside of the USA have thus far escaped major social media bans unscathed. For example, in another sweeping crackdown following the January 6, 2021, storming of the US Capitol Building in Washington, DC, Twitter banned over 70,000 QAnon-related accounts, including that of Michael Flynn himself (Bond, 2021). One report found that this caused significant network disruption, deactivating 60 percent of the QAnon accounts it was tracking (Graphika, 2021). Despite such efforts, however, the Japanese QAnon hashtags remained active (Thompson, 2021). While J-Anon has thus far remained a fringe element, some parts of Japanese society are deeply pessimistic about the future, and as such may still be vulnerable to its spread (Alt, 2021).

While social media bans can help in reducing the spread of conspiracy theories and misinformation into wider mainstream publics, their effects are limited. Groups that existed prior to QAnon, such as France's Yellow Vests movement or non-US hashtags like #J-Anon, have persisted on Facebook and Twitter even after several massive bans from the social media giants. Deplatforming can also drive followers into building their own alternative social media ecologies. These can take the form of what some experts call "alt-tech" (Zuckerman & Rajendra-Nicolucci, 2021) or a modern repackaging similar to how the alt-right attempted to rebrand white supremacy for a new, younger generation. After the major social media bans in mid- to late 2020, many QAnon followers moved to a new app called Parler, which ended up becoming the main platform for the planning of the siege of the US Capitol Building, before itself being deplatformed by Amazon, Apple, and Google. Another unexpected platform that has become an incubator of activity for QAnon is Instagram. Despite being owned by Facebook, Instagram has yet to initiate any bans on QAnon content, which has reportedly become highly prevalent among influencers in wellness and lifestyle online communities, repackaged in pastel colors and heart emojis (Tiffany, 2020). From fashion models to mommy blogs, home cooking to mental health, QAnon content has pervaded these networks, reaching as far as Australia (Bogle, 2020).

Outside of the USA, where Facebook and Twitter are less commonly used, the bans have been less effective. Other platforms such as Telegram and Signal, which offer built-in privacy and encryption affordances, were already widely in use by people outside of the USA. These platforms have become major spreaders of QAnon content, particularly by celebrities who already have large, dedicated followings. For example, NewsGuard found that the German singer Xavier Naidoo was a "driving force" behind the spread of QAnon in his country, sharing numerous QAnon posts with his 84,000 Telegram followers, as did the popular German vegan chef and cookbook author Attila Hildmann (Labbe et al., 2020). Likewise, German QAnon groups "have seen huge increases in membership by the tens of thousands" coinciding with Trump's political attacks on NATO and the European Union in 2020 (John, 2020). One German Telegram group of self-described "Corona rebels" called "Qlobal Change" increased its membership by 100,000 in September 2020 (Mezzofiore et al., 2020).

Even some politicians are taking part. The Italian Member of Parliament and antivax activist Sara Cunial gave a speech in Parliament openly espousing several "Deep State" QAnon narratives, of which she shared a video with her more than 120,000 Facebook followers. Although Facebook flagged the video as false information, it has since been mirrored on other QAnon websites (Labbe et al., 2020). In Canada, the Independent Ontario Member of Provincial Parliament Randy Hillier and a spokesperson for Health Minister Patty Hajdu have both publicly pushed conspiracy theories about COVID-19 internment camps (Tasker, 2020). In Australia, it was discovered that a close associate of Prime Minister Scott Morrison was a significant spreader of QAnon (Ling, 2021). In the USA, newly elected Congresswoman Marjorie Taylor Greene has made numerous posts in the past containing incendiary QAnon content, including calling for the executions of some of her own colleagues in the Senate. Some even argue that QAnon has simply become the "new normal" for the US Republican Party (Ling, 2021).

Conclusion

Despite the defeat of Trump in the 2020 US presidential election, it would appear that QAnon is not going away. If anything, it continues to spread in the USA and abroad, becoming increasingly conspiratorial and militant, while also translating into new contexts and locales, manifesting through alternative social media ecologies, and being spread by public figures like celebrities and politicians. It seems to have become a catchall for a wide variety of conspiracy theories and antielitist sentiment, which are highly resonant in these times of growing socioeconomic inequality and a global pandemic. While Trump's loss and Q's multiple failed predictions – including one that Trump would return to office in a surprise inauguration on March 4, 2021 (Rogers, 2021) – have created doubt and uncertainty among some QAnon followers, especially in the USA, the power vacuum is quickly being filled by online influencers and groups ready to adapt and reinvent the conspiracy theory narrative in new ways. As long as the underlying conditions of economic precarity, distrust in political and scientific authorities, and a thriving alt-media ecosystem continue, then it is highly likely that new manifestations of QAnon will also persist. Sites like the R/QAnonCasualities subreddit reveal how this conspiracy theory movement continues to tear apart families and wreck people's lives.

The endurance of a conspiracy movement like QAnon may also be explained by understanding emotions rather than logic (see also Chapter 6 in this volume). For example, Lepselter's (2016) groundbreaking ethnographic research on American UFO conspiracy theories focuses on the deep emotional and aesthetic resonance of her subjects' narratives rather than on their factual or ideological bases. In Papacharissi's (2014) work on digitally connected social movements, she argues that recent mass mobilizations including Occupy Wall Street, Black Lives Matter, and Make America Great Again all share in common a type of solidarity both online and offline built around public displays of emotion, or what she calls "affective publics." Social media affordances network people together, but storytelling is what connects them emotionally, even more so when they become part of the story. This is precisely the power of Q, whose cryptic drops created a trail of clues or "breadcrumbs" for amateur investigators to piece together and interpret, drawing them deeply into the story and generating a cultish emotional dedication and investment.

Together with the driving force of emotions and affective publics (see Chapter 6 for more on QAnon and emotion), recent developments pointing to a convergence of QAnon with other far-right movements suggest a kind of "nesting" effect where the former finds a hospitable space to exist and thrive in the right-wing political ecosystem. The probability of QAnon enduring in a post-Trump political landscape seems quite high given the movement's adaptation or "crossover" to ideas and sentiments emanating from more established extremism movements and networks (Spoccia, 2021). This QAnon trajectory dovetails with growing far-right extremist groups in North America and Europe in recent years (Jones, 2018; Rotella, 2021), facilitated by an array of alternative social media platforms. As Manuel Castells (2015, p. 9) has observed, by developing autonomous networks of horizontal communication, such groups can invent their own projects and ideas: "They subvert the practice of communication as usual by occupying the medium and creating the message." Embedded in the web of insulated global far-right networks, QAnon seems positioned to endure and possibly flourish in the foreseeable future. Future research should focus on how the exodus of Q as leader, the decentralization of the movement into the far corners of the globe, and the convergence with far-right political groups will shape the course of the movement going forward.

REFERENCES

Alt, M. (2021, March 26). Why QAnon flopped in Japan. *The New York Times*. www.nytimes.com/2021/03/26/opinion/qanon-japan-janon.html

Amarasingam, A., & Argentino, M.-A. (2020, October 28). QAnon's predictions haven't come true: So how does the movement survive the failure of prophecy? *Religion Dispatches*. https://religiondispatches.org/qanons-predictions-havent-come-true-so-how-does-the-movement-survive-the-failure-of-prophecy/

Argentino, M.-A. (2020a, May 18). The church of QAnon: Will conspiracy theories form the basis of a new religious movement? *The Conversation*. https://theconversation.com/the-church-of-qanon-will-conspiracy-theories-form-the-basis-of-a-new-religious-movement-137859

(2020b, May 28). In the name of the Father, Son, and Q: Why it's important to see QAnon as a "hyper-real religion." *Religion Dispatches*. https://religiondispatches.org/in-the-name-of-the-father-son-and-q-why-its-important-to-see-qanon-as-a-hyper-real-religion/

Becket, L. (2020, October 16). QAnon: A timeline of violence linked to the conspiracy theory. *The Guardian*. www.theguardian.com/us-news/2020/oct/15/qanon-violence-crimes-timeline

Benford, R. D., & Snow, D. A. (2000). Framing processes and social movements: An overview and assessment. *Annual Review of Sociology*, *26*, 611–639.

Bogle, A. (2020, June 15). How Instagram wellness became a gateway drug for conspiracy theories. *ABC News*. www.abc.net.au/news/science/2020-06-16/wellness-instagram-influencers-veer-into-conspiracy-theories/12348776

Bond, S. (2021, January 31). Unwelcome on Facebook and Twitter, QAnon followers flock to fringe sites. *NPR*. www.npr.org/2021/01/31/962104747/unwelcome-on-facebook-twitter-qanon-followers-flock-to-fringe-sites

Byrnes, J., & Marcos, C. (2021, January 6). Pro-Trump mob overruns Capitol, forcing evacuation. *The Hill*. https://thehill.com/homenews/house/532951-pro-trump-protestors-overrun-capitol-forcing-evacuation

Castells, M. (2015). *Networks of outrage and hope: Social movements in the internet age* (2nd ed., enlarged and updated). Polity Press.

Dias, E., & Graham, R. (2021, January 11). How white evangelical Christians fused with Trump extremism. *The New York Times*. www.nytimes.com/2021/01/11/us/how-white-evangelical-christians-fused-with-trump-extremism.html

Djupe, P. A., & Burge, A. (2020, November 6). A conspiracy at the heart of it: Religion and Q. *Religion in Public*. https://religioninpublic.blog/2020/11/06/a-conspiracy-at-the-heart-of-it-religion-and-q/

Farivar, M. (2020, August 15). How the QAnon conspiracy theory went global. *VOA News*. www.voanews.com/usa/how-qanon-conspiracy-theory-went-global

Festinger, L., Rieken, H., & Schachter, S. (1956). *When prophecy fails*. Harper & Row.

Finkelstein, D., Donohue, J. K., Goldenberg, A., Baumgartner, J., Farmer, J., Zannettou, S., & Blackburn, J. (2020). Covid-19, conspiracy and contagious sedition: A case study on the militia-sphere. *A Report by the Rutgers Miller Center for Community Protection and Resilience and the Network Contagion Research Institute.* https://networkcontagion.us/reports/covid-19-conspiracy-and-contagious-sedition-a-case-study-on-the-militia-sphere/

Fuller, M. (2021, January 12). House Democrats briefed on 3 terrifying plots to overthrow government. *HuffPost.* www.huffpost.com/entry/democrats-briefed-plot-overthrow-government_n_5ffd29a4c5b691806c4bf199

Gjelten, T. (2021, January 19). Militant Christian nationalists remain a potent force, even after the Capitol riot. *NPR.* www.npr.org/2021/01/19/958159202/militant-christian-nationalists-remain-a-potent-force

Graphika (2021, January 22). DisQualified: Network impact of Twitter's latest QAnon enforcement. *Graphika.* https://graphika.com/posts/disqualified-network-impact-of-twitters-latest-qanon-enforcement/

Harwell, D., & Timberg, C. (2020, November 10). "My faith is shaken": The QAnon conspiracy theory faces a post-Trump identity crisis. *The Washington Post.* www.washingtonpost.com/technology/2020/11/10/qanon-identity-crisis/

Harwell, D., Stanley-Becker, I., Nakhlawi, R., & Timberg, C. (2021, January 13). QAnon reshaped Trump's party and radicalized believers. The Capitol siege may just be the start. *The Washington Post.* www.washingtonpost.com/technology/2021/01/13/qanon-capitol-siege-trump/

Ingersoll, J. (2017). *Building God's Kingdom: Inside the world of Christian reconstruction.* Oxford University Press.

Ingram, M. (2020, August 13). The QAnon cult is growing and the media is helping. *Columbia Journalism Review.* www.cjr.org/the_media_today/the-qanon-conspiracy-cult-is-growing-and-the-media-is-helping.php

John, T. (2020, July 30). A baseless US conspiracy theory found a foothold in Europe. New research shows how. *CNN.* https://edition.cnn.com/2020/07/30/tech/qanon-europe-covid-intl/index.html

Jones, S. G. (2018, November 7). The rise and of far-right extremism in the United States. *Center for Strategic & International Studies Brief.* www.csis.org/analysis/rise-far-right-extremism-united-states

Juergensmeyer, M. (2017). *Terror in the mind of God: The global rise of religious violence* (4th ed.). University of California Press.

Kanno-Youngs, Z., Tavernise, S., & Cochrane, E. (2021, January 6). As House was breached, a fear that "we'd have to fight" to get out. *The New York Times.* www.nytimes.com/2021/01/06/us/politics/capitol-breach-trump-protests.html?action=click&module=Spotlight&pgtype=Homepage

Kristian, B. (2020). Is QAnon the newest American religion? *The Week.* https://theweek.com/articles/915522/qanon-newest-american-religion

Labbe, C., Padovese, V., Richter, M., & Harling, A.-S. (2020). QAnon's Deep State conspiracies spread to Europe. *NewsGuard.* www.newsguardtech.com/special-report-qanon/

LaFrance, A. (2020, May 13). The prophecies of Q: American conspiracy theories are entering a dangerous new phase. *The Atlantic*. www.theatlantic.com/magazine/archive/2020/06/qanon-nothing-can-stop-what-is-coming/610567/

Lepselter, S. (2016). *The resonance of unseen things: Poetics, power, captivity, and UFOs in the American uncanny*. University of Michigan Press.

Ling, J. (2021, January 6). QAnon is Trumpism now. *Foreign Policy*. https://foreignpolicy.com/2021/01/06/qanon-q-trump-republican-party-election/

Mezzofiore, G., Polglase, K., Lister, T., Pleitgen, F., Croker, N., & Hernandez, S. (2020, October 7). "It's like a parasite": How a dangerous virtual cult is going global. *CNN*. https://edition.cnn.com/2020/10/07/tech/qanon-europe-cult-intl/index.html

Moscovici, S. (1987). The conspiracy mentality. In C. F. Graumann & S. Moscovici (Eds.), *Changing conceptions of conspiracy* (pp. 151–169). Springer.

O'Conner, C., Gatewood, C., McDonald, K., & Brandt, S. (2020). The boom before the ban: QAnon and Facebook. *A Report by the Institute for Strategic Dialogue and NewsGuard*. www.isdglobal.org/wp-content/uploads/2020/12/20201218-ISDG-NewsGuard-QAnon-and-Facebook.pdf

O'Donnell, S. J. (2020, September 12). Demons of the Deep State: How evangelicals and conspiracy theories combine in Trump's America. *The Conversation*. https://theconversation.com/demons-of-the-deep-state-how-evangelicals-and-conspiracy-theories-combine-in-trumps-america-144898

Papacharissi, Z. (2014). *Affective publics: Sentiment, technology, and politics*. Oxford University Press.

Possamai, A. (2005). *Religion and popular culture: A hyper-real testament*. Peter Lang.

(2012). *Handbook of hyper-real religions*. Brill.

(2018). *The I-zation of society, religion, and neoliberal post-secularism*. Palgrave Macmillan.

Possamai, A., & Lee, M. (2011). Hyper-real religions: Fear, anxiety, and late modern religious innovation. *Journal of Sociology*, *47*(3), 227–242.

Rauhala, E., & Morris, L. (2020, November 13). In the United States, QAnon is struggling. The conspiracy theory is thriving abroad. *The Washington Post*. www.washingtonpost.com/world/qanon-conspiracy-global-reach/2020/11/12/ca312138-13a5-11eb-a258-614acf2b906d_story.html

Rogers, K. (2021, March 26). QAnon has become the cult that cries wolf. *FiveThirtyEight*. https://fivethirtyeight.com/features/qanon-has-become-the-cult-that-cries-wolf/

Rogers, R. (2020). Deplatforming: Following extreme internet celebrities to Telegram and alternative social media. *European Journal of Communication*, *35*(3), 213–229.

Rotella, S. (2021, January 22). Global right-wing extremism networks are growing. The U.S. is just now catching up. *ProPublica*. www.propublica.org/article/global-right-wing-extremism-networks-are-growing-the-u-s-is-just-now-catching-up

Snow, D. (2004). Framing process, ideology, and discursive fields. In D. Snow, S. Soule, & H. Kriesi (Eds.), *The Blackwell companion to social movements* (pp. 380–412). Blackwell Publishing.

Snow, D., Rochford, E. B., Jr., Worden, S., & Benford, R. (1986). Frame alignment processes, micromobilization, and movement participation. *American Sociological Review*, *51*(4), 464–481.

Spocchia, G. (2021, January 26) QAnon merges with white extremists and spreads new conspiracy Trump will be president again on March 4. *Yahoo News*. https://news.yahoo.com/qanon-merges-white-extremists-spreads-135605633.html

Stone, J. (2000). *Expecting Armageddon: Essential readings in failed prophecy*. Routledge.

Tasker, J. P. (2020, October 20). PM, health officials warn Canadians against believing COVID-19 "internment camps" disinformation. *CBC News*. www.cbc.ca/news/politics/covid-19-internment-camps-disinformation-1.5769592

Taylor, M., & Colbert, M. (2017). *The Trump prophecies*. Defender.

Taylor, V. (1989). Social movement continuity: The women's movement in abeyance. *American Sociological Review* *54*(5), 761–775.

Thompson, N. (2021, January 13). What drives "J-Anon," QAnon's Japanese counterpart? *GlobalVoices*. https://globalvoices.org/2021/01/13/what-drives-j-anon-qanons-japanese-counterpart/

Tiffany, K. (2020, August 18). The women making conspiracy theories beautiful. *The Atlantic*. www.theatlantic.com/technology/archive/2020/08/how-instagram-aesthetics-repackage-qanon/615364/

Timberg, C., Harwell, D., & Lang, M. J. (2021, January 9). Capitol siege was planned online. Trump supporters now planning the next one. *The Washington Post*. www.washingtonpost.com/technology/2021/01/09/trump-twitter-protests/

Tumminia, D., & Swatos, W. H. (2011). *How prophecy lives*. Brill.

van Prooijen, J.-W., & Douglas, K. M. (2017). Conspiracy theories as part of history: The role of societal crisis situations. *Memory Studies*, *10*(3), 323–333.

Waldman, P. (2021, January 20). QAnon is mortally wounded. But the right's conspiracy theories will never die. *The Washington Post*. www.washingtonpost.com/opinions/2021/01/20/qanon-is-mortally-wounded-rights-conspiracy-theories-will-never-die/

Walker, J. (2021). Conspirituality.net. Keynote Panel 2 at (Con)spirituality, Science and COVID-19 Colloquium, Deakin University and Western Sydney University, March 26.

Ward, C., & Voas, D. (2011). The emergence of conspirituality. *Journal of Contemporary Religion*, *26*(1), 103–121.

Wright, S. A. (2009). Martyrs and martial images: The volatile link between warfare frames and religious violence. In M. Shterin & M. Al-Rasheed (Eds.), *Dying for faith: Religiously motivated violence in the contemporary world*. I.B. Tauris.

Zuckerman, E., & Rajendra-Nicolucci, C. (2021, January 11). Deplatforming our way to the alt-tech ecosystem. *Knight First Amendment Institute, Columbia University*. https://knightcolumbia.org/content/deplatforming-our-way-to-the-alt-tech-ecosystem

Index